Tomorrow, God Willing

Tomorrow,

Unni Wikan

God Willing

Self-made Destinies in Cairo

The University of Chicago Press ❖ Chicago and London

Unni Wikan is professor in the Department and Museum
of Anthropology at the University of Oslo. She has
served as visiting professor at Harvard University and
the Johns Hopkins University. Her earlier books include
Behind the Veil in Arabia: Women in Oman and *Managing Turbulent Hearts: A Balinese Formula for Living,*
both published by the University of Chicago Press.

The University of Chicago Press, Chicago 60637
The University of Chicago Press, Ltd., London
© 1996 by The University of Chicago
All rights reserved. Published 1996
Printed in the United States of America
05 04 03 02 01 00 99 98 97 96   1 2 3 4 5
ISBN: 0-226-89834-2 (cloth)
       0-226-89835-0 (paper)

Library of Congress Cataloging-in-Publication Data

Wikan, Unni, 1944–
    Tomorrow, God willing : self-made destinies in
Cairo / Unni Wikan.
          p.   cm.
    Includes bibliographical references (p.   ) and
index.
    1. Cairo (Egypt)—Social conditions.   2. Poor—
Egypt—Cairo.   I. Title.
HN786.C3W55   1996
306'.096216—dc20   95-26658
                                              CIP

♾ The paper used in this publication meets the minimum requirements of the American National Standard
for Information Sciences—Permanence of Paper for
Printed Library Materials, ANSI Z39.48-1984.

If nothing but the bright side of characters
should be shewn, we should sit down in despondency
and think it utterly impossible
to imitate them in *anything*.
The sacred writers . . . related the vicious
as well as the virtuous actions of men;
which had this moral effect
that it kept mankind from *despair*.

Samuel Johnson

Contents

Acknowledgments   xiii

A Note on Transliteration   xv

Cast of Characters   xvii

Introduction   1

Prelude: *Talking Together Makes Wise*   22

Part One
Woman, Mother, and Poor

1   A Broken Dream   27
Presentation (*anno* 1982)
The dream
"And ever since have I neglected my looks"

2   Tomorrow, God Willing   31
"The man should have his freedom, but not at the
     woman's expense"
"The man is like a child"
"God helps him who helps himself"

3   The Back Street Environment   34
The way in
Shoes make people
The modern quarter
The *baladi* quarter

4   A Woman and Her Man   41
Umm Ali
Mustafa

5   The Children   46
Rights to intercourse
Hit-or-miss contraception
Maternal love

6   A Life in Poverty   51
Living quarters
Life without schedule
"People *think* we are well off"
Figuring time and money
A closer look inside the flat
Priorities

A house of one's own
Tomorrow, God willing

7   **Seven Brothers and Sisters**   62
Ali
Amin
Hoda
Mona
Afaf
Anwar
Nosa

8   **For the Children's Sake**   67
"I don't care if they starve or they die"
"If only the children were happy"

Part Two
Umm Ali Speaks

9   **The Source of All Misery: Mustafa and the Money**   73
"As if 'never mind' can fill a belly"
"I, without earning a penny, have to be the provider"
"But you are poor and that's no shame"
Simple treason
Securing one's due
"The shepherd is responsible for his flock"
"It's not *you* who will be shamed"
"It's brains he lacks, not money"

10   **Manchild Mustafa**   81
11   **Marriage and Love**   87
"Like a third-rate girlfriend"
A flop
Sharing responsibility
"It's a heavy burden to carry unreciprocated gifts"
Would you call *this* happiness?
"Marriage makes a man of you"
"He goes one way, I go the other, and never the
    twain shall meet"
"Like a stranger from the street"

12   **Might and Vulnerability**   94
"In many a house, she is the man and he the woman"
"For if I hit him, he wouldn't be a man"

To control oneself
To strike first and think afterwards
The house of obedience
A blessed chicken
"The man is the wife's best doctor"
"Only four times have I demanded divorce"
"I neither love nor hate him"

13   **Three Desperate Attempts at Self-Help**   100
The job: "So I can walk apart and look at him"
An accursed car and a heartbreaking savings club
The house site that gives wings to a dream

Part Three
The Back Streets as a Social Environment

14   **Everyone Begrudges Others Everything They Have**   117
Envy
The people's talk
Gossip
The evil eye
Invidious comparisons; or, Why everyone else seems
    better off

15   **Materialism and Want**   123
Status symbols
The material measure of a person's value
The vulnerability of women

Part Four
Daily Life and Rhythm

16   **Typical Days in Umm Ali's Life**   133

Part Five
Growing Up in Poverty

17   **The Child in the Family**   143
The problem of assessing experience
"Egyptian children are kissed, not disciplined"
Nature and nurture: The roles of mother and father
Brothers and sisters
Squabbling over food

Different faces of poverty
Bickering over clothes
Sharing
Self-defense

18   **The Everyday World of Children**   158
A small world
Home versus street
The new age: TV
Toys
One day is like another
School: Pathway to the future
Social intelligence and competence

Part Six
Three Ways out of Misery

19   **Amin's Death**   171
20   **Afaf's Illness**   177
21   **Hoda's Spiritual Conversion**   182

Part Seven
Some Important Persons and Events in Umm Ali's Life

22   **Childhood and Youth, 1934–1949**   189
23   **Amira: Sister-in-Law Who Has Enough with Her Own**   192
24   **Ahmed: Beloved Brother**   207
25   **Farida: Sister Whom Life Did Not Spare**   213
26   **Umm Magdi and the Friendship That Broke Up**   222
27   **Some Who Were Not Mentioned**   229
28   **Houseguests Holding Their Ground**   232

Part Eight
Young Today

29   **On Freedom, Choice, and Love**   241
But freedom is not all
30   **Ali: Freedom at a High Price**   246
31   **Hoda: "As If *He* Could Decide over Me"**   253
32   **Mona: "Marriage Is Like an Unopened Watermelon"**   258

Part Nine
A Hope for the Future

33   **Fulfillment**   277
34   **Talking Is Therapy**   278

Part Ten
Epilogue

35   **What Happened Next?**   291
36   **Cairo—City Victorious?**   297
Four political regimes
Education
Standard of living
Recession
The Contract with Egypt
Population explosion
Building and renting out
Savings clubs: A reprise
The rent freeze
Project Home
Life at the margins
Safety and human supports
Changing times
The fundamentalist upsurge
Making a future for the children

Postscript: Fieldwork   325
References   331

Acknowledgments

My deepest respect and thanks go to my friends in Cairo, first and foremost Umm Ali, Mustafa, and their children. But I wish to thank everyone who has welcomed me into their lives and let me be their friend. Words are poor to express what I owe them.

All names in this book are pseudonyms. I have tried to cover up real identities by changing aspects of personal lives so that the personas that emerge might have been real without betraying real persons. Where I may have failed, I sincerely hope that none will feel I have betrayed their trust, and that in giving an account of grinding poverty and the dignity and zest of people fated to make do under such circumstance, I have borne witness to their oppression and struggle while testifying to the immense potential and capacity of the people. It makes the sins of omission of the government even more glaring. And it shows what could be achieved if in a cooperative venture people were better helped to help themselves.

With hindsight I find it difficult to use the word "poor." True, that's what they called themselves and true, that's what some of them still are. But only in a partial sense. The word seems to connote a poverty of spirit that is wholly alien to the people I know.

Beyond the back streets, others lent me courage and support. My deepest gratitude to Dr. Laila Shukry El-Hamamsy, director of the Social Research Center at the American University in Cairo. Without her faith in me and practical support, I might not have persevered. My gratitude also to the late Dr. Chris Thoron, president of the American University in Cairo, for his support.

I am indebted to the Egyptian authorities for granting me de facto permission to do the research, and to the Ministry of Higher Education for their generous offer of a scholarship. My fieldwork since 1975 has been financed by the Norwegian Research Council for Science and the Humanities (NAVF) which also provided me with a year's scholarship to write in peace. I gratefully acknowledge this support.

This book is a rewritten and expanded version of a book that was published in Norwegian in 1983. I am grateful to Suzanne Palme, book agent, for first suggesting that I bring out an English version, and also to Linda Sivesind for help with the translation of some chapters.

To Arthur Kleinman, my gratitude for his vital encouragement and his advice to rework the book in the best English of which I was capable, rather than translate the original text. I am also grateful to Sarah and Robert LeVine for their encouragement, to David Brent, senior editor at the University of Chicago Press, for his unwavering support, and to Jean S. Gottlieb for superb copyediting.

To Anna von der Lippe, my heartfelt thanks for coming with me to Cairo and sharing in my world. Her competence in developmental and clinical psychology has made our collaborative work on the children's future a gratifying experience.

Thanks also to my son, Kim, for twice coming with me to Cairo and sharing such a vital part of my life.

As always, my husband, Fredrik Barth, has played a crucial role in my work. He translated parts of the original Norwegian text, read and commented on the manuscript at several stages, and gave me invaluable advice. Though he never participated in the fieldwork with me, his admiration and affection for the people, whom he met only once, has sustained my own sense of their truly extraordinary qualities.

This book is dedicated to Umm Ali's family and to the memory of Tove Stang Dahl, beloved friend and colleague. Tove did more than anyone over the past few years to encourage the project which here comes to fruition. Together we had embarked on a collaborative project that brought us together to Cairo once, and eventuated in the publication of her book, *The Muslim Family—a Study of Women's Rights in Islam* (1992), just before she died. An internationally renowned professor of women's law, Tove was overcome with admiration for the people, for their competence and resilience. And her love and admiration was more than reciprocated. I dedicate this book to her memory.

A Note on Transliteration

In spelling Arabic names and words, I have tried in as simple a way as possible to provide the nonspecialist reader with an idea of how the words are pronounced while at the same time rendering them recognizable to one who knows Arabic. I have not distinguished long from short vowels, nor have I indicated separately the several distinct consonants that to an untrained English ear can be grouped under "s," "t," and "h." I use the sign "'" for a guttural sound rendered in Arabic by the letter ayn, and "'" for the glottal stop hamza. The letters "kh" and "x" indicate a sound quite similar to the German "ch" (as in *Nacht*), and "gh" indicates another, related sound farther forward in the mouth. The soft "th" sound of English (as in "the" rather than "think") is represented by "dh" or sometimes "z."

Umm Ali's family (ages in 1982, except where otherwise noted):

Umm Ali	47
Mustafa	56
Ali	son, 31
Amin	son, died at 19 (1972)
Hoda	daughter, 27
Mona	daughter, 24
Aleyya	daughter, died at 4 (1964)
Afaf	daughter, 17
Anwar	son, 15
Nosa	daughter, 10

Other persons in Umm Ali's life:

Abdou	brother-in-law, married to Feyza
Adel	brother-in-law, married to Shaddya
Ahmed	brother
Amina	Mustafa's sister
Amira	sister-in-law, married to Ahmed
Farida	third oldest sister
Feyza	oldest sister
Hamdi	Mona's husband
Karima	Mustafa's foster sister and cousin
Khadiga	second oldest sister
Khalid	Hoda's ex-fiancé
Nefeesa	daughter-in-law, married to Ali
Sayyid	brother-in-law, married to Farida
Shaddya	youngest sister, died at 28 (1972)
Zenab	Umm Ali's given name
Umm Fathi	best friend
Umm Gamal	Coptic neighbor
Umm Magdi	former best friend

Introduction

At a time when Islam is perceived as the new enemy by many in the West, a book like this carries a special significance. It lets you meet people, human beings, who would like nothing more than a peaceful world: a world where they were free to pursue their superordinate goal, to make a future for their children; a world of equity and interpersonal respect, of human dignity and compassion; and a world where we could meet people of different cultures and talk to each other. "Talking together makes wise" is the dictum of Umm Ali, the main character of this book. And she means it not in a narrow sense. Rather, she and her familiars would reach out to you—as they reached out to me—and draw you into their world, if you meet them with courtesy and respect. It is from such beginnings, such human bonds, that a better world can be forged. And it is in this spirit, and to such a purpose, that I lay this book before you.

You will hear the voices of people living in poverty in a third world megacity, telling what it is like to be human in their world. It is an account of lives and living conditions, told from the perspective of a few real persons and in large part in their own words, an account from Umm Ali and her circle of their concerns, struggles, dreams, and realities. They are, inevitably, stories of disappointments, anger, misery, and despair, of hardships that often seem at the point of overwhelming people, as their fate certainly overwhelmed me when I first met them as a young anthropologist twenty-five years ago, and over the years as I have come ever closer to them and their struggles.

I see no other way of communicating such lives with any degree of faithfulness than by the massive detailing I give in this book of everyday events, everyday relationships, and enduring particular concerns, through major segments of whole lives. There can be no way to concentrate it as a text or distill it as statistics without purging it of the human message it contains, bearing witness to the conditions of life that Umm Ali, her family, and her neighbors share with millions of others.

But once this baseline of pain and inequity is grasped, there are important other sides to these life stories and persons, which emerge with gathering force. For one, it is remarkable to realize how through their endless trials and defeats, nearly everyone, nearly all the time, perseveres; and how they do not allow their personhood to be destroyed, or their sense of value, their robust claim to worth, to be stifled. Indeed as the stories will show, people seem to retain to the last their ability to forgive each other and forge new beginnings.

And as for Cairo's back streets, with their smells, ugliness, and conflicts, I have only slowly come to realize how different this urban habitat seems to be from many other megacities, at least as they appear from the descriptions we have of them. For all the drawbacks of poverty, overcrowding, pollution, and contention, Cairo's back streets still remain an environment hardly touched by violent crime, unterrorized by mafias, devoid of street children and pavement dwellers, with a population of stable families where nearly all children are born in wedlock. Perseverance and hope triumph in the face of bitter realities to make the children in turn emerge as responsible and nurturant parents. This suggests another reading of these stories of struggle, frustration, and disappointment: a reading informed by the realization that the sum of such people's efforts, conflicts, concerns, and strivings is in fact an urban lifestyle that creates in its aggregate an urban society less destructive to personhood and dignity than what we find in much more favored inner cities in Europe and North America, and in many other big cities in the world.

Questions, enigmas, and a message for the world

Thus the story of Umm Ali and her circle poses a series of questions and enigmas:

1. What is the connection between the objective conditions of poverty and their interpretation as a context for human lives? What is the lived experience of being part of this world?

2. If we use as our evidence of that lived experience people's own assessment and narratives—what they tell each other as well as what they tell me—are we then in danger of being misled by a style of representation, a rhetoric of complaint that misrepresents that experience by ignoring the unsaid in these messages and the self-evidences of the lives of which the rhetoric is a part?

3. In my role as an anthropological investigator, how can I hope to come close to knowing and judging the lived experience of others suffering such extreme circumstances? And how can I best supplement and modify my understanding of what they say with the evidence of what they do, as well as what they achieve in the long run?

4. And, finally, in my role as author, how should I communicate so that my readers can share my understanding, judge the validity of my rhetoric as well as the import of Cairene rhetoric, and grasp the ramifications of events and relations for those whose lives are being told?

I wish to present the urgent yet humdrum words and lives of Umm Ali and her circle in such a way that these enigmas are made visible—possibly even resolved to some extent—so we can move forward toward a fuller understanding of the life of cities. I do not attempt to analyze the macro-forces that determine the economic and social inequities that create poverty. Instead, I am trying to show how the particular forms of poverty and misery are experienced, and how they are actively shaped and transformed by the people who suffer them.

I do so because I want to bear witness to the plight of the people. But I also believe that a grasp of what happens in Cairo's back streets has even more to offer us. If we can understand how the resilience and buoyancy of this population arises, and what factors allow its members to live with a degree of integrity and hope—sometimes even transcending the impediments imposed on them and creating better lives into the bargain—then there is a message of general importance and relevance in these materials. A life of poverty in a big city can still be led in such a way that it neither brutalizes people nor turns neighbor against neighbor in the destructive way we see in so many other cities. The neighborhoods described in the following pages may not be benign, but their residents have numerous qualities of humanity, humor, cooperation, and compassion for others. The patterns of relation and interaction that are revealed are not the kind that draw people relentlessly into antisocial activity or violence, destroying the milieu as a whole as well as the individual perpetrator. On the contrary, Umm Ali's quarter is a place that allows people to nourish dreams and realistic hopes, where one can make persistent efforts to better one's lot and obtain constructive support from others, and where there are functioning collective institutions to facilitate such cooperation. There are too many urban environments in the world where none of this is true.

This, then, is the way I invite you to read these materials: search behind the immediate froth of despair and contention for that which stops the more irremediable forms of hardship and defeat from eventuating. What prevents the corrosion of lives and morality in Cairo that is so common in poor districts of many other cities? The answers are here somewhere, buried in the particulars of how Umm Ali and the others grapple with their relations and their circumstances. Realizing that, the task of understanding her story takes on a much greater significance.

There is renewed concern in the social sciences today about the urban poor and human misery, motivated in part by the decay of inner cities in the United States and Europe and the realization that unless we act now to try to change this state of affairs, it may be too late.[1] Increasing violence,

1. The literature on the deteriorating condition of the poor in U.S. inner cities is vast. Let me just mention three works here: Freedman 1993; Lavelle et al. 1995; Wilson 1987

drug abuse, deprivation, and demoralization seem to be the order of the day, and the privileged classes can no longer stand back and let it happen, for the future of their own children is at stake.

But such deteriorating conditions, inevitable though they may seem to us, are the man-made creation of particular ways of life, which means there is hope: they can be avoided. Identifying the mechanisms that open the way for other options is a major challenge to social science and is of practical importance to policymakers.[2] Umm Ali's story teaches the need to go beyond descriptions of poverty and misery to look for the human potentials and cultural competences that enable people to survive and even, in some cases, to thrive. Her story does not romanticize their lives— there is nothing romantic about poverty—but it gives us a more realistic grasp of the human condition.

It makes one somber to ponder the fact that at a time when Islam is portrayed as the new enemy in the West, and many Muslims feel that they are all characterized as a bunch of potential terrorists, it is in Cairo's back streets (rather than in the inner cities of Washington DC or Detroit) that we find (relative) peace and order.[3] Fundamentalism cannot be given credit for this, however. Contrary to widely held stereotypes in the West, the fundamentalists or Islamists draw their main support not from the poor but from the intelligentsia and the middle class (Elon 1995). Umm Ali's story helps us to understand why. People at her level are a pragmatic lot who long for a stable and predictable life of relative comfort. They condemn terrorism, hate oppression, and admire regimes—of whatever civilization—that promote equality and cooperation among people and protect the lives of their citizens. During the Gulf War, Saddam Hussein was unanimously cursed by the people I know for instigating war and killing innocent people. The Islamists likewise are condemned for re-sorting to terrorism and social upheaval.

The people I know do not want a social revolution, not even a social experiment; they want peace and order and a dependable, decent income that enables them to feed and clothe and educate their children. They have tried a revolution—that of President Nasser in 1952—and it was a disappointment. The revolution fell pitifully short of delivering what it

2. I am currently at work on a book which explores these issues in a comparative study of poverty. The groundwork was laid in Wikan 1995.

3. Public concern over violence in U.S. inner cities is mounting and has spawned extensive literature on the subject. Homicide now ranks as the number 1 cause of death for black males between the ages of fifteen and twenty-four in the United States, and the rate is growing (Lavelle et al. 1995, 111); see also Hawkins 1993.

promised. Rather, it aggravated the problems of common people, who condemned his going to war with Israel, sacrificing their sons, and wasting money on the army. The Islamist movement has likewise not convinced ordinary people that it has the people's good at heart. Why, if it did, would some of its members kill innocent people and undermine the tourist industry which is a vital source of income to many in the lower class? The people I know are religious, not extreme. And their spirituality is one that celebrates compassion for all people, also Christians and Jews.

Experience, achievement, and narrative

Except under extreme circumstances, poverty inflicts damage mainly through the stigma, failure, and hopelessness that go with it. Poverty is a condition of objective material shortage, but it is above all a relative condition; the experience of poverty arises from one's lacking things that some others have. It is not a condition people can take lightly or sublimate through a private philosophy of renunciation. Since one's value as a person is at stake, the effort to overcome poverty tends to be an obsessive battle in which every failure and every negative score is counted and overwhelms the admittedly rarer, positive scores. Thus the testimony of a certain degree of progress over time is easily lost in the clamor of new defeats.

I first became aware of this aspect of life in the back streets when I noticed the material progress people were making in the midst of their daily and disastrous poverty (Wikan 1985). While most public evidence from Cairo reported deteriorating living conditions among the poor, I knew from my small but detailed inventories of property and consumption that the people I knew had, on the contrary, achieved a marginal improvement by the kinds of indicators they themselves would embrace, for example, the acquisition of durable consumer goods. People were also dressing better, which means, in Cairene terms, that they become better able to think well of themselves. And through efforts that were entirely their own and sacrifices by the whole family, they have achieved remarkable gains in the level of education they secure for their children.

I know that these achievements and successes are of great importance to people. Why then are they not more evident in people's narratives? Why do they not stand out cumulatively, instead of falling apart as episodic self-praise and pleas for sympathy? In part because of the relentless interpersonal struggle which means that most people, most of the time, are competing and comparing themselves to others who seem slightly better off. But also, the style of people's expression is one that overplays drama and invective in an incessant argument with life and with relations for letting one down. Hence there is not much room for stressing the brighter side of life except as laughter, humor, joking, or as the triumphant display of one's own material successes (which is easily read by others as a way of putting *them* down). While this book may be read as a perpetual complaint, an experience-near account of a life that none of us might like to lead, that is a limited perspective. On another level, it is a story of success, of endurance, holding on, fighting for one's self-respect and social esteem, with some good results in the end. Children generally turn into responsible adults with a firm grasp on life. They are not necessarily happy, for as one seventeen-year-old said, "Happiness, what is that? All life is problems." Yet they carry on in an honorable manner, as striving, family-oriented wives and husbands, mothers and fathers, caring for their own children in turn, and for their parents in old age. Nor does caring stop with the family. A commitment to family and self also entails cooperation and compassion on a broader scale.

This is what I call their achievement, but it is as I experience it from the broader perspective of a comparative view of Cairo. I ask the reader to join me in this perspective. Please offer resistance to the harrowing complaints and tragedies of Umm Ali and others. Acknowledge how horrible their lives, yet how remarkable that people manage so well. Listen to their accounts of envy, gossip, and the endless meddling of other people and say yet how impressive it is that people involve themselves at all. (Said a man last year when I asked him what he thought was the reason for safety and security in the city, "Oh, it's so simple. There are always people about in the streets at night—not like in America—so no one dares to do anyone harm." He would have been amazed to hear that in America the problem is not empty streets but guns and fear of involvement.) Also, every Egyptian I know has a social network, a security net, that picks up those who fall by the wayside. Even though it is not always successful, there is comfort in such companionship. People do not just drop in and out of relations; they remain linked with others while engaging as active partisans in the drama.

The resulting story is not a beautiful one, for lives in urban poverty are not beautiful. Indeed, a most compelling message I want to convey concerns the corrosive effect of poverty on all social relations, how it undermines people's efforts to do well and to think well of themselves. But the story is impressive for what people manage and endure while striving to protect self-respect through ceaseless attempts at defiance. Resistance is a favored concept in contemporary social science, and these lives I depict can be read as exercises in resistance against the state, against the family, against one's marriage, against the forces of tradition or change, against neighbors and society—even against oneself. But it is resistance that seems to follow a hidden agenda to manage and endure in ways that respect the humanity of others.

It is this combination of respectability and resistance that makes the people in Cairo what they are: a people full of individuality and charm who delight in zest and humor, and whose hope of self-realization lies in honoring their social commitments. That is precisely why poverty is so tragic to them. It undercuts their ability to be what they truly are: hospitable, good humored, generous, and just. Therefore, for those who are trapped by this kind of life, the dark side predominates; hence an account in people's own voices will not be entirely transparent.

Remember also that Egyptians talk worse than they act. Their tendency is to dramatize events in florid language, laced with invective and hyperbole, that exaggerates feelings, black or white. The ugliest accounts about others or about one's own plight should therefore be taken with a grain of salt. Not that they are not earnest, they are, but life is played at a fever pitch and people let themselves become intoxicated by words. For those bred to a more circumspect style, it is necessary to remember this. Nor are people's curses necessarily directed at the ostensible target. Take a father who threatens to kill his baby daughter for breaking a glass; his fury is certainly intensely felt, but his words are as much a cry of despair at his own failure to sustain a proper life as they are meant for his baby daughter.

Poverty is also demeaning in the way it drives people to use language to give vent to their pain; the language itself inflicts pain, as when husbands call their wives "daughter of a slut" at the slightest provocation. Nerves worn to a frazzle, the root cause of such speech is monetary misery. But the pain cuts as deep, nevertheless. And we realize that poverty infects even one's vocal chords.

Methodology and anthropological authority

A major methodological concern for me has been the interpretation of utterances and words, the very style people use to express themselves. How is it possible to escape the conlusion that their lives are lives of unmitigated misery when that is what people themselves seem to be saying in their acting out of emotions and their manner of talk? Put differently, how valid are expressions as an entry to experience?

For me, the answer is deeply colored by the long-term perspective. It took intimacy with people over time, and attention to how they coped throughout life to appreciate what seemed a discrepancy between expression and experience, with the former more a rhetoric of complaint than I had realized at first. What began as a documentation of misery (Wikan 1980) has turned partly into a story of transcendence. What has emerged through the years are massive data testifying to people's resourcefulness and competence. What began as a study describing their deprivations and failures has turned into a testimonial to their resilience, vitality, and zest.

But is it right? Am I fooling myself and the reader? After all, I have changed through the years. No longer the inexperienced youth who had never really seen poverty, and who was overcome by the indignities visited on the Cairo poor, I have come to see them in a broader perspective that takes into consideration poverty in other parts of the world.[4] From this perspective, people in Cairo emerge as quite capable, resourceful to a degree I have rarely come across elsewhere. But what relevance does that have to their experience of themselves and of their world? It is only through first understanding the particulars of their perspective that we can later compare and identify the sources of their strengths.

It has been argued that anthropological authority is established in the writing (Clifford 1988; Geertz 1988). I disagree with that. It is not so much from one's narrative—making one's account *seem* plausible—as from doing that and also being explicit about one's methods that one's reader is afforded the insight to judge the validity and authenticity of an account. Because the structure of this book disguises my methods, it is all the more important that I lay them out explicitly, and that I also discuss how this book was actually composed.

When I present it as an "inside account," I am drawing on twenty-five years of experience with the people, and a total of approximately thirty months of actually being with them. In addition, I lived in Egypt for two years before the fieldwork began, and this gives me a wider perspective on Egyptian society and culture.[5] The initial fieldwork took place in 1969–70, but I have continued to return to Egypt annually—with the exception of two years—revisiting Umm Ali and others (see postscript for a description of how I came to know the people and how I conducted my relationships with them). The major part of this book draws on material gathered over fourteen years, from 1969 to 1982, but my subsequent visits add depth and scope to the story. I have also written an epilogue

4. I have since worked in Bali, Indonesia (Wikan 1990b), and Bhutan (Wikan 1994). I have also had ample occasion to travel and observe the conditions of the urban poor in such places as Jakarta, Katmandu, Calcutta, New Delhi, Beijing, Mexico City, and the United States. Besides, I have had a rich comparative literature to draw on.

5. I lived in Alexandria for one year (1964–65) in a cosmopolitan community incorporating Egyptian families of Greek, French, Turkish, and Armenian heritage, as well as many foreigners. I also lived in Cairo for more than one year in 1968–69, studying Arabic at the American University in Cairo and associating with Egyptian upper-class families.

that brings the story up to date. Language, familiarity, and mutual affection over the years have combined to create a great sense of intimacy in our communication. I started by studying Arabic in Egypt for a year before I did my fieldwork and have maintained a considerable fluency over the years. Moreover, I sense a curious affinity between colloquial low-class Egyptian and my native dialect, north Norwegian. Both draw on an arsenal of metaphors and figurative speech and are replete with hyperbole and drama.[6] Both use "simple" phrases, down-to-earth language, and sweeping, declaratory statements. I felt remarkably at home with my friends in Cairo's back streets, participating in their conversations and their lives. All my thinking about them has been in either one of two languages, Arabic or Norwegian. Writing about them in English has been a real challenge.

The book should be read as a story; I have wanted it to come across as though it were a novel—even when all facts are documented—to give an experience-near account of life and society in Cairo. It is based directly on my presence as observer and participant in much of what it tells, though I choose to let Umm Ali's voice be privileged. But the material was not collected as a narrative. It accumulated as I participated in innumerable events and conversations, one-on-one and in groups, as part of the interminable flow of speech, and as an interested and sympathetic party to people's thoughts and concerns. The same stories, the same life incidents, surfaced again and again; I know them and now I am used as witness: "Just ask Unni, she knows, we have been friends for more than twenty years"—as indeed we have. Over time, the stories have appeared in many contexts and have been used for many purposes, and I have acquired an ever-increasing fund of observation and detailed information as my context for listening and understanding.

I have tried to combine a narrative approach—the stories people tell— with a perspective that foregrounds life's "urgency and necessity" (Bourdieu 1990), the obstacles against which people battle, and the real-life constraints that facilitate or impede their actions. I cannot see how even the best self-account by Umm Ali could do justice to her life, her triumphs, miseries, victories, and defeats. An Egyptian narrative would necessarily seize on one's own successes and on the failures and betrayals of many

6. Indeed, both also have an affinity with black American English, as was brought home to me when Alice Walker's *The Color Purple* was translated into Norwegian, and the translator used the north Norwegian dialect rather than standard written Norwegian. One might think that African Americans from the deep South and north Norwegians from beyond the Arctic Circle would have little in common by way of speech. But the translator's choice was superb, and came out just right (Rogde 1984). Black American, North Norwegian, and colloquial low-class Egyptian have much in common.

others. There is nothing exceptional in that; perhaps such a tendency is panhuman though more pronounced in societies where self-praise is culturally acceptable. But in order to ground a self-account in a real world that both adds to a person's stature and cuts her down to size, I judge it necessary to provide the added perspective that comes from observing actions, on the one hand, and from assessing them from multiple vantage points, on the other. How do Umm Ali's actions stand up in the world? What are their effects and consequences? And how do her social others, both contestants and familiars, judge those actions?

My basic method thus brings together (1) observation of acts and events in which the person engages, (2) self-narrative, and (3) contesting or supplementary viewpoints from people simultaneously engaged in the subject's world in matters of common concern.

First, I give priority to observation and participation in spontaneous interaction. This concern with natural observation as my primary method means that all the stories I report were part of people's spontaneous conversation, either among themselves, and/or with me. I committed these stories to memory, which was easier than you might think, for people naturally tend to repeat themselves when there are things that really matter. I have heard many of these stories countless times, in different fora, with different audiences, but the story remains basically the same, even over a time span of ten to twenty years, unless there are drastic changes in relationships, as, for example, when a friendship turns into enmity or vice versa, or an engagement comes to an end. Because I regarded people as friends, not informants, I never took notes on the spot or used a tape recorder. What I relate is rendered from memory.

Second, much of the material I use is gathered from hearing people talk—not telling stories—on such humdrum matters as what one is going to eat or how to get hold of the money or who's going out to borrow it or how to simply endure. Pertinent here is the Egyptian predilection to always talk: they are a people given to words, who delight in sound and clamor. How often have I not felt quite exhausted by all this vocalizing that centers on the most routine and trifling matters. Yet my basic understanding has drawn on precisely such sources of experience: how to make do and manage. Could I have fathomed what it means to be poor if I had contented myself only with the narratives, the stories?

Third, it follows from my basic methodological stance that all verbal materials are grounded in observation of the resistance life offers to people's efforts to think—and speak—well of themselves. It is from observing their daily struggles that I know most of what I think I know—not from listening to their stories. The obstacles comprise both sheer material constraints and the barriers others put up by being in the selfsame world and having their own concerns (Barth 1966). I have been Umm Ali's confidante and a recipient of her self-narrative in a real world composed of many actors, where there is also no dearth of obstacles against acting as she would wish.

George Ainslie (1982) has observed how daydreams fail to be satisfying because they "are not governed by scarcity." In daydreams, everything is possible. The opposite applies to Umm Ali's world. There is no shortage of scarcity; it is the only thing there is plenty of. And so she comes up against the wall all the time, both subjectively and in an objective sense (as when her efforts to talk well of herself are undercut by the electrician's coming and shutting off the light because the bill was not paid). My understanding of all her narrative and talk depends on my having seen how it happens.

Fourth, because every event and every person can always be viewed from multiple perspectives, I tried to understand how people differently positioned regarded the same or similar events; and I tried to identify areas where there were convergences as well as real differences of opinion and value judgment: should children have the right to choose their own spouse? Does a man have the right to beat his wife? What is the meaning of freedom? The examples could be multiplied. To this end, my account comprises the views and actions of people of both genders and various ages, statuses, and personalities. Bringing them together here also shows them as children of one culture in the sense of sharing some knowledge, values, and predicaments, even as they disagree.

Much as I sympathize with a project of "writing against culture" (Abu-Lughod 1992) to reveal the vacuous generalizations that often disguise people's humanity and make them seem more "other" than they actually are, there is no denying that cultural differences exist and are of major relevance to cross-cultural understanding. "Culture" is an abstraction, a construct, but the acts and events produced by people under the influence of cultural knowledge and values are real enough. The anthropological project must strive to render the distinct humanity of each person we "write" while uncovering the conditions that make them human in ways that, in many instances, even hinder the realization of their potentials and happiness.

It is now accepted wisdom that culture works in many ways to distribute pain unequally in populations (Das 1994). My account of people in Cairo would not do its job if I did not seek to expose the formidable cultural constraints under which they labor and that they also, in many instances, re-create through their own actions. The material measure of persons (epitomized in the saying "Egyptians look only to the appearance, not to the character") is one example of a cultural value that works to the detriment of the poor, conferring stigma and eroding self-respect. The man's right to force sexual intercourse on his wife is another example of culture lending itself to the infliction of pain. My method seeks to trace the constraints that obstruct people's efforts to lead satisfying lives while it also reveals their individual and culturally facilitated resourcefulness.

One might deplore the fact that my access to people's lives has been limited by gender. I could not move about among men and observe and participate in their interactions. Though I was free to sit and talk with men in the domestic sphere, I could not follow along with them to work or to the cafés. As a result, my understanding of men's informal interaction is limited, based on their own reports, episodic observation, and hearsay. But such is the essence of our shared humanity in all social life. We are all gendered; there is no ungendered vantage point from which to enter into a "neutered" relationship to everyone. More perceptively one might say that my access was empowered by gender: it positioned me and gave me a meaningful perspective (meaningful to them and to me) from which to engage in relations and participation. Indeed, as you will see, in Cairo, access to women's worlds is crucial to an understanding of the society as a whole.

Likewise, my access to people was shaped by my personal relationships. Thus, while I would have wanted to hear Mustafa's own account of his life and marriage with Umm Ali, that was impossible. Mustafa is exceptionally shy, and I did not have the heart to intrude on his privacy; nor would it have been right. My relationship to Umm Ali positioned me in a certain way; I had loyalties, and Mustafa sensed it. I trust that he knows my affection and respect for him. But I regret that his voice is not heard in this book, except second-hand. It means I have not done justice to him, in the way that I hope I was able to with men who were more forthcoming, for instance, his brother-in-law, Ahmed.

Ahmed reached out to me to impress on me the sheer despair of being in his shoes. But even more important, I had occasion to observe him time and again in a variety of settings, in his own home and in the homes of relatives and friends, and also while riding his ready-to-collapse taxi through the maddening Cairo traffic. In other words, I have a picture of Ahmed as a well-rounded individual interacting with others in a variety of situations. And I have the "resistance" to his own account provided by his wife, his sister on good terms, his sister on bad terms, and so on. For the account I provide, such composite material is essential.

Let me make a last comment on methodology. At no point have I been interested in concepts, utterances, or phrases per se for what insight they might convey into Egyptian culture, self, or emotion. With my fluency in the local language, it would have been easy to enter into a study of words, text, discourse at a time when such a preoccupation dominates much of anthropology. But my overriding goal has been instead to focus on people—unique individuals—and the predicaments they face.[7] That meant tuning in to the source of their deepest pain, the unceasing material shortage, and to what was most critically at stake for them: the fracture of relations and the onslaughts on self from the eroding effect of sheer material need.

The best way to write against culture may be to work against culture—by which I mean to go out among people who struggle so hard to make do, that for the anthropologist to concern herself with "culture" or any other concept in vogue would seem absurd. Transcending such interests and reaching out to people in a world shaped, among other things, by cultural facts, provides a more powerful way to understand what life in the city—or any other place—is all about.

Such an understanding builds on, as well as conveys, the lived experience of residents in the city. We need to situate their actions and their choices in the world as they see it, construct it, and thereby (in part) create it. And so we return to the enigma of how to interpret their narratives and their statements. Anthropologists, who are taught to attend to "the native's point of view" (Malinowski 1922)—and to this end to be most sensitive to what is said in "their own voice"—should rightly be resistant to taking liberties and imputing views and perspectives to others. The unfortunate result is that experience is often treated as if it were transparent and accessible through people's narratives and utterances. But as Crapanzano (1988) and others have argued, this is a simplistic view; utterances function in a much more complex manner: to plead, beg, deceive, implore, tell the truth as one understands it, and so forth. Thus every statement needs to be interpreted on more than purely linguistic grounds. It is an action, an effort to have an effect on a world of intricate relationships, urgent interests, limited assets, and complexly distributed information; and it is only by sensing the speaker's construction of this world and her intentions in it that we can be apprized of her lived experience, what she believes she is doing, and why. It is necessary and legitimate, therefore, to use all the knowledge we have to interpret what she says—indeed, to let her voice be heard over the gulfs that separate lives lived far apart. Thus I have no alternative but to actively use such knowl-

7. For my position regarding the textual, discourse-oriented approach in anthropology versus a method that *attends* to people's multiple compelling concerns and seeks to understand what is most at stake for them, see Wikan 1992.

edge as I have to interpret and convey to you what Umm Ali and her circle are thinking about their world.

Experience, I have come to appreciate, is much more age-specific and life-cycle-specific than anthropologists allow when we try to pinpoint "the" experience of, say, marriage or poverty in "the" culture as if there were such a thing to behold. The now outmoded studies of social organization had at least this advantage: they took an overall view of the more stable aspects of social relations and institutions (the roles of mother, in-law, neighbor, and so on still persist in this Cairo neighborhood in much the same form as they did twenty-five years ago, as do political institutions), whereas the *experience* of persons filling those roles is shifting. To this day, all I can say of my attempts to get at experience in another (or my own) culture, is that I can know only something of some aspects and then only from a partial perspective. Little do I know what it means to be old, for example; nor can I know truly how life is experienced when joy and happiness recede before sorrow and regret, as in the stories some people tell of the indignities they are forced to endure in the back streets of Cairo.

From methodology to composition

The narrative of this book has been pieced together entirely by me. The stories Umm Ali and others tell, and that I render, are strung together in a sequence composed by me, even when I feel they might have done it in just the same way. The flow of the experience as it appears from this account is what I understand their experience to have been, though there is no way they would render it like that—in part because of the way life impinges on their stories but not on mine. I can hold my ground and complete my narrative—they cannot. They have to attend to numerous compelling concerns while talking, which adds a lot of noise and detracts from a tidy narrative. But more important, they are driven by their own need to think well of themselves, to extol their own excellence, and elicit their listeners' unqualified support against the injustices of people and circumstances.

The bruises and scars life has left—many of which I have witnessed myself or have heard others talk about—disfigure people's experience of self in ways unspoken yet painfully evident. I take liberties with their accounts in the sense that I reveal some of these scars, not to detract from their claim to pride, but to underscore that claim for the compassionate reader. Thus my narrative is fiction through and through, even though every detail accords with people's own words and is documented by their lives.

The text that appears with an unjustified righthand margin, or, in the case of snatches of dialogue, in quotation marks, deserves special mention. I use these devices whenever I think I recall people's words verbatim. Remember, most of these stories I have heard innumerable times, and even if I inadvertently use a wrong word here and there, I am sure that any passage thus set off carries the original meaning and that people would feel they had spoken just like that. To have used regular text style, or to have omitted quotation marks, would convey the misleading impression that all the materials I render are of the same ontological status; they are not.

With Umm Ali as my main character, it is important that I establish the extent to which she is representative of her time and place, and where she is exceptional relative to others. This I have sought to do by showing how people in her own social milieu perceive her and by presenting actions and events in her life as seen through their eyes. I have given Umm Ali's own narratives considerable space. This implies that repetition occurs from time to time, and that difficulties are accentuated at the cost of the good things in life. But so it must necessarily be if it is her experience I seek to represent rather than an account biased by distance.

The book is composed with a view to providing a kaleidoscopic picture of life in the back streets, with one person—Umm Ali—as the central character, and a host of supporting actors: husband, children, brother, sister, sister-in-law, friend, ex-friend, house guests, enemies, and so forth. The point of bringing them together here, each with a distinct voice, is not just that in actual life they are linked, but that they portray a broad spectrum of human lives and anchor Umm Ali within a particular society and milieu.

The book may be read as the account of a certain woman and her family, but it is intended to be much more: an entry into a social world with its own ground rules and networks of relationships. Umm Ali provided my entry point. But my story does not end with her. It carries beyond to other families struggling in similar ways and to structures and patterns confining but also empowering people: to what may reasonably be called their society. These structures are in part imposed from above, in part created from below. For each person, they consist of external obstacles that maintain an obdurate hold on people, thwarting their opportunities for betterment and brighter lives. But people are not simply pawns; they work with or against these circumstances, molding their own lives and society through myriad little acts. By moving between Umm Ali and a host of others, letting the perspective shift, I hope to give a sense of a world coming into being, of social relations making and remaking themselves within the overwhelming constraints of poverty and destitution.

My angle on this world is experience-near (Wikan 1991b), a close-to-the-bone, bitter-to-the-heart experience of fighting with all the odds against you. But the struggle takes place in a social world that, for all its heartlessness, still empowers people to survive and cope and find moments of fleeting happiness. *This* world, not any particular person, constitutes the subject of my account.

Having a broad cast of characters also highlights the contested nature of lives and values. By letting the perspectives shift and compete, Umm Ali does not hold the center completely. She has to step back and let others do to her what she is doing to them: critically appraise their actions. The object is not to diminish her, but to make her a more fully rounded human being than her own narratives would allow. The object is also to highlight real differences in opinion and value, areas of contestation and ambivalence within a broader consensus. Because I know so well the people who speak, each from their different viewpoint, offering their not always subtle commentaries on Umm Ali's person and life, I can assess their views—much as I provide resistance at times against Umm Ali's assessment of others.

It is in this sense that I enter the scene. I have opinions, and I express them. I make assessments of people to the best of my knowledge. And I side with people at times or challenge what they say. In this way, I take my participation seriously, as do my friends in Cairo. But I do not engage in the sort of reflexive anthropological writing that foregrounds the anthropologist's dialogue or encounter with "the other." This book is about Umm Ali and her circle, not about me. And my reflections on and assessments of persons and critical events are made solely with a view to enhancing our understanding of their world—compared with which I am quite insignificant.

Basically, then, in this book I attempt to bring to life conditions and constraints under which millions of people in Cairo live and labor. How many there are, no one really knows. Poverty is not easily defined; disagreements prevail regarding standards and measures. But my conservative estimate would be that at least one-fourth of Cairo's approximately fourteen million people could be considered poor or lower class. To the best of my understanding, Umm Ali's life, unique as it is, is still subject to the same constraints, aims at the same small victories and joys, and shares in the defeats and problems—the never-ending hopes and suffering—typical of Cairo's lower class. This assessment is borne out by my intimate knowledge of scores of other families in seven disparate quarters of Cairo where I now work.[8] It is my hope that the reader, by sharing in Umm Ali's life and the lives of people close to her, will come to understand the predicaments that affect millions of people in Cairo, women, children, and men. For though this book is inevitably female centered, its subject matter is really people.

Some might say that to realize such a project, I should have made an analysis of the political economy and macrosocial conditions. But that would be another book. I intend here to give a lived quality, an experiential sense, to poverty and oppression and thereby also to show how what social scientists call factors and separate into neat units typically run together in the ordinary person's life in an unpredictable and chaotic fashion. People commonly have multiple compelling concerns that cannot be shed but that keep pushing forward and thwart our best efforts to maintain control and keep abreast. This is a recurring experience of the Cairo poor: life is really too much for them given what they have to do to cope. And so the felt impact of the political economy is not just a crushing sense of injustice and outrage but sometimes an overwhelming feeling of chaos that threatens to do one in—epitomized by the cry for *nizam* [system, order] to take the edge off the onslaught on body and mind.

An understanding of why Islamists have made so little headway among the Cairo poor lies in people's quest for order, peace, and predictability, not upheaval or social revolt.

Wellsprings of vitality

"Tomorrow, God willing . . ."; the words invoke hope and trust in the future. For that is the reassuring message of this often repeated phrase: that by helping yourself, and only by helping yourself, life will bear fruit. Fate, destiny, even poverty—all those excuses people give to exonerate themselves—will just land you in that selfsame misery. Whereas when one works wholeheartedly to better one's own situation, chances are one may succeed little by little. [*habba, habba*]

Such is the life philosophy of Umm Ali and of many other Egyptians I know, that God helps her who helps herself. [*Rabbina yisa'id illi yisa'id nafsu*]. As she says, man must, while saying "God willing," decide in his heart, decide in his soul, put it into his mind that he will work to achieve results. [*yi'zim bi qalbu, yi'zim fi nafsiyyitu, yihutt fi moxxu innu*

8. See Wikan 1995. The quarters are Imbaba, Omraniyya, Talbiyya, Kafr Tohormoz, Haraniyya, Munib, besides Umm Ali's quarter. Works by other scholars on lower-class quarters in Cairo also bring out many common features; see, e.g., Atiya 1984; Early 1993; Rugh 1984; and Singerman 1995.

bayi'mil, bayif'al ikkalam]. Any other use of the words, as in well-worn attempts to escape responsibility, she regards as a mockery of God.

When, despite poverty and degradation, people continue to cope and persevere, when they show the buoyancy and create the relatively benign environment I have noted, it is because this basic philosophy mobilizes enough of them, enough of the time, to sustain their struggle against adversity. It is the wellsprings of such strength I ask the reader to look for, in the pain and contentiousness of Umm Ali's life. Where are they lodged?

Basically, I see them in the overwhelming commitment of mothers to their children, a commitment that motivates wives and mothers to hold their families together, to discipline and drive their men to support the children, to take the long view and think of the future. "Project Children" may be a fitting name for this supreme orientation to life, which they call "making a future for the children." [*yi'mil mustaqbal lil 'ayyal*] Throughout the book, you will hear the voices of women—and the supporting voices of men—clamoring for this orientation, this priority, in their eternal battles with scarcity and despair. Nor is this a commitment that ignores people at other points in the life span. "Project Children" naturally requires a milieu, a proper place for children to grow and thrive. And that environment is best secured if children are part of a larger network that includes the elderly. Moreover, "Project Children" aims to foster a commitment in those, once vulnerable, who saw their own caretakers struggle on their behalf, so that when the relationship is reversed, the elderly are secured some human supports. And probably the attention and commitment on the part of the mother creates in each child a deep security and sense of self-value that even the indignities of poverty can never fully erase.

Given the supreme priority of "Project Children," other elements also fall into place as positive supports. The force of Islam and its control of family life and sexuality in some ways strengthen the hand of the *sitt il bet,* the matron of the house. The impact of Islam as practiced in this population also bans alcohol among women, and deters its use among men, thus effectively countering the ills of alcohol and drug abuse. The importance of hospitality and generosity that is a distinguishing mark of Egyptian values may be a recurrent cause of shame and failure, yet it serves to regulate the forms of socialization in the community. Savings clubs create mutual commitments to the future and empower people to manage their assets as they would not be able to on their own. And even the gossip, gloating, and public shaming of enemies, though it causes pain, also transmits lessons and affirms the validity of ways of coping, proximal goals to pursue, and the importance of standards. In assessing the environment that Umm Ali and the others describe, there are submerged synergies to uncover that help us find the wellsprings of people's resilience and capacity for self-help (Wikan 1995).

That people mobilize such strength and resistance in no way exculpates governments from their active oppression or passive negligence with respect to the poor; on the contrary, it only adds to their moral responsibility. And the Cairo poor are relentless in their condemnation of three governments—Nasser's, Sadat's, and Mubarak's—for their indifference. But trusting the government to help is like waiting for the world to turn upside down. Meanwhile your children will suffer. So for the sake of making a future for the children, people must also struggle to better their own condition. Poverty of material means does not excuse poverty of the spirit.

If this book can work to change an ingrained perception in the West that the urban poor are simply that—destitute—then something will have been achieved. If it can also lead us to learn ways in which people are enabled to cope with adversity against all odds, then Umm Ali's dictum, "talking together makes wise," will have borne fruit.

Responsibility and ethics

How does Umm Ali react to having her life laid bare in a book, to exposing her most private feelings and problems? And what of her family and relations: her husband, children, daughter-in-law, and others who might recognize themselves in this account?

To take Umm Ali first; I have discussed the composition of this book with her in detail. She knows which stories I use, and in what context I place them. But I have not translated the text for her, so she cannot know the total impression I convey. Yet she says she wants her story told. She believes in openness and trust, not just among intimates but across the world. "Talking together makes wise" is her motto.

Equally important, most of the problems I expose she regards not as private in the sense of the word as we use it. The disclosures I make which she feels are most intimate have nothing to do with her sexual life, the physical violence in her marriage, or the many problems with the children. Everyone has these kinds of difficulties, they are in the nature of things, as people see it; it would be absurd to try to pretend otherwise. Umm Ali and her associates are blessedly spared my own society's demand for the happy marriage and the happy façade. Rather, people talk openly of their marital and family problems, secure in the knowledge that they will receive support, and that it helps and heals to share such problems with others. Umm Ali herself does it daily. Every story I recount I have heard her tell numerous times to close and distant relations alike.

What she does not talk openly about, because it is private and shameful according to her society's values, has to do with debt and material need. This is where her circle of social others might criticize her, this is where she stands most exposed to ridicule and shame. That the world should come to know that her husband did not bring her a chicken when she had given birth to their child is more serious than our being privy to the fact that he has broken her front teeth. That he was two months behind in paying the electric bill is worse than his trying to force intercourse on her by kicking and hitting her.

And yet we have agreed that these dark secrets have to be told. God willing, may the reader be compassionate.

But what of the innocent accomplices in the dramas here told, people who were not asked if they would grant their permission to let themselves and their lives be used? Might it not do irreparable damage to them and their social relations if the book's contents seeped back to them?

The answer is, yes, it could. And yet, when I choose to put them at risk, it is from the vision of a broader motive. The only way to inspire our compassion and respect for people mired in poverty is for these individuals who stand forth in all their humanity with their tragedies and their triumphs to bear witness. If in such a story of suffering and triumph, there are some sordid accounts, so be it. God willing, may people in Cairo, too, read the book as it is meant to be read: as a rhetoric of complaint, a cry of despair and protest against all those powers that would trap one. And may they see through even the blackest stories some glimmer of hope and joy that reveals people's love and care for themselves and each other, without which, as they well know, they would indeed be lost.

Fortunately, there is the added circumstance that the stories told here belong to the past. Life and relations change, and though the stories will be repeating themselves in other lives and other versions—and even in these same lives in new versions—so that my account is in that sense up-to-date, there is the comforting circumstance that time draws a veil between past events and present vulnerabilities. Also, any one account is always a partial one. Much of the blame should be placed on me, if thereby others go scot-free.

Probably the gravest accusation that can be made against me is that I use the label "poor." An incident regarding my first book (Wikan 1980) is revealing. I had brought it with me to show to my friends, and was especially antici- pating the happiness of the old woman who is featured on the cover with a crowd of children. I could just envision how proud she would be. She was. But her daughter was furious. The only one who could read a little English, Gamila made out the word "poor" in the title—"*Life among the Poor in*

Cairo"—and raised hell. Pointing to her color TV, she screamed, "Poor, is *that* what you call us? Do *you* have a color TV? [She knew I did not, just black and white.] Shaming us before the whole world!" I was distraught and tried to defend myself, when her brother turned up. Taking her to task, he admonished her, "Now stop it! You know she has told the truth! Poor, that's what we are. Is *that* any shame?"

Gamila's reaction is paralleled by that of some Egyptian officials who were also distraught that I had used the word "poor." Their position was, Egyptians are not really poor. In both cases, vested interests are at stake. As for Gamila, she was in love with a boy of better position whose family had rejected her. Her experience was particularly painful in that the boy's sister and she had been best friends (they had met at a sewing course). But when Gamila threatened to become part of the family, she was rejected—simply for being poor. Thus the worst indictment that had been made of her, and that had cost her her love, had been repeated by me. And I had gone public with it, branding her for all time.

Fortunately, Gamila's fears proved untrue. She is now married to her onetime beloved; and she has risen to lower-middle-class status both by virtue of this alliance and her own university education.[9] But her reaction portends judgments that may be launched against me by others. At the time, she was the only one I knew to take exception to my use of the term "poor," which they all used about themselves. But now things have changed. Now many of the children aspire to middle-class status, and some have even attained it, enhancing their parents' status in the process. For them this book may be like a fist in the face. I sincerely beg them to forgive and reconsider. Unless we give poverty a human face, we cannot expose the dignity and drive that have made these children what they are, and we cannot rehabilitate their parents without foregrounding the parents' achievements. Unless we expose the indignities visited upon them by an unjust system, we cannot expose the absurdity of people being forced to live in this way with a view to enlighten those with the power to change the state of affairs.

How people in Cairo struggle against all odds to compose dignified lives is the main thrust of this book. May it stand as a testimony to a remarkable woman and a remarkable people.

9. To tell of her achievement, she never attended primary school, her family was too poor; but she read by herself in the dim light of the night after she came home from work. By the force of tremendous will power, perseverance, and good brains she made it in the end through university, graduating at the age of 38.

Talking Together Makes Wise

"I like talking with people," says Umm Ali. "Talking together makes wise. Where had we humans been, and what had we understood, if we did not tell each other what each of us thinks and feels, and why we are happy and why we are sad. It is a life necessity to be able to talk. You get the problems *out* of your body that way. Talking together, like I and you do now, purges you of sorrow/anger [*za'l*] and invigorates your soul."

And she remarks about her daughter Afaf, "It was because she sat silent, never letting her problems out, that she got sick in her soul. If only she had been able to talk!"

Umm Ali practices what she preaches. Like most people in the back streets, she will talk to just about anyone who can be made to listen about her deeply felt concerns as well as the minor—but no less urgent—trivia of everyday life. Both women and men seem to have a persistent urge to let their feelings out, and to compel others to become engaged, even sitting them down to make them listen. Thus the air around them is vibrant with talk, and life resonates with perpetual high drama.

Life in the back streets is never dull. It may be hard, dismal, desperate, and sad, but it is perpetually full of commotion to the extent of making people long for some peace and quiet, some escape from this torrent of events. Often it is talk [*kalam*] that gets the thing going, triggering events that then proceed with their own momentum—to the sheer exasperation of the main actors.

When they talk, people employ all the theatrical and rhetorical skills with which they are richly endowed and enter with body and soul into their act. The audience, too, joins in with running commentaries, roaring exclamations, and vigorous head wagging to express their heartfelt concern. Often several of them have their own story of what really happened, or how it all went. They will try to drown each other out in a crescendo of clamor and sound. It is as if one hears the air crack—as if its powers to absorb all this talk were bursting.

Life revolves around talk, as it revolves around food and sleep. Through

Talking together makes wise.

talking, people assert themselves, they realize themselves, they project their longings and aspirations. Through talking, one seeks an outlet for anger, consolation for sorrow, a testimony to love and loyalty, and togetherness in the group. Talking is the essence of all social interaction. And the quiet and taciturn are losers in this milieu.

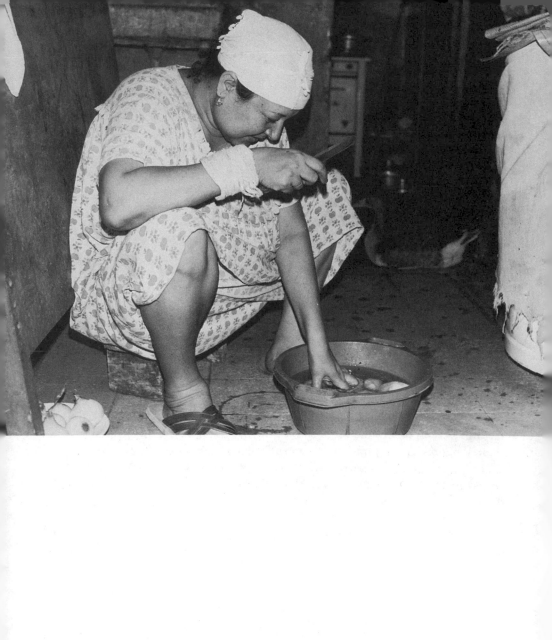

Part One

Woman, Mother, and Poor

One

A Broken Dream

Presentation (*anno* 1982)

Umm Ali is her name, and she has borne eight children. Ali is thirty-one years old, he is married, and drives a taxi. He still has no children. Then there was Amin who died when he was nineteen. He set fire to himself. He was wise and handsome and attended high school. Next is Hoda, now twenty-seven, she works in a factory. She quit school after tenth grade because her fiancé demanded it. He was a traitor and left her. Next is Mona, at twenty-four; she also works in a factory, the same as Hoda. She quit school after eighth grade because her fiancé demanded it. He, too, was a traitor and left her. Then there was Aleyya who died when she was four. She was the most beautiful of all the children. Next is Afaf, now in eighth grade. She has been sick in her nerves, but now she's better, thanks be to God. Then there is Anwar, who goes to seventh grade. And last is Nosa, in third grade now. Then she bore a boy who died in her stomach, praise be to God, for he had diabetes, just like his mother.

This, roughly, is how it would be told if Umm Ali were introduced by a woman of her own milieu. This is how women in the back streets introduce each other to third persons.

They are mothers, and such are their achievements.

The dream

"To have a husband who looks after his wife and children with all that they need of food and clothes; who shows his wife affection and sits home with her when he is free from work, or takes her and the children out for leisure—that's all in the world for a woman. . . . But only one in a hundred ever reaches it."

Such is women's dream of the good life—and their experience of life's harsh reality.

"And ever since have I neglected my looks"

I was only fifteen years when I got married, and marriage seemed to me something frightening because I was so young. Mustafa used to come home to us to visit my sister's husband, Abdou—they were friends—that's how he got to see me. First, he asked Mama permission

27

"You should have seen me before,
how beautiful I was." Umm Ali
at age seventeen.

to marry Farida [older sister], but she refused because he is black. But
I thought he was handsome and followed Mama's advice to marry him.

Mustafa was not the first suitor who came to me. There had been
two before him. The first one was as lovely as a movie star, he looked
just like King Farouk! But Mama refused to accept him because he
already had one wife—and that though he promised to place us each
in a separate flat. Oh, I wanted to marry him! The second she refused
because his job was no good—I've forgotten what it was; perhaps he
was a doorman or something. . . . When she agreed to Mustafa, it was
to please Abdou ['ashan xatr Abdou]. Baba [Father] protested and said
that Mustafa was no good because he smoked hashish. But Mama said
that Abdou said he was good/ kind [tayyib], "and so tomorrow, God
willing, he'll be good, you wait and see!"

We were engaged in great haste. I knew nothing about it in advance.
One morning as I awoke, Mama said to me, "Today is your engagement
day!" Baba didn't know it either, so he had gone to work, and didn't
even attend the party. Mustafa only gave me one ring, no engagement
gift like a groom should to make his bride happy—a bracelet or necklace or such. I cried at the party for I was completely taken by surprise
and didn't know what I was in for. And Mama scolded me and said that
it was a shame to cry at one's own engagement party.

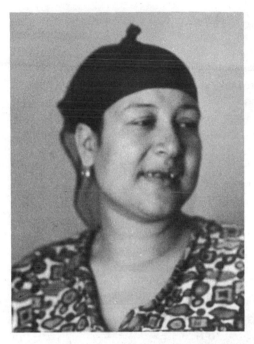

"And ever since, I have neglected my looks." Umm Ali at age forty-one.

It was just a very small party, with Mama, my sisters, Abdou, and two of my aunts on Mama's side. From Mustafa's family, nobody came. And even at the wedding, there was only one person from his side, his brother-in-law. His sister could not come because her children were sick. And his foster mother was angry because he didn't marry one of *her* daughters. So neither she nor her husband came!

We were engaged for ten months. It was a happy time. Mustafa used to take me out together with my sister. We went to the movies, cafés, and to the zoo. But our happiness stopped the moment we were married. Mustafa spent all his free time in the company of his bad friends, smoking hashish and drinking whiskey with them. I had known that Mustafa used to do these things before we were married. But I had thought that all would be well once we had our own home, and he came free of the influence of his bad friends. Instead, the opposite happened. Mustafa ignored me completely. He came and went as it suited him, and beat me and abused me if I ever so much as asked him where he had been, or tried to warn him about the dangerous path he was following. That's how I lost my two front teeth. Mustafa used to flog me with his belt against my cheeks and back and ears, till my back was black and blue, and I nearly lost my hearing on one ear. . . .

But really, it wasn't Mustafa's own fault that he behaved the way he did. It was his friends and most of all my brother-in-law Abdou who made him do it. They told him to bully me and not accept any interference, to act the strong man.

All day long I was left to myself and my sad thoughts. I cried as I paced back and forth, back and forth, in the flat. Late at night, when Mustafa eventually came, things only became worse. For he beat and abused me, and tried deliberately to pester me—to dominate. For instance, he would make me set the table, then remove it, then set it again, then take it all out again. I had eaten long before he came, and slept some, too. When Mustafa came, I would get up and warm up the food and put out the *tabliyya* [the Egyptian low table] and serve him. But I wouldn't have any food myself since I had already slept a bit, and it has always been impossible for me to eat just after I've slept. That's how I had been taught in my mother's house. But Mustafa cursed me and commanded me to eat with him. When I still refused, he flew into a rage. He flung the dishes at me and ripped off his belt and flailed me, then made me remove the food. No sooner had I done it than he demanded to be fed again, and so I had to fetch it all out again. . . .

Afterwards, when we had gone to bed, he wanted to sleep with me, while I cried. How could he imagine that this kind of life was possible, first scolding and beating and outright neglect, and then together-together [*sawa sawa*] in bed! How could he ever think that I could bear to sleep with him?

I was terribly unhappy 'cause I had expected marriage to be sharing, doing things together, just the two of us, for Mustafa to come home from work, and then we would sit together and talk together, we two; and on holidays, we'd go walking together in the park or visiting the relatives. In the beginning, I used to make myself so beautiful for him. I prettied myself with rouge and mascara and met him in the door when he came, dressed in my chiffon negligée, all adorned and beautiful for him. But then I saw that it made no difference. And ever since, I have neglected my looks. . . .

Two

Tomorrow, God Willing

"The man should have his freedom, but not at the woman's expense"

I tried to make Mustafa understand that we must be open with each other and mutually adjust—that we must tell each other what each of us liked and wanted from life, so we could make each other happy. But he just scowled and said, "I do as I please!" [*ba'mil mazagi*] and "I'm free!" [*ana hurr*]

He thinks he is free, but nothing could be farther from it! He has taken his freedom the wrong way [*xad hurriyyitu 'ala il ghalat*]. As a child, he was kept very strictly by his foster parents, his father's brother and the wife, and so when he came free of them, he never knew how to use his freedom and behave decently [*yitsarraf tasrif salim*]. The first thing he did was move in with his friends, and all *they* did was have parties and smoke hashish; they used all kinds of stuff. And *that* he thought was freedom!

And this is how he has continued. What he's really doing is acting against himself, not by means of his freedom [*biyi'mil ghasb 'annu, mish bi hurriyyitu*]. Of course, the man should have his freedom, but not at the woman's expense!

"The man is like a child"

But it really isn't Mustafa's own fault that he behaves the way he does. He just follows the example of those who reared him. His foster father was just the same; so was my own father, too. They smoked hashish and drank beer. His foster sisters, too, are to blame for how he became. For they reared him up by means of abuse and beatings and bullying, so they created resentment in him. Freedom is good and right, otherwise children will do twice what they were kept from doing when they were small. And look at Mustafa now! He does just the same wrong to his own children as others did to him!

I pity Mustafa that he never had a mother who could teach him about right and wrong, and to live decently in the world. Men are like children—they need kind words and love and compassion. Because the man must leave his mother when he marries, and go to his wife, the wife must give him all that his mother used to do, and be in her stead. I tried to be in a mother's place to Mustafa. I wanted to teach him about life so he

31

could tell right from wrong, the things he never learned because he was separated from his mother as a baby. But he has kept doggedly to his old ways. That way he wore himself out, and us, too.

If a marriage is to succeed, the hearts of the two must be together. Just like two who start a business together: It is doomed to fail unless they cooperate.

"God helps him who helps himself"

Whenever I ask Mustafa for money for food and household expenses, he is cross and grumpy and abuses me for squandering and wastefulness. He doesn't have the faintest idea what it costs to feed a family, nor does he want to know, either, for he lacks all sense of responsibility. He says he'll give me some [money] as soon as he gets some. But *when* will that be? I need it regularly, not just now and then! Always he says, "Tomorrow, God willing" [*bukra insh'allah*] or "Nothing doing, never mind" [*ma'lesh*] or "Later" [*ba'den*] or "May God make it possible!" [*Rabbina yisahhil*] But all his "God willing"s are just empty talk. To begin with, I *believed* him when he said, "Tomorrow, God willing, I'll bring you some money." But then I learned that his words have no connection with reality. God will not help those who do not struggle to help themselves. Man must, while saying "God willing," decide in his heart, commit himself in his soul, put it into his mind that he will *act* to realize what he has said. Mustafa only creates false expectations and then destroys your hopes.

He has no intention to make an effort to put his promises into effect. He just stands there as if he expected the money to materialize from thin air. What's more, he even bungles those lucky breaks that come along. He always excuses himself saying he has bad luck. But I have told him, it's not his luck that's bad, it's his behavior!

God rewards those who are honest and upright and responsible. Mustafa is false and fraudulent—*that*'s why nothing works out for him. . . .

I have never been in a position to trust him, never known if he would bring us money for the next meal. It's always been me who had to manage somehow to provide the children with food and clothes and money for school, still their crying, and requite their needs. Always me who had to borrow and save and manage. Mustafa is so negligent that he doesn't even ask what I paid for a thing, or where I got the money from. If the children show him clothes I've bought, he just says, "Great!" without even asking what it cost, or how I raised the money. If I complain that we are broke, he just answers, "Praise the Lord for what He gives you!" If I

A view over the rooftops in Umm Ali's quarter.

ask for money for food, clothes, or the rent, he just says, "Tomorrow, God willing" or "May God provide!" But his calls upon God issue only from his mouth, not from his heart. I have asked if he really expects God to step down here himself and *hand* him over the money! No, the Lord has said, "Be alert, my servant, and I shall help you; sleep, my servant, and I shall desert you." God helps him who helps himself.

Three

The Back Street Environment

The way in

She lives on the second floor of a run-down four-story house in the back streets of Cairo, about six miles from the center of town [*midan ittahrir*]. The closest bus stop is about fifteen minutes' walk away, and the road passes along narrow market streets so crowded with people and stalls you have to elbow your way through. After a while you arrive in a broad main street. *Hitta frangi*—modern quarter—the people call it. The street is noisy, dusty, and littered, with hordes of people and deafening traffic and a chaos of buses and cars, bicycles, and motorcycles, donkey carts, horse carriages, and pedestrians by the thousands in every conceivable direction. All your senses are awhirl. Here a cyclist in reckless abandon, one hand in his pocket and balancing a tray of bread on his head, scattering swearing people, barking dogs, and cackling hens right and left; there a wreck of a bus, with the driver's foot on the gas and elbow on the horn, lurching wildly with a number of male passengers clinging to its outside—in breakneck maneuvers. The din is enough to burst your eardrums, not just from the thundering traffic but also from music, song, and soap opera blaring out of radios, loudspeakers, and cassette players. Shrieking voices in high falsetto cut through the racket, shouting and joking, fighting and laughing.

The odors are equally numerous and strong: hot fresh bread from a few bakeries and many bicycle vendors offering their lovely *'esh baladi*—native bread—at one piaster a loaf;[1] the smell of spicy foods served in the innumerable sidewalk cafes where men like to take their meals mingles with the odor of urine from an assorted animal population of stray dogs, cats, donkeys, horses, and the occasional sheep, and the pungent aromas from unrefrigerated butcher shops and fruit stalls.

Everywhere there are people—people moving about and finding their way through a chaos which to them has both rhyme and reason. The place is aswarm with people—of every age, size, and shape. But the women are in the majority, or so it seems, watching their heavy, ponderous and self-assured figures striding through the crowd. Men, by comparison, seem slight

1. An Egyptian pound is divided into 100 piaster. Between 1969 and 1995 the pound has generally fallen in value against the U.S. dollar from a high of approximately $2.30 to a low of about $0.30. Around 1982 the pound was worth about $1.50.

At the market.

and insignificant with their weak and often skinny bodies, haggard faces, and shuffling gait that undermine any attempt to appear forceful and assertive.

What help can Arab culture offer them, with its ideology designating men the select, set to govern womankind, when everyday reality is a desperate struggle to survive and to wrench a modicum of respect from their fellows, an effort at which they often fail, and through which many lose whatever trace of assurance and self-confidence they once had. They know so well, these men, that it is said about them, "The man does as the wife says" [*irragil biyisma' kalam miratu*], "The man tags along after his wife" [*irragil mashi wara' miratu*], or "The women rule" [*issittat biyuhkumu*]. Indeed, the men say so themselves—about *other* men.

Shoes make people
The main street is an arena for self-display and a center for commerce and recreation. Along the sidewalks, like pearls on a string, are the tightly

Two friends, one dressed in the black *milaya*, the other in a long turquoise silk dress, choose tomatoes at the market. Note the woman with her back toward the viewer; today it would be unheard-of to dress like this, whereas into the 1970s it was quite common.

packed shops. Some are big, like the pharmacy and the government co-op, but most are mere holes in the wall. Along the gutter is parked a nearly solid line of the handcarts of peddlers selling fruits, vegetables, bric-a-bric, and "special offers." These vehicles, pushed by country folk—*fellahin*—trying to make a penny in town, arrive early in the morning and leave late at night. Trading is brisk, with loud bargaining and histrionics. Most customers are women and children. Division of labor in the family is such that nearly all shopping falls on them.

The importance of the occasion can be read from the way people dress. Women are either clad in the impersonal, respectable *milaya*—a black, sacklike Mother Hubbard that covers all save hands and feet and perhaps the bottom of the *gallabiyya*—a nightgown-like inner dress—that shows below the hem, or else they are done up to the limits of their ability. To go to the market dressed in the long silk evening dress, the one used for marriages, is quite within the ordinary. Everyday wear is conspicuously absent.

Bargaining is usual at the market.

The reason, people say, is that they are being inspected by an army of critics bent on finding faults and errors in their dress, "so we must dress up just to go to the main street as if it were to a wedding we went!" they complain.

Till the late 1970s, men wore Western clothes almost exclusively: slacks, shirts, and jackets. Very few still dressed in the traditional Arab long tunic (in Egypt called *gallabiyya*), and then mainly in the evening when relaxing at their regular cafe after the stresses and strains of the day's work. Since the early eighties, this has changed. A number of men, perhaps one in three, now wear the *gallabiyya* regularly.[2]

2. This reflects two circumstances, as I understand it. The traditional Arab dress/ tunic is worn with pride and dignity by the new masters of the Arab world, Saudi and Gulf Arabs, who seasonally invade Cairo to escape the tormenting heat of their home countries and to enjoy forms of entertainment not permitted them at home. Due to their power and wealth, they have set the fashion in many fields, including dress. Also, the fundamentalist resurgence, though it does not find many adherents at lower-class levels, has set its mark on dress for both genders.

Mona at the corner where the road leading into Umm Ali's lane takes off to the right at the far end of the main street. The street is broad and good by local standards.

Through all these years (since the late 1960s), young girls had dressed in bright colors and the newest Western fashion, whether mini, midi, or maxi. But since the early eighties, the style has changed markedly for them also in the direction of religious conservatism. The cut is more modest, and the colors subdued. Tight pants have disappeared, as have tight skirts and sweaters. Now the skirts are full, blouses are long sleeved and loose, and they are often hidden beneath an ankle-length wide Islamic dress which is now in fashion and worn by many, but not all, females of whatever age (save children). Colors that used to be thought dull and ugly and that I never expected to see used for dressy clothes are now regarded as fashionable and modern: beige, gray, pale rose, and dark blue. Young men are also very fashion conscious. But among them, no radical change has yet occurred. They still favor narrow slacks, shiny shoes, flashy shirts and sweaters, and hairstyles well cut and tended.

Shoes are particularly important for both sexes. People complain that what everyone *else* is doing while waiting at the bus stop, for example, is inspect each other's shoes. Little children, however, run about in pajamas and plastic sandals, if they have anything on their feet at all.

The modern quarter

Hitta frangi—modern quarter—is the term grandly applied to the main street by the local people. Thus they invoke a vestige of its former grandeur and present relative poshness: the large and well-built façades, the width and surfacing of the street, and the good manners of the residents. "Nobody sits in the doorway and stares at what the neighbor's husband brings home for dinner. Nor do they hang out of their windows and hurl abuse at passersby, or lash out at each other in the street. Everyone stays in her place."

That is how things should be, they imply; neighborhood obliges. Whoever lives in an area as classy as a "modern street" must keep up to its standards. And that, of course, implies refraining from the kind of despicable manners that demean life where one has to live.

By any other standards one would hardly find the main street "classy"; and Cairo's better-off citizens would doubtless scoff at the pretensions of the term *afrangi*. The houses may be large, but they are overcrowded, the plaster is peeling off, the blinds hang akimbo, and the filth is thick up along the walls. The street may be wide but trash and garbage abound, and the crowd bears vivid testimony—in dress and manners—to their low status. A "modern quarter" to back street residents is a "simple quarter" to the affluent.

The *baladi* quarter

A few hundred meters down the main street, beside a whitewashed little mosque, you turn right, and you enter another world. "*Hitta baladi*— native quarter—the people call it, and mean by that that the neighborhood is second rate and the people uncouth and rude. The lane is narrow, just five to six meters from wall to wall. The houses rise straight up from the street, like the sides of a narrow canyon. Garbage piles up in great mounds, and the stench of the open sewer hits you in the face. But life abounds— mainly there are women and children, besides an assortment of animals— sheep, donkeys, and stray dogs—that throng around the garbage piles.

Until the mid-eighties, no cars passed here.[3] At night, there might be a

---

3. Nowadays, it is common to see cars in the area, especially at night. With the terrible state of the public transport system and the increased distances within the city (Cairo is expanding rapidly and both one's work and relatives may be at opposite ends

Umm Ali's lane.

couple of cars parked, but a taxi driver would scoff at the mere idea that he should be willing to enter with his precious motorcar. A narrow sidewalk runs along each side of the lane but is blocked here and there by handcarts and donkey carts or similar obstacles. You do best to hold your breath to block out the stench of the sewer, and you zig-zag along the middle of the street, keeping clear of the larger mounds of garbage.

Fifty meters farther along, you turn off to the right again, into an even narrower lane. This passage is only three to four meters broad. A characteristic, pungent odor hits you as you round the corner; it comes from stagnant, rotting refuse. The lane is dark. In contrast to the one you just left, the sun rarely reaches down to the ground here. The back street is like a narrow niche, flanked by tall-seeming (though only three- to four-story) buildings torched by sunlight only on the top floors. All the houses are brick; all of them were originally plastered though much has long since flaked off. There are shutters over the windows (to keep out the inquisi-

---

of the city) plus the fact that driving a taxi is a main source of income for many men, the incentive to buy a poor quality second-hand car is very high.

tive gaze of neighbors), and balconies on the second and third floors. Like other adults, you step gingerly to avoid the rotting garbage, whereas the children don't mind and play on top of it.

At the third entrance on your left you enter—through a dark, low passage—you have to crouch to clear the doorbeam—and walk over a mud floor and up a narrow staircase that stinks of urine from dogs and from the communal toilet on the ground floor. It is so dark that if you arrive in the evening, you have to grope your way up the uneven staircase to the second floor. There, on a tiny landing, is one door to the right, one to the left. You reach for the one to the left and knock hard, several times, to drown out the clamor of TV and clattering voices inside. Finally, the latch is pushed aside, a child opens the door, and you have arrived.

Four

A Woman and Her Man

Umm Ali

This is the home of Umm Ali, her husband Mustafa, and five children ranging in age (in 1982) from twenty-seven to ten years. The family has lived here for twenty-eight years. When I came to know them, in 1969, there were two more children: the eldest son, since married and living elsewhere, and the second oldest, now dead; the youngest, Nosa, was not yet born.

She is a striking woman, tall and poised and beautiful. Well, maybe she is not actually beautiful, in the strict sense of the term, but her warmth and personal magnetism give her a presence that is best described in such terms. Her body is solid—she must weigh fully 220 pounds—but her own complaint is that she has lost so much weight. I should have seen her before when she was plump and beautiful, she says, and pulls forth, for the umpteenth time, a dilapidated album of photographs, faded and torn from a thousand showings. The ideal of feminine beauty among these Egyptians is "the fatter, the prettier," and to emphasize one's own good qualities is not regarded as bad form, but is expected and accepted. Her face is pear shaped, her skin so light she is truly called *be-e-e-da* [white] with a praise-ringing long vowel, in a culture singularly conscious of nuances in skin color, where white is beautiful, black is ugly

Her forehead is high, her eyebrows narrow, with a natural arch. Her hair is curly and still black, without a trace of gray, and is combed tightly back under a head scarf that reaches half-way down her forehead, in the style favored by women. Her nose is long and narrow, lips shapely and curved over practically toothless gums that flash unabashedly at you when she smiles, talks, or laughs—as she does almost constantly. Umm Ali loves to talk. Conversation makes wise and creates closeness between people, she says—in an eternal argument with her husband who is of a different temperament and takes a different view of the matter.

But the most beautiful feature of Umm Ali is her eyes, radiant eyes that twinkle and laugh, and shine with warmth and wisdom; eyes that may turn bottomlessly dark from sorrow, or narrow in anger and fury, yet never quite lose their touch of humor and joy of life, sparkling eyes framed in a fine pattern of wrinkles from her smile.

She is forty-seven years old now. Actually, she does not keep track of it and know her own age. But her daughter Hoda has worked it out that her mother must have been born on 24 December 1934.

Her skin is still tight and smooth; her hair has thinned but still has its shine and vitality; only the body shows signs of age. Though her back is still straight, she moves ponderously and with effort. And she always feels ill, she says, ever since her diabetes struck in 1972 after her son Amin set fire to himself and died. She is convinced that it was the shock of his death that brought on the disease. She spends much time in bed, is tired most of the day, and lies restless and sleepless much of the night. This has been her condition ever since her son died. The pain of his loss has threatened to crush her.

Some more teeth have also been lost through the years (in addition to those Mustafa knocked out). Sorrow and bitterness erode the gums, she says, to make the teeth fall out. And yet I am struck by a feeling that in a sense she has only grown younger and younger. No doubt, this is partly because I have grown older and changed my attitude toward age. We met when I was a student of twenty-four and she, at thirty-four, was the mother of six, so the difference in our ages then seemed much greater than it does now, when I, too, am married and a mother. And I see in my diary that on our first meeting, in September 1969, I thought she looked close to sixty! With her weight and presence, both physical and spiritual, she gave me a deceptive impression of great maturity, of having lived very long. Yet in a sense, I was not so wrong.

At thirty-four, Umm Ali had been married for nineteen years and had shouldered responsibility ever since she was a small child. In her mother's house, little Zenab—as she was called until she became a mother and took the name of her firstborn—had lived a life of many duties and few amusements. In her own home, the responsibility for eight children—and a husband—has weighed heavily on her. As she says, "I, without earning a penny, have had to support us all!" and "After thirty years of marriage, I still feel like a girl [*bint*], for I have never been the wife of a *man!*"

Life and fate in her world and mine differ so much that personal age likewise becomes incommensurate. Yet I cannot understand now that I ever thought of her as being sixty: She is incredibly well preserved, and is younger in body and mind than many women her age in my society. The reason, above all, lies in a deep difference in attitude toward age between her society and mine. We fear aging and try to disguise its traces, but the fear itself takes its toll. Egyptian women of lower class value the authority and respect that age lends, while savoring the reduction in toil and responsibility it brings. No one likes to grow old. But there is no doubt about it, Umm Ali has flourished with every child raised to maturity. If her health does not go too fast, she may still have the best years of life ahead of her.

And it is incredible how well her health stands up despite ten years of diabetes which she has had neither the money nor the energy to treat properly. She has never taken regularly the medication prescribed, nor could she afford the protein-rich food the doctor tells her she needs. Yet she continues to use sugar in her tea—not so much each time, but surely ten times a day—and she lives on, if not in the best of health, then at least in surprisingly good condition!

Mustafa

Umm Ali's husband, Mustafa, is her diametrical opposite in body and soul. He is short and dark, indeed, so dark that people refer to him as black (*iswid*), a term implying African, rather than using the word *asmar* (brown); and I have given up taking his photograph. Most people in the neighborhood love to be photographed, and they usually implore you to take their picture; but Mustafa is always so disappointed with the result. He complains that my camera makes him look even darker than he is. And in Egypt, as in much of the world, the judgment is categorically that the whiter, the lovelier, the darker, the uglier.

Mustafa, poor man, is well aware of his handicap. Umm Ali tells me how he accuses her, when they quarrel, of despising him because he is black. According to him, that is at the root of their troubles. "Not at all!" she will say that she answers, "it's not you I condemn but your behavior." And I believe her. There is nothing to indicate that she looks down on Mustafa for his negroid features: the black skin, thick lips, flat nose, and kinky hair. But the conventions associating such traits with ugliness are

A man who resembles
Mustafa.

so ingrained that Mustafa can hardly escape an inferiority complex. Umm
Ali herself has reported at least one experience to confirm his fears: He
originally wanted to marry her sister Farida, but she refused him because
he is black.

In sharp contrast to his wife, Mustafa is tactiturn and shy with people.
He cannot even get himself to eat with guests but prefers to have his food
served separately after they have eaten—unheard-of behavior in Egyptian
society where the sharing of food is the essence of conviviality and hospitality. Anyone but Mustafa would risk being dubbed highbrow and hostile
for doing such a thing. But Mustafa is so obviously helpless in his relations
with people who visit his house (how he acts outside, when he is in his
own circle, I have no way of knowing), that he is excused. Countless
times I have seen him fidget and fumble before guests that Umm Ali has
forced on him, trying to be as friendly as he could but so ill at ease that
I could not help but come to his rescue by engaging in conversation with
his guests.

Umm Ali also takes pity on him. "The poor man, he has never learned how to behave with people, because he never had a mother!" Mustafa's father died when he was still a baby, and his mother remarried swiftly. As is generally the case with stepfathers, her new husband refused to feed another man's child, so Mustafa was given to his father's brother and his wife as a foster child. The worst fate Egyptians can imagine is to have a stepmother, and being brought up by kin on the father's side is nearly as bad. Mustafa was either bullied and beaten or outright neglected. Except when it came to money, Umm Ali wryly adds. His foster mother would empty his pockets every night to rob him of whatever meager earnings he had.

Mustafa worked as an apprentice with his uncle who was a well-established mechanic. How good the training must have been is evidenced by the fact that Osman Ahmed Osman—one of Egypt's richest contractors—likewise took his early apprenticeship with Mustafa's uncle and worked his way up from poverty. Mustafa, too, became a competent mechanic, there is no doubt about that. And for a brief moment in time—when he inherited a small sum of money from a childless aunt a couple of years after his marriage—he had the drive to start up his own workshop. So he is *sahib wirsha* [garage owner], a position that ought to provide both money and status. But Mustafa lacks—I have to grant Umm Ali that—a knack for both business and judging people. There must be countless strangers and friends who over the years have taken advantage of him. For Mustafa *is* simple and kind—character traits that will not do in a society of quite crass materialism. For Umm Ali, the workshop has turned into an endless source of worries and expenses, a dripping drain rather than a source of plenty.

Times were better, Mustafa says, when the British were here. Then he had a government job, and in those days there was order and system in the country. This is a widely shared judgment among people who have personal recollections of those times. Mustafa is proud to have been associated with the British. He has kept the government post as inspector [*muhafiz*] since the government became Egyptian. But nothing is the same any more; now, he and many of the people say that corruption, neglect, and disorder reign.

When he goes out of the house, Mustafa always dresses in Western clothes: slacks, jacket, and shirt or sweater. At home he always changes into a pair of striped pajamas, and unlike most men, he never uses the *gallabiyya*. On his head he wears a small Sudanese-type skullcap.

Mustafa is hopelessly devoid of aspirations—or blessedly free of pretensions, whichever way you choose to look at it. Those rare times when he has his picture taken, Umm Ali will look him over, and straighten the collar of his pajamas, to Mustafa's mild protests, "Leave me be, I am the way I am, *baladi kida—baladi* like this." To most people in the area, *baladi* is a derogatory term; they would not dream of using it about themselves, nor allow others to do so. A literal translation might simply be "native" or "of the people", but it is generally used in these circles in the sense of backward, uncouth, rough.[1] That Mustafa uses it about himself reflects perhaps his efforts to distance himself from his wife's and children's aspirations—from their eternal ambitions. Mustafa is resigned; he has accepted his lot in life, unlike them.

Mustafa is the outsider of the family. As his children sometimes say, with a mixture of triumph and regret, "We never tell him anything!" In this family, as in so many others, mother and children form a coalition against the father. Secrets are kept from him, evasions and white lies resorted to when needed for the sake of the children, and to keep peace in the house.

Mustafa probably knows it, and therefore feels resentment. Only in his relation to the smallest children—now there is only Nosa left—and when he watches soccer on TV, does he soften up. When he comes home at night, he is eager to see if Nosa is in bed yet. If she is asleep, he goes to her bed and strokes her, kisses her, tucks the covers around her. If she is awake, he takes her onto his lap and cuddles her. Thus he reveals a longing for tenderness—and an ability to give love—which he could not live out and have satisfied in his marriage, as it has developed, because of him, and because of her. As Umm Ali says, "He goes one way, and I the other, and the two never meet."

Five

The Children

Rights to intercourse

Nine children they have conceived—nine children through simple physical union. "You cannot refuse me my right!" Mustafa has screamed, when

---

1. For a different usage of *baladi,* see El-Messiri (1978) and Early (1993) who in describing practices in two old quarters of Cairo show the positive connotations that can be applied to the term. *Baladi* is here used to connote good old values like honesty, integrity, hospitality, and so on.

she has tried. And understandably so. As a man in a Muslim society, he has an unquestionable legal right to demand intercourse from his wife, and she has the duty to give. Kisses and physical caresses do not belong here—at least not among the poor. With them it is difficult enough to arrange for intercourse when it must take place inaudibly in a room shared with the children, and often in a bed shared with some of them. The women are frantic that the children might notice something, and they complain that the men have no sense of shame. Umm Ali told a story of one time when Mustafa was impatient to sleep with her, and Anwar and Afaf who lay in bed with them, would not fall asleep. Mustafa ordered them to sleep, making it all the more impossible for them. The angrier he got, the more restless they became. When midnight came, and they had not yet dozed off, he tried to force her nevertheless. She got out of bed and went into the hall where she sat down. There she was safe. There he would not pursue her. Intercourse belongs in the bed.

During the past few years, some of the younger women whose husbands have worked abroad have started to complain that their men have presented them with new demands that they should be naked during intercourse! The women will not hear of it. Such lack of modesty and decorum! What is more, nakedness excites the man so he spends longer "doing his thing," whereas they prefer the sexual union to be done with as quickly as possible so that the children will not wake up.

No wonder that, under such circumstances, women say they experience intercourse as a nuisance. Whether they are tired or depressed, or truly sick, the right to intercourse prevails. There are no mitigating circumstances, even if the man has just beaten or abused the wife. Umm Ali and many other wives have time and again been the victims of what we would call rape within marriage. But they do not see it as such; it is not in their way of thinking. They may be harsh in their condemnation of the man for his lack of sense and lack of feeling, when, for example, he fails to see that intercourse requires a modicum of affection, or when he thinks he can beat the wife one moment and lie with her the next. They are also upset that the man often signals his wish by grabbing his wife's arm or kicking her leg. And they resent his resorting to threats of withholding money for food as a sanction to urge compliance. I know women—not only Umm Ali—who say they feel treated like a third-rate girlfriend, that the man's only real interest in them is for sex. And yet they accept the man's right to intercourse, and rarely do they resist. Umm Ali refused Mustafa once only, and had her pants torn and her body beaten. And when her best friend's husband used to come to her and complain that his wife refused to sleep with him, Umm Ali scolded her, "You have to sleep with him. You must give him his right [*haqqu*]. It is written in the Quran."

Islam's emphasis on the man's sexual needs and his right to have them satisfied does not preclude acknowledgment of the woman's sexual drives and needs. In contrast to Christianity, Islam is explicit in its recognition of sexuality as a need that must be satisfied in both sexes. Proof of impotence, in all Muslim countries—Egypt included—guarantees the wife the right to obtain a divorce. According to Islam, women have strong sexual drives that must be satisfied by the husband or society may erupt in chaos and despair (Mernissi 1975). But women among Cairo's poor would scarcely create havoc if they were left in peace sexually. Most would, I think, experience it as a real relief. And that can in no way be explained by the fact that they are circumcised.[1] Cramped quarters, material deprivation, marital conflicts, stress, strain, and drudgery and frequent pregnancies add up to a much more effective means of sexual repression than any form of circumcision.

Despite my intimate knowledge of the lives of a number of women, I do not know of a single case of infidelity among them. Even the "people's talk" [*kalam innas*], which is usually rife with attributions of all kinds of evils to people, does not accuse women of such things. Somehow, the scenario of a woman luxuriating in a man's erotic embrace does not ring true. Women have more satisfying ways of gratifying themselves: in their emotional engagement with their children from whom a woman derives her deepest sense of value and affirmation. A few friends and relatives are also important as sources of love and loyalty, whereas sexuality is regarded as having little or no value in itself.

What might a lover give? Passing satisfaction at the risk of eternal shame. Besides, women are at heart deeply loyal to their husbands. They have an eternal longing to be loved by the man to whom they are wedded. And when they sometimes seem to say something else, by word or deed, it is because their prime goal—making a future for the children—does not leave them any other option. Submitting to the man would thwart that very project. But there is a limit to a wife's recalcitrance. She will not be unfaithful. The husband can at least be assured of her loyalty in that respect.

Hit-or-miss contraception

Nine children they have conceived. The first seven were wished for, whereas the last two were "accidents." And Praise be to God, the last one

---

1. The form of circumcision practiced here is of a relatively moderate kind, involving removal of the tip of the clitoris. Circumcision is commonly practiced in Egypt, though it is now prohibited by law.

was stillborn. The mere thought of how it might otherwise have been makes Umm Ali shudder. A diabetic child, with all that would have implied in expenses and worry. She cannot afford to treat her own condition, and she knows so well that if she had had a diabetic child, all her concern and resources would have gone to it, rather than to herself. Her vitality is spent, so it was a blessing that the child died. "You should have seen him, how he looked, he was huge! His head was so big, they could hardly get him out of me, because he had diabetes. The doctor said he died in my womb only fourteen days before the birth. Thank God that he died!"

Eight live births, two of whom died later—a common enough fate in Umm Ali's generation. Six children were reckoned a suitable flock. That she has had only two accidents is the result of some effort and a good deal of luck. To limit the size of the family, she and her husband have used various methods: in part coitus interruptus,[2] in part a traditional method in which she stuffed her vagina with a particular mixture of herbs to block the flow of the semen. Furthermore, she has nursed all her children till they were two years old, and the last two till they were nearly four. Though nursing does not prevent conception, it does reduce the chances. She will not take the pill. It produces nausea and makes her sick, she says. Not that she has ever tried it, but she knows from others who did. The pill can be obtained at a nominal charge from a nearby clinic. But knowledge of its use is pitifully inadequate, and most women who try it beget complaints—and children. The spiral (intrauterine device or IUD), which she can have inserted free of charge in a neighborhood clinic, she refuses, like most women, even to consider as a possibility. It is widely reputed to cause hemorrhages and to damage the male organ.[3] But after her last accidental conception, when she also nearly lost her life during the birth, she has panicked and will take no more risks. *Haram!* [Sin in

2. Women complain that this technique often fails because the husband does not honor his part of the agreement either to refrain from penetration or to withdraw in time.

3. The pill has been without doubt the preferred form of contraceptive among lower-class women, but it is highly ineffective, as most of them learn by failure. At present the IUD is becoming quite commonly used, though women thoroughly dislike it. However, the disadvantages of the method are being weighed against its efficacy, which is widely known to be far superior to the pill. The problem with the pill is inadequate knowledge of its use, plus the fact that it needs to be taken regularly which is difficult in the chaos and turmoil of a life in poverty. Motivation for family planning has been remarkably strong among lower-class women, which is partly why Egypt has had such success in lowering the national birth rate from an average of six to three children per woman (cf. Cochrane and Messiah 1995).

the eyes of God] she says, when Mustafa wants to sleep with her. That he accepts her refusal is no doubt because he himself was in mortal fear that she might die during her last birth. What should he have done then? Who would have looked after the house, and brought up the children? They now have a silent compromise: one intercourse—interrupted—once a month.

Every time she has given birth, Mustafa has left the house. All the children, apart from the stillborn, were born at home with the assistance of the local midwife. Umm Ali is distressed that Mustafa has gone off every time. She would have wished him to be close, with the sense of sharing and comfort that would have provided. But Mustafa, poor man, could not have managed to be close (in the neighboring room), even if he had wanted to. The strain would have been too much for one so softhearted; he cannot even bear to be close to an ailing pigeon. "Do something! Take it away!" he begs Umm Ali in that case. He has even been known to wake her up in the middle of the night because one of the family pigeons was dying, and the thought of it made him sick. When their son Amin stood aflame, it was she who had to quench the fire. He was incapable of acting at all.

Maternal love

Nine births and six living children—a common enough fate for a woman of her generation. That does not mean that women are resigned to the events and accept the loss of a child with grace. Nothing can so completely shatter a mother. No sorrow is more difficult to bear.

When Umm Ali's Aleyya died of diphtheria, in 1964, at the age of four, Umm Ali was paralyzed, in utter limbo, for four months. She could neither speak nor perform the simplest tasks. Her sisters took turns helping her out and looking after the children. After Amin's death, she sat mute and paralyzed for seven months. And it took her years to come back to normal—if she ever has. The tie between a mother and each one of her children is so strong that the sense of bereavement from the loss of any one child overwhelms her completely. Umm Ali's mother sat paralyzed with grief for seven years after one or her seven children died in an accident.

Children are the focus of women's lives in many societies, but here perhaps more completely than anywhere. Women who cannot give birth—those unfortunate few, for they are few—become a foster parent to one of their sister's children[4] and name themselves after that child. The identification of mother and child is so fundamental that every mother is always known as "Umm" (mother of) her firstborn, whether a girl or a

4. Adoption is forbidden in Islam.

boy. Only her parents, and perhaps her elder siblings, will continue to use her maiden name. And whereas men are also known by their first-born's name, the identification is less absolute for them, and the public may also use their given name. Indeed, the wife generally refers to her husband by his own name, whereas he calls her "mother of ———."

It is not just that women realize themselves by embracing their role as mother. Children are truly loved in this society, not just wanted for the security they give to parents in old age but loved for what they are in themselves, an integral part of mother's life, appreciated as if they were her whole life. No one can love a child like its mother. And no mother can love another's child like her own. The good stepmother is inconceivable, likewise the impartial mother. In any controversy between children, the mother will always side with her own, and clashes between children are the most frequent source of enmity between women.

The mother is likewise the focus of children's deepest, most lasting attachment, the linchpin of everyone's life. When Umm Ali is so sympathetic with Mustafa, it is largely because of the pity she feels for him that he never had a mother. Especially when they are small, children are showered with love and affection. As they grow older and more demanding for material things, the relation between mother and child becomes problematic and may turn hostile at times. For in this culture where it is so accepted that feelings should be allowed expression, love and hate run together without causing fear and distress. A mother's love remains inalienable; and a mother's love contains within itself the whole gamut of emotions. As Umm Ali says: "I love all my children equally, but how well I *like* one or the other depends on how they behave and comport themselves" [*ilmu'amla, ittabaq bitu'hum*].

Six

A Life in Poverty

Living quarters

The first impression of the flat is one of decay, dirt, and mess. All colors have faded to brown or gray. The walls shine with a pale turquoise only where the plaster is still clinging. The floors are stone. Belongings lie spread about where they obviously do not belong: a pair of shoes atop a folded tablecloth on top of the radio, and another pair on top of the bed.

But perhaps there is a certain rationale to this arrangement, since shoes are among one's most precious possessions.

Clothes are bundled and stored everywhere, littering the beds, bulging out of cupboards, hanging from door handles and hooks. Pieces of bread are also floating about on top of the beds, on the floor, on the chest of drawers. There seems to be a surfeit of furniture, especially beds, until one realizes the stark need considering that seven persons live and sleep in a total area of twenty-four square meters.

Consisting of no less than thirty-eight square meters, Umm Ali's flat is indeed relatively spacious by the standards of the poor, and it is of fair quality: not too damp and cold in winter, not insufferably hot in the summer. It is fairly light and airy with good facilities: one front room, two bedrooms/ sitting rooms, a kitchen, and a bath. Many families in the neighborhood make do with much less: dark ground floor rooms, water faucet and toilet shared with other tenants in the same entrance and so forth. In the winter, such flats may be so damp that mildew grows on the walls, and in summer they can be so hot that people haul their beds out into the street to be able to sleep at night. Others again, the poorest among the poor, live in windowless basement rooms or in shacks and shanties built on the rooftops.

Umm Ali is fortunate. She even has a balcony, with a view of the lane. There the children loll over the edge when there is nothing better to do, and there she keeps her dozen pigeons and a few rabbits for occasional meat supplement. It also gives her a place to dry her washing; tenants on street level are dependent on the goodwill of those higher up for a place to hang their laundry, and such goodwill is not always forthcoming.

Another advantage of living above the street level is that it makes it easier to impose a restriction dear to most mothers: keeping their children from playing in the lane. It is a battle fought with single-minded determination from the day the child can walk, but with the mother the winner in most cases. Yet the children will out, and seek to exploit any opportunity to escape. Living above ground level enhances the mother's chances of emerging victorious in this battle.

The rent for such a flat is very moderate: five pounds ($1.5) per month plus a fee for water and electricity. The rent has been the same ever since the family moved in 27 years ago, due to a law imposing a rent freeze on all leases.[1] Umm Ali's landlord and his family live on the third and fourth floors of the house.

---

1. Thanks to this law the people have security of tenancy and drastically falling rents over time. But an unfortunate result of the rent freeze is the deterioration of housing since there is no incentive for the owner to spend on maintenance.

Life without schedule

Regardless of what time of the day you arrive, there is no telling what or whom you will find. Life in the back streets does not move by the watch, it is rather unpredictable. It has its recurrent themes, set by a number of activities that must be performed each day to sustain life and health, but they are often carried out in a haphazard and disjointed manner as if there were no standard pattern or rhythm.

Each task runs on through whatever time it takes, which is usually a great deal. One sleeps, cooks, eats, watches TV, has visitors, goes visiting, does homework, quarrels, fondles, and fights in random succession at just about any time of the day or night. After thirteen years during which I, too, have come and gone at all times of day and night, all I can report of regularity is the following:

Between two and six in the morning it is night; then everyone usually sleeps. But otherwise, there will nearly always be someone sleeping, regardless of the hour. Sleeping is a way—often the only way—of escaping the clamor of the house in a situation of no privacy, so people just fall asleep on the bed where others sit watching TV at full volume under the neon light. Sleeping becomes a way to withdraw and create a private space. Meals, and which family members partake of them, are likewise unpredictable. Breakfast is eaten any time between 6 and 11 A.M., lunch between 1 and 5 P.M., dinner may be at six o'clock, or eleven. Whoever is home, awake, and hungry joins in the meal. One tries to put aside something for household members who are not there—if there is anything left over. If not, one of the children will be sent out later to buy more of the same, or something else, and food is cooked anew when the others arrive. An example of a typical day is 16 October 1976. My field notes read:

> We had dinner at six thirty, Umm Ali, Mona, Afaf, Nosa, and I. It consisted of fried potatoes, bread, and a salad. Anwar came home from playing just as we were finished, but then there was no food left. So Afaf was sent out to buy more bread and potatoes, and Mona told to fry potatoes and make a salad. Shortly afterwards, Hoda woke up: she had been asleep all afternoon. She did *not* want potatoes, and so Afaf was sent out again, this time to buy beans [*ful*]. By the time she came back, her mother had discovered that there were no tomatoes left for a salad for Mustafa and Ali when they would come—and so Afaf was sent out again to buy half a kilo tomatoes. One muddles along without much foresight, and with a spectacular waste of time.

People themselves complain about the lack of system and order [*nizam*] in their lives. Daily life is just a mess, they say, and the absence of plan

A basement room without windows is the home of this widow and her children. Boxes and baskets are her only furniture.

and foresight wears on body and soul. They attribute the disorder to the chronic shortage of money which prevents long-term planning and gives life its character of continuous improvisation and brinksmanship. Time, on the other hand, is something women have plenty of, since little is spent on tidying and cleaning, and the children are entrusted with many tasks and errands. And yet the subjective experience is one of always being pressed for time, in part because of the strain of managing life with little more than the bare essentials. Thought takes a lot of time, and thought is what the women have to employ continually to get through the pitfalls of everyday life: securing food, borrowing money, paying off debts, managing social safety nets, keeping the children off the street, stilling their incessant clamor for things which ought to have been their due but which no power on earth can provide, given the state of the world.

Thus when women, to escape work and relations, proclaim, "I've no time" [*mafish waqt*], it is not simply an empty excuse. Otherwise, being pressed for time is the man's lot. Most men hold down two jobs and put in an average of sixty hours per week. Some take no holiday. The jobs are both in the formal and informal sector of the economy, but it is from the latter that men derive their main income, even when they hold regular employment in the public or private sector. Jobs in the formal sector have the advantage of giving social security in the form of job tenure plus old-age pensions, paid sick leave, and so forth, which is why such employment is eagerly sought by nearly everyone (Egypt has no general social welfare system). But the wage is exceedingly low. The informal sector has been paying much better for decades, and even the educated work in the evenings as painters, electricians, taxi drivers and so forth. The informal economy is what keeps people going, and it also explains why unemployment is rare among most men I know, though Egypt has high official unemployment of about 14 percent.

From seven in the morning till eight at night, Mustafa is usually at work. From 8 A.M. to 2 P.M. he tends his job as inspector at a government automobile center. Afterward, he goes to his own workshop and labors till the evening. On Fridays, which is the government's day off, he usually sleeps late and then goes to his workshop. Sundays, he takes time off to watch soccer matches on TV. Now that Hoda and Mona work in a factory, they too are regularly away until about 3 P.M. The elder, Hoda, always takes a long nap when she comes home. Mona does most of the housework, watches TV, chats with visitors, takes a short nap, and makes the rounds to borrow money, if necessary. Umm Ali sleeps intermittently till eleven in the morning or noon or even two in the afternoon, depending on whether there are visitors she wishes or feels obliged to see. Visitors can arrive at any time of the day or night, from six in the morning till two at night.

Overnight guests are also frequent. They may settle in for months or just for a night. Generally, they are friends or relatives of Umm Ali who have quarreled with their husbands, but relatives of Mustafa or friends of the children can also come. Finding a place for guests to sleep is never a problem—except if it is someone one really does not want to lodge. Up to eight persons can sleep in one double bed, arranged alternately head to feet. Often, someone will also sleep on the floor, and if necessary, some of the children will sleep under the bed.

"People *think* we are well off"

Umm Ali's flat may be fairly high quality, but its furnishings are rather poor, considering the family's economic level. Relatives and neighbors criticize her for squandering money on clothes for the children and not caring how the house looks. Amira, her brother's wife, told me how Umm

Ali's in-laws quarreled with them at Amin's funeral because the couch they had put out in the street for guests to sit on during the Quran reading was dilapidated, without a slipcover. "It was an eyesore!" Amira said, "and Mustafa's relatives abused him and said he could not blame poverty, what with him being a workshop owner and all!" To which Umm Ali would have retorted, "People *think* we are well off, just because Mustafa has the workshop—but they should only have known!" And that they ought not to talk without knowing. Besides, clothes are more important than furniture. And it costs to have two—soon three—marriageable daughters. What is more, it is not with her blessing that the girls wallow in clothes; they don't care what she says, just go and buy on credit, and then present her with the bill! So what can she do?

Just the other day, Hoda came home wearing a new dress, bringing a bill of one and a half pounds from the seamstress. Umm Ali thought there was something familiar about the dress, and on closer scrutiny she saw that it was the beautiful black silk dress I had given her as a gift from Vivi Täckholm![2] Hoda had simply taken the dress and cut it up and had a dress made for herself from the material! Umm Ali was so furious, she tore the dress to pieces.

Figuring time and money

Umm Ali can enumerate every object found in the flat and tell exactly what it cost and how she raised the money. She cannot recall which year it was—1967 or 1975, it makes no difference—but she can place every purchase in relation to vital family events, such as "the year Nosa was born," or "the summer Anwar fell off the balcony," and so on. Numbers are useful to measure cost, not to measure time. She cannot add two and two on a piece of paper, but she can perform the most intricate arithmetic in her head, and has a formidable memory for numbers. But then money is the key to everything, truly the source of happiness, as people see it.

A closer look inside the flat

The flat is divided into three main rooms, besides a tiny kitchen and a bath. A solid brown door separates the landing and the front room. The door is always closed with a lock to keep strangers out, and visitors must knock and pound to be heard. Use of space changes from time to time to accommodate the different demands of the life cycle. But from 1969,

2. A well-known Swedish professor of botany who lived and taught in Cairo for forty years until her death in 1976.

when I first entered the family, until the early eighties, the pattern was more or less like this:

The front room [*sala*] served many functions: sleeping, eating, doing homework, receiving guests. Above all, it contained the TV. The family was one of the first in the neighborhood to obtain one, in 1968. Had the flat been larger, the front room might have served as a dining room, as is often the case among the middle class. But here, lacking both money and space for a dining table, it serves multiple, seemingly disparate, uses.

The walls, as in the other rooms, are alternately splotched turquoise and unpainted gray. A narrow window opens onto a light well. A naked electric bulb, hanging by its cord from the ceiling, provides the light. There is a rusty basin and a cold water tap on one wall—the only tap in the flat. Furnishings consist of an old, green chest of drawers, a tattered couch, two straight chairs, a brown cupboard, and an old schoolroom desk. On top of the desk is a torn plastic cover. A yellow-grey rag in the window niche serves as a curtain.

Two doors on the inner wall lead to the two main rooms of the flat, the bedrooms. To the left are the kitchen and bathroom. The bathroom walls reach only two-thirds of the way up to the ceiling. That was why they immediately saw the flames when Amin set fire to himself and died. The kitchen is an open niche behind the bathroom, without a door but with a bench and some shelves. The butane stove, which the family bought in 1976, is strategically placed by the entry for all visitors to see. It is rarely used, Umm Ali finds the primus both cheaper and easier. Besides, she prefers to sit on the floor to cook rather than to stand, as do most women here. The bath has a hand shower with cold water and a hole-in-the-floor toilet. It also has a great number of cockroaches.

From the front room, special guests—such as men, the daughters' friends, and some women—are led into the room to the right. This is the bedroom of the two eldest daughters, besides other family members, variable over time. Overnight guests also always sleep here, since the husband and wife (and some of the youngest children) sleep in the other room. When Umm Ali and Mustafa are not on speaking terms, he sleeps in the front room.

The right-hand room is roughly three by four meters. It contains a double bed, a large wardrobe, a couch and a small table. Between them, the bed and the wardrobe fill about two-thirds of the room. A door leads onto the balcony. The pane in the door has been broken, and the hole has been covered with cardboard on the outside and a torn yellow sheet of paper on the inside. The door to the balcony is generally left open, so the doorway is shielded by a flowered piece of cloth, tacked up to prevent the neighbors (only a few feet away across the lane) from looking in. Two bricks are stacked under each leg of the bed, to raise it sufficiently to make room for sleeping under it as well. The wardrobe has two doors with cracked mirrors, broken in one of the many marital fights. On top are packed three wicker baskets, a half dozen shoe cartons, and a suitcase. Underneath are several pairs of shoes. Inside are clothes, bundled and stuffed so they bulge out all along the edge of the doors. Towels and clothes are draped over the head of the bed. Clothes hang on the walls; clothes hang on the door handle; clothes are on the floor and in the corners.

The couch, which serves as the place of honor for guests, is covered with a gray and brown striped pajama material. In front of it is a table— once white but now roughly the same shade of gray as everything else. On the table a newspaper is spread out to serve as a tablecloth, and on it are spread crusts of bread, some tea glasses with the remains of cold tea, an ashtray full of cigarette butts.

Umm Ali and her husband sleep in the left bedroom, in separate beds. There she also prefers to receive her guests and friends. A green door with flaking paint opens into the room. On the door handle hang clothes. A small window opens to the street side. One windowpane has been broken and replaced with cardboard, the other is cracked and mended with scotch tape. A rag of a curtain is always let down to afford privacy from the neighbors. The room is dark, lit by a hanging bulb as in the front room. The walls are bare, except for a 1964 calendar with a picture of a film star, a color postcard of another film star,[3] and a bar with six hooks loaded with clothes. On the floor is a tattered, dark rug. The furniture consists of a double bed, a single bed, a sideboard with a large mirror and glass doors, and a tiny table. The single bed is piled with three mattresses, bulgy and worn. Originally, they were rose-colored. Now they are gray and splotched (partly because diapers are not used, and so the children's urine soaks in where it falls); they are covered with a sheet gray from use, and over it is a gray and brown checked blanket. Toward one end is a pile of gray, hard pillows—they are offered as support for your back when as a guest you are invited to sit on the bed. A tattered prayer rug has been thrown over one of the bedposts, and on the bed itself is an assortment of clothes and half-eaten pieces of bread.

Three pigeons roost under one of the beds—in the daytime they wander freely and fly about the room. Under the other bed is a breadbox and

3. These were removed in 1981 at Hoda's insistence following her religious conversion.

a *tabliyya,* the Egyptian low, round wooden table around whic
on the floor to eat. Between the beds stands a small wooden tab
once painted white; now it is gray. A newspaper is spread on top
as a tablecloth; and on the newspaper are a pair of children's sh.. s and
an ashtray. Between the glass doors of the sideboard a few cups and glasses
and numerous packets of medicine are on view, as well as some empty
liquor bottles.[4] On top of the sideboard is a newspaper, covered with
medicine bottles and boxes of pills, a black plastic handbag with a torn-off
strap, a couple of aluminum bowls, a tea glass with a bit of milk in it,
some half-eaten pieces of bread, and a radio—with a pair of shoes on top.
In the corner by the sideboard is a wooden crate packed full of clothes,
on top is a wicker basket with clothes, and on top of that again bundles
of clothes piled a meter high, precariously balanced. It all bears witness
to crowding, wear and tear, and despair, and, as many of Umm Ali's neighbors would add, a good deal of neglect [*fawda*].

Priorities

The lack of money cannot fully explain why Umm Ali's flat looks quite as
depressing as it does. Several of her neighbors, worse off than she is,
manage to have homes that look a good deal more presentable—at least
from time to time when they get their heads above water. It is partly
because they have different priorities from hers, partly because they are
at a stage of life when it is more feasible to have other priorities. With
two, soon three, marriageable daughters, Umm Ali must be prepared to
spend a sizable part of the family income on clothes. How well a girl
dresses is quite decisive for her marital chances. Clothes and jewelry are
perceived to reveal the family's status, and thereby what kind of match a
particular girl represents.

By now Umm Ali's two eldest daughters are approaching the class of
old maids—they are twenty-seven and twenty-four years old—so she cannot afford to be petty about their clothing. But there are indications that
she is even more worried about this than they. Recently, she had saved
and hoarded to be able to buy them gold bracelets. But they asked to
have a washing machine instead!

A house of one's own

The present flat is the second the family has had. For the first two years
of their marriage, Umm Ali and Mustafa lodged with her father. But then
her sister Farida and her husband also moved in, and life became a perpet-

---

4. In 1981, the remaining crockery was broken by Mustafa in a quarrel.

ual quarrel. To top it off, her father remarried—for which Umm Ali could never forgive him, so she moved out. The new flat she found through acquaintances; it is only a ten-minute walk from the old one. At that time it was easy to find vacancies, and flats were cheap. Now you have to pay several hundred pounds as a down payment, and flats as central as this would be effectively out of reach.

She has lived here for twenty-seven years, but she still does not feel at home in the neighborhood. People have such bad manners, she complains, "They sit in the doorways and stare at what the neighbors are doing, and hang out of the windows and loll over the balconies and snoop and gossip. Everyone begrudges others everything they have!"

In harboring such attitudes, Umm Ali is in no way exceptional. Women in general heap abuse on their environment and distance themselves from "the others" in no uncertain terms. The neighborhood children, they complain, are filthy and ill mannered, and are a bad influence on one's own. Umm Ali is not satisfied with the flat, either, for there is never sun; only at the height of summer does it barely reach down across the houses in front. And sun is so important. Her mother used to say that sun is even more important than food.

Her dream is to have a house of her own built on a plot of land she owns out by the Pyramids. She managed to buy the land through a formidable, sustained effort of savings and management. Mustafa never supported the project to begin with; later he actively boycotted it, and finally, in a terrible quarrel in 1978, he tried to steal the deed from her and sell it. Ever since, Umm Ali has kept the document with a friend. The problem is that neither her husband nor children want to move, and without their cooperation, she cannot hope to raise the money to build.

She reckons she will need one thousand pounds to build just the ground floor.[5] That equals about three times Mustafa's yearly salary from the government. To manage that, the whole family would have to stand together and make great sacrifices in all other respects for a long time. They will not, and she feels dejected and bitter. A couple of her friends have managed that and have moved—admittedly, into unfinished houses with dirt floors and no water or electricity—but even so—it is a beginning; the rest can follow by-and-by. . . .

She has many acquaintances in her immediate neighborhood, nearly all her close kin, and her few close friends, yet none of these is so precious

5. By 1995, this sum has risen to approximately 2,500 pounds which is equivalent to about three years' salary with the government for a recent university graduate.

that she could not do without them. And if they really loved her, they would come and visit even if she moved. There are plenty of buses. . . .

She is so tired. All she wants is peace and quiet. Through all the years I have known her, this has been her perpetual dream: peace and quiet and escape from a nerve-racking struggle. Hundreds of times I have heard her threaten her children that she would go away and live by herself as soon as a certain debt has been paid off, or the daughters have been married (for it is she who must assemble their dowries); as soon as this and as soon as that. . . . A thousand things must be put in order first. "Tomorrow, God willing" sustains her hopes that some day, some way, things will be better. *Ba'den*—later, another time, if only God will. . . .

Tomorrow, God willing

"*Bukra insh'allah!*" [tomorrow, God willing] This phrase can drive foreigners in Egypt to despair because it seems so empty of meaning other than false expectations (God is so rarely willing, it appears), but what does it not contain of hope and dreams and faith, both faith in God and faith in destiny, and of life-sustaining flight from reality for people doomed to a life in despair? These are people who have long ago given up every illusion that the future belongs to them, or that they are masters of their own fate.

They also know full well that *bukra insh'allah* may be just a cover for cowardly attempts to evade responsibility. And Umm Ali is relentless in her condemnation of Mustafa for doing precisely that. She firmly believes that God helps only those who help themselves. But precisely therefore *bukra insh'allah* can carry a person like her, a person who has almost lost hope, across the abyss of total despair. And the belief that God does not act randomly but has a purpose in what he does can soften the hardest blows.

But tomorrow comes, and the next, and the next—and Umm Ali sits there, captive of a harsh reality, torn between her love for the children, and her wish to escape from it all.

"When I threaten to go, they come running after me and cry, 'Don't leave us, Mama, you know we love you so!' But I reply, 'You don't love me for what *I* am, but only for what I can do for you!'" ['*ashan masla-hatku bass* (for your own interests only)]

Seven Brothers and Sisters

Ali

Ali, Umm Ali's eldest, had passed from childhood by the time I entered the family. He was seventeen years old, a shy and taciturn boy with stooped shoulders and diffident movements. He worked as his father's apprentice for the nominal wage of two pounds a month. Umm Ali complained that the boy became extra clumsy in his father's presence and lost all confidence in himself. Ali wanted to quit, but his father would not let him. A son should and must help his father. And besides, where could Mustafa find such cheap labor?

Ali had undergone rough treatment from his father as a child. His mother tells how Ali was interested in mechanics and sometimes took things apart. His father would be furious and beat him for this "destructiveness." She tried to make him understand that it was curiosity, a desire to explore things—really good qualities—that motivated the boy. His father only scoffed at that.

Ali quit school in sixth grade. He can read a little but not write. After nearly three years of military service, when he had only three more months to go, he deserted the army and fled to Libya.[1] He returned to Egypt a year later and was caught. To avoid serving years in jail, he paid a fortune in bribes. That is, his mother paid, for it was she, naturally, who raised the money. Later, he got engaged to a girl of dubious reputation. She left him to marry another, and had a child by her husband. But when that marriage broke up, she came back to Ali. She tempted him, Umm Ali says. She and Mustafa were furious, so Ali married the woman behind his parents' backs. In retaliation, he was thrown out of the family. He has tried repeatedly to have a reconciliation, but the parents are adamant. Umm Ali says, "He is dead to me—dead like Amin."

Amin

Amin died at the age of nineteen by setting fire to himself. When I first met him, he was fourteen—a tall, handsome boy with bright eyes and an air of self-assurance. Umm Ali always spoke of him as the one of her children most like herself. He was ambitious and hardworking, and had

---

1. Military service is one year for university graduates, two years for high school graduates, and three years for all others.

made it to the second year of senior high school by the time he died. He promised to be the most successful of the children. Perhaps therefore the feeling of inferiority became most acute in him. He had friends of higher social position; and in Egypt, as in many societies marked by sharp inequality, the poor child who rises above his or her position faces harsh depreciation in many ways. In Amin's time, it was still rare for children of his background to attend high school.

The last month before he died, Amin was irritable and tense, unlike his usual self. The family thought it was because he was desperate for new clothes. School was to begin after the holidays, and he would soon be meeting his superior friends; he must have good clothing and this he could not get. His sister, Mona, explained, "Clothes are *so* important here whereas personality counts for nothing. Egyptians look only to the appearance, not to the character!" [*Ilmasriyyin biyshufu ilmanzar bass, mish il axlaq*]

Hoda

Hoda was fourteen in 1969 a talkative, lively girl who ingratiated herself with people and had many friends. She seemed innocent, curious, and quite naive. In due course, she was to develop into a willful young lady with a firm hold on life, endowed with her mother's managerial powers. But this only bloomed after she married and had children and took charge of a realm of her own. In her youth, Hoda was the terror of the family.

She developed into a headstrong person who needed no physical force to pester the family. Her conceit and stubbornness coupled with high rank in the sibling hierarchy (after Amin died and Ali moved out, she was the eldest) gave her a position as inviolable as any weapon.

Thus she persisted until, at the age of twenty-six, she changed again. She became deeply religious. She had suffered one broken engagement by then, and two attempted suicides. She was extremely thin, perhaps anorexic, and was twice brought home from work because she had fainted. Her last suicide attempt was described to me by Mona.

Hoda was up for exams in French and dreaded it. She asked Mama for ten piaster for a copybook. Instead she bought fifty aspirin. She took them all and laid down on the bed and cried. She had thrown the wrappings for the pills in the garbage. I was making dinner and discovered the wrappings. There were lots of empty boxes. I asked Anwar who had bought them, and he said Hoda had. Even then I had no inkling of anything wrong. Then I started to tidy the house and found a note under my pillow saying, "My dearest sister, Mona, I have taken pills.

Please, ask Mama and Baba to forgive me, and give my love to my friend Amal . . . ," and so on. I screamed, and rushed to Hoda and hauled her out of the bed. She was not really asleep, and fell heavily to the floor when I tried to raise her. I ran to Umm Gamal [a neighbor] and had her sit with Hoda while I dashed to the workshop to have Baba bring a taxi. But I found only Ali and my cousin, Kamal. When we finally came with the taxi, Umm Gamal's husband had already gotten hold of one and rushed Hoda to the hospital. Baba arrived just after us, and was furious, he wanted to beat up Hoda. "First my son kills himself, and now you do this!" he screamed. "And have I ever harmed you? People will say you wanted to die from shame because Khalid [her ex-fiancé] did something to you!" The doctor had to hold Baba to stop him from hitting Hoda. He said she needed to have her stomach emptied, and then peace, not war.

So Baba went home and abused Mama instead: "First you kill one child, and now you kill another! *You* must have driven her mad since she does this to herself!" Mama answered, "By God, I haven't done her anything!" And she was very angry with Hoda for being the cause that Baba scolded her like that, and because now people would say that Hoda had wanted to kill herself because Khalid had taken her honor.

Mona

Mona was twelve years old in 1969, a chubby, cheerful girl with bright, intelligent eyes and kinky hair. The hair was her great despair. She strove tirelessly to straighten it.[2] But unlike Hoda, the failure of the endeavor did not make Mona grumpy. Mona is by nature fair, not just in skin. Umm Ali talks of her as the one of her children now most like herself—since Amin died. She says Mona has got brains that she uses, looks to the bright side of life, does what the others refuse to do, and tries to smoothen things out when they have gone wrong.

Mona grew into a pretty young woman, thick-set, which Egyptians value, with her cheerfulness retained. She is the bridge builder of the family, the soother of sorrows, and everyone's friend. Apparently she does it all without great effort. But appearances are deceptive. Once she sighed with despair, "Look at all the problems I have met in life, and I am only

2. Straight hair was so important in the sixties to mid-eighties that virtually all young girls, and many boys, used to wear a tightly wrapped towel or a ladies' nylon stocking or a cap on their heads when they were at home to press the hair flat. They would wet the hair first. Now, this is less common.

Two sisters and a friend. By now, they have all graduated from college.

eighteen years old! Often tears well forth without any reason. I just can't take any more!"

Afaf

In 1969, Afaf was the beauty of the family, just six years old, but stunning in features and looks. Her golden brown skin and delicate features framed big almond eyes and dimples as deep as they come. She had an innocent look about her that radiated purity and was her father's decided favorite. Perhaps he saw in her a vestige of what he himself might have become, had Nature been more benevolent to him. For Afaf, too, was negroid. But in her this heritage metamorphosed into singular beauty and charm.

Afaf has kept much of her beauty and innocence. But like her sister Hoda, she, too, metamorphosed into a sullen and unruly child. From around age nine, she was most trying to have around. At fourteen she developed a nervous illness; she started roaming about at night, and could not account for where she had been. "But I haven't been *anywhere!*" she cried when her parents and siblings interrogated her and tried to extract the truth by force. Finally, her mother realized that Afaf did speak the truth; she didn't know where she had been. Thanks to her mother's insight and some medical care, Afaf became better. No demands were made on her, she was allowed to be, cradled in her mother's love. But she never fully recovered. Her mother thinks she knows the main reason. "Because she sat quiet, unable to talk and get her problems *out* of her body."

Anwar

Anwar was only two years old and the apple of his mother's eye when I entered the family. He has probably had the easiest life of all the children—at least until 1979 when he became, by default, the "eldest" son in the family—following Amin's death and his parents' break with Ali. With three older sisters whom he could order about, since he was a boy, he has been rather spoiled but seems none the worse for it. He has always been a tease, and rather too lively, but good at heart and quite clearly intelligent. Umm Ali always says that Anwar and Mona are the nicest and brightest of the children. "But," she sighed, when Anwar had just turned eight, "now Anwar is learning bad manners from the others!"

And by the time he was fourteen, Anwar drove her and Mustafa to despair. He had started staying out at night, and they would prowl the streets searching for him. One night, they found him and a pal asleep together on the roof of the building where they live. They could not understand what had happened: "And he who used to be so good!" They tried scolding, beating, "house arrest"—to no avail. And they were so afraid. By then, he was the only son they had.

(Though I should add, their fears were quite unfounded. Anwar never engaged in deviance, his staying out all night was just youthful rebellion that lasted only a few weeks. But his parents' quick reaction is telling; it reveals the strict control under which youths are kept—a supervision that aims at protecting them from all evil and guarding the family honor.)

Nosa

Nosa was not yet born when I entered the family. She is four years younger than Anwar. In looks she resembles her brother Ali, and in nature her sister Hoda—not the best combination. She is stubborn and headstrong, and has tantrums unless she gets her will. To keep the peace, the others

often dance to her tune. Perhaps they think what I th[
not had an easy life. She was only nine months old wh[
her mother fell into her state of stupor [*sadma*]. And unl[
who fall victim to such an unhappy fate, Nosa had no on[
mother's place. The whole family was hit: sisters, aunts, u[
was in shock. What a trauma for a little child to be so su[
of her mother's loving care and thrust into such a bleak existence. Perhaps
that is why Umm Ali nursed her till she was almost four, to compensate
her somehow.

This description of Umm Ali's children has focused on the dark side of
life, on the problems and crises, rather than on the smooth passages; on
the sources of anxiety and distress, rather than on the joy and content-
ment—in keeping with Umm Ali's own experience. This is why the children have been given such unequal attention. The problems are there to
be solved; and they are so many and so overpowering that they displace
the joy, or the peace of mind to savor the joy, of what goes well. Therefore
I have passed quickly over Mona; so does Umm Ali. Admittedly, Mona has
had her problems too. But they were related to other persons and did
not tax her relation to her mother in the way that Hoda, or Afaf, or Nosa
constantly do.

Life is one perpetual series of problems, as Umm Ali (and most other
women in her neighborhood) see it. And it is she who must solve them
all—alone.

Eight

For the Children's Sake

"I don't care if they starve or they die"
Countless times I have heard Umm Ali sum up her life in words like these:

My health is gone, and it doesn't help me whatever I take of medicines, they don't make me any better. The doctor has said that I *must*
try not to get worked up or angry [*za'lana*]. But it is impossible, with
all the problems and quarrels in this house. None of the children heeds
me. They do as they please and don't give a damn what I say. Those
children have turned out just like their father—stubborn and willful

and stupid. I swear by the Prophet that as soon as this savings club is over, I will go away to a place where no one can find me so I can have peace and relief from the problems of the house. It would serve them right, those children! Let them fight and tear each others' eyes out for *that's* what is bound to happen when they don't have me to go between them and straighten things out. I won't care if they starve or they die, for none of them cares about me! I work myself to death to make life good for them, and what do I get in return? *Araf!*" [disgust]

"If only the children were happy"

The next moment she can say,

I would happily do without everything—food, clothes, and all, if only the children were happy! When once in a rare while we have something good, something extra—like yesterday, we had chicken—I always give them parts of *my* share as well, even though I'm the one who most needs nutritious food! The doctor has said that my diabetes would get much better if only I had protein-rich food. But even more do I need to soothe my nerves, and that can only be when the children are happy. And they relish good food!

. . . And clothes! You should have seen Afaf yesterday how happy she was for the shoes I bought so she will have something new for the Feast [after Ramadan] this year. Myself, I haven't had a new pair for five years. Look what mine look like [and she gropes under the bed and pulls forth a pair of shoes so ragged and torn that they ought to have been dumped into the garbage long ago]. But it makes no difference, if only the children are happy. . . .

So Afaf had her shoes, they cost four pounds. But Nosa started screaming because *she* didn't get anything—though I had bought her two pretty handkerchiefs at five piaster each to console her, since she is the smallest. And Hoda was furious because *she* didn't get new shoes. If Afaf's shoes hadn't been much too large for her, I'm sure she would have taken them for herself. And Anwar was grumpy! So if one of the children is happy, the others get angry. How fortunate are the rich! Just think, to be able to give *all* one's children something each all at once. Oh, to live to see such a day! . . .

Everything I do is for their sake. Every savings club I ever made for Mustafa, it was all for the children's future. My brother criticizes me for loving them too much. As if there ever was a mother who could love her children too much! They are all that she has in life.

This is how Umm Ali experiences herself: as someone whose whole existence centers on the children, nurturing them, protecting them, securing their interests, coming to their rescue, and teaching them to know right from wrong—thus helping them make a future.

And she shares with many mothers all over the world the feeling that her reward is—ingratitude.

Part Two

Umm Ali Speaks

Nine

The Source of All Misery:
Mustafa and the Money

"As if 'never mind' can fill a belly"

Through the twenty-five years we have been married, Mustafa has
never given me his wage into my hand, just a little now and then, and
only as it suited him. Never according to the needs of the house and
the family. I have begged him to give me a fixed daily amount—just
thirty piaster—that's the absolute minimum we need to live. But he
won't hear of it. *Never* has he got. Or he claims that he owes so and
so money, or so and so owes him and didn't pay him yet, or he has
unforeseen expenses at the workshop—always! He has no sense of
economizing or planning. I have told him that he seems to believe that
if he feeds the family one day, he can with good conscience take off
the next, and the next, and the next . . . !

Often we have to go to bed hungry because he didn't leave us one
piaster when he left in the morning, nor bring us one piaster when he
came home at night. Yesterday, Anwar was sent home from school
because he didn't have ten piaster for notebooks. The day before, Afaf
was sent home because she didn't have a nice and clean school uniform.
Now Nosa is sick with a fever and cough. It's already been a *week* since
I brought her to the doctor who wrote a prescription and said, "Bring
her back in three days!" But Mustafa hasn't brought the money for
medicines yet. He doesn't have a thought for the children and the needs
of the house, for he is lacking in all responsibility and caring. To everything we ask, he just answers, "Tomorrow, God willing!" and "*ma'lesh!*"
[Never mind], and "Later!" *That*'s what the family has lived on! As if
ma'lesh could fill a belly!

I have no idea what he earns or what he spends, for he doesn't tell
me anything, and besides, he lies and fools me. Truly, I don't know a
thing about him.

"I, without earning a penny, have to be the provider"

It is not that I ever *ask* Mustafa what he earns or how he spends the
money. All I demand is that he keep the children with food and clothes.
Yesterday I asked him if he had received his salary this month. He said
no, but I don't believe him. "How come *you* didn't receive when all

73

the others have?" I asked. I'm sure he has spent it all in the workshop, and on paying back loans. He owes lots of money, all over the place, for the workshop devours money; and besides, he's very generous with customers, always treating them to cigarettes and tea. That's what Ali tells me. Mustafa also smokes a lot, three packets of cigarettes a day, while he relies on *me* to satisfy the needs of the house! *I*, without earning a penny, have to be the provider! And it is true, were it not for me, we would be in the street by now, begging!

Whenever the children ask him for money, he says, "Go and ask Mama!" He expects *me* to ride out the difficulties and *borrow* money if necessary, whereas he is never willing to borrow for us. He would be ashamed, he says, "You go instead!" I've asked him if he really believes that *I* too do not feel ashamed? The truth is, I feel so humiliated that I send the children instead. I tell myself they're still too young to feel the shame. But it's not true. Already the big ones refuse, and I have to plead with the small ones to go.

Once Amin needed money for private tutoring in French and math, thirty-five and fifty piaster, and so he came to me and asked for it.[1] I didn't have any, so I sent him to his father. But Mustafa said he didn't have a penny. Amin knew that a workmate of his owed Mustafa three pounds—for Ali had told him—and so he asked to be allowed to go and get it. But Mustafa wouldn't hear of it! He is ashamed even to ask money from people who owe it to *him!* So Amin came to me and said, "What am I going to do, Mama, skip the lessons? Please, Mama, help me, borrow wherever you can!" And so I did, this time like all the others.

"But you are poor and that's no shame"

Another time there was a friend of Mustafa, a rich man—he used to come and visit us—and one day he said that his wife had masses of clothes which the children had outgrown. "You, Umm Ali, would do us a big favor if you would accept them!" My heart swelled with happiness, and I thanked him profusely. Again and again I begged Mustafa to go with me to fetch the clothes. But he was furious and screamed, "What d'you think I am, a beggar?"

"Far from it, but you are poor and your children lack clothes, and that's no shame!" When he still wouldn't go, I asked him to give me the address so I could go on my own. But he refused. And the rich man probably understood that he had offended Mustafa, for after a

---

1. Because of the poor quality of government schooling, it is usual for students to take private tutoring, nowadays even from grade one.

while he stopped coming. I was so furious with Mustafa that I exploded, "God's curse be upon you!"

There was another time when we were going, the whole family, on a trip to Helwan [recreation area half an hour by train outside Cairo]; it was the only time we've ever been there. When the conductor came, Mustafa asked for seven tickets instead of two. The children should go for free! And he refused to go back and admit his mistake and ask for his money back. I was on the verge of tears for wasting so much money. The whole trip was spoiled for me. And once, when we had taken a taxi for twenty piaster—I know, for it had a taximeter—Mustafa paid fifty piaster and *didn't protest* when he got only twenty back! I made a big quarrel with him and said, "You act as if you were a rich man!"

Simple treason

Sometimes he admonishes me to let the children go without food. "So let them starve to death!" he says. Even Ahmed [her brother] has supported him in that. "So let the children fend for themselves!" They talk as if they were crazy! The children are hungry, and yet you shouldn't give them food!

There was a time, just after we'd moved here, that it happened like this: we were new in the place and so I didn't have anyone to borrow from, we were completely dependent on Mustafa. One day he went out in the middle of the day, it was a Friday and free day, and said he would be back soon with some money for food. I said it was plain to see that he was heading for a soccer match. He denied it. Only at eight at night did he come back—penniless—and with a studiedly desperate look on his face. He said he had lost his pocketbook on the bus and spent hours trying to find it. I said he had wasted his time, he should have searched at the soccer grounds instead. In the meantime Hoda, she was nine years, had been sitting by the kitchen window, right across from Umm Gamal [neighbor], and whined, "Please, auntie Umm Gamal, I'm so hungry, please give me something to eat!" And I was so relieved that Umm Gamal wasn't home and couldn't hear her. And the smell of fresh bread simmered up from the bakery below. And I sent Ali to my sister Feyza to borrow two piaster for bread. But she said she didn't have. She only cares for herself!

Securing one's due

Umm Ali says she knows people say she is to blame for her own situation. They say she is at fault because from the start she didn't persist in her demands and retaliate when Mustafa said, "No money!" and "Tomorrow,

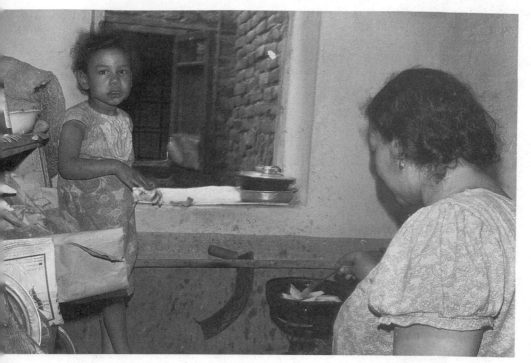

Nosa at the kitchen window right across from Umm Gamal's. It was here that she sat and said, "Oh please, Auntie Umm Gamal, I'm so hungry—please give me something to eat!"

God willing," and similar things. They say that by backing down from her demands, "Give me, give me!" she taught him to be negligent.

But in the name of the Prophet, it's not true. She didn't even know about duplicity and deceit before she met Mustafa, and so she couldn't ever imagine that he would let her down. She was so sure that he would naturally care for his family. For this was when she was still innocent and had trust in people.

And what she thinks is true: people do talk just like that. Her brother's wife, Amira, for example, says, "Umm Ali is to blame for her own misery since she never taught Mustafa to carry responsibility. From the start she kept quiet [*sikit*] when he said, 'No money' and '*Bukra insh'allah!*' She *borrowed* money to help him, and thereby she taught him that he could always rely on her! *She* reared him [*rabbitu*] to be irresponsible!"

Umm Ali would only sneer at that. To her, Mustafa is a victim of his own poor judgment, caused by a lousy upbringing and a group of lousy

friends. Poor man, when he also didn't have a moth
expect?

"The shepherd is responsible for his flock"

One day they came and cut [off] the electricity becau
hadn't paid the bill for three months. The same day his fi
Karima, came here and asked for money from him. Mustafa ... ne was
sorry he only had twenty piaster, and gave her half. When she had
gone, I picked a big quarrel with him. "You let your own children
starve and thirst, while you are generous to others!"

"But she's my cousin, not a stranger from the street!"

"It doesn't matter! It is written in the Quran, 'The shepherd is responsible for his flock.' It will not help you in the least that you're
pious in prayer—it is the behavior God looks to. On Judgment Day he
will send you straight into the fire because you ran away from your
responsibility. *First* you must feed and clothe your own children, and
then, if you show mercy to others, God will reward you."

I asked her if she also was not angry with Karima for asking for money.
She had told me herself that Karima was far from needy at the time; she
worked as a teacher and earned sixteen pounds a month, and she had
only two children.

No, I quarreled only with him. Karima couldn't really know how
bad our situation was, although—I *had* told her, when she came, that
the electricity people had just been here and cut off the light, and that
the children were starving. . . .

Mustafa also used to give his sister, Amina, a lot. He loved her very
much. She used to visit him in the workshop and sit and drink Pepsi[2]—
don't think *she* was contented with tea! And when she was leaving, she
would ask him for money for the bus. And Mustafa gave—fifty piaster
or even a pound—whereas the bus cost ten piaster! When he came
home in the evenings, he would tell me, "Amina greets you and says
she's sorry she didn't have time to come and see you today!" He had
to say *something* since Ali is with him in the workshop and would be
telling me of Amina's visit. I retorted that if Amina visited *me,* I would
love her, otherwise not. And that it was only an empty excuse this
thing that she didn't have time to come—it takes only ten minutes to
walk from the workshop to here!

. . . I was angry with Amina because she took advantage of Mustafa's

2. Pepsi, costing five piaster in 1982, is served only to very special guests.

love for her to ask money from him. At the time, she was far from needy, for it was before her husband had left her. . . .

Also Karima took [money] in a sly way. She lived by herself at the time for her husband worked abroad, and she paid five pounds in rent from the sixteen that she earned as a teacher. She smoked a lot, two packages of twenty [cigarettes] a day, and so she asked Mustafa to keep what was left of her salary once the rent was paid so the whole thing wouldn't go up in smoke;[3] she would come and fetch a little from him every day. After ten days, the wages were gone, and she continued to fetch!

"It's not *you* who will be shamed"

Mustafa never takes care to pay the rent punctually, either at home or in the workshop. Once it went so badly that the landlord came time and again and threatened to sell our furniture if we didn't pay immediately. I panicked. I told Mustafa that if he only paid three pounds a month, I would manage the rest. So I took a couple as tenants for two pounds a month. I gave them the big room, and pressed the whole rest of the family—we were six then—into the other. But Mustafa, traitor that he is, didn't keep his part of the agreement, and so the landlord started coming again with his threats. The tenants panicked that he might sell *their* belongings too! And so they left.

Not long after, Mustafa owed the rent once more, this time for three months. And so the landlord put his threats into effect, filing a complaint with the courts. An official was sent to write a list of everything we owned—everything *I* owned, for they are *my* belongings. I have a list [*qaima*] certifying it all as my property.[4] But it wouldn't help me in the least. *First* the court would sell the things, and *then* I could complain!

I went to the shopkeeper on the corner and begged her for help. She—God bless her—first lent me five pounds to cover the next month's rent, and then she said we would make a savings club together. She would recruit five members, and I five, each would pay thirty

3. She had picked up the habit when she lived abroad. Women in the neighborhood never smoke.

4. Customarily, the bride's parents have the groom sign a list (*qaima*) specifying every piece of furniture and equipment that the bride brings to her marriage (whether given by the groom or her parents) and making it her personal property. Any piece of furniture acquired after that date becomes the man's property since it is bought with his money. But some parents feel that writing a "list" is a sign of distrust, and so they refrain—an act for which the daughter may have to pay dearly.

piaster a day, and I would appropriate the whole am[ou]
after five days I would have fifteen pounds in my han[d]
and kissed her and said, 'May God reward you!'

But Mustafa—God damn him! When I complained t[o]
him for the fifteen pounds, he just shrugged his shoul[ders]
didn't have any, and "*ma'lesh,*" and "May God help us[!]
mumbo-jumbo. I said *he* could take it easy, for it was not *he* who was
being shamed. And that the next time the landlord came, I would send
him to Mustafa in the workshop, so he could stand there and make him
a laughingstock for all the world to see! That would serve him right!
Then he could feel for himself what it's like to be publicly put to
shame. . . .

The whole thing almost ended in divorce. And Mustafa had to promise, in front of my father and father's wife, that he would pay the rent
and the electricity bill every single month. I said the rest didn't matter,
that we had food and clothes, as long as the rent and the light were
paid.

When I went to pay the fifteen pounds to the landlord, I asked
him—for the first time in my life—for a receipt. I thought that when
he was so heartless that he wanted to throw us all into the street, then
there were no limits to what he might do. And so I went to him and
asked him to prepare a receipt while I fetched the money from Mustafa.
I was afraid to pay first, for then he might say, "The receipt later." The
landlord was insulted and accused me of lack of trust. And it's true, I
did not trust him! And Mustafa scorned me and said it was foolish, this
thing with the receipt. But I told the landlord that it was Mustafa who
wanted the receipt!

"It's brains he lacks, not money"

One day in 1969 as I was sitting with Umm Ali, her brother Ahmed came,
bringing bad news. The day before, the police had closed Mustafa's workshop because he hadn't paid taxes for eleven years and owed the government thirty-three pounds ($68). Ahmed said he knew Mustafa had re-
ceived many warnings before that if he didn't pay within a certain time,
the workshop would be closed. But he had ignored them all, and now the
warnings had been put into effect.

Umm Ali was distraught that Mustafa had not told her this himself. She
strongly feels that spouses must be open with each other and tell their
problems to each other so they can try to solve them together. She feels
hurt and rejected every time she learns from others things about Mustafa

that concern her. And Ahmed warned her not to tell Mustafa that he had told her this.

The next day Ahmed came back and reported that Mustafa had borrowed the thirty-three pounds from a friend, so the workshop had opened again. "And who will repay the friend?" asked Umm Ali curtly.

A couple of days later Mustafa brought up the matter with her and asked her to help him borrow the thirty-three pounds. She could make a savings club, he suggested. He would repay her generously as soon as he got money himself. But he needed it immediately. And she helped—in the hope that this time, God willing, he would keep his promise. But afterward came bitter days.

In October 1975 again, the police issued a warning that the workshop would be closed unless Mustafa immediately paid forty pounds that he owed in rent. This time it was Ali who brought his mother the news. Mustafa himself did not say a word. "Because he is ashamed," Umm Ali said. "This workshop is the fifth he has [had]. Every other one he lost because he didn't pay the rent." Ali told her that Mustafa had been given fifteen days to settle his debt. He owed rent for seven months.

Two days later, Mustafa "opened the story," as Egyptians say, and asked her to help him borrow the money. She could go to her brother-in-law, Adel, he suggested. Umm Ali was furious and reminded him that she already owed Adel vast amounts due to Mustafa's negligence; besides, Adel was in great need himself. And she lectured him on how she had always helped him before, but now it was the end—when he can never learn to help himself. To me she said, "There's nothing wrong in making mistakes if one only learns from them. But Mustafa never learns. He makes all his mistakes over again, and twice over each time!"

But in the end she took pity on him—to save the children and herself while she assured him that this was definitely, absolutely, the last time she would help.

There were to be many more.

She complains, "The workshop swallows money and gives nothing in return. People *think* we are well off because Mustafa owns a workshop. Even my own brother thinks that. If only they had known! Even if Mustafa went to work in Saudi Arabia, it wouldn't help us in the least for he is completely lacking in economic sense and foresight. Khalid, Hoda's ex-fiancé, used to say that it's not money Mustafa lacks, but brains!" [*moxx*]

Ten

Manchild Mustafa

Through all the years I have known her, Umm Ali has complained to friends and relatives, acquaintances and strangers—just about anyone she met—about the incorrigible Mustafa. In detail she has laid bare his failures, lies, and deceit. As she sees it, he alone is to blame for her family's deplorable situation and her own nerve-racking life. Sometimes I have heard her carry on with Mustafa sitting a hair's breadth away, doubtless able to hear, had he wished to. He has not batted an eyelid.

What might he have said? How might he defend himself? He is as aware as she is of his own dismal failure.

Not that Umm Ali thinks there is anything wrong in making mistakes. She is really quite tolerant of human faults and failures. What she cannot forgive Mustafa is that he is unable ever to learn from his mistakes, and that he fools her with empty words into thinking he will mend his ways and emerge a responsible man.

By criticizing her husband so candidly, Umm Ali disregards a basic value of Egyptian culture that she also cherishes: the wife should show the husband unconditional loyalty and respect. But I doubt that she sees it this way. She knows full well that she criticizes her husband. At the same time she admonishes her daughters that the woman should show the man respect. "Look at me, I tell your father 'as you please' [*hadr*] in all and everything. And does he ever make me happy? But it is written by the Prophet, 'The wife must obey the man!'" And when Hoda defied her fiancé's orders regarding how she was to dress, Umm Ali used to say to him, "Just beat her! You have my permission! The woman must obey the man!"

Perhaps this is the way Umm Ali sees it: that loyalty and respect consist in performing one's duties and obligations rather than selling one's soul. How could she defer to Mustafa when his behavior goes against everything she believes a man should do and against God's own injunction, "The shepherd is responsible for his flock." Thus she can expose Mustafa's failures before an attentive, private audience and still see herself as the epitome of the dutiful wife.

Is it not she who comes to his rescue every time he has gotten himself embroiled in problems? Is it not she who saves him, time and again, from being made a laughingstock for all the world to see?

She always emphasizes how she, unlike most women, is ever loyal and steadfast to her husband. Anyone else would have given as good as she got, emptied his pockets every evening, and cheated him as he cheats her, whereas she always fulfills her wifely duties.

In Umm Ali's view, no one but Mustafa can be held responsible for the life that is hers. Neither the government with its exploitation of the poor, the population explosion with its pressure on public resources (particularly housing and jobs, which are most critical to the poor), nor the staggering inflation (price rise, she would say) can be blamed for her own and her children's plight. It is all Mustafa's fault. Admittedly, Umm Ali is just as harsh as other urban poor in her condemnation of the government for its passive negligence rather than active oppression. But a simple individual, such as she, is powerless before the government, which represents a set of constraints one simply does best to accept. The human being must bow to her fate while striving to make the best of it. Mustafa doggedly makes the worst.

For a poor man, he has been given several exceptional opportunities in life by means of which he might have pulled himself up a bit and out of his misery. He has held two good jobs: as a government inspector with security of employment, and as the owner of a workshop. He has been offered a house lot, cheap as dirt. Anyone but Mustafa would have known enough to use these opportunities for the children's benefit. He, by contrast, lays waste all possibilities.

Once he was offered a house plot out by the Pyramids for fifty piaster a square meter. And turned it down! "No, thank you!" he said. NO! You would think he was mad!

"What would I want property for?" he said, "I can't take it with me where I'm going."

"But you can leave it for your children!" I said.

In her lighter moments, Umm Ali knows that Mustafa is neither worse nor better than most other men. But she usually feels so bitter and neglected that he seems the worst, whatever he actually is. Moreover, what help would it be to her if others were just as bad as he is? Why compare him with the worst? Man must aspire to live by the highest standards.

In criticizing her husband so candidly, Umm Ali is in no way unique. Most other women I know resemble her in feeling deceived and neglected by their husbands and therefore freed of the duty to show them deference. Where Umm Ali stands out is in her exceptional eloquence, deep psychological insight, and remarkable personality which lead her to assert herself with unparalleled force and verve. She finds words for some of the things that others suffer mutely or can express only weakly and vaguely, though by our standards, even they are remarkably articulate. Egyptians are a verbalizing people; their ability to put their thoughts and feelings into words is truly impressive.

Since Umm Ali started telling people's fortunes in the coffee cup,[1] she has also helped others, men as well as women, to articulate their deeply felt concerns. It is striking how those who come to her share a common complaint: their problems center on the relation to the spouse. As dependent as man and woman are on each other in a system like this, it must inevitably be thus. It hardly helps matters that most couples get off to such a bad start.

Many women share with Umm Ali the experience of a happy betrothal period that ends abruptly with the marriage. People themselves explain this sudden change in terms of the man's distress with the heavy economic burden that overwhelms the young husband. From the position of being generous and praised for it whenever he brought gifts to his betrothed, he is now suddenly sole provider and falls miserably short whenever he does not bring his wife what she and the children need. In return for his support, the family should obey and respect the man, and the wife should also serve him, keep house for him, submit sexually to him, and teach his children to respect their father. The basis for the relationship is reciprocity [*tabadul*]. But what becomes of reciprocity, women ask, when the husband fails so dismally in his duty?

The dilemma of the poor man is that he is practically destined to fail. And though he may argue that it is hardly his fault, he is doing as well as he can, his wife will be of another opinion. If he would only act responsibly, spend less money on himself and his cronies, and struggle a good deal harder, he could surely do better. The very basis for the reciprocity between them, as she sees it, has been undermined. When she is not granted her right [*haqq*], she will not meet her obligations.

So she feels free to borrow money whenever the family needs it, not only when it can be done without a loss of face for him, or for priorities and purposes *he* deems legitimate; now *she* will decide without deferring to him. And she abuses him before the children and many others. But

1. Umm Ali's mother used to tell people's fortunes with cards, and Umm Ali started telling them with coffee grounds after people who had known her mother and thought the daughter had inherited her gifts, started urging her. In the late sixties, when I first knew her, she used to respond to at least a dozen requests a week. At first she read the coffee grounds gratis, but from the mid-seventies on, her spiritual siblings [*muluk*], who had bestowed this gift on her, told her to take a small fee. She stopped telling fortunes in the mid-eighties when her sight started to go.

sabotaging her housework or denying him his sexual rights in her would be going too far—except when she really cannot take any more and leaves the house, seeking refuge with a friend or relative, until the husband, subdued, begs her to come back with a promise of a complete change of heart.

Much is at stake for women and children. The man's failure has quite heart-rending consequences for them. Admittedly, they are rarely reduced to hunger. But they must go without most of the things that they wish for in life and are forced to pinch and scrape to exhaustion. Moreover—and this is more important in a way—the man's failure undermines their chances for self-respect and status in the community. When others discover the extent of your poverty, when they see that you are without food or shoes or whatever, you lose face and lose position and are shamed. For here, as in most places in the world, women and children depend on the husband and father for their social position. What counts is what he brings home in the way of material things or money that is transformed into material things and made visible to others.

It is against this background that Umm Ali's criticism of Mustafa must be understood. But it also reflects the fact that she lives in a society that allows her to speak candidly about her marriage. She and others are trying to salvage something of their reputation and self-respect by distancing themselves from the man. They refuse to let their self-esteem and their social identity be dependent on him and his inadequate efforts or be destroyed by his failure. And they can do this without the cost that a similar course would entail in my society, branding oneself a failure in one's marital role. Norwegian middle-class culture has required success and harmony in marriage; to expose other realities behind the façade would reflect on the woman who committed such indiscretions and would cause her to suffer feelings of personal defeat and fear of loss of esteem. It was only with the feminist movement that these attitudes started to change. But in Cairo, the outlook has long been different.

The Egyptian women I know are children of a culture that does not demand happy marriages. Rather, conflicts and problems are so much an acknowledged part of life that no one would wish to deny them, in marriage as in any other relationship. What is more, women like Umm Ali have been brought up to think of themselves as persons with their own identity, separate from that of their husbands—so they can stand apart from him without sinning against social norms that demand unity and fusion between the spouses. Man and woman in Egyptian culture are different but linked: she may be dependent on him economically, but she

Female friends commiserating with each other about their husbands.

is not one with him. So the woman need not always make up a moral team with the man. In this respect, Cairene women are indeed more emancipated than many Western women.

Their problem is that women's social position and prestige depend overwhelmingly, as they and others see it, on the material contributions they receive from their husbands; and from this situation there is little escape. Women have little influence on the structure of values applying in society at large. But they can choose to some extent what values they apply to and among themselves. They can argue, as these women seem to, that what really counts is not material things but a person's moral qualities and religious piety.[2] They can declare that they, as women, will embrace other standards than those professed by society at large. Thus they can defend their own self-respect and help others think well of themselves, too. And that may be seen as more important than social rank and prestige.

2. See Wikan (1980, 43ff.) for a development of this argument.

Their responsible and independent role they enact in other contexts also: for example, when they serve as arbitrators in conflicts in which they play a forceful and independent role, and especially through their economic activities in the management of loans and savings clubs (see below). Wage labor, on the other hand, has been beyond the reach of most women of Umm Ali's generation. But many have regularly found themselves pressed into taking on economic responsibility when their husbands have failed or left the family in the lurch, thus forcing the wife to cope. Women also on occasion seize an economically independent role by borrowing money when they judge it necessary, even over the husband's veto. Moreover, they run the whole informal credit market in the form of a series of savings clubs, ranging from small to very large indeed. Finally, it is almost exclusively the women who plan systematically for the distant future and make investments, be it in education for the children, enhanced level of living for the family, or improved housing, perhaps even home ownership.

By these various means they can alleviate and reduce the defeats their husbands perennially visit on them, but they can never truly escape. For they cannot free themselves from the dominant values of the larger society and its emphasis on material wealth—which they reveal by their own eagerness to show off things whenever they get something of value. And their rebellion against their husbands more often takes the form of verbal ambush than of active revolt. As Umm Ali says, "What would it help me if I dug in my heels? It would only make bad worse." Woman, man, and children are trapped in a system of mutual powerlessness and dependency.

Yet the relief and moral satisfaction women derive from denigrating their husbands and complaining about how useless they are should not be minimized. Perhaps it is essential for their mental health.

In my society, women can resort to antidepressants, sleeping pills, psychologists, and social workers. Women like Umm Ali must cope by themselves.

The question arises, Why do women hope against reality? Why do they continue to hope that their husbands will change and their lives will change when experience overwhelmingly tells them it's no use: men are what they are? Why do hopes ignore reality when reality crushes hopes time and again?

It is as if hope is bred in the bones of these people. The whole social environment is one that teaches people to persevere; good effort will bring good results. Giving up is like showing lack of faith in God and his superior scheme. So people struggle along, railing against fate, family,

spouse, and government but persevering all the way.
them their stamina and vitality. And it is also what gives
in the good example and man's ability to remodel himself.
belief in the human being's ability to change and come to
remarkable. It accounts for the basically optimistic outlook o.
accounts for the ability to forgive. A person's bad behavior is t.
be just that, behavior. It does not reflect on the individual himse.

Marriage and Love

There are many reasons why the material contributions from man to
woman remain essential, however much women might try to deny it.
They are indeed the only unequivocal expression of love in this milieu.
It is shameful to show affection between man and woman in public. To
the world, the husband's love for his wife can only be expressed by means
of "gifts" in the widest sense. He who looks after his wife and children
conscientiously and gives them what they need in the way of food and
clothes is the epitome of the loving man.

Men rail against this notion and claim that it leads to squandering
and wastefulness on women's part. Men accuse women of showing off
needlessly just to be able to say, "Look what *my* husband has given me!"
The man feels he does the best he can, and the wife should be understanding and accept whatever he provides as the best he can manage. Most
men hold down two jobs and have an average working week of about
sixty hours. But their labor is poorly paid, and their own private expenses
are quite high. A man needs considerable resources to be a man among
men. He wins respect in his own and others' eyes by being generous, like
Mustafa was when he tipped the taxi driver so liberally. It also matters to
smoke a great deal and perhaps drink a little now and then. On average,
men use one-third of their income for these purposes, and some men
spend one-third of their wage on smoking alone.[1] In the wife's eyes, this
is treason.

1. The place of cigarettes in the enactment of the male role can hardly be exaggerated. Until the early eighties, it came out in the pose men invariably took for a photo,
nearly always with a cigarette in the mouth. Though nonsmokers make up only a tiny
fraction of adult men, the attitude toward smoking is changing. It is now used more

Naturally, women are not blind to the man's dilemma, that to be a man he must be generous and spend liberally on his friends. But she then feels it is her right to demand, in keeping with the principle of reciprocity, that he compensate her for what he fails to give by means of other contributions that she values. And it is entirely possible for the man to do so. He can show loyalty to her when the children are sick, and care and affection for her when she is tired or distraught. He can show concern for her constant struggle to make ends meet by giving her a fixed monthly sum for household expenses. He can sit home with her at times when he is free or take her and the children out for a picnic or to the zoo, as described in women's tales of the good husband. In all these respects, Mustafa fell miserably short.

"Like a third-rate girlfriend"

He has treated me like a third-rate girlfriend. I have accused him of having taken me just for the sake of intercourse. He has no feelings at all. I feel as if he had just seen me in the street and come to sleep with me, like I were a prostitute. . . .

When we were newly married, I used to make myself so beautiful for him. I waited for him in my nightgown of chiffon, and with my hair flowing down my shoulders, oiled and brushed to a shine. Then he came. He would pound on the door and burst into the room, his face contorted and exclaim,

"I feel awful the moment I see you! Here I come happy from the street, and what do I meet? An apparition so ugly I want to turn back. You look like a man!"

"Do you see any moustache?"

"Well, then you must be a ghost!" [*afrit*]

I was *so* unhappy, naturally. I used to stand in front of the mirrors and scrutinize myself. What was wrong with me? I didn't see anything. And if I looked so ghastly, why didn't he divorce me? I felt like in a prison. . . . Every Friday he used to go out with his friends while I was left to myself. When I begged him to take me with him, he just snapped,

"The flat is good enough for you!"

"But I am also a human being, I need exercise."

"So do it in the flat! Walk up and down!"

"And fresh air!"

"So open the window!"

---

to calm one's nerves; I know several men who were committed to not smoking but took it up from overwork and tension.

A flop

Mustafa is never willing to take the family out for leisure. He him gets all the relaxation he wants. But me and the children! I've tried to make him understand that the children *need* amusements. They must have exercise and a change of air. But Mustafa turns a deaf ear. "So get Ali to take you out!" he says. He knows full well that Ali is just like himself: ashamed to go out with the family.

When Amin lived—Amin was wise, he understood about life—he used to say to his father, "You are her husband. You should take her out!"[2] But Ali is just like his father, complaisant in words, but not in action. He has no brains!

Only twice in my life have I been to the movies, both times alone with the children, and only to still their nagging. I can't bear to go without Mustafa, for I feel people staring at me and wondering why we are alone, without a man. They must think that my husband doesn't care about me! Once when we were standing in line to buy the tickets, a man offered his help. I was grateful and gave him the money, and he got the tickets for us. He was very friendly and bought us snacks—for two piaster. But when we went into the movie hall, he followed after us and sat down beside us. I was annoyed. What was he up to? All the time he chatted in friendly fashion with the children. When the movie was over, I acted as if I was waiting for Mustafa. "Why do you think, Ali, that your father is so late?" The friendly man asked, "Do you go out?" I answered that I was much too busy for that; and besides, why did he want to know? Because then we could have gone out together and amused ourselves! I said he should be ashamed of himself to make such a suggestion. And that if he wanted to be compensated for the snacks he had given us, he ought rather to say so. "Not at all!" he replied. "I'm married myself and have children of my own. But I'm just like your brother, and your children are like my own."[3] I laughed scornfully and said that in that case, he ought to take his own wife and children out! Then I took out two piaster and threw them at him and marched off.

When we got home, I told Mustafa what had happened.

"Is it so that you *want* men to make approaches at me since you let us go alone to the movies?"

"I presume that's what *you* want, since you insist on going!"

---

2. I doubt that Amin actually said it to his father, but he might have said it to his mother.

3. The saying "I'm just like your brother" is a common way to indicate intimacy mixed with respect. Young lovers address each other as "brother" and "sister."

"Insist on going! Can't you understand that it is the *children* who want it; and they need it, too!"

And I lectured him on how I struggle incessantly to keep them from playing in the street so they won't learn disgusting manners; and how impossible it is, for the children seek any opportunity to escape. So I resort to threats and punishment and promises to keep them in. I say I shall take them to the zoo, or on a picnic, or to the movies; and what's more, if Mustafa thinks I get any enjoyment out of taking five kids to the movies, he should think twice! For the bus is jammed, and the kids fuss and hassle, and during the movie, soon one, soon the other, wants to go and pee, and I have to accompany them; and then they are hungry, and want a sandwich, or snack, and I run like frantic up and down, hardly even glimpsing the movie!

But it's typical of Mustafa. He has no idea of the children's needs; and even if he did, he wouldn't give a damn!

Sharing responsibility

Mustafa has never been willing to share responsibility with me; he leaves it to me to manage everything. Like that time when Aleyya was ill (with diphtheria). The doctor had said that she *must* have an injection every night. "Don't you ever go to bed before giving her that injection!" One night I was delayed, and so it was late before I could go [to the pharmacy to have the injection inserted; she had the syringe herself]. I asked Mustafa to come with me. But he snorted that he wanted to sleep. "Can't you see that I'm exhausted? Do you think I go idle all day, like you?"

I was seven months pregnant, and Aleyya was a chubby and heavy four-year-old. I carried the girl upon my shoulder as I went out into the dark. We went from pharmacy to pharmacy, there are surely twenty-five in Giza. All were closed. I was just about to break from exhaustion, when I came upon a butcher who was still open, and asked his help. He said I should go to the ambulance station, perhaps they could set the injection. So I did, to no avail. They sent me to the hospital. On my way, I passed the butcher again. He had a customer who offered to drive me in his car. But I refused. It was impossible when I was alone, without a man [male relative]. The man assured me that he would drive me safely back and forth. Still, it was impossible.

At long last I reached the hospital, my spine was about to burst. I asked for the injection.

"We have no injection," the nurse spat out.

"But *I* have," I said, "I just need help to insert it."

The nurse grabbed the injection and stabbed it into the girl so a little went into her body and most went outside.

The way home remained. I was completely exhausted. When I reached the corner by Umm Foad's house, I saw that the lane ahead was pitch dark, and I didn't dare for my life to enter.[4] I went back towards the main street, for it is lit through the night. I found a café with its chairs left out for the night; it was two o'clock already. I sank down, and laid the child beside me on a chair. I decided to stay there till dawn, for there was no way I could walk home in that dark. As I sat there, drowsing, I suddenly caught sight of a figure across the street. I sprang up, thinking it might be a policeman. Then I saw that it was my own father! I cried out, "Ya [oh] Baba!" He turned his head but didn't see me and continued his pace. I panicked. "Ya Baba!" I shouted again.

He turned around, "Who are you?"

"I'm your daughter!"

Then he lit up the way for me with his lantern. [He did not carry the child.][5] He quickly said good night and left, for he was tired.

Early next morning Mustafa woke me up by jabbing me in the arm, "Hurry, get up, you daughter of a slut! You have to give the girl the injection!" I was furious and told him he could at least wake me up in a decent manner. Then I told him what I had done. "Okay, so sleep then," he said, "Go to hell!"

"It's a heavy burden to carry unreciprocated gifts"

Many teeth have I lost. I was only eighteen years old when they began falling out. On one ear I hardly hear, and from the nose I bleed steadily—all on account of the beatings. Not to mention all the sickness in body and soul that sorrow and anger have brought. *Za'l* [sorrow, anger] eats and tears at your body. Everyone thinks that my sisters Feyza and Farida are younger than me, though they are much older. But they have their teeth intact. Yes, they, too, were beaten, but the blows hit them only on the *outside*. They didn't feel *za'l* for their husbands kept them amply provided with food and clothes. Every year

4. Her fear was of *jinn* [ghosts], not human predators. Streets in the neighborhood, as in Cairene low-class quarters generally, are safe even in the middle of the night.

5. In those days it was considered shameful for a man to carry a child in public.

they used to take a clothes loan from the government, and so Feyza and Farida had all that they needed, and even more.[6]

Whereas Mustafa . . . ! Not once in our marriage has he ever bought a thing for me or the children, nor a piece of clothing for himself. He doesn't even know his own shoes or pajama size. I tried to teach him the value of him also bringing something new for the house at times, so I too could be made happy and surprised. I took him with me to the shop to teach him to buy shoes and clothes. But it was useless. He has no ability to judge for himself. To everything the shop assistant said was nice, Mustafa repeated, "Yes, it's nice!" "Not at all!" I said. "Can't you see?" and I held up the material against the children's faces to show him. "Can't you see that what looks good on one, is ugly on the other?" But he can't. It's a pity, for it's a heavy burden to carry unreciprocated gifts.

Would you call *this* happiness?

Once Mustafa came home with a whiskey bottle and said he had got it as a gift from a friend. I believed him, of course, like I used to believe everything then, for it was before I knew of deception and guile. A few days later I and Umm Magdi were walking along the main street. Suddenly Umm Magdi stopped in front of a shop window and asked, "What are those bottles?" She cannot read. I looked and saw that they were whiskey bottles, just like the one Mustafa had just been given. The price tag was on. It said seven pounds. "Mustafa has got one like that as a gift from a friend," I said. Umm Magdi protested that Mustafa couldn't possibly have such generous friends! Then I started to think.

A few days later Mona—she was eight years then—told me a story on the condition that I promised not to tell it to her father. She had been with him in Attaba [central quarter of Cairo] when he had gone into a shop and bought a bottle for five pounds [things are cheaper in Attaba]. Then I understood that Mustafa was a traitor, and that he deceived me. And I who used to respect him! . . .

People *think* we are well off because Mustafa owns a workshop. His sister and foster sister in particular used to come here and sit and talk about how lucky I was to have a workshop owner for husband. Once I got so sick of it all that I tore open the doors of the sideboard, and

---

6. Clothing loans are provided to government employees for the Feast after Ramadan; the loan is given in the form of fabric from government cooperative stores and repaid over ten months through reductions in salary.

showed them the bottles and screamed, "Look—this is what my happiness consists in!"

Umm Gamal has told Mustafa, "One can be a man by virtue of one's personality—drinking and smoking are not necessary."

But Mustafa cannot understand.

"Marriage makes a man of you"

Right from the time we were engaged I understood that Mustafa didn't love me, since he never made me happy. He used to say that he loved me but it was just talk. After the wedding he admitted that he loved another girl, a neighbor, but his foster mother refused to let him marry her. She was angry because he didn't want to marry one of *her* daughters. But Mustafa said he was heartbroken because of that girl, he loved her very much, and so he didn't want to marry anyone else. But even if I had known this before the wedding and told Mama, our engagement would have prevailed; for Mama had set her mind on this. She did me *great* injustice. Love must be there from the start. And it is not enough that one of the two is in love. Both must be.

It was Mustafa's friends who persuaded him to marry. They said he must—or he wouldn't be a man.

"He goes one way, I go the other, and never the twain shall meet"

What has worn me out and ruined my health is that I wasn't given the freedom to choose my own spouse. Mama didn't say, as she should, "What's your opinion?" [*eh ra'ik*] She didn't give me my *right.* I was so bitter that I cursed her and said *"Minnik lillah"* [May God punish you] and *"Rabbina yintihim minnik!"* [May the Lord finish with you] And my sister Farida said I ought to be ashamed for talking like that! But truly, I meant it! For Mama did me a great injustice. That's why I have lived, and will continue to live, a life without love; and that has exhausted me. For I love the people, and need someone, a man, to love me in return. I need tenderness and care so I will be replenished rather than depleted. But Mustafa had no such thing to give. He goes one way, and I go the other, and never the two will meet. With him there was never reciprocity, feelings, and tenderness. He sleeps in one bed, and I in another, and even when he comes to sleep with me, there are no feelings involved. He just asks for intercourse, and then returns to his bed—like a complete stranger.

"Like a stranger from the street"

Truly, Mustafa is like a stranger from the street. This is the way of our "marriage": he comes home at night, asks for food, and sends Mona or Hoda out to buy because there's usually nothing, telling them to hurry because he's tired and wants to sleep. Then he eats and goes straight to bed. And sometimes he comes and wants to sleep with me. Otherwise, I don't see him except if there's a soccer match on TV. He is more remote even than a hotel guest. Hotel guests at least greet you and engage in polite conversation. But Mustafa never says a word about his experiences. I myself always like to tell what I've seen and heard when I've been out. But Mustafa doesn't like talking, it's just noise, he says. "On the contrary," I say, "talking creates understanding and closeness among people." But he neither wants me to understand him, nor him me. He accuses me of being illiterate and stupid as a donkey, and says he is better than me. But I feel I learn about life from talking. I wish our hearts would be together, but he has no interest in that.

Twelve

Might and Vulnerability

"In many a house, she is the man and he the woman"

Mustafa has no thoughts in his head. He's completely lacking in the ability to think, so I have to do it all. I've always masses of thoughts in my head—naturally. For if I didn't, I would not be a human but an animal!

Mustafa hardly acts like a human being. A donkey is better than him. Many people think that donkeys are stupid, but that's just because they don't talk. The donkey understands and obeys his master—which is more than Mustafa can! Sometimes he comes and tells me that so and so at the workshop has advised him to do this or that. Then I remind him that I long ago advised him to do just the same. But he never listens to me or heeds my advice. He says, "Don't think *you* can command over me!" He is afraid to do as I say thinking that then *I* would be the master of the house. And it's true, that's the way it is in many a house, that she is the man, and he the woman. But I don't want any of that—just that we should respect each other.

"For if I hit him, he wouldn't be a man"

He says he wishes he had married an educated girl, and that I am stupid like a donkey. I say he should praise his Lord that he got me.

No one else would have borne such negligence and carelessness without retaliation. Any other woman would have raised hell, and brought down a tornado of curses on his head, and many would have hit him too. At the very least, they would have searched his pockets every night, and stolen his money. But I could never do that because I have breeding [*tarbiyya*]. *That*'s why I still respect him. Countless times I have felt like hitting him, but every time I control myself. For I know that if I hit him, it would be the end of all respect. Then he would no longer be a man.

To control oneself

Mustafa, on the contrary, hits Umm Ali. One incident happened when he and Umm Ali had been married for twenty-eight years.

Mustafa was sick with a pain in his knee, and sent me to call the doctor. The doctor came and ordered full rest for five days. After he left, we were going to eat. The children fussed and wanted fish, whereas Mustafa didn't want to eat at all, just to sleep. So I bought fish for forty piaster and told the children to put aside ten piasters' worth for Ali and Mona, who were not home yet. We ate—I and Hoda and Anwar and Afaf and Nosa—the fish for thirty piaster. But the children were still hungry and wanted more. So I said they could eat it all provided someone went out and bought fish for ten piaster for Ali and Mona when they came. We could borrow the money from Umm Gamal.

When Mustafa woke up, Mona made food for him, his favorite— *gibna rumi* [Greek cheese] and olives and eggs—and served him on a tray in the bed. Meanwhile Anwar had been out to buy more fish, but he came back reporting that the fish market was closed. So I sent him out to buy the same food for Ali and Mona that their father just had. But when Mustafa discovered that the children had eaten all the fish, hell's fury broke loose! "Why didn't you make them save some for their brother and sister?" he screamed. "Why, even when I'm sick, can't I have any peace!" And he flung the plate with olives and eggs at me, and pounded the tray against my chest. And it is a great sin before God to throw food on the floor!

I burst into tears, and went into the other room, while Mona cleaned up the food. Later, Mustafa had excused himself to his sister saying his nerves had been frayed. I said only a fool would think that it was because *my* nerves were so good that *I* kept my control!

To strike first and think afterwards

Mustafa acts first, and then thinks, if he thinks at all. First he strikes, and *then* he says, "*ma'lesh!*" and "*muta'assif!*" [I'm sorry] and "*Ilhaqq 'aleyya"* [it's all my fault] and such futilities. As if *ma'lesh* can undo any damage!

Once, when we were four months married, it happened like this: we had been visiting his father's sister and had a very nice time, so we were in a good mood, and after we went to bed, I tickled Mustafa in the side—just for fun; I've always liked to tease and laugh, it makes life brighter. But Mustafa blew up. "I can't stand that kind of nonsense!" he howled, then went into the other room to lie on the couch. I fell asleep and slept soundly until I was shaken awake in the middle of the night by Mustafa pulling and pounding at me, "Get up, you daughter of a slut, I want to take you to your father's house!" I was startled and asked if Baba or any of my relatives was dead. Not at all! But Mustafa wanted a divorce! I tried to ask him his reason, but all he said was, "I don't want you!" I suggested we could at least wait till the morning to get divorced. But Mustafa was insistent.

Halfway to my father's house he changed his mind, and ordered me to turn back, saying, "It's my fault" and "My apologies" and so on. I said, "You behave like a madman!"

The house of obedience

Something similar happened when I was pregnant with Ali. I had no appetite at all except for *fisix* [dried and salted sardines]; and so I told Mustafa that I would be going out the next day to buy *fisix*. In the morning my sister Farida came and asked me to go with her to change a box of sweets. So I did, and then I bought the *fisix*, and we each went home. Meanwhile, Mustafa had come home and found the house empty. He went to Farida's house to ask about me, and the children told him where we were. When I came home, he was burning with fury. "What do you think I am—a woman, and not a man—to leave the house without my permission?" I reminded him that I *had* told him the night before that I would be going out to buy *fisix*. But he just ignored it and said he was going to teach me obedience. He ripped off his belt and hit me against my cheeks and back and grabbed me by the hair and kicked me to the ground. Afterwards, he asked me to serve him the food. We had some leftovers from the day before, and I heated it and served him. Then he ordered me to eat with him. I said that even if he had offered me a steak of lamb, I could not manage. . . . So he said, "I apologize" and "It's my fault" and that same old song.

A blessed chicken

Mustafa doesn't dare to divorce me. I have told him that I *wish* he would do it, and remarry, and that his new wife would demand her *right*—that right *I* never took—and make him pay for his sins. But he knows how lucky he has been, and so he doesn't dare to do it. There are plenty of women who, when the man neglects the needs of the house, search his pockets when he's asleep and steal from him. At the least, they will sabotage their duties, and let him go without food when they have to borrow money for food themselves. *Biysibu irragil yitfil-liq* [They let the man fend for himself]. Even my brother has urged me to do that. "So let him go to hell!" he says. But I can't do that, for it's God's task, and not mine, to take Mustafa to account. That's why I do not let him pay the penalty for his folly.

For example, that day when they had been here and closed the electricity because Mustafa hadn't paid the bill, I told his sister Amina that I was just about to faint because I had given birth to Nosa the day before, and Mustafa hadn't brought me a chicken.[1] I was lying in bed, praying to God to help me get some food, when there was a knock on the door, and in came Adel, Umm Magdi's son. In his hand he held a chicken which she had bought for sixty-five piaster out of a pound she had borrowed after she had been to see me earlier in the day and found me worn out and miserable. She had even cleaned the chicken, so all that was left for me to do was to cook it. I blessed the Lord that he heard my prayer, and praised Umm Magdi. Then I cooked the chicken and served it to the whole family—Mustafa too! And he didn't even ask me, "Where did you get it from?" Not a word! He ought at least to have asked what it cost and said, "Here is the money!" I told Umm Magdi that I would pay her back right away, but she said there was no hurry; "Today it's you, tomorrow me."

"The man is the wife's best doctor"
In the fall of 1972 Umm Ali got diabetes. She believes herself that the illness had been latent for a long time but was triggered by two traumatic experiences that hit her that summer. First her dearest sister, Shaddya, only twenty-eight years old, died after a tonsil operation. Three months later, her son Amin died at nineteen by taking his own life.

In the following years, she was often sick, not only bodily but psychologically. A nerve-racking story about a car Mustafa bought and expected *her* to provide the money for placed an insufferable strain on an already broken body (see chap. 14). She grew dependent upon an arsenal of medicines that Mustafa never had the money to buy. Her illness turned

---

1. After delivery, women are presumed to have an extra need for protein, and the husband should bring a chicken as gift.

into a new source of conflict between them whenever she needed money for medicines, whenever she had to see a doctor, whenever she was too tired to do the housework. Mustafa used to say that it was madness to waste money on medicines for her when they did not cure her anyway. She felt humiliated and scorned by his attitude. Whenever the doctor prescribed new medicines for her, she would send the children to the pharmacy to ask exactly what they cost so she would not have to ask Mustafa for a single penny too much.

He accused her of having brought the illness on herself. She answered with the counteraccusation; "And was I ever ill before I married you?" She feels it is he who has ruined her health. The doctor has stressed the necessity of her living a regular life: she must get up early in the morning and take the medicines at a fixed hour and eat nourishing foods. But when she asks Mustafa to wake her up early because she cannot manage herself—she lies sleepless till dawn and so is exhausted in the mornings—he just mocks her and says, "To hell if *I'm* gonna be a doctor for you!"

Umm Ali deplores both his attitude and his behavior.

If only he would help me and cooperate, my health would be good as gold. For they have said it on the radio in a program on psychology, "The husband is the wife's best doctor."

. . . Mustafa is never willing to help me. When he was sick with a pain in his knee, he used to ask me to massage his leg, though my arms and back were aching. But he will never massage me. Only twice in his life has he taken me to the doctor: the first time when I lost my speech after Aleyya's death, and the second time after I had given birth to Nosa, when I was so sick I could hardly walk. The doctor said it was tuberculosis.

When I was pregnant with Nosa, I was so huge because of the water in my body that people believed I was going to have twins. I could hardly get out of bed. I used to sleep on the lower bed with Mustafa, and asked him to let me lie on the outside in case I needed to get up and pee. But he refused. "What d'you think you are, that you can order me about as you please?" he thundered. One night as I woke, I couldn't manage to step across him, and I let out a terrible cry, for I was so afraid to pee in the bed.

"Only four times have I demanded divorce"

Even though Umm Ali has been unhappy with Mustafa from the first week of their marriage when he started to beat her, she has demanded divorce only four times. She is proud of that. She feels it is a challenge to master one's fate and one's situation and to endure. She remembers well the circumstances of each crisis. The first time was only four months after the wedding, when she was pregnant with Ali. The second time was after three years, when she was pregnant with Amin. The third time was after eighteen years; and the fourth in connection with "the car," after twenty-five years of marriage.

The first time, Mustafa had hit me so blood gushed from my mouth because I didn't want to sleep with him. I was already asleep when he came home at night; I was lying with my face towards the wall, and he kicked me and ordered me to turn around for intercourse. I refused. I said it was impossible the way I had been beaten earlier in the day. He exploded and hit me hard against my back. I still refused—his breath stank of hashish and booze. He grew wild and beat me so I bled and tore my panties to pieces. "You can't refuse me my right!" he screamed, "I'm free! I do as I please!" I grabbed my clothes and ran out of the house and went straight to my father's and insisted that he free me instantly from the marriage. "I refuse to live with such a brute!" But Baba only wanted a reconciliation, saying things like, "Be patient," and "Tomorrow, God willing, he'll be good again," and "What will people say when you're just married and then divorce?" I said it did not matter what people said, *they* didn't know my situation. But Baba was adamant. So when Mustafa came to fetch me, I had to follow him. But Baba made him promise to control himself and refrain from beating. Mustafa kept his promise one week! . . .

The second time [I demanded divorce] Mustafa had beaten me so my eye protruded like a blue bulge out of my head. We were having guests: my sister Feyza, her husband Abdou, and Abdou's father. Abdou had bought *kofta* [meatballs] for us for dinner, and we had just sat down to eat by the *tabliyya;* the room was crowded, and I was sitting with my back against the door of the sideboard nursing Ali when Mustafa asked for salt and pepper. I stood up, so the [sideboard] door could be opened and went out to sit in the front room. Abdou called me to come back so we could all begin to eat. I replied that I would come soon, I just had to finish nursing Ali first; for children cannot wait, they must be nursed immediately. Mustafa yelled that I must come at once, and I answered again, "Just a moment!" When I had finished nursing Ali and entered the room, Mustafa rose and jabbed his fist into my eye so I lost the water bottle, and almost dropped the child. Abdou's father scolded Mustafa and said, "It's your fault! She hasn't done you any wrong!"

I grabbed my clothes and went to a relative in Sayyida [old quarter of Cairo]. By chance my father came there, and he was shocked to see how his own daughter looked. He was still there when Mustafa came to fetch me. And I got very angry with my father because he didn't side with me and argue my cause but just urged a reconciliation. I bet he was afraid that I might become a burden to *him* by giving him three more mouths to feed [herself, Ali, and the baby in her womb], though I *had* told him that I would never move in with him and his wife. I would get myself a room and a job—any job—and support myself and the children. Later I moved to another relative, and Mustafa came again and asked forgiveness and promised never to beat me again. And because my heart is white, I followed him home.

"I neither love nor hate him"

Abdou, Feyza's husband, used to beat her a lot. So much so that after Mama died, Feyza left him. Mama used to support Abdou and stand up for him. She said he beat Feyza because he loved her too much [*min kutr ilhubb illi huwa kan biyhibbaha*]. But that's just rubbish! Love does not lead to beatings but to closeness and understanding. Mustafa beats because he *cannot* open up and *cannot* tell what troubles him. Scolding [*shitima*] is the only speech he knows. Otherwise, he keeps quiet, and tears on his soul.

I had wanted to be a singer, but Mustafa refused. He said, "You'll be rich and I'll be poor and then you'll despise me because I'm black." He often accuses me of despising him because he is black. But then I tell him, "It's not you I condemn, it's your behavior."

A while ago Ali asked me, "Mama, do you love Baba?" I answered, "I neither love nor hate him, I just live like a wife, that's all" [*'aysha zoga bass kida*].

Truly, I was prepared to love him. But the way he behaved, he didn't let me.

Thirteen

Three Desperate Attempts at Self-Help

The job: "So I can walk apart and look at him"

In the end the cup overflowed. Umm Ali had more than she could bear of accusations of wastefulness and carelessness. So she took the momentous step of seeking a job. It was in 1970—after twenty years of marriage. "I do it so I can walk apart and look at him!" [*mashya bi'id 'annu, batfarrag 'aleh*] she said. By that she meant that she could no longer be held responsible for his household. Now it was up to him to cope without resorting to her as a scapegoat. She was sick and tired of years of accusations that she wasted his hard-earned money. Now he could see for himself what it cost to run a house.

The mere thought that she could take a job required great courage and fortitude. To carry it out necessitated initiative, perseverance, and strength of quite exceptional proportions. Women in this area of Cairo, as in most others, do not work outside the home unless they are educated at least to the level of secondary school. But none of Umm Ali's generation have that much schooling. Even today, when most girls obtain such education, the men usually refuse to let them use it. For the wife to work is traditionally regarded as great shame for a woman, and even more for her husband. Men say they would rather throw themselves into the Nile than let the wife work. That the wife works reveals to the public the man's ultimate failure as a provider. It means that he is no longer a *man*.

But a woman who takes this drastic step also has to pay the price in the form of loss of reputation. About Umm Ali it was said, "*What* a shame! She works who is not at all destitute! Her husband owns a workshop!" Or, despicably, "Imagine, she who is not needy at all! She does it just to get money to build the house. How shameful!" People talked and talked, mostly with scorn and condemnation, but also with a tinge of admiration they would hardly admit for such overwhelming strength of character. Umm Ali said she knew that even her brother Ahmed criticized her for working just to be able to build the house. But no wonder. His wife no doubt regaled him with all manner of criticisms and lies.

She herself was strong enough to rise above people's talk. "They say it's a shame, but shame, what's that? Nothing is shame in itself, one must look to the situation. All things are possible if the situation demands it."

After weeks of struggling, where she spent long hours waiting in the anterooms of various factory offices for the chance to speak to directors and personnel managers, she finally succeeded in the impossible in an Egypt with massive unemployment, she got herself a job. It was in a sweets factory. Her task was to wrap and pack the sweets. The wage was twenty piaster (about 50 cents) per day. Deducting transport costs, she was left with seventeen piaster a day. In addition they deducted—she thought that was plain exploitation of the poor—two piaster tax every time the wage was paid, which was every twelve days. But she was still rather pleased. She had accomplished her goal.

The working day was long; it included three hours of strenuous travel on buses where people stood packed tight as sardines in a box. She had to leave home at half-past six in the morning and did not return until eleven hours later. Then there waited all the housework which her daughters were either too incompetent or too lazy to do: mending clothes or cooking the more complicated dishes like fried fish, for example. Umm Ali was angry about that. She has told them innumerable times that they *must* learn, or else they can never marry. But then they reply, "As if *we* are going to keep house when we're married, we who are educated and everything!" To which she retorts, "And who do you imagine will do it for you? Your husband?"

Mustafa was furious with the situation, and threatened divorce again and again. She was not worried. If he divorced her, she would finally have what she had wished for all these years, freedom from him. Perhaps it was this indifference on her part that made him crack up. One day he exploded, and grabbed her clothes and threw them at her, and yelled that she should take her stuff and get out at once. Umm Ali says she was overjoyed. She rushed to fetch her father so he could help her pilot the divorce safely through. Her father and stepmother came. They wanted to know if it was true that she wanted a divorce so she could marry another man, for that was what Mustafa said. Far from it. All men could go to hell! she said. What she wanted was just peace and quiet and escape from the endless accusations and demands and quarrels, and to live in peace by herself and manage alone. The children all cried, "Don't leave me, Mama! Take me along!" "And me!" "And me!" Her stepmother said, "For my sake, be patient! Tomorrow, God willing, he'll be good again, you wait and see!" She replied that she had waited too many tomorrows already, and that she had been a fool to endure it for twenty years. They ought rather to praise her now that she finally came to her senses. She would work and support herself and the children.

Many of her relations gathered—the father's wife had sent the children to spread the news—both her brother Ahmed and her sister Farida, and Farida's husband, and her best friend Umm Magdi. All of them urged her to be patient and to endure, for Mustafa had long since abandoned his threat. Now it was *she* who demanded a divorce. They all joined in the chorus, "Tomorrow, he'll be good, you wait and see!" "Persevere, and God will give you the money!" "Accept your fate!" "For *our* sake, be patient!" A friend of Mustafa who had also joined them advised him not to let her take any of her belongings with her though they were all hers. She has the list [*qaima*] specifying them as her property. But Mustafa heeded his friend and said that if she wanted her things, she would have to bring the police. In the end, she remained. But for three months, she and Mustafa were not on speaking terms.[1]

In the end, there was a reconciliation through a cousin of hers who extracted a promise from Mustafa to give her thirty piaster in her hand every single morning. Mustafa kept the promise for one day. After that the cousin was sorry and said, "I was wrong. But think if your children had got a stepmother!"

When Umm Ali quit her job she was actually quite relieved. Fourteen months of exhausting double-shift work had worn her down. But whether she wanted to or not, she had in fact no other choice than to give notice after she discovered that her gains were being lost in the getting. As her best friend, Umm Magdi, put it, "You make twenty piaster a day while your home is being pilfered!"

It all began when she became aware of what she felt to be the family's suddenly remarkable consumption of tea, sugar, spices, and sundry victuals. She complained to her daughters and told them that this kind of squandering simply had to stop. But the daughters said, "By the Prophet, Mama, we pinch and scrape all we can. But there are the neighbors who keep coming in and borrowing this and that and they never return it." She asked who these neighbors were, and it turned out they were people with whom she barely had a nodding acquaintance. Plain thieves, in other words.

And then one day she discovered that a large aluminum pot had disappeared. She asked Hoda about it and was told that Umm Gamal had borrowed it, she had needed it because she expected quite a few guests. Days passed, and the pot remained a stranger to the kitchen. This surprised Umm Ali, for Umm Gamal was always punctual when it came to returning things. Finally, Umm Ali went herself to ask after the pot. But Umm Gamal hadn't borrowed it. Hoda admitted then that she had sold it—for three pounds (and it was worth three times that!)—because she was in arrears with her savings club money.

That was how this particular episode came to light. To make the household budget balance, Hoda had begun two savings clubs: one for thirty piaster with daily deposits of three piaster, and one larger, for fifty-four piaster, with daily deposits of six piaster. Mustafa obviously did not give her enough for daily expenses, and without her mother's network of po-

1. Not being on speaking terms [*mitxasmin*] is a strategy which puts the man especially in a difficult position; he will have to go through the children for every task or service he wants performed.

tential lenders, she had seen the savings club as her only possible access
to money. When she did not have money for payments [deposits], she
sold things—clothes, kitchen utensils, and such—to get it.

As if this were not enough, Umm Ali discovered that an assortment of
clothes had disappeared: a lovely, brand new blouse of Hoda's, a new bra
and two pairs of socks, and the smallest child, Nosa's, new pants. All of it
was stolen by guests—guests who saw their chance now that Umm Ali
herself was not there to watch over them with her experienced eye. They
slipped things under their bras, or down their pants (women seldom use
purses). She estimated that they had stolen clothes worth about seven
pounds. A blouse was discovered on the back of one of Mustafa's nieces;
once they saw her sitting on a passing bus, but when they came to visit
the little bird, she had already flown to Alexandria.

Such was life when the daughters were left on their own to take care
of the home.

But in the years that followed, Umm Ali often spoke of how much
happier she had been that time when she worked at the factory, despite
the toil and effort. She was miles away from the worries of the home, and
out of reach of the children's endless "I want, I want" and "Give me, give
me."

She had produced the evidence she needed. It cost Mustafa more to
keep house without her there than with her. She is *not* wasteful.

An accursed car and a heartbreaking savings club

Of all Umm Ali's painful memories, there are few, perhaps none, more
bitter than the saga of the car and of the vacant lot. Both embodied her
dream of happiness and progress, most of all, the car. In both cases it was
she who went out on a limb; she who nurtured the hope; and she who
was left with the shame and the bankruptcy. I don't believe I have ever
seen her as sick and broken as she was in the fall of 1975, when the car
affair was at its worst.

The story, as it was told to me, was short—the consequences apparently endless.

In the spring of 1975, Mustafa came home in high spirits telling her of
a steal of a buy he had the chance to make. They could be rich. What it
was, was a car—a fairly run-down and damaged car, admittedly, but he
and a friend could repair it, use it as a taxi, and make fistfuls of money.
The car cost 540 pounds, so it would only cost them 270 (about $405)
each, and put in order with the know-how of Mustafa and his friend—a
car mechanic—it would be as good as new.

Mustafa carried on or Umm Ali fantasized for herself (it is impossible to be sure just how that went) about all of the car's potential blessings. Not only could they make great piles of money, but what wouldn't the car mean for family happiness? They could go, the whole family together, for Sunday drives, and they could visit relatives in other parts of Cairo without having to wear themselves out on jammed buses. And just think what Mustafa would save in the form of bus and taxi expenses—he who always needed equipment for the workshop which is too heavy to carry except by taxi! Besides, he was getting to be old, his back and knees weren't what they used to be, and who knew how much longer he could put up with ruining his health on public transport, and so on and so forth.

Whether Umm Ali let herself be carried away or was actually convinced is difficult to say. She herself says that what made the difference was the prospect of a better future for the children, and then the possibility of family outings—an eternal longing in a woman from a tradition that re gards the act of a man taking his wife out for pleasure as a key symbol of love.

There was one problem, of course, and that was the money. It went without saying who would have to provide it. Umm Ali did not have 270 pounds, she hardly had one. Women in the back streets rarely have savings in the house. There are so many ways to put a little bit of money to use at any given time that it seems like a physical impossibility to have money within reach and not use it. But because everyone from time to time needs larger or smaller sums of money which can only be obtained through saving, people have developed a solution to the problem, savings clubs. It was this solution Umm Ali now turned to.

The savings clubs are organized and function in the following fashion: One person takes the initiative and as a rule becomes the leader [*ra'is*] for the club. It is also possible for a person in acute need of cash to go to another, well-connected woman and beg her to help out by creating a savings club as Umm Ali did when her family was threatened with expulsion from the house. The leader recruits a certain number of members and each of them makes a regular monthly, weekly, or daily contribution. There are unlimited kinds of membership, from one-sixth to a double or a triple. The members withdraw their savings in an order agreed on verbally at the start of the club. The organizer withdraws first. The guarantee for this savings society lies in the fact that the leader personally knows each member and has confidence in each and every member's willingness and ability to continue to pay her contribution after she has withdrawn her amount. If they don't, the leader is responsible and must pay up herself.

The size of the savings determines the frequency of the deposits; if a large sum is desired, the usual is a monthly deposit (paid the same day wages are paid); for medium-sized sums, weekly deposits are the rule; and for small sums, daily deposits are made. Because women have the contacts in the neighborhood, it is women who run these clubs. Men are only members.

All accounting for the savings clubs is done without the aid of pen or paper. The leader keeps her books in her head.

Umm Ali needed 270 pounds, a formidable sum among the poor. She estimated that the highest realistic membership deposit would be 15 pounds ($22) per month in which case she would need eighteen members. To enlist so many members at such a prohibitively high price was a nearly impossible task. But she managed it finally by using her gift of persuasion and by begging and appealing to people's own best interests as well as to their concern for her and her pressing needs.

It would have been a pleasure to say that everything went according to plan. But that, unfortunately, was far from the case. The "big" savings club, as Umm Ali came to call it—in contrast to the "little" one which she later made to repair the damage done by the big one—ended up an unmitigated disaster. During the course of the first two to four months a total of ten members dropped out, including herself, Mustafa, Mustafa's car mechanic friend, her son Ali, her brother Ahmed, and her best friend Umm Magdi, to name a few. But in an attempt to avoid being accused by the remaining people, who represented eight full memberships and 120 pounds per month, of ruining the savings club and violating their trust, she continued to act as if there were still eighteen members. Had she not, they would have demanded their deposits back immediately, and where would she have got the money? (At the start of the fourth month they had paid in a total sum of 480 pounds). In the meantime she borrowed from all corners, to pay back one loan with another in order to pay back yet another, and so on and on and on in a seemingly endless circle. Nevertheless, she was far from successful in gathering together the necessary 150 pounds extra each month (representing the ten memberships of those who had dropped out), so she had to appeal to the other members' sympathies whose turn it was to make their withdrawal. She had to fabricate an endless series of excuses—how another member had left her in the lurch just that month by not paying—and plead with them to let the debt ride. She had only 80 pounds, for instance, to give the woman who was to make her withdrawal in the second month, and the man who was to make his withdrawal in the third month received only 120 pounds, and so on. In this way she spun herself into an endless web of lies and half-truths which more and more resembled the antics of a beggar: a craven pleader for pity and mercy. She felt herself so humiliated and duped that it broke her health, both physically and mentally. And she swore that when the savings club was over and the debt paid she would leave. That was it! She couldn't stand even the sight of Mustafa any more.

For just what did he do, this man who had gotten them all embroiled in this whole mess in the first place? Was he ever willing to help out and carry his share of the responsibility? Far from it. As always, his refrain was "*Ma'lesh*" and "May God help" and "Tomorrow, God willing, . . ." while she was left with the shame and the debt.

And the car? Well, that was, of course, lies and more cursed lies. It was a wreck beyond repair, but this Mustafa and his car mechanic friend found out only after they had spent 125 pounds trying to repair it. And who paid for it all? *She* did, of course. When she found out that the 270 pounds she had scraped together as Mustafa's half of it was about to go down the drain just as she was on the verge of breaking under all the pressure of the debt and the thought of how she was going to make ends meet and get the savings club back on its feet—*that* just about caused her to come unhinged. And then Mustafa and his friend told her there was still hope—if she paid five, and then ten, and then fifteen pounds for repairs. Which she did, by selling her gold earrings, her aluminum saucepan, and a couple of pillows. One hundred and twenty-five pounds she paid before they finally said, no, there was no hope. And that wasn't the worst of it. Mustafa's friend, the "car mechanic," revealed himself to be the ultimate crook. First, he took advantage of Mustafa every day by playing on how he was ill and needed "loans" for medicine so that he could work on the car. Mustafa, naive and good-hearted as he is, gave him the money and the man bought a hypodermic needle and poured the contents into his tea. It was obviously drugs, said Umm Ali. She was enraged because Mustafa came to her and asked for money for the poor, ailing man. She screamed at him, "*Haram!* [It's a sin] You give *him* food and drink while you let your own children starve!"

But the worst of it was when "the friend" ran off with the car and sold it, and only paid Mustafa 80 pounds of the 270 he had invested. She was convinced that he had managed to sell it for what they paid for it themselves—he was a crook, he knew the tricks. "And Mustafa, idiot that he is, went along with the 80 pounds! If it had been me or Amin! Amin was sensible, like me, he had brains, like me, we would never have allowed ourselves to be fooled like that! We would have demanded our *right!* But Mustafa! . . . And Ali and Hoda will be just like him!"

That the debt had begun to work on her nerves was obvious when I met her in the fourteenth month of the savings club. Four months still remained. She had a haunted expression which, at times, bordered on the look of the mentally deranged. Every thought and all her awareness was concentrated on the debt. She complained of insomnia and even when she was awake there was something of the sleepwalker about her, as if she were locked into her own world. She avoided visits and started at every knock at the door—it could be someone come to demand their share!

That month there were two savings club members whose turn it was to withdraw money. Adel, a brother-in-law who was contracted as one member, had originally asked to have his withdrawal divided over two months. According to their agreement, he would get the first installment, 135 pounds, the third month and the second half in the fourteenth month. But with all the difficulty she was having, Umm Ali wasn't able to come up with more than 120 pounds in the third month. Thus, Adel was due 150 pounds for his second installment. She knew she had no chance of paying him so much and begged him—again—to settle for less. Adel grudgingly agreed to let her still owe him the last 20 pounds, but 130 pounds he had to have before the Feast. (This was the month of fasting, Ramadan, with its subsequent celebrations.)

The other one whose withdrawal was due was Ibrahim, a friend of Ali's. He had contracted as a one-fifth member and should actually have had 42 pounds, but because he had not paid his installments the previous four months (he was ill and unemployed), he was qualified to receive only 30 pounds.

I was witness to how both Adel and Ibrahim came day after day to collect their money, and Umm Ali didn't have it. Each day she had to find new excuses and fabricate new tales and promise, "Tomorrow, God willing." When the next day came she sent the children on frantic missions of mercy, as a rule without success, because her best creditors had lost patience with her. She was in debt all over the place. When evening came, Abel and Ibrahim arrived again and the same scene was played out. Finally, Adel lost all patience and sent his children with the message "Baba says, 'Pay what you can,' but he wants *something*, *now!*" And even then she had to tell them she would send her own children with money the following day. She had in fact, no more than 32 pounds and she knew sending so little would only enrage Adel. She also knew that he was greatly in need as well and was in debt to people who were pestering *him* with their demands. "Yesterday when he was here, he didn't even go and say hello to Ahmed because he was so ashamed—he owes him money."

On 4 October 1975, I noted in my diary:

Umm Ali had an agreement with Ibrahim that he would come around

six and collect his money. He has been here daily for five days asking
for it. She was so beside herself with shame that she could not get
the money together today either, so she left the home in the evening
to avoid meeting him. But he came back at eleven at night. She told
him she felt terrible about it but he simply *must* wait till after the
Feast (in one week) because some members, she lied, had traveled
to Suez without paying her the money they owed. She simply had
no money. Ibrahim refused to be pacified. He said he absolutely *had*
to have the money so he himself could visit his family in the countryside and spend the Feast with them. He would make a big stir [*daw-
sha*] if he didn't get the money.

On 5 October I noted,

Ibrahim came back and got his money. Umm Ali took 30 of the 62
pounds she had painstakingly assembled to give to Adel (she owed
him 130 total), and gave it to Ibrahim instead, "Because it's a greater
shame with Ibrahim, he doesn't know my situation."

She was full of bitterness and felt deceived by so many people. Many
of the members to whom she owed money had cashed in their remaining
installments by not paying in after first having withdrawn their share. Her
nephew, Sami, for instance, had taken his share in the eleventh and twelfth
months, half of it each time. Combined, he should have received 225
pounds because he had not paid his installments for three months. But
Umm Ali had only 200 pounds to give him and asked to be allowed to
owe him 25. Sami reluctantly agreed. But the next month he only paid 5
pounds in his installment instead of 15 and took, in this fashion, 10 pounds
"by force" [*bil qafya*]. And this month he didn't pay at all, thus cashing
in the remaining 15 pounds which she owed him. Umm Ali was enraged
and told him so at the first opportunity. His behavior was a disgrace, she
said, he who was just like a son (it was she who nursed and raised him
after his mother died). To think *he* couldn't wait when others who weren't
even kinsmen could! Sami tried to defend himself saying, "*Ma'lesh*," he
was *so* in need himself. But she scoffed at it and was sure she knew better.
She warned him that she would remember this next time *he* was in need.
And she complained to me and to others, "He's so mean, it's a disgrace.
Last year at the Feast he didn't even come and greet his relatives here in
Giza, and then Ahmed said it was surely to avoid having to bring gifts!"
[*'idiyya*][2]

2. At the Feast, relatives are supposed to visit each other and give the children a
token present [*'idiyya*]. But many abstain, presumably because they cannot or do not
want to give presents.

Every day during this month of October 1975 I heard Umm Ali swear that when the savings club was over four months hence she would leave to a place where I can recuperate and not wear myself out thinking about the family; a place where none of them can find me, or I will never be left in peace. That would serve them right! I won't bat an eye if they starve or are sick, for none of them cares about me. All my life I've carried responsibility for them alone—now I'm going to care about myself only and let them care for themselves. Ali, for example, he should have said, "I must help my mother, who has given me life and upbringing, and wait to get married until these four months are over!" Instead he comes to me and says, "Give me, give me!" I say it's he who should be giving me! It's a sin to neglect your mother like he does. The mother should come *before* the fiancée. He protests that he has no money. But then I remind him of all of the times *I* didn't have, but he was in need and so I *borrowed* money to help him. For example, that time when he was taken for driving without license and fined 100 pounds! To this day he owes *me* money, and yet he still comes and asks for more! I screamed to him yesterday, "I've got two men in the house and not one MAN! . . ."

Doesn't he see that I'm driven crazy? Wherever I am and whatever I do—sitting, eating, sleeping, walking—I think about the debt and how I can get the books to balance somehow. All because of Mustafa's stupidity and deceit. It's *he* who has ruined my health. I wanted to help him for the children's sake—I don't need anything myself—but *they* need to be made happy. You should have seen Nosa how happy she was yesterday with the dress I bought her with the money you gave me. Whereas Mustafa, do you know what he said when I asked him for money for shoes for the children? *"Inshallah ma 'ayyidu!"* [I hope to God they won't celebrate] When I complained to him yesterday about how to get money for Adel and Ibrahim, he just said, "I don't have any! Anyway, I owe money myself!"

I asked him if he believed *I* had any.

"And it's all your fault!" I screamed.

"Ma'lesh!" he answered.

I was about to explode. "And what have I ever gotten from your *ma'lesh?"* I screamed. "What's the use of *ma'lesh?"*

The house site that gives wings to a dream

Given another time and place, Umm Ali could easily imagine working to make money enough to build on the lot. People accused her of doing just that. But in her situation it was out of the question. She could defend her

Umm Ali and her daughter on an excursion to the land lot. Umm Ali's land is the sunlit spot between the two houses.

working as a result of being driven to it by her husband's unreasonable accusations. On the other hand, to revolt against the woman's role in life and cast disgrace over her husband simply because she wasn't satisfied with what he gave her—to insult irreproachable tradition because of simple material greed—such behavior she herself would have condemned.

So her vacant lot remains a bitter dream of happiness. A dream so near fulfillment she can almost imagine it being true—even when, in the grim light of her reality, it always slips away. Others she knows have managed the feat. Umm Magdi, for example, her one-time best friend, has built on her lot and moved there. A thousand pounds Umm Ali estimated it would take her in 1981 to start it herself. And that is just slightly more than the cursed car cost—with repairs!

Hardly a day passes when Umm Ali doesn't bewail her fate, not only to herself, but to people who stop by; she lays bare her wasted life and unfulfilled dreams of which the lot is paramount, and reproaches Mustafa for his role in it all. If it weren't for him and all he's done, they could have built on the lot. And if it wasn't for all her planning and involvement, they would have lost the lot ages ago. Mustafa would have sold it to the lowest bidder! She hangs onto it for dear life.

But to begin at the beginning. It was in 1963 that the lot was purchased, a peaceful little plot of a hundred square meters out near the Pyramids. Two friends of Mustafa convinced him that he should buy. They were going to buy as well and wanted Mustafa along so that all of them could live near each other. Umm Ali paid fifty pounds cash. The rest, 250 pounds, was to be paid back in monthly payments of five pounds. It went just as one could have expected, says Umm Ali bitterly. Mustafa's two friends paid punctually and have long since built on their lots. They themselves, on the other hand, paid now and then when it suited Mustafa. Finally, the owner became so angry that he came and threatened to sell the land to another. That was in 1971. Mustafa wanted to sell, but Umm Ali said, "leave it to me." She saved from the household money, and borrowed some and managed to assure the owner that the monthly payments would be made until they had the deed in their hands. But the lot is still not licensed to build on. That costs 30 more pounds and she hasn't managed to put away that much.

In 1976, says Umm Ali, they were on the verge of divorce because of the lot.

Mustafa wanted to sell the land and buy a new car! A new car, that's right! There you can see what a traitor he is! He claimed he had a buyer willing to pay one thousand pounds for the lot, and we had only put in three hundred! Then he asked for the deed. I answered "over my dead body," that he could choose between me and the lot. He insisted on selling, I insisted on divorce. He refused to give me a divorce, I refused to give him the deed. I said, "The lot is neither yours nor mine, it is the children's. *We* don't have money to build with, but maybe *they* will in time." I threatened to report him to the police and take him to court. I told him I was going to shame him before the whole world if he sold the lot. The next day I took the deed, which I had hidden under the mattress, to Umm Badr [her friend] so that Mustafa would not be able to take it with force. Mustafa commanded Hoda to find it for him and she was so afraid she searched the whole house. Afterward, I told Hoda and Mona where I was keeping the deed so that they would know in case I die.

One problem with the lot, and deep inside Umm Ali is aware of this, is that neither the children nor Mustafa want to move. I went with her and the two oldest daughters out to the lot one time, and while she praised the peace and quiet, the clean air, and the sun illuminating the place, the daughters spoke only of how dead it was and how far it was to walk to the grocer's and that there weren't any other shops around and how few people there were and how far to the bus. Those features which for Umm Ali mean peace for her nerves—quiet, light, one's own entrance, and people at a remove—have little appeal for them.

They have their roots in the dark and narrow back streets and the surrounding area. And this is the way it often is with children and teenagers: they like it; it is the mothers who complain and want to get away.

Nor have I ever heard Mustafa, man of few words that he is, either praise or criticize his domicile, but I would believe that he is quite satisfied. His workshop is nearby, and shops are within easy reach. On the main street there are life and activity, entertainment, plenty of cafés, plenty to see. In comparison, the lot seems isolated and remote. And unlike his wife, he has never, as far as I know, had any ambition to become a home owner.

She herself insisted that whether or not the family chose to move there, they ought at least to build and rent out the house.[3] At least twice a year she makes the trip out to the lot. She takes a friend with her. The older children are uninterested and the younger are a nuisance to take on the bus. She says just seeing the lot gives her peace of mind.

She remains alone with her vacant-lot dream of happiness.

3. It would also be a good investment. With the present housing crisis and the high rent for new flats, Umm Ali would be able to collect about thirty pounds per month (in 1982; by 1995 this has risen to nearly 100 pounds) for a two-room flat plus the advance ("key money") of one to two thousand pounds (by 1995, approximately 4,000 pounds) from which half the rent is deducted until the sum is repaid. She could use the advance to build the next story, as is common procedure.

Part Three

The Back Streets as a Social Environment

Everyone Begrudges Others Everything They Have

From my first day in the back streets people cautioned me, "Don't get involved with people [*matruhish 'and hadd,* literally, don't visit anyone], it just leads to trouble. The people here begrudge others everything they have!" [*innas mish biyhibbu ilxer li ba'd abadan!*] Over the years these warnings have taken on a semblance of truth for me. Not because it is true that nobody wishes anybody else well, but because the people themselves are so convinced of the veracity of the statement that they live their lives accordingly.

I have sometimes asked myself how, in an environment like this, one could possibly convince another that one truly wished her well. Smile most sincerely and impress upon her how happy you were for her? It is not likely to work. The fortunate one would know in her heart that you were covering up your feelings and were being two-faced. She knows she is enviable, so she takes envy for granted. Indeed, she would feel a bit cheated if she were not made an object of envy. It would be like denying the value of what she had gotten. Envy is itself a form of recognition, though a curious form, I admit.

Only in the rare case when the person who expresses her joy over another's good fortune has previously demonstrated good feelings for her (e.g., by giving her generous gifts or lending her money regardless of her own needs), only then will the object of good wishes believe that they were, in fact, sincerely meant. But in an environment such as this, few possess the means or the ability to live up to such exacting standards.

Apart from her children, a woman may have a special friend, possibly a brother or a sister or two, whom she can fully trust. Many have none but the children. Umm Ali was lucky until 1975. At that time, she had a friend, a sister, and a neighbor. All had in common that they were better off than she was. But then the sister died, and the friendship broke up. In 1981, the neighbor, Umm Gamal, died. Umm Ali grieved deeply. Umm Gamal was a Christian (a Copt), and that, Umm Ali said, was the reason why she was so good hearted. Had she been a Muslim, she would have coveted the success of others. "No matter how fortunate they themselves are, Muslims always begrudge others whatever they have." This is a common sentiment among the people.

Envy

"Envy [*ghira*] is like a national scourge," people say. "It's as inbred as people's needs for food and clothing. People envy anyone who is better off, nicer looking, or more beloved than themselves. If a woman sees another who has a nicer bed or dresser than herself, it becomes like an obsession that she must also have. It's no use saying, 'Wait a moment, sister! You don't need it straightaway!' No, she must have—immediately!"

Men accuse women of many things. Lack of respect for themselves is a prime point of contention, but topping the list are extravagance and wastefulness. Men condemn women for squandering their hard-earned money with nary a thought for how they must toil to earn it. A prime example of such capriciousness, say men, is when women "rush off to the fish market when the fish is at its most expensive just so they can boast to the neighbors, 'See what *my* husband has given me!'"

When women deplore the neighborhood in which they live, as most of them do quite often, their complaints sound alike: "Women sit in the doorways and stare at what the neighbor's husband brings home for dinner!" When friendships break up, one party may berate the other for having been a terrible bother because she was underfoot all the time. "She was always sitting here gaping at everything my husband brought home, and whining, 'I want one too!'"

Envy is perceived to be as old as humankind and to stem from the marriage between Adam and Eve. Adam and Eve were brother and sister, and all siblings are jealous. Through the fateful circumstance that all people are descended from a pair of siblings, envy has become the mother of us all.

Egyptians do not distinguish between envy and jealousy, but subsume both under the word *ghira.* This is connected with the fact that the giving of things stands as the most potent symbol of love. Thus, when a woman is jealous of her daughter-in-law, as mothers-in-law generally are perceived to be, people see envy as the reason—not that the son gives his wife love, but rather that he presents her with money and things. When stepmothers—predictably—pester their stepchildren, again the reason is seen as jealousy of the material things that the husband/father gives, rather than resentment of his love as such.

Envy is perceived to permeate the air and suffuse everything. It is destructive of the environment and of oneself. Next to poverty, people see envy as the source of most of their misery. Because of envy, they say, there is no trust [*mawadda*] and cooperation [*ta'awun*] among people. "Everyone looks only to their self-interests."

The people's talk

The belief in envy as a fundamental aspect of human nature is part of a larger worldview that shapes people's perceptions and actions: it serves both as a guideline for their own acts, and as a framework for finding meaning and motive in the acts of others. Closely connected with envy in this view are three phenomena that can be separated in theory but not in practice: the people's talk [*kalam innas*], gossip [*xobs*], and the evil eye [*hasad*]. A person who gives in to envy will surely gossip and feed the people's talk, and she also risks casting the evil eye. The people's talk, gossip, and evil eye are all born of envy, and beget more of the same. They make up a vicious circle.

To illustrate the power of the people's talk, and a person's helplessness in the face of it, people tell the following story:

Once upon a time long ago there lived a man named Goha. One day he was to journey to town with his little son and a donkey. He placed his son on the donkey's back and walked beside them. All along the way, people laughed and pointed at them, "What a fool, to walk when he could ride! How will the son ever learn respect for his father!" Goha was annoyed. He lifted his son down, and rode the donkey himself. Now people hissed and shouted, "What a selfish man, to be so lacking in compassion! Just think, to ride while the poor child walks!" Goha was exasperated. He lifted his son up and placed him in front of himself. Then they both rode on. Now people taunted him and screamed, "What a brute! Is he going to kill that poor animal?" "What can I do?" thought Goha. He jumped off the donkey and lifted his son down, then they both walked on. Now people rolled on the ground laughing, "Look at that idiot—to walk when he could ride!" Goha was at his wit's end. He lifted the donkey and carried it on his shoulders the rest of the way. People screamed with laughter, "What a madman!"

The moral is, Whatever you do, people are going to find fault. Since the dawn of time, people have talked, and until the end of the world, they will be talking. The best you can do is ignore it and follow your own conscience.

But that is easier said than done. Everyone deplores the people's talk and its power over their own lives, but few have the strength to resist it. Umm Ali rose to such heights when she defied her husband and time-honored traditions by taking the job in the factory. But she has the backbone to follow her own convictions against popular opinion. Therein lies some of her special quality. For most others, the price would be too high. The people's talk is like a physical barrier before which you have to bow. There is power in the people's talk. A friendship, an engagement, a reputation can be wrecked. It takes exceptional faith in oneself and one's own judgment to stand up to such pressure.

The people's talk is perhaps that part of their local environment that people condemn most frequently and intensely. Because of it, they complain, there is no freedom [*hurriyya*]. Their fear of *kalam innas* is so pronounced, it is almost tangible. The concept is on everyone's lips all the time. In everything they do, people tend to think, "But what will the people say?" And they do not mean what will they think or believe, but how might they warp and twist one's every action?

The people's talk consists precisely in taking loose bits of hearsay or information and twisting them beyond recognition if not to the point of utter malice. If a mother is careful to give her children good and nourishing food, she can be sure that people's talk will say that she is eating up the money. "It's a shame! She should see to it that her children were properly dressed instead!" If she does the opposite and gives priority to clothes—in a situation where she can't have it both ways—then, surely, people will say, "What a shame! Wasting money on clothes! What those children need is nourishing food!" Fighting the people's talk is like fighting windmills—you're bound to lose.

When Umm Ali worked in the factory to refute her husband's allegations that she was to blame for the family's large household expenditures, people said, "Imagine, she's working *just* to get money to build on the lot!" Their comment is typical of the people's talk, and reeks of envy, not because Umm Ali had got herself a job—most women would not dream of sinking so low—but because she actually does own a lot and might possibly be able to build on it sometime. Had people cared to give the matter a moment's thought, it would have been plain to them that the chances of that were miniscule. Umm Ali would have had to work for at least four years, and save every penny she earned just to get starting capital to build the ground floor.

But the people's talk is not interested in understanding. Its driving motive is to find fault. The point of the criticism of Umm Ali's working outside the home was that she defied tradition and revolted against her husband because of pure covetousness and greed.

It would be too much to contend that such distortion is a conscious maneuver. People work with the information they have at hand and place it in the context of their understanding of life and humans. The interpretations they make seem both probable and plausible to them, even when they often also contain an element of rejoicing in the misfortune of others.

People blame envy as the source of *kalam innas.* They say envy breeds a fierce need to find the faults and defects in others. By belittling others, one can hope to aggrandize oneself.

Gossip

Gossip [*xobs*] is different from the people's talk in that it has both a face and an origin. Whereas *kalam innas* arises without anyone quite knowing where or how, gossip has a definite source: someone has gone and told what she has seen or heard. *Kalam innas* is like the wind which suddenly starts to blow, perhaps from several directions. Gossip is like a cold gust from one particular corner. *Kalam innas* is based on loose conjecture and hearsay. Gossip involves spying, exposure, and betrayal of trust. The tattletale [*xabbasa*] has gone to others and told them things she should have kept to herself, not because they are necessarily shameful to the object of gossip, but because one should not reveal the secrets of others. The standard accusation is that the gossip has come as a friend or a guest to a home, and then betrayed trust by splashing about private information. People call it *yigib sirat ilbet* [passing on family secrets].

Umm Ali makes a point of telling me how she never, on a visit to anyone, asks them, "*'amla eh?*" [what have you been doing], in itself an entirely conventional and innocent greeting. No, she sits down and waits until they themselves, perhaps, tell her. In other words, she takes precautions so she won't be suspected of poking and prying into their affairs. It is only a small step from making a friendly inquiry to being accused of prying. In fact, many people say that if you want to avoid trouble, you'd better not visit anyone. For every visit gives the hostess the chance to say later, "Guess what she came here and told me!" And you are hard put to defend yourself. After all, you were there!

People try to accommodate their actions to this view of humanity. They are exceedingly careful in friendships. Women rarely have more than two or three close friends. They show the utmost caution about personal information of a potentially compromising kind so it won't be twisted or distorted (see Wikan 1980). They publicize their victories and try hard to conceal their failures and defeats.

The evil eye

The evil eye [*ilhasad*] is another manifestation of envy. "The eyes curse anyone who is better than oneself," people say. Just as with envy and the people's talk, the evil eye stems from times past. People tell a parable about the Prophet's daughter, Fatima, who had given birth to twin sons, Hassan and Hussein. One night, God came to her in a dream and said she should remove the boys from the crib because she would have a visitor next day—a *husudiyya* [woman who casts the evil eye]. Instead, she should place two rocks under the blanket in the crib.[1] Fatima did as the Lord said. The woman came, threw out her arms and exclaimed, "Imagine, you having *two* sons, Fatima!" After she left, Fatima removed the blanket and found the stones crushed to pieces. The evil eye works through the eye of the beholder and the tongue of the speaker. It is not a deliberate power under the person's control. The evil eye works independently of the person's will.

But, people say, one can take precautions so one reduces the chances of doing harm in this way. Thus one should never talk about what others have. It is all right to look at their things but not to dwell on their successes or harp about it. The more composed you are, the greater the chance that they can keep their belongings in peace.

Egyptians do exactly the opposite, people complain. Umm Ali says,

Whether a person is poor or rich, people *must* find fault and cause damage to her. If a poor woman has so much as one kilo [of] *good* tomatoes, people must whine about it [*yiqurru 'aleha*].[2] "But what *fine* tomatoes you have!" they cry. Envy is in their blood. "Imagine, her husband empties his purse into her lap *every* evening!" cluck the women. Or, "Her husband brings her *bags* full of fruit!" They talk as if an injustice had been done to themselves. Also, they talk without knowing. Myself I always ask, "But did you *see* him emptying his purse?" The next day, perhaps, the man no longer turns the money over to his wife because the evil eye has changed his mind. Maybe he now spends it on cigarettes and hashish instead. . . .

When women mimic the way others give in to envy, they act in a characteristic way: they fling their arms about and throw their heads back while whining harshly and shrilly, "And she who's already got everything!" or "What a lovely dress! Where did you get it from? I want one just like it!" Says Umm Ali,

People talk without knowing, as when they say about me, "Like *she* has reason for complaint, she who has a workshop owner for a husband!" They have perhaps visited me once, but do not know my situation. I usually tell them, "What's the matter with you, to be talking about others like that!" My own heart is happy when others get something, whereas they grow black in their hearts. When Umm Gamal got

---

1. At the time, and even today in parts of the Arabian peninsula, it is customary not to let a visitor look at a newborn child.

2. *Yiqurr* means talking in a special way so that one stirs evil spirits that can destroy that which one is talking about; in other words, so that one invokes the evil eye.

the butane stove, I said to her, "Congratulations! May God give you a refrigerator!" When she got the refrigerator, I said, "May God give you a washing machine!" *Bahibb ilxer linnas!* [I wish others well] Whereas they . . . ! You should have seen Amira how she acted when Ahmed asked her to show me the coat he had bought for her in Libya! She pretended she didn't hear. He had to ask her several times before she finally opened the closet door just a crack so I could barely glimpse the coat! She herself begrudges others what they have, and so she thinks that I am like her!

. . . People used to say about Umm Magdi, "She's so lucky, with all that money and everything!" But I always told them, "It's not true! You should feel sorry for her, she has many children and problems in the house. May God have mercy on her!" I am rich in my soul because I rejoice at the happiness of others, and so God will reward me. I am happy, whereas most people fret.

Invidious comparisons; or, Why everyone else seems better off
Faith in the evil eye has quite sinister consequences, especially for the men. This is not because men believe in the evil eye more than women— the contrary may, in fact, be true—but because women's conviction that others believe and therefore hide what they have gives them inflated ideas about how much others actually have, and as a consequence, how hardworking and supportive *their* husbands are! The would-be wealth of others becomes the measuring stick for one's own worth, and the pillory for one's husband. How many times have I heard women say of others who were obviously much poorer than they, "You can't see it, but their closets are *full* of clothes!" And there is practically nothing you can do to try to shake such beliefs. You can open your closet door wide and shout, "Look here! This is all I have got!" People will still believe that you were keeping things under cover.

Fifteen

Materialism and Want

Status symbols
There is an apparent paradox in the way most people relate to both their ordinary and their more precious material possessions. Fear of the evil

eye coexists with a virtually unyielding passion to display whatever one has. It is as if one were trying to defy envy, to draw it out into the open. New and valuable acquisitions are usually placed where they are sure to be seen by visitors, rather than where they functionally belong. Refrigerators, which a few fortunate women whose husbands have worked in oil-rich Arab countries have acquired, are always placed in the living room, never in the kitchen. (The kitchen is shunned by visitors with any self-respect for fear they will become known as snoops.) The butane or bottled gas stove which ranks second on the list of status symbols—after the refrigerator but before the TV—is placed in the kitchen, but inevitably right in the door opening, where it is visible to visitors. In addition, people often seem to engage in an escalating process to try to outdo others materially, using any means at their disposal.

Women boast not just of what they have but what they are going to get, and how much better than the neighbor's it will be. In open quarrels between women, played out in full view in the lane, one may brag about how much richer, and therefore better than the opponent, she is: "I eat better, drink better, and go better dressed than you!" or, "*My* husband makes more money than yours!" (Wikan 1980:131).

There is sense to such exclamations. People live in a society—Egyptian urban culture—where materialism provides a bedrock of value. "People look only to the appearance, not to the character" is the scathing experience of these "have nots."

In their contact with the larger society, people cannot throw off the mantle of poverty. It reveals itself in the way they walk and talk, in the texture of their skin—coarse, blemished, and baggy—in facial expressions, in the timbre of their voices and in their dialect. Yet among themselves, they can savor some self-respect and esteem from others by a simple means; they can outdo others by means of the nuances inherent in the quality of a bedcover, a wardrobe, or a pair of shoes, meaning they paid more. When everyone has too little of everything, just about any material thing takes on the value of a precious object.

But a question remains. How can people be so eager to outdo others materially if their fear of the evil eye means that they might actually lose what they have by disclosing their precious possessions?

There is nothing out of the ordinary about holding inconsistent beliefs. What is strange is, rather, the Western preconception professing consistency as the moral norm. Egyptians have great tolerance for such aspects of human nature as ambivalence, ambiguity, and inconsistency—especially in themselves and their dear ones. One incidence to which I was a party is telling:

Women baking before the feast after Ramadan. It is important to avoid the evil eye when carrying the cakes to the bakery for baking (since people have no stove at home). Most women prefer to go in the middle of the night.

Umm Nagwa, a neighbor of Umm Ali's, told me one day the startling news that Umm Ali had baked fifteen kilos of cakes [*kahk*] for the Feast that year! I said it was impossible; she hadn't baked anything. Oh, yes! protested Umm Nagwa, she certainly had, for Umm Ali baked huge batches of cakes every year. I said it was not true; she hadn't baked anything last year or the year before, for I had seen it with my own eyes, nor had she even baked a single cake this year. "All right then," grunted Umm Nagwa, "so she hasn't baked anything this year—because she's *working* and has no *time!*" (implying, *what* a shame!)

There is no shame in misinterpreting people's behavior or in holding logically incompatible views. Indeed, much of one's own confusion can be blamed on others. As unpredictable as they are, you just *never* know! . . .

It is one thing, however, to hold contradictory views, quite another to have a basic fear of something and then do what triggers the fear. If a man with fear of heights straps on skis and leaps off a cliff, he must either be mad, or he doesn't really have acrophobia. If people in Cairo have such a burning desire to show off valuables they own, can they really be so afraid of the evil eye?

I think not. The evil eye is not a pressing fear so much as a conviction, a belief. And just as many believers fear the wrath of God if they commit a skin but do so nonetheless, so people believe in the evil eye and its destructive power without letting it run their lives. They take a pragmatic stance. The evil eye functions less as a guideline for one's own behavior than as a framework for assigning blame to *others*. Events we would label accidents have for them a highly rational cause: the oil that splashed on the woman's hand and burned it while she was frying fish, or the cakes that fell off the tray while she was going to the bakery to bake them (people do not have an oven at home) are proof of the evil eye. Someone no more than glanced at the fine catch or the lovely cake with envy in her heart, and the deed was done. The evil eye serves to explain why misfortune hit me but not you. You also had fish today, but luckily for you, you didn't meet anyone who gave you the evil eye. The belief in the evil eye is a warning to others to contain their envy lest they cause harm, rather than an injunction to oneself to conceal one's possessions so as not to arouse envy. When misfortune strikes, it is because others let their envy run away with them rather than because you got what you deserved for being foolhardy and tempting envy.

The material measure of a person's value

The consequences of having to hide one's material possessions would be simply absurd when people live in a society that makes material things the measure of the person, the essence of status and respect. A story will illustrate how deep-seated these notions are:

A friend of mine, Nadya, was beside herself with anger and despair because a suitor had arrived on her doorstep wearing a pair of sandals on his feet. "Imagine!" she hissed, "Sandals at thirty piaster! The kind *children* wear! Had it at least been sandals from Bata (major shoestore) at one pound! Now people will say, 'They will accept anyone just to get her married!'"

The greatest shame is of being ridiculed as poorer than you really are by people of your own kind—the people in the neighborhood. In the cutthroat struggle for recognition, the poor can be just as ruthless toward one another as any representative of society at large. One might think that they would stand together against the larger society and its emphasis on material things. But they are children of the society that spawned them, bred to Egyptian culture. It may even seem as if they assign material things particularly great value among themselves, making the curse of poverty even a bit heavier for themselves and each other to bear. The reasons are several.

When relations between people suffer from general mistrust, material objects rise above that distrust. They stand, impervious to the judgments of others, whereas good deeds and intentions can be twisted and turned inside-out by the people's talk. Second, when everyone feels the pinch, you know that material objects are what everyone else wishes for. So when you yourself experience envy, you can be sure that others will likewise envy you. Third, when your close relations with others are few, you can reach a large audience by publicly displaying signs of wealth. Finally, and most important, material things satisfy needs that can never be sufficiently satisfied in a poor population, so the person herself experiences them as *the key to happiness.*

When the proud mother parades her children in pretty new clothes but only meets with criticism, "She should be *ashamed* for wasting money on such costly clothes, what those children need is nourishing food!" then the critique is a testimony to her victory, and both mother and children bask in the glow of envy.

The vulnerability of women

The curse of poverty strikes women and men differently in their struggle for status and prestige. Admittedly, I know less of men's predicament since I could not participate in the male world. But I have seen men refrain from bringing friends home with them and heard them explain that it was for fear the friend might go out and "reveal the secrets of the house." They might say, "The wife was ugly" or "The furniture was awful," and so on. To minimize the chances of such disclosure, men generally prefer to find their friends outside their own neighborhood, thus reducing the chance of accidental visits. Let this incident I witnessed stand as a testimony to what is at stake for men. It also illustrates an important difference between women and men in the stratagems each can deploy to project a valued self.

Kamal, a young man from one of the better-off families in the area, attended technical college. He was always extremely clothes conscious and dressed in the latest fashion, whereas his brothers and sisters wore rags. They cursed him for his selfishness while admitting that some of it was justified. "Kamal keeps company with engineers, officers, and doctors. If he didn't dress as well as them, no one would be his friend."

One day, a group of Kamal's friends came to visit. They had found his house by asking people along the way for directions, but stopped, a bit perplexed, when they were shown to the bottom of a narrow flight of stairs, filled with rubbish. The shoemaker down below was sent up with a message to Kamal that they wanted to see him. The family was frantic. The smaller children ran out on the balcony to catch a glimpse of Kamal's fancy friends through the broken railings. Kamal's younger brother was sent down with a message saying no one called Kamal lived here, but he forgot his lines and returned reporting he had said that Kamal was not home! Then an uncle was sent down with a new message, no one named Kamal lived here. But the visitors insisted on what they had been told by people in the neighborhood, the shoemaker, the brother, and so on. So a new messenger was dispatched, this time in the person of Kamal's father. He said that a man lived in this house who had a distant *cousin* named Kamal; was it perhaps this Kamal they were looking for? If so, they must go out to the Pyramids (an upper middle-class area), for that was where Kamal lived. Kamal's friends meaningfully shook their heads and left.

Men in the poor quarter can do as Kamal does: dress in their very best and shake off some of the taint and stigma of the home. They can go out in the world and act as if they were better than they are. But women are trapped within the world of the neighborhood and its squalor. All the stains and blemishes of the home cling to them. Their gender and class mean that they have restricted freedom of movement. In theory, they are free to visit friends and relatives in other parts of Cairo.[1] In practice, they are bound by their duty to look after the house and the children and be always present when the husband comes home. Moreover, it is considered shameful for women not to keep to the house. Even minor infractions of this unwritten rule will easily earn one the reputation of "roaming." Cafés are not women's venue. Therefore, if women are to meet with others, it must necessarily be within the home.

There their bitter defeats stand glaringly, in full view of visitors: the torn and stained couch, the ragged carpet, the third-rate, blotched tomatoes. No wonder women are much more eager than men to spend money on consumer goods. The men would rather have plenty of cash to lavish on their friends and acquaintances, thus to enact a semblance of surplus.

---

1. By the 1990s, this freedom has been severely curtailed for young wives who must have the husband's permission to visit even their own sisters.

Typical are Mustafa's tipping the taxi driver ten piaster; and his refusal to ask for money back from the conductor when he had paid too much.

Even when the man fails in his role as provider, a duty for which he bears full responsibility, it is his wife who suffers the shame. Umm Ali raged at Mustafa when the landlord had been on her doorstep, claiming the rent which Mustafa owed. "*You* can take it easy for it's not *you* who're being shamed! But just wait, the next time I'll send him to the workshop to you so he can stand there and make you a laughingstock for all the world to see!" Thus she can threaten, but she knows her threat is hollow. Her instinctive reaction after years of struggle when she has been left to fend for herself is to marshal every ingenious device to save the sinking ship rather than letting it sail rudderless. For that is what would surely happen if she were to rely on Mustafa.

But her lifesaving operation comes at a cost. The sting of bitterness pains. She works it off by maligning Mustafa through daily detailed laments to friends and relatives. But publicly humiliating him would be going too far. Besides, that would reflect on herself. What counts is to maintain some self-respect and the children's life and health, not to degrade the man unnecessarily.

What counts above all is not to expose the family's material shame.

Part Four

Daily Life and Rhythm

Sixteen

Typical Days in Umm Ali's Life

The dream of a house of her own and peace and quiet and all the good things she thinks would follow in its wake—order, plan, neatness in life— stand in glaring contrast to Umm Ali's life today. She constantly complains how it is a mess, and how the chaos and disarray eat into body and soul. Not that she thinks the harried living conditions have anything to do with cramped quarters. People are so used to living tightly together that they seek to be close, even when there is space. Closeness runs in their blood; it gives a feeling of security and belonging. No, the chaos is all on account of the money, or want thereof. It is that which prevents foresight and planning, that which gives life its character of tortuous improvisation. If only one had a fixed monthly sum to make do with! The house would not remedy that, she knows so well. And yet, the dream of a house of her own carries with it the dream of a new life. For Umm Ali, as for many of us, happiness is where she is not. Now her daily life is like this; I render some notes from my diary.

27 September 1975. As usual, it's around one before she gets up, and then very reluctantly. She complains that she has had an even worse night than usual. First, she had to get up several times to change Nosa who wet her bed because she had a cold. Then, at seven in the morning she was up to drink tea with Mustafa and Anwar and Afaf, before Mustafa went to work and the kids to school. But then she was so tired that she went back to bed again. She cannot sleep at night because of the thoughts of all her debts. In fact, she was awakened at one at night by her father's wife who came and demanded one and a half pounds which Hoda owed her for a blouse she had bought.

I said, "By the Prophet, I don't have a penny!" And that the girl wasn't *allowed* to buy anything. She's got piles of clothes, while her sisters sit almost naked. Yesterday, Afaf sat crying because she doesn't have a single pair of shoes, just worn-out sandals. "You're making me a laughingstock!" she cried. Hoda is gluttonous. She begrudges others everything. And still she expects me who is up to my neck in debt to fork over so she can have one party blouse more!

Father's wife answered, "You are her mother, so you are responsible. Either you have to pull her by the ears so she behaves, or else you fork over!"

I said she could have half a pound now, and I'd pay her the rest when I got it. I'm flat broke. But she wouldn't hear of taking only half a pound. "I want everything all at once!" she said. And she is right! If she takes a little now and a little then, the money just evaporates in the house. Better to get it all at once and spend on something proper, like meat or medicines or something.

Umm Ali raises herself laboriously up on the edge of the bed and gives her *gallabiyya* a shake. It's the sixth day and night she has been wearing it, and it reeks of sweat and food smears. But today she is going to change because it's Thursday and tomorrow is the day off.[1] Yesterday, she tells me, Anwar was sent home from school because he had a hole in his sleeve. She had told him to tell the teacher that he *was* going to get a new uniform in just one week, once his father got paid. But the teacher scolded him and called him a slovenly lad, and he came home crying.

Umm Ali goes to make herself a glass of tea, while spewing forth a stream of complaints: Mustafa left only thirty-five piaster for food this morning, and not a penny for medicines. It is ten days already since she was at the doctor's who wrote out a prescription for insulin for her diabetes. Now she feels so poorly, she gets dizzy every time she tries to stand up. But Mustafa doesn't give a damn. The doctor has said that she *must* try to live a regular life, get up early in the morning and eat properly and take her pills. But it is impossible because she gets too little sleep. If she goes to bed early, the children wake her up with cries of "Mama, where's my this? Mama, I want my that!" In the morning when she wakes up, she asks for a glass of tea so she can take the medicine. But she must ask a dozen times before anyone cares to listen. So she gets tired and lies down to sleep again. "You have seen it yourself, when I ask for tea, it takes two hours before anyone brings it!" Mustafa is mad because she can't get up in the morning. She asks him to wake her before he leaves, but he mocks her and says that if she can't wake up on her own, she can go to hell and sleep there! The doctor has said she needs a lot of nutritious food. But that's impossible in a house like this. For

1. It is common to bathe and change one's clothes only on Thursday night, unless one is going out. Otherwise, people wear the same clothes day and night. Children in school, however, have to wear clean and newly ironed uniforms.

the children beg, and she doesn't have the heart to say no. Like yesterday, Mustafa bought ten eggs for thirty-three and a half piaster and cheese and olives for seventy piaster so there should be plenty for dinner. He would get two eggs, she would get two, and the children would get one each. But then Anwar, Afaf, and Nosa all asked for more, and Mustafa said Anwar could have a bite of his second egg, then she herself divided her second egg between Nosa and Afaf. And there went those nutrients!

Today Umm Ali wants *ta'miyya* [beans] for breakfast, and she asks Afaf, who is sitting half hidden over by the window eating a piece or two of *gawafa* (fruit she had stolen from the top of the refrigerator), to go out and buy her some. The girl answers, "*Hadr, ya Mama*" [as you please, Mama] and doesn't budge. The mother waits a few minutes, then calls out again, and again. . . . And Afaf responds, more irritated each time, "*Tayyib, ya Mama*" [Okay, Mama] and doesn't move. Then the mother tries Mona to see if her luck will be better. And Mona gets irritated because her mother keeps calling out "Mona" and doesn't call Hoda (who is such a sourpuss that the mother doesn't have the energy to ask her). Then the mother tries Hoda, who is in the other room, and either doesn't hear or pretends not to hear. Every time she wants anything done, she has to call out at least ten times before anyone bothers to listen. Hours can pass before anything gets done. She seems resigned to the situation, and chooses the path of least resistance, which means nagging relentlessly at Afaf, who seems to be the most cooperative at the moment.

Hoda makes the bed, airs the bedclothes, and tidies. Today, on the eve of the holiday, she also washes the floor. Mona washes clothes. The daughters have taken over all their mother's duties except cooking and feeding the pigeons. Afaf does most of the shopping. Because of the lack of system, this means she is sent out ten to fifteen times a day. She is also the one who is most frequently sent to borrow money.

Nosa whines a lot and seems to demand her mother's undivided attention. She throws terrible tantrums if she doesn't get her way. She torments the poor pigeons (kept on the balcony but roaming about in the flat). She doesn't obey any orders unless it suits her. Hoda yells at Afaf all the time, without any apparent reason. She hits Anwar when he's been out running an errand and has stopped a few seconds too long with the boys in the street. Anwar screams. Then he comes up from the street crying that someone hit him. Anwar hits Nosa just to tease her but triggers her howls. The mother scolds him, and he just smiles, then he hits the girl again, and the mother scolds and he laughs. . . .

28 September 1975, 1:30 P.M. Umm Ali is getting dressed up to go out. The whole family is invited to her brother-in-law Adel's for *fitar* [the meal held at sunset during Ramadan]. They are all eagerly look- ing forward to it. Umm Ali hasn't been there for several months, and she hasn't set foot outside her home for several weeks. The children are excited, swishing around, getting dressed up. Then Mustafa comes and says he has to go on an errand, and takes Anwar with him. Umm Ali is furious. She knows full well that that "errand" is just another word for soccer game. And one's word is one's word. Mustafa had promised that the whole family would visit Adel to- gether. I encourage her to take the children and go by herself. But she couldn't do that because Mustafa would get angry when he came home to eat and found no one to wait on him.

4 October 1975.   Mustafa stops by the house at about 3 P.M. He doesn't say a word to Umm Ali. After he leaves, she tells Hoda that she will be going out in a minute. Hussein, Mustafa's apprentice, is going to take her out for some fresh air since she has been feeling so poorly. She is going to pay a call on Hussein's father, who is ill.
   "And who's going to make dinner?" frets Hoda. "Baba was going to bring fish."
   "But why? We *have* food for today! And why didn't he say any- thing to me when he was here?"
   "*You* should have asked him what he wanted and what his plans were!"
   "And why should *I* always ask him? If he has something on his mind, he could tell me without being asked!"
   "No, you should have asked, not just sat there ignoring him when he stopped by."
   "But he stops by every day, without any reason!"
   "Now he went away angry, and ——"
   "So what? We *have* food for today, and I *am* going out! Fry the fish yourself!"
   "As if I know how to fry fish!"
   "Well then it's high time you learned! How can you ever get married when you don't know a thing!"
   The upshot was that Hoda and Mona "ran off" and didn't come

home until midnight. Umm Ali was thus forced to stay home and make the food. Otherwise Mustafa would have been irate. The next day the apprentice, Hussein, came over and chewed Umm Ali out for not showing up at the appointed time and making his family sit there, waiting with dinner all prepared for her!

11 October 1975, 2:30 P.M.–4:45 P.M.   She is up for a change when I arrive because the father's wife has been there again trying to collect the money Umm Ali owes her. She is sitting all wrapped up in a double layer of blankets, with one scarf on her head and one around her neck because she has a headache as well as a toothache. She seems terribly depressed, and her depression seems to get deeper by the day. All her spontaneous chatter is either about illness or Mustafa's injustices to her. But today she and Nosa are going to the doctor; maybe just getting a few minutes' attention from him will pick her up a little. Her whole life is limited to the flat now, she hasn't set foot outside for at least two weeks, so she can concentrate fully on the problems there. She talks about taking me to visit a friend that she would like to thank for giving her a loan. I encourage her to visit the friend alone today, on her way back from the doctor's. She says yes, if she can manage to make it up the stairs to the second floor. But when she mentioned taking me along, there was no talk of any "if." I encourage her to leave the house for a while, to go and visit Mustafa's sister in the country for a week, for example. She answers that it was Aswan she would like to visit, but the ticket is too expensive. A boy she knew in Aswan wanted to send her a cheap ticket, but Mustafa said no. I say, *"Malkish dawa' bi Mustafa!"* [Don't give a damn about Mustafa] She agrees that the next time she won't say anything to him, she will just take off. But, and another but, the children can't manage without her. Even if she were to leave, she would wear herself out worrying about the children turning the house upside down. I think to myself, How long is she going to treat the children like babies? Finally she agrees with me that traveling to Mustafa's sister in the country is better than nothing. As soon as this savings club racket is over! I protest that she should take a week off now. She says herself how the doctor has told her that she must help herself besides taking the medicine. She must stop her worrying and quit being sad and angry. He has said that she is sick in her nerves, not just in her body. But I can't see that she's doing anything to help herself, quite to the contrary. She doesn't eat breakfast in the morning and doesn't take the medicine then, as prescribed. She gets going at about 2 P.M. just because I've arrived, otherwise she would have remained in bed.

She looks at Mona washing clothes, she has kept going for eight hours now. Umm Ali remarks that until recently she used to do all the laundry herself and everything else, too. And she adds nostalgically that she wishes she had her health so she could work like before, because she's heard on the psychology programs on the radio that work is so important. "You can put your thoughts (problems) into your work." Now that she isn't up to working anymore, she puts all her thoughts into sleep and the bed instead.

Hoda comes in and sets a tray of *muluxiyya* [green vegetable] to be chopped up for dinner in front of her mother and asks her to finish the job, since she herself has other things to do. The mother grows irritated and protests that she is sick and has pain in her arms, neck, shoulders, and all over her body. Besides, nothing else is as important as getting dinner ready at this moment. After a little while, Hoda completes the work in surly fashion. Then she goes in and lies down to take a nap! What happened to the other things she had to do?

15 January 1979.   We had agreed to go out to look at the lot today, and I came to pick Umm Ali up at 11 A.M. But she was still asleep as usual. The youngest children are up, and Mona is sweeping the floor. They tell me that the mother got up at eight and ate breakfast, but then she went back to bed again. The house is a mess. I go and visit Amira and return at 2 P.M. Umm Ali is still sleeping so we wake her up. I remind her that we had a date to go out and look at the lot again today (for the third day in a row!), but she says right away that there won't be time today if we are going to eat first. I can't understand why there won't be time, sunset is still four hours off. And as incredible as it sounds, we're not finished eating until 6:30, and it's 7 P.M. by the time we've finished drinking our tea, despite the fact that we didn't have to cook anything for dinner today, just had potatoes, salad, and bread. But the potatoes had to be bought, and the salad makings and the bread, and it takes a long time to get the children (that is, Afaf) to do the shopping, and she comes home without getting what she was supposed to get and has to go out again and doesn't obey orders, and then Mona has to go out, and in the meantime Nosa causes trouble, and someone calls to Anwar from the lane, and someone has to go out on the balcony to see, and money is needed for the shopping, and Afaf is sent to search for money under a pillow, but she comes back empty handed, so she is sent to Hoda but returns empty handed again, and Mona has to hunt for money in her mother's brassiere, and Afaf wants to eat raw cucumber, and her mother scolds her because that just leaves four small ones (minute, in fact) for her father and Ali, and the children steal fruit and are scolded, and Nosa throws a tantrum and has to be put in her place with threats of a licking with the ruler, and the mother wants to fry the potatoes and make food while she is sitting in the bedroom rather than in the kitchen, and asks that the primus and the *tabliyya* be moved there, and so on. For every little thing she wants to have done, Umm Ali calls the children, and it takes ages to get anything done because, as she says herself, they don't listen to her at all. She complains that the constant yelling wears her out, and I'm surprised that she wouldn't prefer to do more things herself, like making tea and getting her medicine. The result of her calling and their ignoring is a terrible *nagging* that wears on everyone's nerves.

While we're eating, there are several knocks on the door. And the children command each other to answer it and see who's there. There are shouts of Anwar! and Afaf! from the lane below. And they command each other to go out and see who is there. The meal is one continuous quarrel and the children interrupt constantly; Hoda shouts at Mona from the other room and Mona tries to pretend she doesn't hear because, as she says, Hoda knows very well that she's eating. But Hoda is indefatigable (and Mona has to go because Hoda is older and can command her). Then Afaf hits Nosa because Nosa is eating too much melted cheese and she hits Nosa again for asking for a bite of my piece of cheese. And everyone is always on the lookout to be sure that no one is getting any better food than they are.

Part Five

Growing Up in Poverty

Seventeen

The Child in the Family

The problem of assessing experience

A meeting in Cairo with a Norwegian official representative made an in-eradicable impression on me. The person had been in town for two days and overflowed with excitement and admiration. Egyptians were really happy people, for children more full of smiles and joy, she had never seen anywhere. Egyptians really had a lesson to teach the world, the lesson of love.

I was astonished. By then, I had lived in Egypt for over two years and was deeply involved in life in the poor quarter. My own impression—after six months' fieldwork—was of a life full of misery and sorrow. Children often described themselves, and were described by their parents, as *ga'anin* [meaning hungry, but used in the broader sense of in want of food, clothes, everything]. Their lives were characterized by family turmoil, deep-seated conflicts between the parents, and much sibling jealousy and envy, not to mention the objective deficiencies in the fulfillment of basic needs that poverty entails. The Cairo poor seemed to me amply to bear out Eugene Walter's succinct observation, "The poor have plenty, but it is plenty of what nobody wants" (1966).

With hindsight I have changed my perspective somewhat. But it is worth stating the contrast bluntly for what it reveals of the problems inherent in understanding the lives of children, especially when they live in the most repulsive conditions from a Western middle-class perspective, an urban "slum." How do we bridge the gap sufficiently to understand the experience of growing up under such conditions? How to avoid the error of, on the one hand, being overwhelmed by the misery and want which are all too objectively real, or, alternatively, falling into the trap of the Norwegian representative who saw nothing but joy and happiness in the equally real smiles?

The problem hinges on a double stereotype, the romanticization/demonization of poverty. The Norwegian rejected my observations, saying they stemmed from the preconception that poverty is misery. I on my part suspected her of harboring the opposite stereotype, that poverty breeds genuine human values through its freedom from materialism. In my defense, it may be said that my perspective was more in tune with the people's own views. They often say how surprised they are that the rich have any problems, "when they have no *reason* for it!"

143

To live in poverty is to go without most of the things that one wishes for in life, and to experience material things as the essence of happiness and the key to harmony and health. This perspective permeates all daily acts and experiences of the Cairo poor; it is at the base of their life philosophy and view of the person. But can we therefore conclude, as I did, that the notion that "life is misery" is at the core, so to speak, of their lived experience? To what extent can we take "the native's point of view" as an adequate representation of what life is for a child?

Now when I set out to describe aspects of children's lives, it is with some trepidation, aware of the yawning gap that separates them and me. Not only am I disadvantaged by my position as an adult, which means that I can naturally identify more with the lives of grown-ups, but also, children cannot express themselves with the perspicuity and wisdom of many of their elders, so they are hampered in getting their views across. Third, and most significant, my efforts to penetrate the worlds of children and adults alike suffer from a major constraint: the language they use to express themselves. It is a rhetoric of complaint, replete with expletives, virtual cries of dissension, protest and pain—how can I separate out "experience" from this flood of suffering? For there is more to their lives than gets expressed in this outpouring of pain and high drama.

How do anthropologists get at experience? The standard procedure is to take people's statements—their stories, utterances, and talk—as a basis to infer feelings and thoughts. Some also look at acts and gestures—expressions in behavioral terms—as a means to infer experience. But what does it mean when these expressions resound with a thundering message, "We are hungry hence unhappy"? Are we still justified in concluding that this is the key to their lives? And what when daily life sounds like a jumble of hissing and swearing? Are these people's lives so different from others' similarly placed in poverty, who pride themselves on elegance and grace? My own experience in Bali springs to mind (Wikan 1990b). The Balinese set their sights on grace and poise even when they are in the throes of despair. Do they therefore "feel" suffering less and lead a happier life?

To some extent, probably yes. Expression does seem to leave its mark on experience and affect the way we feel. Experience can be shaped, to some extent, by emotional expression, so the Balinese probably feel less distraught than the Egyptians who dramatize their own suffering.[1] On the other hand, there seems to be a common core to poverty that makes for some commonality of experience across cultural boundaries, even when that ex-

---

1. I explore this problem in Wikan 1988. See also Wikan 1990b, chap. 8.

perience is always overlaid or shaped by a cultural style. But what is the relevance of these observations for our understanding of children's lives?

The problem of the interface between experience and expression haunts me in my own efforts to come to grips with the lives of children in Cairo. Indeed, I contend that the problem cries out for methodological consideration in anthropology. With hindsight (writing now in the nineties), I believe that the lives of the children cannot have been quite as bad as I depict in the following chapters, to judge from how well they managed later in life. But I need to stress this point: were it not for the fact that I have followed them for a very long time, I should not have known. I would have thought that my interpretation of their experience as one of pervasive and harmful deprivation was true. Now, instead, I have the evidence of their later development to shake me out of my conviction and compel me to ask, What actually *were* the children's own experiences of growing up? Consider the facts. Practically all of them are well-adjusted, responsible adults. No one is a delinquent, a street child, or drug addict. None misuses alcohol. No girl has had a child out of wedlock. Nearly all the children—many of whom are now married and have their own children—lead orderly and respectable lives centered on the family. There is clearly evidence of a resilience here that warns against exaggerating the influence of the deprived environment in which they grew up.[2] There is a term "dandelion children" to describe this phenomenon of children who should have been doomed but who thrive nevertheless. The children I know in Cairo are such dandelion children.

But how did it happen? To identify the circumstances that further such developments is too extensive a task for this book. But I shall point to certain formative conditions. In retrospect, I realize that life was a school for the children where they were inculcated with the deeply moral family values and practical survival techniques that constitute a true competence for life. Growing up in stable families in a society with strict social control, they were steeped in the norms of propriety and orderliness combined with respect for age and wisdom. Exposed to the realities of daily life in ways that do not shield children from the world of adults, they learned about marriage, parenting, nurturing, conflict resolution, and death by observation and participation. Thus they also learned about the necessity for perseverance and hope, the lack of which amounts to a lack of faith in God. But when children retain such hope and trust, it is not just because

2. On how later experience can counteract some forms of deprivation in childhood, see LeVine et al. (1994).

Islam, as practiced in their local context, bids people to persevere. Early childhood experience is also crucial. Small children are smothered with an affection that seems to create a basic trust in oneself and one's lovability, helping one endure the lean years of growing up. We turn to an exploration of how it is fostered.

"Egyptian children are kissed, not disciplined"

The first two years of life are like a golden age. The child lives in her mother's arms, lap, and bed. At the slightest sign of discomfort, the child is nursed or cuddled and so receives nearly constant bodily contact. Egyptians vie with each other to hold and caress a child, and the child often moves from one lap to the next. Basically, however, the child is with the mother wherever she goes, whatever she does. There is no notion of "bedtime" for a child. Children learn to sleep at any time or place, impervious to the clamor and ruckus that surrounds them.

The child is showered with love and affection and constantly told how beautiful and clever she is, while discipline is nearly absent for the first couple of years. As one woman said, "Egyptian children are kissed, not disciplined." Even parents who were beside themselves when they found that the wife was pregnant again, and who tried by all possible means to induce an abortion, remark how happy they are to have the baby—while she is young. Not until they grow older and begin to demand money and material things are children experienced as—sometimes intensely—problematical.

If the child remains the last born, this privileged time, along with nursing, may continue. Umm Ali nursed her two youngest till they were nearly four; otherwise two years is the norm. Almost every child is nursed. I have never seen a baby bottle in use except as a supplement when the mother is at work. But to facilitate nursing, the working day for women is reduced from six to five hours until the child is two (this after maternity leave).[3] People are so convinced of the superiority of mother's milk that powdered milk is making next to no inroads. In the rare case that the mother does not have milk, she will use a friend or a relative as wet nurse, with the proviso that the child cannot later marry any of the wet nurse's children; nursed from one breast, they will be like real brothers and sisters.

3. Maternity leave for workers in the public sector (some 90 percent of the workforce) is three months with full pay for the first three children. The woman is also entitled to a total of three years' leave without pay and a guarantee of getting her job back.

Nature and nurture: The roles of mother and father

Almost every child is born to parents who remain together for life. The divorce rate in urban Egypt is less than two percent (cf. Singerman 1995, 53) and even less among the lower class. As people say, "Divorce is for the rich who can afford it." Unwed mothers are a rare exception. Thus the child's life unfolds in the context of a stable parental relationship, marked by frequent conflicts and fights, but bound in a commonality of fate. And though the father is absent most of the day, there is no absence of male role models for a little boy, owing to the presence of older male siblings, relatives, or visitors.

Relations between the parents follow a standard pattern; child rearing is chiefly the mother's task, whereas the father's role is quite peripheral. He functions, naturally, as a role model for the children, and mothers often complain that they take after him and his example. But in society's view, he is blameless. The mother bears full responsibility (cf. von der Lippe, n.d.).

In daily life, the mother delegates much of the care of young children to older daughters. But they do not share her responsibility, just her duties. The mother remains, in everyone's awareness, the key person in a child's life. No one can love a child like its mother, and no one can love another woman's child like her own. Hence no one is pitied more than a child who loses its mother. Not only will she be bereft of an all-enveloping love for life, but also of the guiding hand to steer her through life's adversities. The good stepmother does not exist, she cannot even be imagined. For she would love *her* children, not anybody else's.

The bond between mother and child is so strong that all other relations fade by comparison. Even for adults, the mother often continues to be emotionally more important than the spouse. By contrast, the father is quite insignificant, however loved and appeciated he may be. Losing a father by death, for example, is rarely considered a catastrophe except if it also entails loss of the mother—as when she, to provide for the children, marries another and has children with him. The result, people say, is that she comes to love the children from her new man more than the others. But to steer clear of such a predicament and its worst aspect, that the children should be ill-treated by a stepfather—no man will want to feed another man's child—women strive to remain single if they have small children, even when they face poor prospects of managing on their own. One reason Amira, Umm Ali's sister-in-law (cf. chap. 23), adores her mother so is that she knows what the mother suffered to remain single and provide for her three daughters after the husband died. A widower, on the other hand, will generally remarry swiftly after his wife's death. Many men wait only the obligatory forty days, as did Umm Ali's brother-in-law, Adel, after her sister died.

The mother is the child's anchor in life whereas the father is remote and irresponsible. This is one of the first lessons children learn. It is conveyed not just by the way the father behaves, but also by the way the mother apprehends and judges his behavior vis-à-vis the child. Because he so often fails to provide the family with what they need, because he usually leaves it to her to sort out the problems and borrow money to cope, and because what little he gives them usually reaches the children through her, the children experience the mother as the provider—whereas he is the prodigal who spills the water down the drain.

Children also have ample opportunity to form their own opinions of the father as they witness almost daily confrontations between the parents over money. The father gets furious and abuses the mother when she, usually on the children's behalf, asks him for money for food, clothes, school books, or whatever. Up to her neck in bitterness and despondency, she tells them whenever they lack anything, that she cannot supply it because their father is neglectful and selfish. Thus the children come to experience the mother as their benefactor and protector, whereas they feel bitterness against the father for leaving them in the lurch. "He just uses the home as a hotel, doesn't give a damn whether we starve or wear just rags," said one thirteen-year-old girl.

Parents generally agree on the goal of child rearing: to cultivate *adab* [obedience, good manners, and politeness] in the child. But the father stresses obedience more, whereas the mother underscores a spectrum of good qualities: kindness, diligence, and helpfulness. The father is more uncompromising, the mother more pragmatic. He intervenes rarely in child raising, and then often with abuse and beatings, whereas she uses a variety of disciplinary techniques such as praise, threats, scoldings, and (more rarely) beatings. This parental difference is partly grounded in gender; the father should be authoritarian, the mother loving and tender (*haniyyan*). But when the behavior of each veers toward extremes, the reason can be found in their marital conflict.

The mother courts the children's affection, and she needs their loyalty and support. In the conflict with the father, they are her allies. The father feels slighted and excluded and becomes defensive; he sees signs of lack of respect everywhere and tries to extract by force the respect he regards as his due, which they do not grant him willingly. His behavior drives the children further over to the mother's side. Umm Ali related the following example:

Mustafa is awful in striking the children. Once as I was frying potatoes, he grabbed Ali and beat him so badly that I thought he might kill the child. The boy's eyes swelled like balls protruding from his face. I tried to go between them but was kicked and hurled to the floor. The reason for Mustafa's rage was that Ali and Amin had broken the window in the balcony door while playing soccer in the flat. When his father had finished hitting and kicking him, he ordered Ali to get out of the house for good. "As you please, Baba!" Ali replied, and asked Amin to get him his shoes. Amin did so, with the result that Mustafa hit *him* for *helping* his brother! I protested that Ali could not possibly go barefoot in the street, but Mustafa snarled that he was no better than a beggar. So Ali went—barefoot. After a while Mustafa felt remorseful and went out looking for him and said, "Hurry up, boy, get home!"

And this is also characteristic of fathers. They feel remorse and regret their own loss of control. Take another example:

Once Ali was so afraid of his father's fury that he ran away from home. He had quarreled with Amin, and in the heat of it had torn Amin's shirt to pieces. He was sure his father would beat him black and blue when he got home. So he took some money his mother had given him to give to his uncle, and bought himself a ticket to Aswan instead. On the train, he met a boy who invited him home. Back in Cairo, the family was in despair. They searched everywhere; his father went asking at every hospital and prison in town. After a month, the boy from Aswan came to them and asked if they had a son, Ali, with such and such clothes. The father took the first train to Aswan. He and Ali fell into each other's arms and wept as they met.

There is no doubt that fathers harbor genuine love and concern for their children. The man's predicament is that he is hard put to show it given that the gift of material things symbolizes love like nothing else. This is an exercise in which the father is practically destined to fail. He is in a no-win situation, for Egyptian culture does not encourage fathers to show affection for their children through emotional displays. The relationship between father and child has been traditionally marked by distance and respect: a father of Mustafa's generation could not even carry his own child in public. Hence the father is forced into a predicament that compels him to use power and authority to be the figure of respect—or so he hopes—which his actual situation of poverty subverts.

Now, there is nothing wrong with the use of violence as a disciplinary technique from an Egyptian perspective: beating is regarded as sheer necessity. Apprised of the news that in my society we do not beat, just reprimand and scold children, people looked at me aghast and said, "You mean talk only? Then it must be because children are *born* better behaved with you than with us!" That you could teach children to behave without punishing them so it really hurt seems absurd to them. It falls to the father as master of the house to mete out the major blows. Mothers sometimes appeal to him to take action when their own measures have failed.

What parents disagree on is not the legitimacy of beating but the justness of a given measure and its degree of harshness. Mothers complain that fathers are needlessly rash and violent, whereas men regard women as soft and under the children's thumb. Also, the father tends to leap into action at the slightest provocation, whereas the mother resorts to threats without putting them into effect. The following is a typical example:

Umm Ali complains that the children steal food from each other and blame each other. "They got a lashing yesterday, and now see, they do it again." Hoda overhears and says, "It's Mama's fault because she doesn't hit them!" The mother says that she will hit, and that she has asked a hundred times for the ruler, but no one brings it; and in the meantime Umm Asad came visiting, and it is a shame to beat in front of the guests—the children are embarrassed—but now she will beat them! In the meantime, the rascals have escaped. And this is characteristic of the mother's style of child rearing that much time passes between the mischief and the sanction, and that threats come pouring out without being followed up.

Many mothers complain that the father, by his example, socializes the children to lying, obstinacy, and deceit. Parents must teach by their own good example and show that truthfulness pays. A favorite example of Umm Ali's concerns the time Mustafa ordered Mona to go to school, though she had been doing the laundry all day before, and so had not had time to take a bath. This was the first day of the month and the inspector was sure to expel any child whose hair was not newly washed. Still, Mustafa ordered Mona to go. She wept and protested, but to no avail. So she dressed and went to the school gate, only to head straight home. In the evening her father asked her if she had been to school. She said yes. But her mother told the truth, "but in such a way that he wouldn't beat her. He has no right to beat. It is useless to flaunt principles in the face of reality. One must look to the situation."

Egyptian culture teaches women that they must bring up their children to show unconditional respect for the father. In reality, many do the opposite. Men are fully aware of this power on women's part and resent it bitterly; "You have completely destroyed my children! What's the use of the father holding back with one hand, if the mother gives with the other? Then they will come curse him because she lets them think he is selfish and unfeeling. Then one day they will hate me and mock my orders, and I will no longer be master of my own house!" screamed one man in despair in a fight with his wife.[4]

The preceding description may give the impression that parents are always at loggerheads, caught in a tug-of-war. But this is not the case. Though the conflict of interest between them is real, the couple is bound by a shared goal: making the children's future. This is the raison d'être of a woman's life, and if the man seems to be a reluctant participant in the project, this is only partly true. He does toil long hours for the family; he does abide by his duty as provider; he does remain with the family for life in most cases, though it would have been easy to opt out. In a comparative perspective, the fathers I know are diligent, loyal, and steadfast; and the parents' dedication to making the children's future provides a partnership of sorts.

With education, the father's role is changing. In the younger generation, men engage in more deliberate cooperation with their wives, and they take an active role in child raising (see Wikan 1995). Young fathers cultivate an emotional bond with their children and are proud to carry a child in public. The contrast with the mother's role still exists: she remains the emotional fount of the family, the focus of children's deepest attachment and love. But education is freeing both father and child from the shackles of a distant, authoritarian relationship that engendered much mutual hostility and inhibited the expression of love.

Brothers and sisters

Age and rank in the sibling group are important factors in a child's life. The oldest and the youngest child have a favored place. Otherwise, much depends on how close the children are in age, how many there are, their personal qualities, the mother's sense of vitality and energy vis-à-vis a child, and the presence of other caretakers. The maternal grandmother is treasured, whereas the paternal grandmother is more usually shunned, "for she will love *her* daughter's children" (that is, the children whose maternal grandmother *she* is). Similarly, maternal aunts are preferred to paternal aunts.

The firstborn has the power over her siblings by virtue of her age. An oft-cited proverb goes, "Whoever is a day older, is a year wiser." And though the formula is not literally adhered to, it is often invoked, as it was the time when Ali, who was one year old, had hit his younger cousin, and the cousin's mother got furious, saying Ali should know better since he was older. A senior place in the sibling hierarchy confers the power of command, though gender is a moderating factor, and boys can often (but not always) command

4. The case is described in detail in Wikan (1980, 115–20).

their older sisters. But though the firstborn occupies a privileged place, jealousy may also hit her especially hard when she is superseded by the next one in line. Parents make little effort to still jealousy in a child, believing that jealousy and envy are inborn in humans. To be the youngest, however, is always good, and the last born tends to be spoiled like no one else.

I have sometimes heard mothers invoke the principle that to discourage jealousy among the children, one should never compare a child favorably to another when the latter can hear it. Umm Ali criticized Mustafa, "Ali was always told how stupid he was compared to Amin—and that in Amin's presence. That's terribly wrong. Now Mustafa makes the same mistake again and compares Afaf to Anwar. It only leads to jealousy, and the one who is depreciated takes it out on the other when they are alone. Like Afaf now—she is always pestering Anwar." But the next moment she may contravene the principle in her own actions. Indeed, in the cramped living conditions of the people, parents have little chance to praise or criticize a child in privacy.

Squabbling over food

Competition for resources marks sibling relations in childhood and youth. Mothers often complain that the children do not know how to share with one another but are gluttonous and greedy. They themselves strive to divide equally but fail because the children steal from each other and then blame each other. The following example is typical:

Nosa, six years old, appears with two dates in her hand. Umm Ali asks her where she got them. Nosa says Anwar gave them to her. The mother gets furious for she had hidden the dates herself on top of the kitchen shelf so they would be safe from the children. What Anwar has done is *steal* from his siblings' shares despite the fact that his father beat him and Afaf last week for doing precisely that. Mustafa had come home with a bag of dates that was meant for the whole family. He took out a handful and gave them to the three youngest children, then hid the bag on top of the kitchen shelf. Umm Ali's sister Farida was visiting and spotted the dates. When Mustafa had left, she asked the children for some; and they fetched a plate and gave her some. When their father came home and discovered the missing dates, he abused Umm Ali, "You haven't brought up your kids!" Umm Ali was angry with her sister for having demanded the dates when she must have known that the father had brought only sufficient for the family [*'ala qadd ilusra*]. But she was angrier with her children for fetching without permission. And she explains,

If a family has a fridge, the children must never open it in front of the guests. Perhaps the mother has placed something special in it for the family, and then it's a shame if the guests see it and are not offered some.

Hospitality is a virtue. But what can you do when you haven't even got enough for your own? A few days back Anwar came in and fetched a bundle of grapes to give to a friend in the lane. I saw him, fortunately, and beat him. He defended himself saying he just practiced hospitality! But far from it! Theft, that's what he commits! If he wanted to be generous, why didn't he take his *own* share and give some to his friend? Yesterday, Mustafa brought a bag of grapes, and look here [she shows me an empty bag] how the children steal! A week ago we had chicken for dinner. I divided it equally so I and Mustafa and Ali would get half a chicken each, and the children one quarter each. Ali wasn't home when we ate, and so I saved his portion for him. When he came, he had eaten already, and so he asked me to keep his share till the next morning. But in the morning, the chicken was gone! One of the children must have got up during the night and devoured it. They all blamed each other, and all of them were beaten; and now see, they do it again!

Different faces of poverty

A book on the poor in Naples (Belmonte 1979) is illuminating for the contrasting light it sheds on Cairo. Beautifully written, it describes family meals that appear as orgies of gluttony from the point of view of the people I know. Delicious dishes, beautifully decked out, are eaten together by all family members. In Cairo by contrast, daily meals usually consist of bread or rice and a vegetable stew, or just bread and potatoes and salad which everyone eats when and where they feel like it. Once or twice a month there may be perhaps a few mouthfuls of meat, or a bit of fish, or in the best of circumstances, a quarter to half a chicken per person. Rice, vegetables, and bread constitute the stomach filler; the standard drink is tea.

I remember the first time I was specially invited for a meal. We were having meat, and the children were bursting with excitement. Half a kilo (one pound) was bought to share between us—five adults and three kids. I had not realized what that meant. Like the others, I let myself be carried away by the thought of the meat (I hadn't had any for weeks). When I realized what had made them so happy—for *they* didn't have unrealistic expectations—I was ashamed: three to four mouthfuls of meat each—and everyone's eyes glued on the others so no one would take more than her share; and bread, huge amounts of bread. The "meat dinner" consisted almost entirely of bread!

Poverty has many faces. For some it is to be without food, for others without clothes, for others again to lack shelter. Poverty defies a universal definition. The Cairo poor may live like kings, compared with Calcutta's poor (Lapierre 1986); the poor in Naples may eat like kings, compared with Cairo's

Getting ready to go out into the main street.

poor. Poverty cannot be measured by a universal standard that specifies minimum requirements of food, clothes, and lodging. Cultural priorities enter to the core of these judgments. Belmonte does not tell us how the poor in Naples dress. Perhaps clothing there counts for less? In Cairo, one's whole person stands or falls with one's clothing. While to eat well and to be seen carrying home status foods like white bread or fish gives you prestige, you will be shamed unless you also dress well. Talk of food and dreams of food fill people's conversations—one elaborates what one has eaten, is going to eat, wishes to eat, and so on, but it is clothes that truly count. Everything seems to depend on *ilmanzar,* the vision or appearance you can project of who and what you are.

Bickering over clothes
When her daughters doll themselves up for hours just to go out in the main street for an errand, Umm Ali complains, "People must think you're headed for a wedding!" But she, too, takes an hour or more to dress before stepping out in that selfsame world, a few minutes' walk away from her doorstep—unless she seeks refuge in the black, respectable but discreet *milaya* [cloak]. Indoors and outdoors are two different worlds, and the persons who move between them seem also to change their skin. Women explain the discrep-

ancy thus: people in the street can say anything they want, and are concerned only with appearances. At home, on the other hand, you can dress as you like, for visitors are obliged not to spread the secrets of the house. In practice, visitors to the home may not live up to this level of discretion, as evidenced by men's reluctance to bring friends home with them. But among women there seems to be a silent consensus that one's private appearance should not be allowed to tarnish one's public standing.[5]

Because self-worth and social esteem are so dependent on clothes, siblings compete for these valued assets. In one case I witnessed, two brothers fought each other with knives over a sweater (Wikan 1980). Mothers strive to share equally, but constantly fail due to several factors. First, clothes must be shared. Parents cannot afford to buy a wardrobe for each child, so they buy a sweater or a pair of shoes to fit, say, four children aged six to twelve. This means that the garment will fit the older, but not the younger. Also, because children compete for use rights, and age gives power, what is in theory common property becomes in practice a monopoly. Second, in the case of personal belongings, the older may simply appropriate the clothes of the younger who cannot mount an effective defense. *All* the clothes I have given Afaf through the years have been appropriated by her older sisters. Afaf is defenseless. She can scream and shout, her mother can scold and threaten, but power prevails.

Another tactic, more rarely used, is to sell the garment of a sibling when it does not fit oneself. The blame can be put on visitors who occasionally steal. Or teenage children can buy clothes on credit in complicity with peddlers who are happy for every penny they can earn. The mother is presented with a fait accompli and the bill, and the others get less.

When little Nosa received dress material as a gift from a neighbor for whom her mother had done a favor, Hoda took it and made herself a blouse. The mother was presented with the bill from the seamstress. She was furious but could not refuse to pay. In society's eyes, she is responsible. As her father's wife said, "Either you have to teach the children to behave, or else you fork over."

Sharing
The loyalty that might have given siblings the strength to stand together against a harsh environment has a slim chance to develop because each

5 With rising ambition, awareness of the gap expresses itself in changing attitudes toward being photographed. Whereas until the mid-seventies people were eager to have their photo taken whatever they wore, now many protest vehemently unless they are wearing their very best, fearing it might diminish their standing in the public eye should a photo fall into the wrong hands.

needs the scarce resources if they are going to excel and *be* something in society. Their recurrent experience is that what others get is at their expense. There are also few tasks to weld siblings together. If they share a task, they tend to perform it successively, rather than together. The only real collaboration I have seen is when teenage sisters help each other to clandestine dates behind their mother's back. Still there is ample evidence that siblings love and care for each other, and that they share mutual concern and generosity. It comes into bloom especially as they grow older and the conflict between them abates because some start working and earning money, or they marry and move away. But as long as the children are trapped in a situation in which the key experience is that what others get is at one's own expense, their conflict of interest usually prevails. Thus they contribute to a split and turbulent family life, to the parents' chagrin.

Why do things go so wrong? Partly because the children are pawns in the parents' game, partly because of the poverty. The children know that the mother needs them, and this gives them power over her. The mother is reluctant to censure them effectively for fear of losing their loyalty and for fear of their revenge. Nor can she appeal to the father for help, for he punishes too severely. Indeed, threats to complain to him seem to be effective only when he is at home. Mother-child interdependence is further enhanced by the cramped living conditions. By declaring themselves not on speaking terms [*mitxasmin*] or throwing temper tantrums, children can make an already impossible life virtually unbearable for the mother. So she chooses the path of least resistance for the sake of peace in the house. In practice, this often means giving in to the most unruly and obstinate of the children who lords it over the whole household; meanwhile she blames the father for her own powerlessness, "By his bad example he has taught the children to follow their self-interests only."

Because age in Egypt gives the right to command and demand services from the younger, older children have a natural privilege which they often exploit. The younger sibling can best defend herself by sabotage, not carrying out a task until she has been asked innumerable times; giving up at the first obstacle and returning empty-handed; "forgetting" what she was supposed to buy; "losing" the money, and so on, and then savoring her own power in due course. I once saw Afaf, ten years old, use her four-year-old sister's party dress as a rag to clean the soles of her shoes. When Nosa protested, Afaf smiled triumphantly. I had more than once seen how *her* older sisters had used *her* clothes in a similar manner.

Indeed, adults who regard themselves as kind and compliant tell how they were exploited as children because of these qualities. Their kindness became a social liability to be used against them.

Self-defense

The fact that children are associated with their family and participate in a conception of joint family honor means that children can be made to suffer for being innocent and defenseless. The mother's enemy can accuse a child of spitting, sticking out her tongue, or being obnoxious, and then beat her up; or she may send her own children in superior force against the child. Grown-ups also occasionally make children scapegoats for misdeeds they will not admit to themselves; or they can make a child carry out actions that would be shameful to themselves. Thus when Umm Ali was desperate to get rid of her sister-in-law who had lodged with them for months, she asked Amin, then ten years old, to ask his aunt to leave. His aunt got furious with Umm Ali, who defended herself on several occasions, saying it was not she but Amin who had asked the woman to leave! And once when a visitor had offended Umm Ali, she put a good face on things, then sent Mona—twelve years old at that time—after her to say, "Why do you always come here and upset Mama? It's a shame!"

Children can even be used by their own family as pawns in a battle against enemies. It is a well-known strategy for adults to threaten to hurt themselves and report the enemy to the police as causing the injury. Children can be used as hostages, too: an adult may dangle a child over the balcony and threaten to drop her unless the enemy agrees to certain concessions.

However, the child will not be dropped; the drama epitomizes the weapons of the weak in a society where many people are pitted against others and feel they are under constant assault. Involving the children is a way of impressing on them the notion of joint family honor in which all family members are mutually responsible and vulnerable. Also, children must be taught practical survival techniques that may not be moral in terms of abstract principles yet are the only reasonable ones, given the state of the world. Getting a child to reprimand the neighbor who upset Umm Ali or to reproach her sister-in-law who would not move is a way of saying that the family is as one against the world, sharing in both happiness and vulnerability.

Many of the reactions of people as described here may seem unduly harsh. But it is important to realize that in such a milieu, the person will regard her own actions as a necessary self-defense. The corrosive effects of poverty and the people's talk threaten one's self-respect so much that one feels one must use whatever means is available to rise a bit above the degradation and stigma. So people make the shared predicament of poverty a bit harder for themselves and each other to bear—even as they also cooperate and show each other care and compassion at times.

Eighteen

The Everyday World of Children

A small world

The child's world has changed in significant ways during the twenty-five years I have moved about in this neighborhood. Two developments have been crucial: TV and school. Both have expanded the child's vision and lifeworld in ways that might be hard for anyone to understand who has not experienced the confinement that used to be the children's lot. But before we examine the impact of TV and school, let us move back to the time when those who are now young adults were children, the time when Umm Ali's children grew up.

The child's world is a small world with limited opportunities for developing the child's potentials. Basically, children are confined to the flat and the lane right outside it, plus the homes of a few of the mother's relatives and friends whom they visit from time to time. But they do not play with the children when going there; quarters are too cramped and toys generally absent. Visiting with the mother means mainly sitting and listening to the women's talk, their laments and gossip—which can be entertaining as no discretion is observed before children. But apart from such valued outings, diversions and amusements are few.

Life in the flat has a monotonous, frustrating character which constantly thwarts the child's need for stimuli and movement. There is little outlet for physical energy. Children are constantly frustrated in their urge to play or at least do *something*. Adults prohibit any activity that might cause squabbles and fights. So the children's hope of amusement comes to center on playing in the lane. The lane offers breathing space, elbow room, and a chance to scream and shout, whereas the flat is dark and dank and suffocating by comparison.

When Ali had broken the glass in the balcony door while playing soccer in the flat, his mother tried to make his father understand that children need to be able to play inside "since we don't have a yard, and I forbid them to play in the street. We should be happy at least that they obey; the glass can be replaced." But Mustafa fumed, "You talk as if you lived in your father's house. But tenants, that's what we are, and that's what we have to adjust to! Or do you want the landlord to throw us out?"

Little wonder that children's view of the good life comes to center on playing in the lane. Against the parents who are bent on preventing it, children seize any opportunity to escape—but only to the space right in front of the house where the mother can come to their rescue. Boys play soccer with empty cans; girls play tag, blind man's buff, or they just sit and watch. Naturally, children sometimes bump into each other, or strike a bit too hard, but suspicion is so deep that an accidental bump is easily perceived as a deliberate attack. The child screams and shouts for its mother who comes charging over and accuses the attacker's mother of not having brought up her child properly. The premise is, "Right or wrong, *my* child." Often, the result is a physical fight between the mothers with ensuing reports to the police and sworn enmity for life, "whereas the children forget and become friends again quickly," people say.

Indeed, the phrase "the children fought" is used as a justification for almost every one of the countless enmities that occur between women. As children become too old to play in the lane, relations between their mothers improve considerably.

I once asked Umm Ali why mothers always intervene in the children's fights; would it not be better for them to sort things out for themselves? She replied, "Yes, that would be right, for that would teach the children responsibility for themselves. But here the children are so awful, and they attack those who are younger than themselves, so if the mother did not take action, they would strike even harder next time. Moreover, it is *right* that the [attacked child's] mother should complain [to the aggressor's mother] for it is the *mothers* who must teach the children good behavior."

Home versus street
This notion that it is the mothers who are responsible for the children's behavior to the extent of fighting it out among themselves to keep the children from fighting has some interesting repercussions. It explains in part why there are no youth gangs and no leaders among peers. Children are not left to form cliques or gangs. Everyone, young boys included, are individually identified with their own mother and family (even boys in their teens may weepingly seek family protection, for this is a culture in which males' crying is accepted). So when the child gets into a fight, it is to the mother and family that he or she looks for support, not to a group of same-sex allies. Indeed, that's precisely why children stay so close to home, limiting their outdoor play to the spot right in front of their house, so the mother can hear them at the first cry and come to their rescue, which she does.

This is how mothers keep their children on their good behavior. Violence is not allowed to run rampant, it is strictly contained—among the children. If it does run a bit wild, it is when the women, the mothers, attack each other with swear words or even engage in physical combat. But the children are spared.

Why are parents so keen on preventing their children from playing with the children in the lane? The answer is self-evident to them, "Because of their filth and impudence!" [*ilqaraf w'il qillit iladab bitu'hum*] The children who play in the lane are constantly referred to as *wisxxin* [dirty, filthy] by other parents who spare no effort to inculcate in their own offspring contempt for the ways of the street. Egyptians draw a sharp line between home [*bet*] and street [*shari'a*], a line demarcated by a tendency to always keep the shutters down as if to block out the evil influences from outside. The home stands for everything good: polite language, good manners, neatness, and compassion, whereas the street embodies the evils of impudence, filthiness, rudeness, and ugliness. The mark of the good child is that she or he keeps off the street.

Actually, the children playing in the lane are no worse than the rest, and they emerge in time as responsible and respectable adults, just like most others. What distinguishes them is that they come from the poorest families, living on street level in the most cramped quarters. It is not that their parents have different values from others, just that they have fewer means of keeping the children in. They cannot lock the door of their room, for the children need to go and pee, and the toilet is outside; the mother needs to sit in the doorway to do her sewing, otherwise there is no light, and so on. For numerous reasons, the battle to keep one's children in is a losing one in such families from the start.

But that's not how others see it. In the struggle to instill in one's own children the best possible manners, mothers—and fathers—denigrate the back-street environment and heap dirt on "the others" in no uncertain terms. It is a way of distancing oneself and one's family from all "the disgust and filthiness," to refuse to be sullied by the deplorable conditions under which one is forced to live. The battle to keep one's children in is driven by an insistent urge to improve their future by breeding into them respectable moral values and teaching them to rise above the squalor and filth. It's a way of saying, "You can do better; you *are* better"—even if it means looking down on others with contempt.

The new age: TV
Until the early 1980s, it was common to see children lolling over the balconies and peeping from the windows, envious spectators of the play in the lane which favored children living at ground level. Indeed, "street life" was a source of entertainment for all; adults too used to be drawn irresistibly to watch. But now this is history. Now TV captures everyone's attention. Television first made its entry into the neighborhood in the mid-60s, but it was not until the early to mid-80s that it became common

property. Now, TV is usually on in every home from morning to night. It fills the space occupied in my society by children's toys, books, records, sports, movies, extracurricular activities, holidays, and so on. Egyptian TV broadcasts soap operas and sheer entertainment with comedy, music, and dance all the time, a veritable vitamin injection for people who have more than their share of suffering.

Actually, TV has relieved the drabness and monotony of home life so much that most children no longer care to run out to play. They would rather sit and be entertained. Thus the description given above of a dreary and dull home life is how it was through about the first fifteen years of my contact with the people; and I have chosen to keep it in my narrative to highlight the contrast with what came after, for the change was tremendous and was experienced by parents and children alike as a transformation of life. Think of Umm Ali's aborted attempts to get Mustafa or Ali to take her children to the movies—a promise she had made to keep them off the street; now, such broken promises are a thing of the past, nor do children fight and scream from sheer ennui as they used to. Television provides entertainment that keeps them quiet—sometimes spellbound— for hours at a time. For mothers drained by the struggle to get through the day, TV is an unequivocal blessing for it fills the children's minds with images and laughter that divert their attention from the dreariness of life and their own misery. Even the women do not fight much any more; since their children play much less in the street, the "right or wrong, *my* children" impetus that had them at each other's throats before is now activated much less frequently.

But when Umm Ali's children grew up, times were different. Though her family got TV in 1968, one of the first sets in the area, the selection of programs was very limited at that time, so her children grew up bored and grumpy, like most others. The little ones were tied to their mother's apron strings. They tagged at her heels, whined for attention, and begged and nibbled food constantly. They harrassed their siblings and interrupted their mother's visits with ceaseless demands for attention. And though the mother and her visitors both accepted the children's right to interfere in the adults' conversations, the result seemed to be a lack of order and discipline that the mothers themselves decried.

Toys

A memory from fall 1981 remains imprinted on my mind. Nosa, then eight, was rummaging on the floor. I looked and saw that she had found a brick and a piece of wood and made a pair of scales. Then she fetched a newspaper, some sugar and spices, wrapped little parcels, and sat down to weigh them. It was the only example I had seen of a child using her imagination to construct a toy.

Nosa was so happy, and the toy so simple that I could not help but see in my mind's eye the rows of manufactured toy scales in the stores at home, and my own child's overstocked playroom.

But when I, genuinely impressed, asked Nosa the next day to show her toy to a friend of mine, her mother brushed it aside. It was nothing, just a brick and a piece of wood, she said.

Till the mid-80s, children had no toys other than what they could make themselves, which was little. Until 1979, I had never seen a parent give a child a toy. Then the first fathers returned from labor migration in Libya. They brought with them big sleeping dolls with real yellow hair. The dolls arrived in cellophane wrappings, and in cellophane wrappings they have remained, hung high on the wall as adornment.

Another doll came to an even gloomier end. She arrived from Mecca, a glorious thing with golden blonde hair and a baby face, a gift to a girl whose mother had helped another borrow money so she could go on pilgrimage to Mecca. But the girl's brothers received nothing. When next I saw the doll, two weeks later, her arms, legs and hair had been torn off, her mouth and eyes knocked in, and her face blotched with ink, a regular murder.

One father who had worked in Saudi Arabia for five years, earned more money than he knew how to spend. So he bought his children toys. All were broken in no time at all. I was surprised, as his children were unusually well-behaved and careful with things. Their mother explained, "They destroy the toys because they've never been used to such things. Children here know how to take care of their clothes, they have learned that, it's in their habit. But toys—they don't see their value."

Until the mid-80s, the few toys I had given the children all languished atop the fridge or the TV. They were not to play with. Nor did the children care for them much, in stark contrast to the clothes I brought. Toys were just for show, whereas clothes were to make you beautiful and envied. To this day, the pattern persists, with even two-year-olds showing a peculiar delight in clothes. But times are changing. With education, parents (especially fathers) value toys for their children. Toys are perceived as a stimulant to the child's intellectual and mental development. Still, because they are so precious, toys tend to be hidden on a shelf and only brought out under adult supervision.

One day is like another

The children's dream of leisure is to go with the parents on a picnic in the park, to the zoo, or to the Pyramids. But only a few are lucky enough to experience it—at most two or three times in a lifetime. To visit relatives in the countryside is equally desired and equally difficult to realize. For the tickets cost money, and besides, you have to bring a gift. Thus the back streets set the narrow confines around the children's lives. The family lacks the money but also the will and ability to cooperate and organize joint activities. Holidays are just like ordinary days; vacations are spent at home. The only life-cycle ritual for children, circumcision[1] (for boys when they are two, for girls at ten to twelve), is celebrated only occasionally. Over the past ten years it has become "in" to celebrate birthdays for children; this Western custom is becoming a sign of status and modernity in Egypt as in much of the developing world. But its effect is to drive a wedge between the more prosperous families and the others, and to further stigmatize those families—the majority—who cannot afford such celebrations.

What all children look forward to, however, is the three-day-long Feast ['*id*] after Ramadan, the most important holiday of the year. For some, it is the happiest time when they can stroll about in brand new clothes, and savor cakes and sweets. For others, it is a nightmare, and they hide inside in shame because their parents cannot afford to give them anything new. The Feast, which seems to an observer a cascade of joy bringing out all of Cairo's children, is actually celebrated only by the most fortunate among them. Behind the shutters family tragedies are taking place as children weep and mothers rail about the neglect of their fathers.[2] Even in the celebrating families, the expenditures required by the Feast tax family relations badly. As one father said at the end of the Feast one year, "Thank God, it is over! This month and the month before we are up to our necks in expenditures and loans, so the whole world is just quarrels and misery." Indeed, parents are often not on speaking terms during the Feast because of quarrels over money for the children's clothes. In contrast to the tensions engendered by the Feast, engagement parties and weddings provide free entertainment for all when they take place in the lane, as is usually the case; music, song, and dance fill the air till late in the night, to the delight of all spectators.

School: Pathway to the future

In this environment of drabness and monotony, school turns into a favored pastime for a child. Free primary education was instituted in Egypt in

1. Actually, there is one more childhood ritual that is always celebrated, *subu'*, named thus because it takes place on the seventh day after birth. The purpose of the ritual is to propitiate evil spirits and to admonish the child to be always obedient and respectful of the parents, especially the mother.

2. For a description of such dramas as they unfolded during my first fieldwork, and my own, largely aborted, efforts to help in the situation, see Wikan (1980).

Visiting with grandfather.

1923, but it was not until the mid-sixties that it became generally available to ordinary people, and not until the early eighties did all children, even those from the poorest families, attend school. In the sixties and seventies, children used to adore school, at least for the first few years. I never heard a child say she looked forward to the vacation or the weekend. It was school they looked forward to. There they could meet their friends, there things happened. The school yard is the only place where they can play to their heart's content, without fear of the parents' punishment.

The quest for education in Egypt has been tremendous due to a vision of the advantages education offers. It can take you up the ladder into the middle class by way of a government job that offers both job security and social security, neither of which is otherwise available in Egypt. From the time they are small, children will say they are going to school to become a *muwazzaf(a)* (a government employee).

For the first few years, school can be an unmitigated pleasure. But with time, it exacts a price in hard work and anxiety. Exams are not introduced

Visiting with
grandmother.

until class 5 (previously 6), when the child's performance will decide whether she can continue in public secondary school or must enter a private school, at a high cost to the parents. But with the poor quality of public education—classes in primary school commonly have fifty pupils, and in high school sometimes up to ninety—it is becoming increasingly common for children to take private tuition as early as first grade. This affects the children's attitude to school. Now many children study hard from the first grade; their parents push them and compel them to do homework all the time; some will even hide the children's toys and only bring them out during vacation time (cf. von der Lippe, n.d.).

The Egyptian educational system is a disaster by all accounts due to overpopulated schools and underpaid and demoralized teachers. Were it not for the joint efforts of parents, pupils, and tutors, the system would collapse. But private tutoring increases the pressure on children who resent both the burden of work and the financial cost to their parents. School, previously a child's delight, is becoming a source of highly mixed feelings.

r of failure looms large, and more so in later years. When chil-
their exams, children and mothers alike shun contacts to hide
shame. However, what is surprising is not that many children fail
have to repeat classes (a pupil is given three chances in each class),
but that many succeed at all. I have seen children lie flat on their stomachs
under the bed—in what seems complete darkness—to do their homework; nor is there ever peace to work in the clamor of their homes. The
educational aspirations and achievements of the people are remarkable,
and mothers in particular go to enormous effort to help their children on
this pathway to middle-class life.

Over the past ten years, a new development has arisen: nursery schools
[*haddana*]. It has become *the* latest thing to prepare a child for school.
Nursery schools are sprouting like mushrooms all over Cairo, reflecting how
high a priority it is for the parents to make a future for their children. Though
the cost of enrollment is high, even destitute parents, uneducated themselves, struggle to give their children this chance. How much children actually learn is questionable. Often, there is only one teacher and one assistant
to take care of a hundred children for four hours. But for the child, preschool
and all it implies—walking or being bused to and fro, engaging in play and
exciting activities—is a haven of freedom and joy. I have seen sullen and
introverted children undergo a metamorphosis from the time they enter
nursery school. It offers the excitement that playing in the lane did before,
but with a stark difference: it is the epitome of status and esteem.

Social intelligence and competence

Mothers in general feel that life is the best school and that academic
schooling serves mainly as a ladder to social status and mobility. Teaching
children to live, however, means exposing them to life's realities. Children
in Cairo are integrated "in life" in ways that Western middle-class mores
and concepts of childhood typically preclude. They have numerous contacts with adults of every age and position, though women are in the
majority; they are expected to behave (rather than be "childish") and are
disciplined when they do not; they learn propriety and respect for the
elders, and to honor the wisdom that age confers; they also learn to subju-
gate their own individual desires to the needs and well-being of the family
that is the source of their attachment, sense of belonging, and security.

Children in Cairo develop a remarkable social intelligence and competence that serves them throughout life. They learn "scripts" for handling
various social scenarios and situations; they develop a repertoire of practical
survival techniques regarding numerous problems such as how to settle a
conflict, to participate in or organize a savings club or deal with a spouse;

Competence for life: a
little boy with his
mother at conflict
mediation.

they learn parenting and nurturing; and they become skilled at networking
and spokesmanship—talents that are of prime importance in a society in
which communications skills determine one's access to many scarce resources: friendship, loans, credit, jobs, and so forth. And they learn that there
is no way except self-help to succeed in life; God helps those who help themselves. Naturally, people differ, and all do not manage equally well, but it is
striking how well developed such skills are in the population. Thus, what
children lack in the way of opportunities for developing their intellectual
capacities is compensated for somehow by excellence in other fields, which
is of prime importance to them and accounts in large part for their resilience.

This is not to minimize the extent of their suffering and struggle. Poverty inflicts constant pain and thwarts the children's efforts to be somebody and think well of themselves. Adolescence is a particularly trying
time in Egypt as in many societies. Three of Umm Ali's children had an
especially difficult life. Their stories illustrate, each in its own way, the
double hardship of being poor and being young.

Part Six

Three Ways out of Misery

Nineteen

Amin's Death

In Umm Ali's life, one tragedy stands out like no other, the loss of her son, Amin, by suicide in 1972, when he was nineteen. She has never recovered from the trauma. "Before" and "after" in her life—the abyss relates to the night Amin died. She was never able to pick up the pieces and carry on as before, not only because of the diabetes which struck her full force after his death and eventually was to make her blind. When he died, she died a bit, too.

The last time I saw Amin was five days before his death when I bade the family farewell after a month's stay in Egypt. He was tense and irritable and not on speaking terms with his parents and elder sisters. Yet no one had a premonition of the tragedy that was so close. His death came as a complete shock to everyone who knew him. The following year, Mona told me this story of what had happened:

It was just before school was to begin after the holidays. Amin had been working during the summer in a shop to earn money to buy himself some clothes. He was terribly clothes conscious and always looked quite nice. You remember? Mama used to tell him—when she thought it was a bit too much—that he was going to school to learn, not to take part in a fashion show!

But it was *right* what Amin did, since he was attending a school [commercial high school] where there were lots of rich boys. If he did not dress nearly as well as them, they would have made him a laughing-stock!

Amin saved all his money for clothes. He neither smoked nor drank. He saved his money in savings clubs [*gam'iyya*] that Mama ran. This time he was a member of a *gam'iyya* at twenty pounds and had signed up for two memberships. He had already withdrawn one membership share as the first in line, and now he came and asked for his second. Mama said it was impossible, this was Uncle Ahmed's month. But Amin got angry and demanded to have at least half a share. Mama said it was impossible, it would only cause trouble if she asked Uncle to split his share. Amin got furious and abused her. He became not on speaking terms with Mama and was hotheaded and quarrelsome with us all. And he who never used to be like that!

Then one morning—it was five days after his fight with Mama—he

171

woke me up abruptly and told me to make tea. He shook my arm so violently, it turned blue. I chided him and said that of course, I would make tea, but he could at least wake me in a decent manner. Amin exploded and hit me hard in the face with his fists, over and over. I cried so hard I was shaking. It was the first time that Amin had ever hit me—he who always used to be so calm! I threatened to go to Baba in the workshop to complain, but a friend of Mama who was living with us—she had quarreled with her husband—warned me not to. She said, "Perhaps your father is very busy and then it looks awkward if you go there and cry!" But when Baba came home at night, I told him everything, and he confronted Amin. He warned him, "If you ever have any complaints against your sisters, then tell me, and I'll take care of it, but don't you ever lay your hands on them or I'll make you suffer for it!" This was about twenty days before Amin's death. He got furious and was not on speaking terms with any of us. To get anything done [tea made, clothes washed, and so on] he had to go through the small ones, Afaf and Anwar.

The day Amin died, Ali had come home on leave from the army. Ali told Mama he wanted fish for supper and she promised to make some for him. Then Mama and Umm Magdi went out to the Pyramids to look at the lot. They were delayed, and when they came home, the fish market was already closed. When Ali came home at nine in the evening, Mama was frying potatoes. Ali got mad as a hornet and gave her a terrible tongue-lashing. He accused her of lying and neglect, and just wasting her days doing nothing, and similar things. Mama exploded, of course, and railed back at *him* for always being demanding without ever contributing a penny to the household. The one curse led to the other. In the middle of the fight Amin came home and took sides with Ali. They heaped swear-words on Mama. She in turn was so enraged and distraught that she told them to get out of the house for good. If they didn't go voluntarily, she threatened, she would get Baba to throw them out. Ali answered "To hell with the whole family," and they left, he and Amin.

They had gone from one friend to the other, we later learned, and sat a little with each. Amin had seemed especially tense and distraught. Late at night, they ended up at one of Ali's friends where they had planned to sleep. But he had only one bed, and so Ali told Amin to go on home whereas he himself would sleep there. Then Amin had said that if Baba upbraided him when he got home, "I must do something to myself" [a euphemism for suicide]. On the way home, he dropped by his best friend, Mahmoud, though it was already one in the morning. Mahmoud was not home, but Amin told his mother to tell Mahmoud to come to him at nine in the morning. "I need him urgently" ['*ayzu daruri*], he said.

All this time, hour after hour, Mama sat in the front room and cried. None of us had managed to eat, just Baba. I and Hoda lay tossing and turning on the bed—unable to sleep. At two o'clock there was a slight knock on the door. Hoda shook Baba awake, and he opened. It was Amin. Baba scolded Amin, but not unreasonably, not more than he deserved. He told him that if he ever again behaved like today, Baba would kick him out of the house to let him fend for himself!

Then all went to bed—all except Mama; she was still sitting up crying. Amin lay tossing and turning on the couch. After a while he got up and went into the kitchen. Mama's friend followed him and asked if he wanted anything. He said no, just to make some tea. She offered to make it for him, but he refused. The next thing we heard was Mama's gruesome screams! We sprang out of bed and saw the flames licking the bathroom wall [the wall is open at the top]. Papa threw himself at the door with all his might so it broke open with a crash. But he reeled back in horror at the sight awaiting him, he cried as if his heart had been torn out. And we ran onto the balcony and tore our hair and tore our *gallabiyas;* and from all the houses in the lane people poured out. Only Mama had presence of mind enough to grab Amin and pull him out of the flames—it was his *gallabiya* that had caused the flames to spread so quickly.

Amin had poured the kerosene from the primus into a tin and set fire to himself. He was terribly burned on his right arm and his right leg from the knee down, his hair was parched, and his *gallabiya* burnt up so he was naked. But his face was unharmed and his body too. Mama wrapped him up in a blanket and cuddled him in her lap, kissing him over and over and speaking soothingly to him. Amin could hardly talk for his vocal cords had been damaged by the smoke, but he whispered barely audibly, again and again, "Please, forgive me, Mama, don't be angry with me, forgive me, for I'm going to die." We called an ambulance which came with its sirens ablast, and then we drove from one hospital to the other—they all said they didn't have space. At last, we were referred to a hospital in Abasiyya [district in eastern Cairo] that specialized in burns.[1] Amin was placed in a waiting room where only

---

1. To commit suicide by setting fire to oneself is the most common method among the people. Women sometimes attempt suicide by an overdose of pills, but no one I know has succeeded. On the other hand, I personally know two people (in addition to Amin) who died by setting fire to themselves. One was an old woman who lived by herself, the other a young wife. I have also heard many stories.

Uncle Ahmed and Khalid, Hoda's fiancé, were allowed in because of all the gruesome sights. Baba wouldn't enter—he was deranged from despair. But Mama wanted to. She insisted on bribing the doctors to let her in, but Uncle Ahmed talked her out of it. He was afraid she would collapse from the sight.

Then we rode home in a taxi. It was three o'clock in the morning. Three hours later they rode back again, Mama and Baba and Uncle Ahmed and Umm Magdi [Umm Ali's best friend] and Khalid, Hoda's fiancé. Uncle Ahmed went in to see the doctor alone. The doctor told him that Amin had died shortly after we left. Uncle Ahmed came out crying, but he didn't say that Amin was dead. He said he cried because of all the terrible burns he had seen. "Your son will be OK," he told Mama. He said that Amin needed rest, and that they could visit him the next day. But on the way home Uncle Ahmed cried so hard that he couldn't drive the car and had to stop at a friend's place to ask him to take over. So Mama understood and said she knew that Amin was dead. All of them came wailing home, barely able to stand. I and Hoda heard them from afar. We screamed and ran out on the balcony and tore our clothes and wept as we had never wept before, and—God willing—will never weep again. And from all the houses in the lane people came pouring out. Everybody cried—even people we didn't know. . . .

At the hospital, they had put Amin's body in a refrigerator. The doctors refused to let us have him, saying a police inquiry would be required first. But Uncle Ahmed bribed them, masses of money, and got his corpse. We had planned to bury him without letting Mama know for she behaved like a madwoman, making strange faces and startling if anyone just came near her. We were afraid she could not sustain the ordeal. But she knew what was going to happen; and we should have known, of course. Whenever there is anything concerning the children, she knows it even *before* it happens.

In the morning, as we were on our way to the funeral, Amin's best friend, Mahmoud, arrived. Just as Amin had told him! Remember, how he had told his mother to tell Mahmoud to come to him urgently at nine the next morning! I was on my way down the stairs when Mahmoud came. And I threw myself around his neck and cried that Amin was dead, and tore at my hair and clothes and cried that Mahmoud was dead! and Amin was dead! and Mahmoud was dead!—and then everything started spinning in my head. Mahmoud thought I had turned crazy. But then a woman came and told him what had happened. He fainted, and we carried him unconscious to the funeral.

Many people came to the funeral—all of Amin's friends that we had managed to get hold of, and plenty of people from our lane and the neighboring lanes. As we were about to bury Amin, several of his friends jumped into the grave and screamed that it wasn't true. Amin was not dead—he had been with them last night! Many of his friends fainted, and I and Hoda too. They had to carry us back to the cars.

There was much discord and trouble in the Quran reading after the burial because of a quarrel between Baba's relatives and Uncle Ahmed about whether to bring a professional mourner. Baba's relatives insisted, but Uncle Ahmed swore that he would beat them black and blue if they did. "We want peace!" he screamed. "The mother of the deceased is sitting mute, in shock, and the father is sitting sobbing! And still you want to *provoke* grief! I dare you to!" No professional mourner came, but to this day Uncle Ahmed and Baba's relatives are not on speaking terms.

After the funeral, Mama sat mute for seven months. It was a terrible time. Baba accused Mama of killing Amin. She was beside herself with grief at his death, and became so even more because of Baba's accusations. She said no, it was Ali who killed him for if Ali had not asked for fish that day, none of it would have happened. But that she only said because she was so distraught, she didn't know what she was saying. Later, when she came to her senses, she saw the truth for what it was. Amin didn't die from the burns. He died because his time was up.[2]

Mama also says, when Baba starts his accusations, "You ask for him today, and tomorrow, and then you'll forget. But I am his mother and will remember him always!"

The day after Amin's funeral a friend of his came to us and said, "It was you who killed him!"[3] We told him to get lost. We said, "You come

2. According to Muslim belief, every human being is given a preordained time on earth. When that time is up, death comes in whatever form—sickness, accident, or suicide—the means is not the cause of death.

3. None of Umm Ali's relatives or neighbors made similar accusations, though many were usually overjoyed to criticize her. Everyone said that Amin was dead because his time was up. Some had heard that Mustafa accused her of causing Amin's death, and rebuked him. He should know, they said, that there are many sons who get angry with their mothers and cease being on speaking terms with their families without taking their own lives. Amin did *not* die from the burns.

Different stories circulated regarding the circumstances of Amin's death. Amira, Umm Ali's sister-in-law, told me that Amin was not on speaking terms with Hoda because her fiancé, Khalid, always used to be around and even to sleep in their home at times. In return, she refused to wash Amin's clothes. The day he died, he had asked her to wash one of his shirts, but she refused; a quarrel developed, and their mother—who was frying fish—sided with Hoda and presented Mustafa with the ultima-

here today and ask about him and then you go away and forget. But we will remember him all our lives!"

It was a terrible time after Amin's death. His death was the fifth, and the worst, in a succession of deaths that struck our family in an incredibly short time—just three months. First, Auntie Shaddya died after a tonsils operation, only twenty-eight years old. Then a cousin of Baba's died when a lorry he was riding in rolled over in the desert. Then Mama's father died—but at least his was a natural death. Three days later Mama's cousin in Alexandria died when a fire broke out in the factory where he worked. When Amin died, the forty-day mourning period for Grandpa was not yet over. Still, all of this we could have managed because such deaths are understandable. Not Amin's—

During these three months, there happened other terrible things too, like that our laundry was stolen from the clothesline (on the balcony) where it hung to dry, including Amin's three best pairs of pants which I and Hoda had taken over. Until then we always used to leave the wash outside at night to dry, but now we won't even hang out so much as a kerchief. In addition, a carpet worth twenty-five pounds was stolen. Baba had received it as payment from a customer who didn't have money. And since it was much too large for our rooms, he said, "We'll put it away till one of our daughters gets married." So we kept it on top of the cupboard. But the day Auntie Shaddya died, we had hung it out to air. Because of the shock of her death, we forgot to take it in in the evening. And the next morning it was gone. Baba blamed Mama and Mama blamed us girls. Everybody's nerves were worn to a frazzle.

After Amin died, people said that we ought to move. The house would be haunted by his *afrit* [ghost], they warned, since he hadn't died a natural death. But where would we have moved? It costs lots of key money (*xilawil*) to get a flat these days.

Mama didn't use the toilet for two months after Amin's death—she went over to Umm Gamal's. We were also afraid, but we were ashamed to ask Umm Gamal so we stood guard for each other when one of us

---

tum, "Either I or your son will stay in this house!" So Amin was thrown out. When he came home at night, the family was eating watermelon (a rare luxury) but they did not give him any. That was the straw that broke the camel's back. Another version had it that Amin was angry with his mother because she had confiscated his alarm clock since he had not paid his savings club deposit after withdrawing his share. It is typical of these two versions, as well as all others I heard, that they are variations on the classical conflict themes: clothes, food, and money.

used the toilet. The first couple of months Uncle Ahmed and Grandfather's wife took turns sleeping with us because we were so afraid. But no *afrit* came, and that just proves that Amin didn't die in the flat. He didn't die from the burns.[4] He died because his time was over.

Once when Mama was in the toilet, her *gallabiyya* got caught in something. She was terrified because she thought it was the *afrit,* but she managed to control herself and swallow her scream. In the night, Amin came to her in her dream and said, "Don't be afraid, Mama, I am with you!"

Twenty

Afaf's Illness

In her mother's eyes, Afaf in her youth was the epitome of beauty. Whenever Umm Ali used to talk of a very pretty girl, and wanted to impress upon you just how lovely she was, she would say, "a girl as beautiful as Afaf." And Afaf *was* beautiful, with her large, almond-shaped eyes, smooth, golden skin, and full, baby cheeks with deep dimples. Her body was tall and supple with a well-rounded bosom—qualities highly appreciated in a female. But for this beauty, Afaf had to pay dearly.

As her mother saw it, it was because of jealousy that she was prettier than they were that her older sisters pestered her. "We dare you to marry before us!" they would threaten. Afaf is seven years younger than the youngest of them, and custom demands that the elder marry before the younger. But custom can be dispensed with when the younger is especially coveted. And as Umm Ali said, "People who don't know really think that Afaf is the eldest because she is the tallest and best developed."

In my diary from 1975 to 1978 I have constantly noted how Hoda and

4. I asked Mona what she thought was the reason why Amin wanted to die. She replied, "It was because he was *midayyiq* [distraught] and *za'lan* [unhappy], and so he lost control of himself and didn't know what he was doing. It happens often like that here—you feel bad about some trifling thing and suddenly you don't know what you're doing. Like Hoda, she tried to commit suicide after Khalid left her. She might easily have come to share Amin's fate."

Mona made life miserable for Afaf. They ordered her about, appropriated her few personal belongings, and upbraided her constantly. Afaf tried to defend herself by sullenness and defiance. But it was a losing battle. The odds were too great. On 17 October 1975, I noted, "I can well imagine how Afaf will take it out on Nosa when she is older." Nosa was only four years old then, too young to be bullied.

But events proved me wrong. The pressure on Afaf became too much, and she got unhinged. Umm Ali told me this story of how it began:

I was in the hospital after giving birth to the boy who died in my womb. And I was so sick of all the problems in the house and the pregnancy and everything that I told the whole family to stay away—I said I didn't want to see a single one of them! And I implored Father's wife to see to it that none of them came. But who turned up but Afaf—with a bloody cut across her forehead! Her father had thrown a chair at her because she was roaming about.

"But where *were* you?" I asked.

"By God, Mama, I wasn't anywhere," she cried.

"But what were you doing?"

"By God, Mama, I didn't do anything."

"And why do you think then that your father beats you?"

"By God, Mama, I don't know. *Ilbet zol*" [the family tortures me].

"What nonsense! You talk as if you were living with a stepmother!"

"It's worse than that!"

Then I understood that she was ill, that she was suffering from a mental sickness [*marad nafsiyya*] . . . I blame myself terribly that I didn't understand it before. I keep saying I wish to God I hadn't beaten her. But we all did. We couldn't imagine that she was actually sick. And she drove us all to despair. She used to go out in the evenings, around seven or eight, and say she was going to see a relative. But then she stayed out till twelve, or one, or two. I and Ali ran like mad along the streets searching for her; we asked everyone we met if they had seen a girl of such and such looks. It was degrading—people must start talking, of course! Sometimes we found that she'd actually been to some of the relatives, but only sat a moment with each, and then moved on. When she came home at night, she couldn't account for where she had been. Ali beat her so the blood gushed from her mouth which swelled to be like so-o-o [shows with a gesture]. Her father beat her with his fists and kicked her with the sole of his shoes so she got black and blue. I also beat her. We all did it because we were so afraid for her—what with her being a *bint bunut* [a virgin].

To tell you the truth, I don't know if she still is.

Afaf has worn me out more than all my other children. I used to think she roamed the streets in defiance. Her sisters dragged her by the hair to drive some sense into her—it was before she cut it short; they beat her with their rubber sandals or any other object they could grab. Nothing helped, naturally. I understand it now, for she *didn't know* what she was doing.

Umm Ali thinks she knows the real cause of Afaf's illness. She always used to sit quiet [*sakta*], taking things to heart, when her sisters pestered her. Hoda in particular was awful. She used to order Afaf about as if she were a servant—against my insistent objections— "Wash! Clean! Sweep! Tidy up! Go, fetch! Do this! Do that!" she nagged constantly. Afaf was extremely unhappy, of course. But anyone else would have fought back and screamed and yelled, and complained to her friends and relatives. And it's right, that's what you *should* do. One must get one's problems *out* of the body. But Afaf cannot. She's just like Amin, neither could he. Ever since she was a child she's been like that—just like Amin. Both of them were wise, and understood about life, but they couldn't talk. . . .

If only Afaf had some friends to confide in and sit with, someone she could amuse herself with, then things would be so much better! But she is taciturn and lonely, always sitting by herself. Even when Amin died, and his body was ablaze, even then she sat silent in shock— while the others ran to the balcony and cried their hearts out.

Afaf has suffered dreadfully from her sisters' jealousy. Hoda in particular used to threaten her, "Don't you dare marry before us!" Sometimes they tormented her, saying, "It's because you eat up *our* food that you grow so fat!" And it's true, she did eat [parts of] their food, but it was only becasue she *didn't know* what she was doing. Still, she was so hurt by their accusations that she's started refusing to eat. Now, she has already lost five kilos, and if she loses more, I will take her to the doctor. . . .

Her older sisters had masses of clothes, while she wore rags. Sometimes she wept and said, "You're making me a laughingstock before the whole world!" She and her sisters were supposed to share the clothes, as you know. But they refused, saying she stretched them [because of her weight] and didn't take proper care. Now she asks to have everything for herself—everything her sisters have, she also wants— and only for herself. I have to explain to her that it is impossible. When they have so much, it's because they're working and earning money.

But Afaf is happy with whatever she gets, so I try to give her some little thing often to make her happy. "Look here, Afaf," I say, "I have a surprise for you!" And she beams like the sun, however small the gift. Had it been Hoda, or Nosa! . . . But there was a real problem. She used to give away her things. When her friends said, "Oh Afaf, how beautiful!" she would say, "Please, it's yours."[1] She is ashamed *not* to give, thinking they might think her stingy. I have had to explain to her that there's nothing wrong about keeping things for oneself. She can just say it's a gift from her mother and father. Now she's better, thanks to God. But her sisters still refuse to lend her clothes and things for fear she might give them away.

—She's so forgetful, cannot keep track of where she puts things. And her mood and interests change constantly. She may pick up a school book and look at it for a moment, just to drop it the next minute. But she's improving, thanks be to God. I gave her a school bag—secondhand, but little used, bought for one pound. She was so thrilled that she has begun to go to a friend to do homework together with her. She has even begun to talk a bit with Mona. But it's very rare that she ever talks with Hoda. . . .

Last year [1978] she was kicked out of school because she danced in the class. The teacher complained that she disturbed the lesson. So she had to stay home for half a year. When I brought her back, the teacher said she would be on probation for a week. If she behaved herself and sat quiet, she could continue. But Afaf danced—poor girl—it is the only way she has to excel. She dances better than anyone else. So she was expelled again. I took her to a doctor who wrote a letter to the teacher informing her that Afaf had to go to school. Health is more important than education, he wrote, and everyone must show Afaf consideration. The teacher protested, but I told her that the doctor had said he would send the police after her if she made any fuss.

Afaf loves to dance. Ever since she was a child, she has shown a special talent. When there's music on TV, I turn up the sound and encourage her to dance. Sometimes she says she's too shy. But then I

---

1. "*Itfaddal(i)*" [please, have it] is the polite reply to someone who expresses her appreciation of something a person has. The other is supposed to decline the offer, even as the person insists on her accepting. But it is, of course, possible to take advantage of the situation, as some of Afaf's friends did. At other times, the owner will be truly happy to give her possession away.

say that being shy is a shame [*ilkusuf 'eb*]. Dancing makes you happy. You can dance your problems *out* of you.

I let Afaf go to school when she likes, and stay home whenever she likes. She shouldn't be forced in any way. It was *that* which was her problem—that she was never left in peace to do as *she* liked.

Even though she's much better now, I can't ever have peace before she's completely recovered. And the thought haunts me day and night: will she ever fully recover? I have taken her to doctor after doctor, dozens of them—doctors for one pound, and two pounds, even *ten* pounds, have I paid! I have asked them all if she is insane [*magnuna*]. But they said no. Then I have felt at peace for a while, but then, when she doesn't recover, the doubt starts haunting me again. I *must* know whether she's insane or not. The last doctor we saw—for ten pounds—I begged to give her an electro-shock. I've heard that's supposed to be so good. But he refused. He asked Afaf, "How do you feel?" "*Zayy izzift!*" [rock bottom, literally, like zero] she answered. And that, he said, was completely telling of her condition. "She's not mad. She just needs love and to be left in peace."

Afaf got both, partly because her older sisters had started working and were not home to bother her in the day, but mostly because of her mother's love and understanding. Afaf did not need to fulfill anything to have it. It was her birthright, as a mother's sick and tormented child. Umm Ali did not know what good she could do, now that she realized Afaf was sick and not obstinate, to compensate her for the suffering she had endured at the hands of the family for so long.

It has been plain to see how Afaf has blossomed. She seeks out and thrives in her mother's company. Even when her sisters—urged by their mother—ask her to join them on a visit to their friends, or to attend a wedding—usually an irresistible pleasure for a girl—she declines. At home she feels secure and content.

Thanks to her mother's insight and efforts, Afaf might emerge empowered, rather than debilitated, by her illness—with more trust in her own abilities, better able to manage her life.

The above came true in part, as I have had occasion to see through the years. Afaf did gain a new self-confidence and ability to stand up for herself—but she also lost as a result of her illness. Her life situation continued to be harsh and, to a large extent, beyond her mother's control. Peace did not descend upon the house when her elder sisters married and moved out, for there was her headstrong younger sister, Nosa, who picked up the battle. Afaf was also plagued by inner voices accusing her of not being a virgin. She became engaged to a man whose lack of drive drove her parents up the wall, and who was also insufferably possessive and dominant. There were times when she earned my deepest respect for the way she took him to task and refused to be treated like a doll. At such moments I realized what a good school her mother's home had been to her.

She married the man at last, partly because she was too old by then, thirty years, to have another chance in the marriage market. But perhaps she also loved him. In any case, any unmarried man is better than no man, for without him, a female cannot realize her prospects of becoming a mother. Everyone hopes that Afaf will soon have a child. I would not be surprised if, as a mother, she blossoms. She has a lot of good sense and managerial powers. And since her marriage, the "voices" have left her alone: she did prove to be a virgin.

Twenty-one

Hoda's Spiritual Conversion

When I first met Hoda in 1969, she was a cheerful thirteen-year-old, who chatted away about all and everything and ingratiated herself with people. Among friends, she was popular, but her mother complained that she was stupid, naive, and easy to fool. Two years later the good-natured girl had been transformed. She was thin as a rail from excessive dieting, and her cheerfulness had given way to rock-hard obstinacy and opposition. The main target was her mother, but her brother and sisters, too, were made to suffer.

Her face had changed, and not only from the weight loss. Her chin protruded, her mouth was pinched, and her eyebrows plucked thin as threads. She uses masses of makeup and spent hours in front of the mirror. In dress and demeanor, she was provocative, to say the least. She wore trousers so tight they left little doubt about the shape of her panties. She was considered sexy, and attracted men like a magnet. Her mother was at her wit's end. The family's honor was at stake. But it was useless to talk to Hoda. Her mother said, "She doesn't heed anyone but herself!"

Thus she continued for about ten years, to her family's dismay. Her sisters tiptoed in her presence so as not to elicit her wrath. The only things she cared for were boys, clothes, and sleep.

But she had little luck in the marriage market. Suitors left her when they discovered how headstrong she was. Hoda might do as a flirt, but not as a future spouse. Increasingly, she realized that she might become a spinster.

The years passed, and Hoda grew old, twenty-six years. She became depressed and twice had to have her stomach pumped at the hospital after trying to commit suicide with an overdose of pills. Twice she was brought home from work in a taxi because of fainting. She was alarmed by her younger sisters' feminine charms. Might they, perhaps, marry before her?

In the spring of 1981, Mona got engaged. Her mother tried hard to get Hoda engaged first, but it was impossible. Hoda was infuriated at the mere suggestion that anyone would "bring her" a suitor. She—alone—would choose the right man.

Not long after, Hoda was transformed once again. She started to pray five times a day, read tirelessly in the Quran, and she dressed beyond reproach. Her tight trousers and low-necked blouses gave way to wide, ankle-length skirts and loose, buttoned-up blouses. She covered her hair, abandoned all makeup, and wore only flat shoes. But pious as her clothing was, it did not satisfy her own exacting standards. She told me how she would have liked to dress in a wide cloak that covered everything except hands, feet, and face—that's how the Prophet's women dressed, and that's what the Quran enjoins. But as long as she could not keep all the *other* injunctions pertaining to women—like staying at home and not talking to any unrelated men—it would be hypocrisy to don such garb. It would have to wait until she married and became a housewife. For the time being, she must work at the factory to earn money to marry. And on the bus and at work she must perforce associate with men.

She explained the reason for her change of lifestyle thus: There was a man at work who showed her the way. He used to read in the Quran, and one day he came to her and asked to be allowed to read to her. Then he read about how sinful it was to dress and adorn herself like she did. She got scared and cried. He lent her some books so she could read for herself and said she must come and ask him if there was anything she did not understand. Since then she has been reading and crying a lot. In the beginning she was haunted by the thought of how she had sinned. But now she is happy. God will forgive, because as soon as he showed her the right path, she followed it.

Hoda is bitter with her parents for not compelling her to follow God before. "Praying is the most important thing in life. The Quran instructs the parents to command the children to pray five times a day from the time they are six years old, to beat them if they don't do it when they are ten years, and to throw them out of the house if that does not help either. That's what my parents should have done. They are both religious people. Both of them have prayed all these years."

Islam is different from Christianity in that it emphasizes pious action rather than pious belief. To be a Muslim is to submit oneself to God by performing the five actions considered the pillars of Islam: saying "there is no god but Allah, and Mohamed is his prophet"; praying five times a day; fasting during Ramadan; giving alms to the poor; and performing the pilgrimage to Mecca (if one can afford it). Islam thus places fewer demands on the person's comprehension of religious tenets than Christianity. Whoever complies with the five pillars of Islam, is a Muslim.

About Hoda's belief, there is this to say: she knows her fate to be ordained by God. God protects her and watches over her. She has had testimony to that on several occasions. For example, twice recently she was prepared to lie for her father regarding why she came home so late, "But both times Baba was not home when I came, and so I didn't have to lie. God didn't want me to sin." Neither does she have to worry about getting married any more. When God finds the time ripe, he will send her a spouse.

Her mother is exasperated. Hoda is confused, for God helps only her who helps herself. She implores Hoda to let well-meaning people bring her a suitor that she can then judge for herself. But Hoda is adamant. "People should not meddle in this. Marriage or not, it is in God's hands!"

Thus Hoda escapes a pitiful fate, to be branded a spinster at twenty-seven. Her fate is not to be blamed on herself. It is ordained by God.

Hoda did marry three years later—a man of her own choice. He is handsome and kind, but what's the use, as her mother says, when he cannot provide for the family. Hoda wears herself out doing double-shift work. She prays every day to God to please let her stay home with her children. Her marriage is marked by tension and strife—in part because she is "better" than her husband, being better educated and better employed; but it began as a love marriage, and retains some of that quality still. Her mother, says, however, "What's the use of love when it doesn't help you to feed your children?" I think Hoda may be silently saying the same.

Part Seven

Some Important Persons and Events in Umm Ali's Life

Twenty-two

Childhood and Youth, 1934–1949

Umm Ali hardly ever mentions her childhood. The memories of it seem submerged under oceans of events in her marriage and present life that dominate body and soul. I have no count of all the times I have asked her to tell me about her childhood—with the same dismal result. She starts telling, just to digress instantly through some association to events or relations in the present—and ends up pondering these in detail. In comparison, the past is a distant country.

But the few times I have managed to get her going, it is always the same picture she draws of a powerful and strict mother, a feeble and irresponsible father, a selfish elder sister, Farida, and herself—Zenab—a complaisant little girl who was exploited by the others because of her kindness. Other family members, three older sisters, a younger sister, and a brother, hardly figure in her accounts at all.

The parallels to her life today are obvious. She emphasizes herself how Mustafa is just like her father; Hoda resembles Farida; Mona is kind and patient, like herself; and she—Umm Ali—is like her mother, but not as powerful and principled as she. But then the mother had a massive advantage over her: she was economically independent, which meant that she was not a captive of her husband's caprices and neglect. She could plan her life with some degree of order. Thus she escaped the despair [za'l] that devours body and soul.

Umm Ali was born in Sayyida Zenab, an old quarter in central Cairo, about half an hour's ride (with the exception of rush hours) from where she now lives. She is of old urban origin, according to herself. Her mother came to town as a small child when *her* mother, a widow, came from the countryside, looking for work. Umm Ali's father was born in Sayyida. He is a second generation urbanite.

Her parents were distantly related before the marriage. "But we children grew up without any contact with Baba's kin because Mama couldn't stand them."

Perhaps what Umm Ali admires most in her mother was her ability to keep order [nizam]. "She never let us children stay up after eight at night, and never let us eat after going to bed. We were raised to be obedient and respectful of the elders. It would be unheard of for any of us to eat *before* the guests!" says Umm Ali, and bemoans her own offsprings' abominable manners.

Zenab was a lonely child. She had few friends and felt she was kept like a prisoner in her mother's house. Housework followed a strict division of labor: her mother cooked and did the laundry, Farida swept and tidied, and Zenab went on errands. But if she lingered an instant when she was out, looking in a shopwindow, for example, she got a beating when she got home.

Zenab went to school for two years. Then she started to become shapely, and so she had to quit as her mother feared she might attract the lascivious looks of men.

Her father loved Zenab more than the other children "because I was so calm," Umm Ali says. He never interfered in the children's upbringing; their mother was completely in charge. And she showed no mercy when she got angry. One memory stands imprinted on Umm Ali's mind; she and Farida were fighting because when Zenab woke Farida up to ask her to come shopping with her to help her carry the purchases, Farida exploded and jeered at her for being no better than a donkey, fit just to carry! So Zenab exploded and threatened to beat Farida, and when Farida dared her, she did. Farida howled, and the mother came charging in and beat Farida, telling her to get out of the house for good. Neighbors had to intervene to reconcile them.

Zenab and Farida were always quarreling, because, Umm Ali says,

Farida was always surly and quarrelsome. Whenever we asked her to help with anything, she snapped, "Don't think I'm going to be a servant! Let Zenab do it!" And because I've always been kind and complaisant, the family exploited me. For example, when the others went out for leisure, or to visit Mama's relatives in the country, I had to stay back to care for my father. My sisters went with Mama time after time, whereas I was never allowed anywhere. Only a couple of times have I been to visit my sister Fawziyya [who was married in the countryside], and then only because she needed help with the children!

Her mother and father quarreled a lot. "But it didn't matter," Umm Ali says,

since Mama was self-supplied with money. *Ilmuluk* [her spiritual siblings] gave her a lot.[1] Baba was exactly like Mustafa, he smoked hashish

---

1. *Ilmuluk* [literally, royalty, from *malik:* king] are a person's spiritual siblings who live underground. Every male has a sister, every female a brother; the *muluk* have children at the same time as their human siblings; they lead lives just like humans, but look a bit different; their eyes are vertical rather than horizontal; sometimes they marry human beings; they have immense powers, and can reach miles with their hands; they are also extremely rich, and have masses of silver and gold; they only reveal themselves

and drank whiskey, and Mama was not happy with him at all. But he was kind too, he did *not* want me to marry Mustafa, it was Mama who forced it through. And when she had set her mind on something, nothing could make her budge.

When Zenab was six years old, something happened that was to change the family forever. Her brother, Sayyid, died, at eleven years of age, in a train accident. The mother was grief-stricken. She sat for seven years immobile, unable to work. She said her hands were tied like with handcuffs. But she could talk and run the family. It was then that her spiritual siblings [*ilmuluk*] came to her and said that she should start telling people's fortunes for a fee. She had already told fortunes in cards before, but at no charge. Now the *muluk* instructed her to take money for her services.

From now on the family managed fairly well materially. They never lacked food or clothes. But the *muluk* made one condition: the mother must sleep in a room by herself. From now on, Umm Ali says, the parents had intercourse only twice to three times a year.

Soon after, the father married again, "because of the people's talk," Umm Ali says. "The people started saying that Mama had gone mad, and that he must have a wife to sleep with."

The new wife was already old, and they had no children. The father moved in with her, but came home a couple of times a week to see his children. Once Farida and Zenab missed him so much that they went to see him in his wife's place. They stayed late, and the mother came dashing to fetch them. When she saw her own children sitting on the floor and munching bread crumbs, she was so insulted that she lashed out against the other woman. The neighbors had to intervene to separate them.

The father was so dazzled with his new wife that he cut work; he was employed in the police. This was in the days of the British, "when there was system and order in the land." He was threatened with expulsion unless he divorced his new wife, so he did. But he remarried her secretly. He was sentenced to jail for a month because prisoners of whom he was in charge had taken advantage of his erratic mind to escape, and he was demoted one rank. The family went to visit him in prison, but the other woman came too! A fight erupted again between his two wives. Each accused the other of having made him so distraught that he, at his wits'

---

to select people. In 1972, when Umm Ali sat mute for months after Amin's death, her *mulik* brother came to her and offered her great riches if she would marry him. But Mustafa refused, although sleeping with a *malik* does not mean intercourse, just sleeping beside, like her mother did with her *malik* brother.

end, neglected his job. After he was freed from jail, the father received a new warning that he would lose his job unless he divorced his new wife. So he did. But he continued to visit her in secret, Umm Ali says.

It was at this time that they moved to Giza—to get away from the other woman, but also from pity for Ahmed, Zenab's baby brother. He had been placed in foster care with an aunt after his mother lost her milk after the shock of her elder son's death. But the aunt neglected Ahmed. In Giza, the mother had another sister, with a good heart, who could care for him.

Umm Ali is sorry that her mother died so early—only fifty-six days after she married Mustafa. Otherwise, the mother could have freed her from the unhappy bond, as she freed Feyza from the marriage to Abdou. Her mother died of an infection after an appendicitis operation.

When the mother understood that she was going to die, she sold all her belongings and gave the money to the poor. She did not want to leave behind any earthly possessions, she said, for that would only cause quarrels within the family.

"As if that didn't happen in any case!" Umm Ali says.

Twenty-three

Amira: Sister-in-Law Who Has Enough with Her Own

Umm Ali can hardly mention her beloved brother, Ahmed, without lapsing into a long, detailed account about his wife, Amira. I find that neither can I. I had meant to tell about Ahmed and his place in Umm Ali's life. But how can I do that when the way Umm Ali sees it, it is his wife, not he, who determines the relation between them? Amira must take priority of place.

Strange how it is possible to give a full-fledged account of the women with only passing references to the men, whereas a man can hardly be depicted without constant references to his wife, mother, and/or sister. Behind every man there looms a woman. No doubt this is partly because of the perspective adopted in this book with its focus on home and neighborhood. Were I to describe the men's domain, women might be relegated to second place—though on deeper reflection, I am not so sure about that! Within the neighborhood at least, men's behavior is seen as contingent on the women.

There are numerous testimonies to that. One is the standard ph used to explain just about everything a man does wrong: *"hiyya sallatih"* [she manipulated him]. Men are perceived as being under the woman's thumb, lacking in independent judgment, so, almost without exception, a woman—wife, mother, sister, or daughter—is cast in the role of scapegoat. When Umm Ali deviates from this in putting the blame on Mustafa himself, it is partly because he *does not have* a mother or sister who might function as scapegoats.[1] Her adherence to the idea that men are easily swayed is shown by her insistence that it was not Mustafa's fault that he bullied her at the start of their marriage. His friends were to blame. Also his foster mother and foster sister are held responsible for his bad behavior.

This view of the man as under the woman's thumb is expressed in other well-worn phrases too. "The man does as his wife says," "The man tags along after his wife," and "It is the women who rule." The standard conception is that men are lax and weak—like children.

The scapegoat mentality serves clear psychological needs. By putting the blame on others, the relationship to the beloved is protected. When Ahmed, for example, does something that hurts Umm Ali, she need not see his behavior as a sign of lack of love for her. The thought, "he loves me, but she incited him" [*biyhibbini, hass hiyya sallatih*] serves to get him off the hook.

She is beautiful. Even Umm Ali has to grant her that. She used to say, "Oh, well Amira is beautiful and intelligent, but what's the use when she doesn't know how to keep order and give her husband peace and quiet!" Like most women, Umm Ali feels that her sister-in-law falls miserably short in giving her brother the care and love he deserves. "Look at Ahmed, he's thin as a rail and dead tired. I have told Amira that she *must* give him a glass of milk every morning. But then she says that she cannot because the children must also have milk and where would she get the money from. She does him great injustice. What if Ahmed got sick and could not work at all? What *then* would the children live on?"

"Proud" is perhaps the word which best describes Amira's stature and posture. She is of medium height, and chubby, in keeping with the feminine ideal. Now she herself feels that she has become a bit too plump,

---

1. Mustafa's mother left him when he was a baby, and his sister married afar and has lived out of Egypt much of the time.

and complains that six childbirths have stretched her stomach. She has turned thirty-five. But I still think she carries herself like a queen.

She has huge dark, almond-shaped eyes, and the most beautiful long hair I ever remember seeing. Her skin is white, and her features delicately shaped. Given other and more favorable conditions, Amira would have been a real beauty.[2] She is quite clearly intelligent, but rather quiet (it cannot have been easy to get a word in edgewise in her mother's house), and exceptionally tidy in her thought. What's more, she is also quite loyal to her husband. I realize that Umm Ali would scarcely grant her that, but let it be: in the course of the years I have been in and out of Amira's house, I have rarely heard her criticize her husband; and that is unusual. Admittedly, she has had little reason to do so, the way Ahmed has struggled for his family's welfare; but it hardly detracts from her feat. I think she loves him, plain and simple.

Even Umm Ali might have agreed with that. *"But,"* she would have been quick to add, "she loves her mother more!" And then she would have launched into a lengthy tirade about the injustice Amira does her husband by giving her mother priority above him. In this view, that the husband should come first, Umm Ali has the community's support. Others also criticize Amira for saying, "My mother is more important to me than my husband for she has given me life and upbringing."

They had been married for twenty years by 1982. Amira has given a moving picture of how the marriage came about.

I was only thirteen years when we got engaged. It was my mother who wanted me to get married. She lured Ahmed. He used to buy *ful* [beans] from her, and one day she said to him, "I have a lovely young daughter with white skin and beautiful hair." Ahmed said he was interested, and they agreed that he would come to see me, together with his sister, Umm Ali. I also wanted to get married for I had to work very hard in my mother's house. She used to scold me, and beat me severely. When she told me that a suitor was on his way, I was thrilled and said, "Oh, I know who he is! That handsome guy with white skin, and green eyes, and yellow hair!" "Oh, no!" said my mother, "he is dark, with brown eyes, and almost bald!" I thought for a moment, then said, "Hair or no hair, I take him!" That tells you how eager I was to get out of my mother's house!

2. However beautiful a woman, she will always carry the stain of her background in her skin, posture, gait, and demeanor. That's what I mean when I say that given other and more favorable circumstances, Amira would have developed into a stunning beauty.

A mother in action in her daughter's kitchen.

There Amira had lived in a windowless, one-room shack, just two by three meters, together with her mother, father, and two younger sisters. Her father was old and sick, and the family managed on what the mother could earn from peddling beans. Amira was left at home to care for the house and the children. Her mother did well in her trade, Amira says, and I do not doubt it. With her quick-witted, bold, and boisterous manner, passersby could hardly escape becoming her customers. As the years have passed, and I have grown used to her, I have come to feel a certain sympathy for this woman. But for years, she repelled me, as she did many others, with her loud, aggressive, almost lewd ways. I can easily imagine the scoldings and beatings that were Amira's lot. But then I have seen her mother lording it over a flock of grandchildren!

She has taken up residence in Amira's flat.

At first, she was merely a visitor there, for some sixteen hours a day, each day, for thirteen years. Then she packed up her things and moved in for good, accompanied by her youngest daughter who was not married yet. She has driven Ahmed to despondency, rage, yes, utter despair. "*Ilbet bawsa!*" [my home is falling apart] he screams. I have seen him come to Umm Ali and rip his shirt to pieces in sheer despair, "*Ha'ish izzayy!*" [how *can* I live in this way] At times he comes there to take a nap because his own house is filled with ear-splitting racket. It does not help him that he is nominally the master of the house. The women's power is pragmatically, not ideologically, based. He can thunder threats of divorce as much as he wants, in practice he is bound to the mother of his six children. They know it so well, both he and she. "What can I do?" he sighs, "marry again and give the children a stepmother? That would only create even more of a madhouse!" Nor could he afford it either.

A man with small children can hardly live alone. Yes, he hardly can, even if he is childless. Whereas a woman is perceived as perfectly able to manage alone, the man is regarded as dependent on a woman for housework and sexual gratification, almost to *be* a man! So Ahmed is compelled to make a life of sorts within the confines of the thirty square meters he shares with three adult women, six children, and every so often, Amira's eldest sister and her kids who come visiting from the country.

Umm Ali is full of indignation.

> Amira does Ahmed *great* injustice because she never gives him peace and a chance to rest. Ever and always, her family is there. Sometimes Ahmed explodes in front of them, and so they back off for a day or two [this was while they still had the one-room shack where Amira grew up as a retreat]. But then they resume their visits as frequently as before. Amira doesn't know how to take care of a husband. Her first duty is to him, the mother must come second. She *must* see to it that he has everything he needs and finds his home in peace and order when he comes home. And then she must leave it to him to decide how he wants to spend his leisure, not complain when he says he wants to go here or there, like Amira does when Ahmed says he wants to go and visit one of his *sisters!* She drives him up the walls with her constant, "But isn't there a taxi available today?" [a reference to Amin's evening job].[3] When the woman keeps nagging the man, she just creates opposition in him!

Many would agree with Umm Ali that Ahmed's life is not enviable. But some have sympathy with Amira too. Her best friend says, "But what can she *do? Tell* her mother to back away? It's impossible!" Amira is trapped in conflicting obligations between her mother and her husband.

Regarding Umm Ali's accusation that Amira nags at her husband to

---

3. The demand for cars rented out by their owners to drive as taxis outstrips the supply.

work harder and that she interferes with his freedom, I think it is unjust. Amira is, in my experience, neither worse nor better than most other women. Amira is still young and ambitious, and Ahmed has shown that he can be driven. As Amira says, "Men are like children. If they are to learn, they must be guided and punished from an early age; otherwise, they will follow the wrong path for life!" Umm Ali undoubtedly would agree with that.

The relationship between the sisters-in-law got off to a bad start. Already before the marriage between Ahmed and Amira was safely contracted, his sister (Umm Ali) and Amira's mother were not speaking, with the result that no one from Ahmed's family attended the wedding. His other sisters were invited, but they stood firm with Umm Ali and boycotted the whole affair. Umm Ali gloats, "Not even our father went!"[4]

A series of conflicts lay at the root of this. First, Amira's mother was offended because once, when she was ill, Umm Ali did not come to visit her.[5] Umm Ali says she did go, but found the door of her shack closed. "She was probably at the neighbors', watching TV!" Ahmed got them reconciled. Then Umm Ali gave birth and Umm Amira came to greet her bringing a generous gift of half a kilo of meat and some rice. Not long after, Umm Amira's daughter was circumcised. Because Umm Ali had her hands full with her newborn, she sent one of the children with twenty-five piaster and the message, "Mama sends her greetings and says, 'Buy yourself a treat for now!'" Umm Ali says she had meant, of course, to go later herself and bring a bigger gift, comparable to what Umm Amira gave her; when she sent her daughter as messenger, it was just to pay Umm Amira her respects immediately. But the child forgot the crucial words "for now"—with disastrous results.

Umm Amira thought that twenty-five piaster was all Umm Ali intended to give, and she was furious. She stormed over to Umm Ali and scolded her up and down, "*I* gave you meat, and you give me twenty-five piaster! May God curse you!" After a few months, they were reconciled again, this time by Amira's aunt who wanted to hasten the wedding. But fate would have it otherwise. Amira's father died, which meant the wedding had to be postponed for another year in keeping with mourning customs. Umm Ali went to pay her condolences. Once burned, twice shy, she saw to it that the gift she now brought was of acceptable dimensions. She also showed up the following Thursday for the Quran reading, but not—alas—

4. It is fairly common for the groom's family to be absent from his wedding. The reason is usually that they disapprove of the bride or have quarreled with her family.
5. This is a very common cause of conflicts, second only to "the children fought."

for the forty-day memorial ceremony. She says she was prevented because Mustafa was ill in bed. But Umm Amira got furious again. When they met on the street, the widow screamed, "May *your* husband die!"

Now Umm Ali had had enough. When, soon after, Mustafa had to be hospitalized, she gave Ahmed orders to see to it that Umm Amira stayed away. She did not want to be reconciled.[6]

But with the wedding now postponed for another year, the two enemies were reconciled once more. Then one day Umm Ali went to visit Umm Amira. Ahmed was out of work at the time, and Umm Amira harped on it constantly. Umm Ali was annoyed. She asked Umm Amira to be patient and understanding. She must realize, Umm Ali said, that when Ahmed didn't take the first offer that turned up, it was because he had Amira's best interests at heart. "Interests!" Umm Amira snapped. "As if we are interested in having him!" That made Ahmed explode, and so the quarrel was in full swing! Umm Ali was deeply offended. "It's a *shame* to quarrel in front of the guests," she says, reiterating a common ideal. She gathered her cloak about her, and marched out, insulted also because Umm Amira chided her dear brother in front of her.

Since then Umm Ali and Umm Amira have made no effort to keep up relations. Rather, both keep their distance. The gap between them as regards temperament and style is too wide to be bridged.

Ahmed and Amira were married at last. He was twenty-four, she fourteen years old. The *maezzun* [scribe] refused to marry them at first because she was under age. "But then," says Amira, "my mother tore up my birth certificate and took me to a doctor saying she had lost it, please, would he make me a new one. The doctor felt my body, and gave me eighteen years."

The marriage, however, did not go so well, as might well be expected. Particularly in the early stages, much depends on how well the respective families get along. If they are at loggerheads or have irreconcilable differences, they will pull in opposite directions and train their own party in stratagems and plots—something they see as sheer necessity. The couple begins its marital life filled with mutual distrust and deep-seated, inveterate stereotypies about the intractable natures of man and woman. What matters is to gain the upper hand from the start. I can well imagine how both Ahmed and Amira must have run back and forth to their respective mothers (for Ahmed Umm Ali would have been in his mother's place),

6. To go and greet someone who is ill is to force a reconciliation.

seeking advice and loading up on ammunition. Amira talks of a happy engagement period but an awful early marriage:

The final straw was that when Ahmed came home at night and wanted intercourse, he kicked me as if I were a donkey! I told him he could just shake my arm, but he quipped that he could do as he pleased. He also came and went as he pleased, and pestered me endlessly. For instance, when I got pregnant the first month, Ahmed demanded macaroni every day. He *knew* I couldn't stand the smell of macaroni and had to vomit every time, that's just why he did it. Ever since, I have not been able to stand the smell of macaroni!

But it wasn't Ahmed's fault that he behaved like this. It was his father's wife who made him do it, because she wanted his money; she hoped he would divorce me.

(If Amira had thought Umm Ali was to blame, she would not have told me.) Amira continued,

Once Ahmed disappeared to Alexandria and was gone for two months without even telling me where he was. I had to sell my engagement ring and necklace to pay for the food and the rent. In the end, I gave up and moved in with my mother. When Ahmed came back, he demanded that I return to him. I said that he would first have to get himself a regular job, which made Ahmed furious. He said he was entirely free to choose his own work! My mother retorted that *she* was free to choose her daughter's spouse! Later my mother said that as we had met as friends, we should part as friends. She paid the scribe, and so we were divorced.

Ahmed moved back with Umm Ali.

When his son was born, Ahmed went to see him. He carried and cuddled the child, and bought him clothes. And so the parents were reconciled, and have lived happily together, says Amira.

Umm Ali's story is rather different. According to her, the reconciliation itself was fraught with difficulties. Umm Amira demanded that Ahmed pay forty pounds in bride-price [*mahr*] the second time. Ahmed was infuriated, so his stepmother offered to find him another bride. But Umm Amira got wind of it, and stormed over to the girl's family and told her family foul things about Ahmed. In the end, Ahmed and Amira got together again and he paid something like ten pounds as a sign of good will.

Though she is too good to say so, I think Umm Ali deplores the fact that her brother did not disentangle himself from Amira. She would have wished him a better life. But she also respects the fact that it is his life, he must make his own choices.

Umm Ali is also bitter because she knows, she says, that Amira's family accuses her of having eaten up the money which Ahmed made those years he lived under her roof.

They say it's my fault that he couldn't pay a higher *mahr*. By God, if there is anything that's my fault, it's that Ahmed could pay anything at all! He earned nine pounds at the time, and it was I who persuaded him to enter a savings club for six pounds so he could save for his future marriage. I got him to buy himself clothes for the money. He said, "What am I going to do with all those clothes?" I said, "When you marry and have children, there won't be anything left for you, so you have to buy yourself enough to last for a lifetime!" I got him to spend his earnings, first on clothes, and then on the bride-price. And still that woman goes and says I ate up his money! Yes, that's precisely what she does, for the people have told me.

With such a history, it was only fair to expect that Umm Ali and Amira would drift apart. As the oldest and the one deserving of respect, Umm Ali might well wish that Amira would nurture good relations. But the strategy Amira has chosen is quite clearly the best for her. By keeping her distance, she minimizes the chances of conflict and interference. More-over, she does have more than enough with her own life. In her place, I think Umm Ali would have done the same.

But she is not in Amira's place, and she feels slighted.

Amira loves only her own family, nobody else! She visits me just two, three times a year, and there are hardly ten houses between us! Her children hardly even know who I am! She does them great injustice by letting them grow up without any contact with their father's rela-tives. Do you know what they say when I go there to visit? They say, "Baba, there is somebody here for you!" *Somebody!* Can you imagine! And they don't even come and greet me, their mother has to *ask* them to do it! Then they stick out a limp hand and mumble something, and charge off. They have no manners, those children! You'd think I was a complete stranger to them!

Even Nosa, little as she is, is amazed at our relationship. Here one day she asked me, "Why don't you ever visit uncle's wife? Aren't you on speaking terms with her?" Even a seven-year-old understands! She thinks we should go and see one another, say, "What have you been doing?" and so on. And she's right, that's how it should be. But when Amira won't visit me, I won't go to her!

When she came here the other day to let me hear the tape that Ahmed had sent from Libya [where he was working], I hadn't seen her for six months. And I'm *sure* she wouldn't have come if Ahmed hadn't told her on the tape to bring it over to me.[7] I told her to her face—yes, you heard it yourself—I said "I'm sure you wouldn't have come if Ahmed hadn't told you!" She excused herself saying she is so busy with the children. But that's just an excuse. She could have *brought them along*! I would have been *happy* to see them! The truth is, she doesn't love Ahmed's family, just her own!

. . . When I visit her once in a rare while, I never eat at her place. She begrudges people the food! Usually, she doesn't even offer hospitality, so *Ahmed* has to do it![8] And *if* she does, she makes it plain that she doesn't want the guests to eat. She says, "Wo-o-ould you li-i-ike something to e-e-eat?" instead of just, "Come on, let's eat!" And if I say no, she never repeats the offer!

Also, when I visit her, she never shows me anything new she has got. She hides her belongings! She thinks *I* am envious, and that I might throw the evil eye. As if I am like her!

. . . She also wastes Ahmed's hard-earned money with nary a thought of how he has to struggle to earn it, spending far too much on clothes for the children. For example, she just bought the three-year-old a dress for the Feast for eight pounds! Eight pounds! It's crazy! The kid doesn't even know how to appreciate the thing, and she'll grow out of it in no time at all!

Amira is equally harsh in her criticism of Umm Ali for teaching her daughters to be extravagant.

When the girls were small, just three or four, Umm Ali used to take them to the shop so they could choose their own clothes. When Ahmed criticized her, she got angry, saying the children should dress as they pleased, not have her taste forced on them. Everything should be by freedom [*hurriyya*]. As a result the girls are not satisfied with anything unless they choose it themselves, and they always choose on the basis of looks, regardless of price. Hoda, for example, buys shoes for six pounds, instead of three or four. And the girls wear panties at one pound a pair instead of twenty-five piaster, and no one ever even sees their panties! The upshot is that Umm Ali is always broke, because she always owes money for clothes the girls have bought. Otherwise, what Mustafa gives her to run the house would have been plenty!

Umm Ali feels hurt that Amira shows no interest in a close relationship

---

7. Ahmed was then a guest worker in Libya; as few people of his generation can read or write, cassettes are used instead of letters. Telephones are exceedingly rare.

8. It is unfitting for a husband to offer the guests food since only the wife can know if there is enough food for hospitality.

with her. "Ahmed says Amira doesn't love his family, but then I tell him, 'If she doesn't love your family, she doesn't love you either, for loving you would naturally mean loving us as well!'" Actually, Umm Ali knows better. That sisters-in-law get along well is the exception rather than the rule. Usually, they will keep their distance, like she and Mustafa's sister did, and many are not on speaking terms for long periods at a time. The relationship is particularly strained when the man's sister is older than his wife, for then the sister has a double right to services and respect by virtue of her age and her affinal position. To protect themselves, many women say they prefer not to be on speaking terms with their husband's elder sister.

Ultimately, the conflict between sisters-in-law is rooted in money and the competition for it. The man's female kin has a moral right to money and help from him when in need, and his sister also has a legal right to his help in an emergency, for example, if her husband divorces her, sickens, or dies. But the relationship between sisters-in-law usually degenerates even in the absence of such conditions. As with Umm Ali, women generally feel that the husband's sisters take advantage of his love to extract gifts and loans from him. Chronic scarcity means that it is necessary to try to protect whatever little one has for oneself. Umm Ali can insist that she wants nothing from Ahmed, just his love. In Amira's mind, she will represent a formidable threat, since love implies gifts.

Umm Ali often complains, "Amira is envious/jealous. She is afraid that if Ahmed visits me, he might give me money! As if *I* wanted any money from him! I just want to sit with him and talk with him, perhaps eat a little together. Am I not his *sister?*"

The relationship between Amira and Umm Ali is neither better nor worse than that between most sisters-in-law. They see each other at most two to three times a year. That is perhaps less than most sisters-in-law and reflects the fact that both of them keep their pride and their distance. Because they see each other so seldom, they are usually on speaking terms, for the chances of a confrontation are small. Their children, too, have little contact; once in a while one of the younger children will accompany Ahmed on a visit to Umm Ali. Until Amira got a TV, she also used to come, along with her mother and sisters, to watch soap operas on Thursday and Sunday nights. Umm Ali used to say then, "She only comes for the TV, not because she loves us. Just wait and see when she gets her own TV!" And she was right. But Amira says that she does not come anymore because of the children. Then she had only two—now there are six.

Regarding the women's mutual criticism that the other wastes money and lacks all ability to plan, I think Umm Ali's criticism is the more unjust.

For Amira has proven beyond the shadow of a doubt that she knows how to plan. She is of a tougher caliber than Umm Ali, and also more pragmatic. Amira does not let her compassion for people or a desire for peace in the house dictate her actions. She works slowly and assiduously in a way that is quite rare in this environment and, I think, very impressive. Umm Ali would hardly agree. But here is the story:

In 1975, Amira, her sisters, and her mother inherited a considerable sum of money from Amira's half-brother (from her father's first marriage). The three sisters received 100 pounds each, and the mother 70 pounds. Instead of each using the money to buy some of the countless things they each wanted and needed, they decided on a joint investment. Ahmed, who saw his chance to realize his age-old dream of a taxicab, pleaded with the women to help him to that. But Amira snapped, "And what when the car breaks down? Where do we stand then?" The women had another plan.

Amira sold a bed, a wardrobe, and a carpet (they were her personal belongings) for a total of fifty pounds. The bed brought twelve pounds, the wardrobe twenty-eight, and the carpet ten. That meant that they had a total of 420 pounds between them. Then the mother gave up her shack, and moved in with Amira. For that, she managed to extort 100 pounds from the landlord who could now rent out the room for a much higher price.[9] Next Amira's youngest sister sold her gold engagement bracelet for ninety pounds, bringing the women's cache to 610 pounds. They invested the money in a house that cost 1,100 pounds.

The house contains two small flats and one room, and brings in a total in rent of ten pounds a month. They financed the house purchase in the following way: a loan of 500 pounds was granted by the former owner. He gets half the rental income each month, that is five pounds (sixty pounds per year). The loan is interest free.[10] To speed up the repayment of the loan, Amira and one of her sisters (who is working and earning some money) have joined a savings club for five pounds per month, giving a lump saving of fifty pounds (since there are ten members). The former owner rents a room in the house for two pounds a month, but the contract specifies that he will move out when the entire purchase price has been paid. Then the sisters can let the room for two and a half to three pounds

9. Egyptian housing laws provide that the rent is frozen and cannot be raised after the contract is made, even if this was generations ago (a son can inherit the tenancy at the original rent). Nor can a tenant be evicted save through gross violation of the contract. The only way to raise the rent is to get a new tenant.

10. The Quran forbids the taking of interest, and though this principle is not always heeded, among the Cairo lower class all loans are interest free. The effect of this on people's chances of improving their lot cannot be overestimated.

per month, so that each sister will get a monthly net income of three and a half pounds. Later, when they can afford it, they plan to build a new and better house on the foundation of the old one. They have already applied for a condemnation permit since such matters take years.

I have seldom come across such a long-term, carefully conceived plan either among women or men. Others who want to build for the future do so by investing in education for their children and/or in a plot of land on the city's outskirts. Only a few actually manage to move, for as with Umm Ali and her plot, they are dependent on their husbands' cooperation. Amira, her mother, and sisters have no ambition to move. Unlike Umm Ali and many others, they are attached to the neighborhood and consider it their home. Here they were born and raised, here they belong.

Recently, Umm Ali, who is perennially hopeful about her husband and never seems to learn from his mistakes, managed to buy him the car he had been craving for years. It cost 500 pounds, and she has managed to get her hands on 300 so far. The car runs—for now. Ahmed almost went mad with envy, she says, when he saw it. And she criticizes Amira, "She doesn't know how to help her husband. Ahmed shouldn't stand for it. But Mustafa says that Ahmed has gotten used to fending for himself without any help from his wife."

Ahmed has not wanted so much as to see the house the women bought. He doesn't even know its location. Umm Ali on her part is merciless in her censure of Amira for failing to buy him his long-desired car.

Thus they live, the two sisters-in-law, so near in space and yet so far apart, so intimately related and yet so far removed. Each has her own circle of friends and acquaintances, and there are few both of them know. Thus when a relative of Amira's died in a tragic accident a while ago, Umm Ali knew nothing about it until I happened to mention it a year later. Ahmed had not told her. He is otherwise the only bridge between them, but he goes from one to the other without instilling confidence and trust. Why should he? All he wants is peace. If he brought them together, it would surely bring discord sooner or later. The best he can do is to minimize the information each has about the other and keep up the truce by keeping quiet when they churn out complaints against each other. He always defends his wife against his sister's recriminations, and vice versa—even when he himself agrees with the critique!

Umm Ali and Amira are divided by a strong conflict of interests—with one important exception. When the *honor* of one of them is at stake, they join forces. Thus, when Umm Ali wanted revenge on a woman who had seduced Hoda's fiancé, she called on Amira. (She did *not* turn to Ahmed.)

Amira mobilized her mother and sisters to go and beat up the seductress. Likewise, when Amira was severely distraught because Ahmed paid attention to his father's young wife, Umm Ali joined Amira in condemnation of the stepmother. The two sisters-in-law mounted a joint rescue operation. The background of the story is as follows:

One evening in 1969 at about 10:30, as I stopped by Amira's, I found her sitting alone knitting. She seemed distraught, and I asked about Ahmed. She gave an anxious reply. She doesn't know where he is, he didn't come home for lunch today; she has no idea of his whereabouts or what has happened. If only he had a regular evening job, then she could at least have gone there and inquired. Now she is so helpless.

I sympathized wholeheartedly and then her confidences came pouring forth about Ahmed who, in the past two months, had strayed on a dangerous path, manipulated by his father's young wife.

I hardly ever see him at home these days. Whenever he is free, he goes to his father's and sits there smoking hashish, playing cards, and telling jokes. Sometimes he doesn't even come home for lunch but goes straight to his father's place. On other days he just stops here for food, changes his clothes, and goes to his father. Then he comes back again at about nine at night to get Abdullah [his best friend]. They say they're going to see one of Abdullah's friends. Sometimes he even tells me he is going to drive the taxi. But I don't believe him, and so I wait a little and then send Mohamed [son] to his grandfather to see. Always, Ahmed is there. One day I went myself and surprised him. He got furious and cried, "Are you coming to spy on me, you bitch, you daughter of a slut? I'm free! I'm going to divorce you after Ramadan!" [Divorce during Ramadan is sinful.]

Also, Ahmed spends a lot on clothes and entertainment for his father's family. Last Tuesday, for example, he bought material for a *gallabiyya* for each of the six members of the family; and my sister has even seen Ahmed's new shoes—which cost him a whole one pound and thirty-five piaster—on the feet of Fathi, the stepmother's son!

Amira is especially bitter because this is the month of Ramadan when her own family has extra need of money. The family owes rent for two months, and she has had to sell her gold earrings to buy the children new clothes for the Feast.

This life has been going on for two months now. But last night when Ahmed came home at midnight the third night running this week, I exploded. I lectured him that he is making life impossible for me. He is my husband, and so I expect him to come home from work every day, change his clothes, eat, then have a rest, and on his evenings off to sit with me and the children, or take us out for a walk. I told him that the house that he leaves, he should also return to [*ilbet illi xarig min, mafrud yirga'lu*], not like now go straight to his father's after work. Ahmed got furious and screamed, "I'm free! You have only the right to your food!" [*liki takli bass*] I replied that I used to eat in my father's house too so that was *not* why I married him. And if he expected me to keep quiet so long as he gives me the food, he can pack his things and move in with his father for good. Then I know what I have at least—a house without a man—and can accommodate to that, rather than being constantly disappointed like now because I am hoping and waiting.

Amira compares their life now with their engagement time.

At first, I didn't care much for Ahmed because I was so young, just thirteen years, and didn't understand about life. But as I got to know him, I came to love him, and he loved me. He used to come to our place almost every evening and sit until midnight, and he cared a lot for me [*kan biyxaf qawi 'aleyya*]. If I so much as had a stomachache, he wanted to rush me off to the doctor. We went to the movies, for walks, and to visit the relatives. Look at the difference now! Now he leaves us in the lurch and doesn't care about a thing. When he comes home late at night and finds me and Umm Hani [best friend] sitting here, he just snorts, "Excuse me!" [*'an iznuku*] and goes straight to bed. In the morning, when I try to wake him, he is sour and grumpy and calls me daughter of a bitch and a whore. I hardly manage to get him up. Then he drinks a glass of tea with milk, without a word, and goes off.

And that's how it usually goes. With time, a wife becomes cheaper to her husband [*bitiqba arxas 'aleh*].

But Ahmed still loves me—that's not the problem. All our troubles are just because his stepmother manipulates him.

The desperation of her situation made Amira swallow her pride and appeal to Umm Ali. And Umm Ali came to her rescue, for though she was full of indignation with Amira for neglecting Ahmed, she was even more critical of her stepmother who she believed would stop at nothing for the sake of Ahmed's money. So she sent the children to summon Ahmed, saying she wanted to see him at once. When he came, she urged him to stay away from his father's house. Ahmed immediately sensed the signs of female conspiracy and blew up. He was free, he said, to do as he pleased. When this maneuver failed, the women (successfully) tried subtler tactics. One episode in particular impressed me.

One evening after we had eaten at Amira's place, Ahmed grabbed his shoes to go out. Everyone suspected he was heading for his father's house, and Amira made an instant move. She grabbed one shoe, and pulled it away from him playfully saying, "No, no, not tonight! Tonight you're going to stay with us! You were with them this morning! Aren't we also humans—or are we animals?" As they pulled at opposite ends, with Ahmed trying to shake her off, she continued, "Okay, if you want to go, then why not take me along?" "Because you can't converse!" Ahmed snapped. Then Amira started persuading him that they should go to Umm Ali instead and watch TV. "Let's go to Sawsan's aunt, she loves Sawsan so much!" By playing on how happy he would make his sister by bringing his baby daughter to her, she finally managed to make him yield—with the air of a father who reluctantly gives in to a sulky child.

Amira shone with pride and happiness as they left. As an observer, I was mightily impressed by her tactics. It was plain that she could never have achieved the same result by nagging and scolding. That would have been perceived as an infringement of the man's freedom, and would have forced him to retaliate. But when I congratulated Amira on her victory the next day, she told me it was Umm Ali who had given her the bold stroke! Thus two women chose to underplay strong conflicting interests between themselves in order to score against a common enemy.

On the larger canvas of life, these conciliatory alliances are fleeting, however. They emerge suddenly but wither away, leaving no lasting traces, for each woman's yearning for the man's—husband's or brother's—love and loyalty is too painful and enduring.

Twenty-four

Ahmed—Beloved Brother

Ahmed is tall and thin with a haggard look. His back seems bent even when he walks upright. He is a handsome man, with fine features, thin brown hair combed straight back from his face, and brilliant brown eyes that sparkle with zest and humor or cloud in sheer despair. His affinity with Umm Ali is obvious. His mind is sharp, and his understanding of life deep; he talks as if the whole suffering of humankind had somehow zeroed in on his body— which, for those who know him, does not seem so far from the truth.

Life has been hard on Ahmed. He was just a baby when his mother was stricken with shock, sitting lame and mute, after her elder son Sayyid's death, and Ahmed was placed in foster care with an aunt. She beat and abused him, so he was moved to another aunt. At fourteen, he moved in with his sister Umm Ali who had just married. He was happy there. But six years later, his father demanded him. The father had meanwhile remarried, and wanted Ahmed's help to feed his family. Ahmed did not want to go, but that was irrelevant. A father has the right to his sons.

Ahmed fell in love with his stepmother's daughter. But his stepmother wasted his money so, says Umm Ali, there was nothing to marry on. The offer of Amira must therefore have come in handy. Since her family was dirt poor, they could only ask for a small bride-price. Umm Ali tells me that Ahmed asked her to come along the first time he was to see Amira. She agreed, so he would not have to go alone, but afterward when he asked her for her opinion, she declined. "You've got to make up your own mind! It's you who're going to sleep in her arms!" she reported saying—a most unusual abdication for a woman. But Umm Ali is special, and I believe her.

Through all the years I have known him, Ahmed has been in the depths of despair, so skinny that his ribs have shown through his shirt and his back has been bent as if he toiled under some constant heavy burden. And that's precisely how he has felt. Time and again he has wailed, "Ever since my father died, I've prayed that God would take me too!"

His father's death in 1972 left Ahmed with the financial responsibility for his father's four young children and his widow, in addition to his own four (later six) children, wife, mother-in-law, and sister-in-law. When soon after his sister Farida walked out her husband because he took a second wife, Ahmed became responsible for her, too. In sum, this gave him thirteen mouths to feed, plus his own, and two flats to pay rent for. His wages at the time amounted to fourteen pounds a month. He worked as a truck driver with the government.

To manage it all, he worked himself half to death. He just stuck his nose in the door after work, gulped a quick lunch, and then went out to drive a taxi far into the night. In this way, he could earn two more pounds a day. He was rarely in bed before midnight and up at six the next morning to start all over again. No wonder he was cross and grumpy when Amira tried to shake him awake, or that the children tiptoed to steer clear of his anger. Trouble seemed always close at hand. I remember one episode in particular.

The family was sitting around the *tabliyya*, having lunch. There was barely room for us all, so we sat tightly squeezed together. Amira held the baby on her lap. Suddenly the baby waved her arms so Ahmed's glass slipped and broke. Ahmed lashed out against the child, "I'll kill you, daughter of a whore! Do you think I'm rolling in money?"

Ahmed is, nevertheless, a caring man as father, husband, brother, and guardian. In contrast to most men, he buys all the children's clothes himself and sees to it that they are well dressed and have enough to eat. He is also one of the few men in the area to take his family on an occasional outing. Before his father's death, when Ahmed's mandatory contribution to his father's family was "only" two and a half pounds a month, both Amira and Umm Ali agreed that he gave much more, although he had protested at first against supporting his father's family. "Ahmed is *haniyyan*" [tender/softhearted], Umm Ali says.

Ahmed's father was nearly seventy when he remarried—a woman only in her forties. Soon the lump-sum pension (from the police where he had worked) was exhausted, but four children had been born. Ahmed was called on to help. He protested, saying that if anyone should help, it ought to be the stepmother's two sons. But his father took the matter to court, and Ahmed was sentenced to pay up. His heart got the better of him, and he paid more than he was actually required to. But it cost him dearly. Sometimes, when his stepmother's daughter dropped by as he was visiting Umm Ali, he burst out, "Don't you dare tell your mother that you've seen me, or she'll come running, whining for money! And I just can't take any more!"

Since 1979, however, life has improved for Ahmed. Aware that he would literally collapse if he continued to try to feed all the mouths he was responsible for on the meager wages he earned in Egypt, he went to work in Libya in 1977. He earned a lot, more than 300 pounds per month (five times what he earned in Egypt from his main and secondary jobs combined). But he was homesick. The tapes he sent gave vivid testimony to that. So Amira said he should just come home. She would rather have him healthy than wealthy. He had been gone for one year by then.

Ahmed came home, put on some weight, and started a new job. Life was easier, he saw light at the end of the tunnel. He had come through the worst of it financially. No longer did he feel he had his back against the wall—labor migration was always a possibility.[1] And though he was dismayed at the women for not buying him his long-desired taxi, he has,

1. By 1982, the cup had again overflowed, and Ahmed was planning to go to work in Kuwait. They were then living, six adults and four children, in thirty square meters. Besides going mad from the ruckus, Ahmed was irate because the crowded conditions made it practically impossible for him to sleep with Amira, and he threatened her constantly with divorce. This was when she started searching for the new flat where they are now living though it meant a down payment of 1,000 pounds and a rent ten times more than for the old flat (which they chose to keep for the children's study since it costs only three pounds per month). Ahmed wanted to go abroad to finance the new rent and the rising expense of the children's education. All the children were then getting private tutoring, and some were in private school because of having failed

as Mustafa says, become resigned to his lot. He has only himself to count on. As Ahmed says, "He who lives, lives, and he who dies, dies—it's all in the hands of Our Father."

Ahmed's visits to his sister Umm Ali are neither regular nor frequent. He may go there once a week or once every two months, depending on how he feels. If he is particularly desperate for moral support in a conflict with Amira, or for peace and quiet because his own home is filled with ear-splitting racket, he goes to Umm Ali. Not that her house is especially peaceful, but everything is relative. Compared with the ruckus his mother-in-law stirs up, Umm Ali's home seems quiet as the grave. Moreover, Umm Ali is nearly always ready to give him the solace and sympathy he craves. Usually, she is full of indignation with Amira for neglecting him and not granting him due respect. But she must be careful about how she phrases her reproach. If she is too severe in her criticism of Amira, she risks stepping on Ahmed's toes. After all, he is the master of the house, he should be able to compel respect. Usually, Ahmed insists that Amira has done nothing wrong, it is all her mother's or her sister's fault. Umm Ali refuses to swallow this, and so they quarrel a bit about it before Ahmed says, *"Xalas!"* [enough] Reluctantly, Umm Ali changes the subject.

Ahmed is just as touchy when Amira criticizes Umm Ali. Then his loyalty is always with his sister.

Umm Ali and Ahmed's relationship is colored by the fact that she was like a mother to him for years, and they are therefore particularly close. But it also bears the mark of gender and age: the relationship between an older sister and younger brother can be very close, whereas when the relationship is reversed, it is marked by respect rather than intimacy, as in Ahmed's relationship with his younger sister, Shaddya. But gender plays a part in other ways as well. As a man, Ahmed is subject to extensive material and moral expectations from his sisters. His relationship to his other two older sisters has suffered much because they often pressed such demands. Umm Ali, however, has rarely done so. Even the few times she has run away from home, she has not sought refuge with Ahmed, but with distant relatives on her mother's side. She does appeal to him for loans from time to time, however, and is sometimes hurt by his reply. The last time I saw her, she swore that she would never again ask Ahmed for help, "Because I got so angry recently when I asked him to help me borrow

---

in public school. So even though Ahmed was earning moderately well—by working until midnight and never taking a day off, he could make 120 pounds per month—he felt he had no other choice but to leave for the Gulf. In the end, however, Amira persuaded him not to because she feared for his health.

fifteen pounds and he declined, saying the people would say, 'But he's poor!' Okay, poor, that's what we are. Is *that* any shame?" She feels she has stretched herself to the utmost to help him time and again, without concern for what people might say, whereas he puts his honor above her.

Most relationships in this milieu suffer from the fact that each party feels that the other has failed in her commitments. The desire for total support and total affection is so strong as to make it virtually impossible for anyone to live up to such expectations. The fact that each person is simultaneously committed to many others means that no one can give full priority to any one person. Not only are material resources short, but love and emotional support are also in short supply if you feel that what a beloved gives to another is given at your expense.

To avoid being disappointed or hurt, Umm Ali tries not to turn to Ahmed for help except if she has no alternative; and then only for non-monetary purposes. Over the years, there have been important occasions when she has called on him as her closest male relative, for example, when she and Mustafa have been on the verge of divorce. Sometimes Ahmed has taken her side, sometimes not. "You are grown-ups and have daughters to marry off! No way I will enter into this!" he said the last time. And she was bitter about that.

When Mustafa opposed the engagement between Mona and Foad (chap. 32), Umm Ali mobilized Ahmed who cornered Mustafa and said, "As the girl's uncle, I now take the matter into my own hands!" To her children, Ahmed is second only to their father in authority. Her daughters complain that he criticizes their dress and hairdos far more than their father does, and that is quite likely. Children's relationship with their father is generally quite formal, whereas they can be much closer with their mother's brother. Thus when her daughters are annoyed because they never get to go to the movies, they sometimes say they will ask their uncle Ahmed to take them—to which Umm Ali retorts, "And what do you think Amira would say!"

Amira stands as a barrier between Umm Ali and Ahmed. Take the following incident which took place after Ahmed returned from Libya in 1979. Umm Ali told this story:

> They didn't even send for me! Can you imagine, they didn't even send for me, his own sister! I sat there and didn't know that he had come. I would have wanted, of course, to go immediately and say, "God bless you that you have arrived safely!" He had been home a full three days before I even knew, and that by pure coincidence. I was on my way to the doctor, when I suddenly ran into Ahmed and Amira and the kids in the street. I almost fainted! They were on their way to Samia, Amira's sister. Ahmed was extremely embarrassed and tried to excuse

himself saying how he'd been so tired after the journey that he didn't manage to come and greet me. He said he'd asked the children to go and tell me he was back, but they were lazy. I was deeply insulted and made it quite clear to him. "And am I not your *sister?*" I said. "No matter how sick and tired I had been—even if my legs had been too weak to hold me, I would have dragged myself over to you to greet you, my own brother! *But,*" I said to Amira, "I bet *you* were afraid that I expected homecoming gifts! But I can tell you, even if you came with a crown upon your head, I would be better than you!" Ahmed tried to excuse Amira, but I was deeply offended and just marched off.

It's all Amira's fault. Do you think *Ahmed* had any desire to visit Samia? Amira drags him with her! In the evening they came to me, straight from Samia. I put a good face on things; I sent the children out to buy Pepsi, and invited them to stay for dinner. But they refused to eat. They just stayed for a moment because Atif [one of the children] kept whining that he was hungry. I said, "But stay and eat with us, we've plenty of food!" But he said he only liked his mother's food. Talk about manners! Her children have no breeding! When I drop by them, they don't even come and greet me! . . .

The next day I went over to Ahmed with two kilos of rice, half a kilo of butter, five bars of soap, and a kilo of sugar as a gift. He was embarrassed and our conversation was awkward. He told me that they had taken a suitcase from him in the customs with goods worth 320 pounds! I said it didn't matter, I didn't expect anything from him, just to sit with him and rejoice that he had returned safe and sound. Then he went and got a few things and apologized again that it was all he had since they had taken this suitcase in the customs. It was two meters of dress material, of poor quality—not like what Ali brought me when he returned from Libya—and a pair of trousers for Anwar that were too tight. I said, "Give them to your daughter!" Mustafa only got a pair of socks. Ahmed excused himself saying he had wanted to bring everyone a gift, but with this suitcase. . . . I gave him two pounds and asked him to buy Anwar a pair of pants the next time he, or any of his friends, traveled to Libya.

He is not a man! Umm Ali complains.

Biymashshi kalamhum humma! [he does as those women say] Remember that time when he promised Farida by his own eyes that he would protect her if they so much as lifted a finger when she moved in with him? And the next day he stood silent as they kicked her out! He is weak, and those women know it. When I was working, Ahmed used to say, just like the people, that I did it just to build on the lot. As if *he* didn't know better! But no wonder, what with those women dinning it into his ears. Now he's telling me to sell the lot and buy a house in a poor area like his wife has done. He's envious, but not so much. I tell him that never in my life will I give up that lot by the Pyramids!

"So what are you gonna do with it?" he asks. "As if *you* can ever afford to build!"

"Then perhaps the children will," I answer. "The land is for them and their future."

He also criticizes me for helping Mustafa by organizing savings clubs. I tell him it's not Mustafa I'm helping, it's the children. Always, it's their interests I have at heart. "But so don't come afterwards and ask for a loan and say you're in debt [*madjuna*] and excused!" [*mazura*] he says. I tell him that if he doesn't have anything good to say, he can just keep quiet. I do nothing wrong as long as I work for the children and their interests. If he doesn't want to help me, he can keep his advice to himself. Myself I always say, if somebody is in trouble, "May God make it easier!" [*Rabbina yisahhil*] When Ahmed is upset, I always try to soothe his nerves. I say things like "*Ma'lesh*" [never mind] or "To-morrow things will be better" [*bukra hiyibqa ahsan*], "Stretch your patience" [*tawwil balak*], "May the Lord help" [*Rabbina yustur*], "The Lord is with you" [*Rabbina mawgod*], "Be patient" [*usbur*], "Perse-vere" [*istahmil*], and so on. Whereas Ahmed, on the contrary, says, "Let the kids fend for themselves!" [*sibil'ayyal yitfillqu*] "Let them go to hell!" [*sibihum fi sittin dihya*] "Let them starve to death!" [*xallihum yimutu min iggu'*]

But that's just because those women bait him!

Twenty-five

Farida: Sister Whom Life Did Not Spare

Because I know Farida through Umm Ali who always calls her sister by her maiden name, it is natural for me to do the same. Actually Umm Ali ought to have said "Umm Nadya" which is what Farida now is called by virtue of her eldest child. But old habits are hard to break. True, Farida has managed it, and calls her sister Zenab by the name of Umm Ali. But there are several reasons for that.

First, Umm Ali steadily functions as if she were the elder of the two. It is she who gives advice and counsel, she who takes charge and protects. Farida often comes to her, whereas she goes rarely to Farida. The two sisters usually meet in Umm Ali's place, and here consideration for Mustafa also enters. Mustafa would surely feel disrespected if Farida did not acknowledge that *her* sister is first and foremost the mother of *his* children.

Though with reference to respect, among the things Umm Ali chides her sister for is that she does *not* show Mustafa the proper respect. For instance, she once sat down to remove the hair from her legs in Umm Ali's bedroom with Mustafa sitting in the front room; he might well have had to go in to get something! Umm Ali was burning with indignation.

Revealing your legs to an unrelated man is the epitome of indecency, almost like asking him to sleep with you.

Umm Ali is often indignant with her sister, and with quite good reason. Telling is the time Farida asked Umm Ali's children to fetch her some fruit from the top of the fridge where Umm Ali kept it to ensure that it was justly shared. Where else could she keep it in a house where there is no other hiding place except under the mattress? But Farida ignored the principle of equity and wolfed the fruit to her heart's content. Surely, she herself would have been enraged by such "unguestlike" behavior.

Umm Ali also criticizes Farida for being two-faced—"she wears one face before you, another behind your back"—and superficial—"she feels things only with her face, not with her heart". That, says Umm Ali, is the reason why Farida looks like the younger of the two though she is actually five years older. Life does not leave its traces on her.

But life has indubitably taken its toll on Farida. She is fairly well endowed by Mother Nature, with white skin, fine facial features, compelling brown eyes, and straight brown hair. Both the light skin and the straight hair are qualities highly appreciated. I can well imagine how Farida once must have been quite lovely looking. Farida also has all her teeth and is in reasonably good health. But her mouth droops, her gaze is stiff, and her stomach and chin protrude.

She looks as if she expects the worst from life. And truly, it has treated her badly.

Farida tries to cover up by layers of makeup and a youthful appearance in hairdo and dress. Her mouth is a glistening red, her cheeks rosy with rouge. She wears her hair loose, like young girls but not married women, who should cover their hair when going out. Umm Ali and her daughters frown with disapproval, saying it's a shame the way she decks herself out, and that she does it only to drive her husband mad with jealousy. She wears her dress a bit too short, and on the tight side.

Farida is fairly thin— contrary to the feminine ideal and much against her will. (That her stomach protrudes is due to a high-calorie, low-protein diet, plus nine deliveries, and a stooping gait.) She laments that it was because she was so thin that her husband took a second wife. "He wanted something solid to hold on to, someone he could sleep with every night!" And she moans with the insight born of regret, "Had I only understood that it was sleep with me he would, all those nights he called to me from the bedroom, 'Whatever are you doing in the kitchen at this time of the night?' Had I only understood in time! And now it's too late."

Poor Farida, she has reason to grieve. After twenty-five years of marriage and six children, her husband urged her to take a holiday one day. Wouldn't she like to visit his relatives in the country? he suggested. Farida was quite overwhelmed. Here he had just bought her a new bed and a new wardrobe, and now this—What a testimony of love! Elated, she took off. On her return a week later, the upsurge of "love" found its explanation: a co-wife was installed in one of Farida's two rooms—the one with the new bed and wardrobe! The "gift" and trip had been a pure cover-up operation!

Farida wept with rage and stormed out of the house with her youngest sons, ten and thirteen, crying, on her heels. She did not even collect her wits enough to grab her clothes—which she was to regret bitterly. Off she fled to Umm Ali's, where she installed herself with her two sons. She was warmly received, naturally. She was given food and drink and bed space and clothes besides moral support and physical protection for ninety consecutive days. Then Mustafa threatened to move to a hotel, and Umm Ali suggested that her sister move instead.

No wonder Mustafa, accommodating as he is, was fed up; Umm Ali was too. The flat which before was cramped, was now bursting at the seams. To sleep, Farida barely managed to squeeze into the bed with Hoda, Mona, Afaf, and Anwar, while her two sons slept under the bed, on the floor. Bedclothes, which were always in short supply, now had to cover three more people. Food, which was often short and triggered bickering among the children, now had to stretch for three more mouths. Clothes had to be shared, for Farida had no more than what she wore, as was also true of her sons. Everything had to be shared: combs, toothbrushes, shoes, and so forth. And though people are used to sharing what little they have, the necessity of doing so for a long time naturally frazzles everyone's nerves.

And Farida is not one to hold back. One day she let down the hem and sleeves of a dress belonging to Hoda and Mona! Umm Ali was so furious, she turned several shades of red. But she could not say a word.

Three months with Farida, even in the best of conditions, can be trying. In her current state, living with her became no less than a debacle. Her husband was bent on having her return to him at any cost. And so should *his* sons! Farida was equally set that no power on earth would bring her back! Moreover, she wanted *her* things—those few items that were hers and only hers: a dress, a nightgown, three pairs of panties, a slip, and a tattered album with photographs. All the other things she had, she owned jointly with someone else, like her eldest daughter. And she wanted her furniture: a bed, a wardrobe, a couch, a primus burner, and three aluminum pots! Granted, she had no legal right to those things, for when she had married her mother's paternal cousin, her mother had said that as proof of their trust they would not write a "list" (*qaima;* see chap. 9, no. 4). It was impossible, her mother said, that there could be problems in a marriage between relatives. Now Farida had to pay the price of that trust. But list or no list, she had decided that the furniture was hers. She would go to court and complain that she had had a list, but her husband had stolen it and burned it. The stage was set for a major showdown.

Not one battle but many, ensued. Almost every day during the first two months there were grisly sometimes violent scenes between Farida, supported by Umm Ali's family, and Farida's oldest son Abdullah, who had been sent by his father to bring his mother and brothers back. One scene in particular appalled me. Abdullah grabbed his youngest brother and held him dangling over the balcony railing, threatening to drop him if Ali didn't surrender his mother and brothers at once. Another time he showed up when Farida and her sons had gone to the Nile to get some fresh air. He sneaked up on his mother, tied her hands, and tried to drag her away by force. A ghastly scene ensued, drawing a large crowd of people. Farida managed to send a message to Umm Ali who came charging over with Ali and Anwar and rescued Farida. Farida let out a howl as she left that if her husband wanted anything from her, he could come to her stepmother's house, for that was where she was heading. (The stepmother's brother was married to the sister of Farida's co-wife, so the stepmother was in a particularly good position to arbitrate.)

Her husband went to the stepmother's, and a new hot scene erupted. As Farida tells the story, she screamed at him, "What d'you want?"

"I want my sons!"

"So take them! What else?"

"I want their clothes!"

"Help yourself! Just come to Umm Ali's house—if you dare—and take them!"

Her husband grabbed hold of his two sons and tried to drag them by force. But the ten-year-old cried so agonizingly that the stepmother admonished him to let the boy stay, "It's useless, he'll just run away!"

That was just what the thirteen-year-old did. The next day he was back at Umm Ali's. Then followed at least five successive rows where he was fetched, escaped, fetched, escaped, and so on, until the father gave up. Umm Ali says their father showed no interest in his sons until he heard that Farida would sue for divorce. Then he got afraid that he might have to pay alimony for them.

As for the clothes, the husband actually came to collect them. But in the meantime, Farida had hidden them. They were her guarantee that she could keep her sons; their father would not be willing to buy them new clothes, she reasoned; that much they were surely not worth to him. She, for her part, could not afford to buy new clothes, so if *she* was to keep her sons. . . . The husband had to leave defeated.

Other pathetic scenes revolved around Farida's clothes. Nadya, her twenty-year-old daughter, was also dispatched by her father to bring her mother to her senses.[1] Instead, it came to serious blows between the two several times, so people had to intervene to tear them apart. I remember these scenes as especially harrowing. "But take it easy, control yourself, isn't she your *daughter!*" people would scream as they tried to prevent Farida from tearing Nadya's eyes out. "And aren't I her *mother?*" half cried, half wept Farida. The battle concerned her clothes, those threadbare few items that were absolutely priceless to her. She insisted that her daughter bring them to her. The daughter made excuses saying they were in the wash, in the ironing, dirty, in the wash. . . . Farida cried that they had stolen her clothes to prevent her from traveling to the country and seeking support from her relatives.[2] They knew that without her good dress she could not go. An especially agonizing scene took place once when the daughter arrived wearing that selfsame dress. Farida attacked her so ferociously, I thought she might have killed her daughter if people had not intervened. Rarely have I experienced the curse of poverty so painfully as at that very moment.

1. It is unusual for children to support their father thus. Umm Ali explained why. The father had "bought" the son's loyalty by bribing authorities to exempt him from the military service. The daughter, too, had a self-interest in supporting her father: she was getting married and needed money for her trousseau.

2. Because they were related to both her and her husband, they were in a good position to arbitrate.

The effect was the same one day when the daughter arrived, and her youngest brother, who was an apprentice in a beauty shop, discovered that she had two of *his* bobby pins in her hair. They nearly tore each other apart. A fight to the bone over two ordinary bobby pins of the simplest type, the kind we throw about like bread crumbs! The incident sent a shiver down my spine.

Throughout the entire situation, it was clear where Umm Ali's loyalty lay. Farida had her full support. Had her husband placed his wives in separate flats, she reasoned, then Farida could have gone back to him. But in the same flat! Impossible! Even his father must understand, she lectured Abdullah, Farida's son (who was steadily there as his father's envoy), how heartbreaking it was for a woman to *see* her husband go into the other room to sleep with the other woman! The poor son could not say much one way or the other. Umm Ali also said that it was not a genuine catastrophe for a woman to have a co-wife. Actually, she wouldn't mind it herself, it might even make life easier because the man would have *two* women on whom to vent his bad moods and sexual urges. But before she would ever consider consenting to such a scheme, her husband would have to promise to provide enough food and clothing for her and the children. Farida's husband, on the other hand, was so stingy that he kept an eagle eye on every penny they spent. He earned good wages, fifty-four pounds per month, while he begrudged her the food. What's more, he was a terrible gossip, worse than any woman! I couldn't believe how he sat around at the café, filling people's ears . . . ! The men themselves had told it!

Farida's husband provided Umm Ali and Farida with a common target for their disdain. For if Umm Ali disliked Farida, she detested her husband. Her antipathy dated all the way back to the time when the two sisters, each with husband and child, had shared a flat. The children bickered constantly, and the upshot was that Umm Ali drew the shortest straw and moved out. Umm Ali says that Farida kept accusing Ali, who was just over a year old, of hitting and pestering her little Abdullah, who was four months younger. Farida held that Ali ought to have known better, since he was older. She also insinuated that Umm Ali had pilfered food from her, and once her husband came right out and accused Umm Ali of having stolen money from him! "But then," Umm Ali recalls, "I smacked him right in the face! I'm not afraid of *anybody* when I'm really angry!" Farida's husband also fretted and growled that Umm Ali left Farida alone in the same room with Mustafa. "He is morbidly jealous and suspicious," Umm Ali says. And he served Umm Ali's father stories about a love tempest brewing between Umm Ali's youngest sister, Shaddya, and Mustafa; so

Shaddya, who had been living with Umm Ali, was forced to move in with her father and stepmother.

Now Farida claims that it was her husband's fault that she quarreled so at the time. He urged her on, saying, "Just drive Umm Ali mad so she'll move and we'll have the flat to ourselves!" It was also her husband, Farida says, who urged her to convince her father to remarry. Umm Ali has never forgiven Farida for that.

But despite all her sympathy, the cup had overflowed. Mustafa and Umm Ali were both fed up.

At this point, Ahmed realized it was time he paid his dues in this family drama; and he suggested that Farida move in with him. Farida hesitated. She gets along even worse with Amira than Umm Ali does, and Umm Ali strongly opposed the move. But Ahmed swore that he would treat Farida like a queen and give Amira a good beating if she ever so much as foisted herself on or bothered Farida. Three days later he stood silently by and watched his wife throw Farida out!

There are different versions of the history of this dismal scene. Farida claims that she had just hinted, as a mere joke, that Amira would surely have preferred to have Ahmed to herself, but that Amira and her mother flew into a rage and said that *their* family was not as selfish as hers! Amira's version was that Farida had started slinging mud at her family by saying how her own family never made such a racket as they did because *her* family had breeding! Both versions sound equally plausible. Farida can't stand Amira, nor is she at all diplomatic. If it is also true, as Farida claims, that once as they sat down to eat, Mohammed (Amira's eldest son) said, *"Mataklish illa ta'miyya!"* [you can only have *ta'miyya* (the cheapest food)] then it's no wonder she cracked up on the third day. Farida was also insulted that when Amira had her photo taken during that time, she wouldn't even give a copy to Farida! I can't even imagine what Farida would do with a picture of a woman she cannot stand, but that is beside the point. Amira had refused to give her one, and that is an insult.

Sputtering like a boiling kettle, Farida reappeared at Umm Ali's. Umm Ali chided her for not heeding her advice and keeping away from Amira. "Ahmed is no man, you know that!" she said. But Farida swooped down on everyone who dropped by Umm Ali's during the next few days—and there were many, as news of the exodus had spread far and wide—with fuming accusations about the way Amira manipulated Ahmed.

Now Umm Ali herself had had her fill. She was so exasperated that she actually took Amira's side and expressed sympathy with her. Farida must realize herself, she said, that it is natural for a woman to react as Amira did; all women like to have the husband to themselves and not share the things he gives with anyone. If there were enough food and clothes, things would have been different. She herself had been distressed, she reminded Farida, that time when Mustafa's sister moved in with them, and in the end she had asked her to move.

Farida had no choice but to move out. Umm Ali helped her find a room, and Ahmed paid the rent. Umm Ali loaned Farida a bed and a mattress and a small wardrobe. Ahmed loaned her a pillow, a blanket, and a sheet. The room was in a basement, dank, cold, and dark. But at least it was her own. Her two youngest sons moved in with her.

For Umm Ali's family the arrangement meant that three of the daughters must sleep on the floor for a year until the court helped Farida get her own furniture. However this disadvantage paled compared with the relief they all felt at getting rid of Farida.

Well, "getting rid of" is an overstatement. Farida kept coming daily to Umm Ali until the relationship between the sisters fell apart and they became enemies.

It was in 1975. Farida had brought five kilos of *sholek* [sweets] from her husband's relatives in the country to sell for a profit. She offered Umm Ali two kilos for ninety piaster. Umm Ali told Farida that she had just bought two kilos from a friend for less (seventy piaster). "How can you who are my sister charge more?" Farida said, "*Ma'lesh*" [never mind], she had bought them at a higher price and was only making five piaster per kilo profit on the deal. Umm Ali was appalled and said it was a disgrace to make a profit from a relative. If she couldn't have the two kilos for the seventy piaster she was offering, she did not want them. Farida then took the sweets to Ahmed and offered him two kilos. He was willing to pay her asking price of ninety piaster. Farida told him that Umm Ali was also taking two kilos and asked him to deliver them to her. Umm Ali accepted the *sholek*, thinking she was getting them at the seventy-piaster price she had proposed. At that time, Farida was a member of a savings club Umm Ali ran. When she did not show up when it was time to pay her dues, Umm Ali went to Ahmed and asked him to pay *her* the ninety piaster he owed Farida for the *sholek*. Then, adding the seventy piaster she herself had agreed to pay for the sweets, she sent a message with the children to her sister, saying Farida now owed her a balance on her savings club dues of one pound and seventy piaster, an amount arrived at by deducting the money Umm Ali and Ahmed would have paid Farida for the sweets. Farida raised hell. She accused Umm Ali of having manipulated Ahmed and stolen money from her. The upshot was a whopping row about what they really *had* agreed on and Farida got in the last insult when she sent the children around with one pound fifty piaster (instead of one pound seventy piaster). After that, Umm Ali cut off relations with Farida.

Not that this was the first time the sisters had quarreled. Their relationship had always been stormy, and they had never really been friends. The reason, Umm Ali says, is that Farida was always jealous of her and never wished her well. But the cup was now full. Umm Ali would *not* be reconciled.

When Umm Ali was in the hospital in 1978 to give birth to her last child, Farida managed to insult her once more. Her daughter, Nadya, was getting married and Farida went to Umm Ali's children and invited them to the wedding. They declined on the grounds that their mother was ill. "*Ma'lesh*," said Farida, "just come over and have a *little* fun!" Umm Ali was outraged when she heard about it. "It just proves how self-serving she is! Imagine, enticing my children to have fun when their mother is so sick she thinks she's going to die!"

A further story illustrates how deep-seated their enmity was. One day when I knocked on Umm Ali's door, Mona answered saying, "Mama is over at Umm Gamal's [neighbor across the hall]. Sit down and I'll go and get her." She knocked on Umm Gamal's door; no reply; she knocked harder; still no reply; she pounded on the door; still no answer. "How strange," said Mona, "I'm sure Mama's there." Then she said that her mother had marched out half an hour before under the nose of Farida who had come to patch things up.

An hour later Umm Ali came. "I *thought* you must have come by now," she said to me. She also said she had heard the pounding on the door but feared to answer thinking it might be Farida. And she continued,

I was lying asleep in bed, when someone shook me awake. I startled and looked straight into Farida's face! She said "My children told me you were sick, and so I came to wish you well!"

I gazed straight into the blanket.

"How are things going with Afaf?" she inquired.

"*Ilhamd'lillah!*" [Thanks be the Lord] I said. I didn't look up or move a muscle!

"And how is everything with Ali?"

"*Ilhamd'lillah!*" I kept staring blankly. Then I got up and marched out right under her nose! [Umm Ali beams at the thought.] As if *I* want to patch up things with her!

And Umm Ali goes off on another tirade about Farida's atrocities and her wholly obnoxious personality.

One thing is certain, marching out under the nose of a person who has taken the initiative for reconciliation is a devastating insult.

In a nutshell, this is the rest of Farida's story. She sued for a divorce and custody of the two youngest sons. She also claimed alimony for one year and the furniture she didn't have a list for ("because her husband had stolen it and burned it"). After many trials and tribulations and large legal fees (which Ahmed had to cover), she finally got her divorce and alimony for one year: three pounds a month. She did not get her two sons or the furniture. But the sons kept escaping to their mother until the father tired of fetching them home and let them live with her. The boys took any job they could find and supported their mother. Four years later, Farida even returned the things she had borrowed from Umm Ali and Ahmed.

The sisters got back on speaking terms in 1982. Umm Ali was hospitalized for diabetes and Farida came to wish her well. To turn her back on such a gesture would have been utterly disgraceful.

Twenty-six

Umm Magdi and the Friendship That Broke Up

Umm Ali and Umm Magdi met on a summer's day, twenty-five years ago, as each was sitting in the doctor's office, a restless child in her lap, trying to pass the long hours of waiting. They lived only fifteen minutes' walk away from each other but had never seen each other before. For though they frequented the same main street and market for their shopping and so forth, so did some five thousand other people.

The meeting marked the beginning of a friendship that was to develop into a very close, stable relationship that lasted for twenty years, interrupted only by two brief periods when they were not on speaking terms. It is extremely rare for friendships in the area to last so long and be so stable, and Umm Ali had every reason to be proud. She set great store by her friendship with Umm Magdi and often talked about what uncommonly good friends they were. She used to say that Umm Magdi was the only person, apart from her sister Shadyya and her (Coptic) neighbor, Umm Gamal, who truly wished her well.

Umm Magdi was a heavyset woman, even by local standards. Rolls of flesh peeked out in every direction. She did not have a double chin—it

Umm Ali's new best friend.

was triple or quadruple. The word that comes to mind when I attempt to describe her manner and way of walking is that she waddled. Her voice was high and shrill, her behavior and expressions crude. I never could really understand what Umm Ali saw in her. She did not have the warmth and humor of so many neighborhood women, or their insight, intuition and wit. Umm Magdi appeared to me, I have to admit, rather sluggish and dull.

Now I have to say that Umm Ali never praised Umm Magdi for her lucidity or breadth of vision. On the contrary, she often remarked how Umm Magdi was older than she and therefore ought to have known better, and yet it was always Umm Ali who handed out guidance and advice.

Why, I wondered, would a person of Umm Ali's caliber choose a friend like Umm Magdi? The answer is perhaps that she never actually chose, but she knew how to appreciate what she got. Friendships among the people do not grow on trees. They must be carefully tended and cultivated and are the object of endless complications and encroachments by "the people." Umm Magdi admired Umm Ali and offered to be her friend; and that is a gift so precious that few women would reject it on the basis of some paltry requirements regarding special personality traits.

One demand is made, however, and it is unconditional. It was expressed every time Umm Ali said, "Umm Magdi loves me and I love her." A friend is someone who loves you, and that is the evidence that she is of the noblest breed. Quality is always judged as kindness or affection for oneself.

Umm Ali had undeniable proof of Umm Magdi's love for her. First, Umm Magdi visited her regularly, every other day or so, and only people who really love you do that. Moreover, she was always willing to come up with a loan when Umm Ali was in need, like that time when Umm Ali had given birth and Umm Magdi brought her a chicken. Also, Umm Magdi showed Umm Ali complete and rare trust by never refusing to eat at her place. Umm Ali told me, "Whenever Umm Magdi comes to me after vis-iting her *sister,* she says, 'I'm so hungry, please give me a little something to eat!'" It is difficult to appreciate what a declaration of trust this is unless one has lived in the area. Women generally refuse point blank to eat in each others' homes for fear that the hostess might go around afterward and say, "Imagine, she was so greedy that she ate the food from my own children!" or, "Imagine, she was starving 'cause she had no money for food, and so she came here and ate up mine!" So deep-seated is this suspicion that even good friends rarely eat at each other's place. Umm Magdi, on the other hand, showed Umm Ali a degree of trust she did not even show her own sister. And as Umm Ali often said, "I love anyone who eats at my place."

Umm Magdi was married, but I have never seen her husband. They had eight children. Umm Ali tells me how he used to come to her sometimes when he had fought with Umm Magdi and needed help making up. The root of their quarrel was usually that Umm Magdi refused to sleep with him. "But then I told her," Umm Ali says, "'He's your husband. You have to sleep with him. It is written by our Prophet!' And when Umm Magdi quarreled with her daughter Laila, who is bold and disobedient, I always said to her, '*Ma'lesh!* Don't take it so hard, she's your daughter. And be grateful for your other daughter Soher, who is gentle and kind.'"

In the fall of 1975, when the friendship was on the wane, Umm Ali said with an air of self-satisfaction, "Now Umm Magdi has no one to solve her tangles, and I've heard that she's always quarreling with her husband and daughter."

That was a year and a half before things really began to go wrong—or at least openly wrong between the friends. Personally, I think the root of the conflict goes farther back, two to three years in time. Umm Ali herself never said so, but then the incident I have in mind was of such a nature that she couldn't very well admit that she had been insulted. But she recounted the story in painstaking detail time and again. Umm Magdi had not committed any clear and obvious mistake, as in the more recent incidents that Umm Ali gave as the real reason for their breakup. But these later incidents were so minor that they would not have brought the friendship to an end, had the parties themselves not wanted to break off.

Umm Ali complained, "Umm Magdi has changed and so have my feelings for her. She used to visit me all the time, but now she hardly ever drops by. She says she's sick and doesn't have the energy. [Umm Magdi had developed diabetes.] But I don't believe it. People say they're always seeing her on the street." And Umm Ali felt she had ample reason to believe that Umm Magdi had really changed. She confided the following to me:

The two friends had both wanted a butane stove for a long time, and they each joined a savings club for the purpose. Together, they went to buy the stoves in a distant part of town from a shopkeeper who was reputed to have the lowest prices. But the shopkeeper had no *amboba* [tank] for the stove. So they agreed that he would send a message to them when he got the merchandise, which he did. Umm Magdi went and got hers. She did not pass the message on to Umm Ali. She said later that she was sorry, blaming it on being tired and weak. "But that's no excuse," Umm Ali said. "When Umm Magdi needed something, I always used to offer to go with her, no matter how tired or poorly I was; and if she didn't have money, I said it was no problem, and took and lent her; and if I didn't have any money myself, I didn't mind selling things to help her—like my golden bracelet. . . ."

Not long after, there was a story about cotton filling for blankets and pillows.[1] The two friends were once again going across the town to buy. They had thought the cotton would cost twelve pounds, but it turned out to have gone up to fifteen pounds. So there they were, several hours' bus ride from home, lacking three pounds each. They asked the shopkeeper for credit, but he would not give it.[2] He said either they could come back with the rest of the money within ten days or he would sell the cotton. Once again, Umm Magdi went by herself, not notifying Umm Ali. "And that though *she* owed *me* money!" Umm Ali says indignantly.

Then there was a story about Umm Magdi's sick son, who was down with influenza and diarrhea. Umm Ali tells how she twice sent Mona and Hoda to call on him, once with bananas, and once with some money. In

1. When Umm Ali tells this story, she typically refers to all the blankets and pillows in the house and calculates what each one has cost in filling and covers.

2. This was unusual; shopkeepers usually give credit even to customers they do not know who live at the other end of the city, if the husband has formal employment. In that case, the guarantee lies in the fact that employees receive their salaries on the first day of the month, so the creditor can just show up at the place of work if the debtor does not honor his obligations.

other words, she fulfilled her obligation in an irreproachable manner. But Umm Magdi got angry because Umm Ali herself did not come. Umm Ali apologized and blamed her illness. "I can't manage to climb all those stairs at your house [Umm Magdi lived on the fourth floor]. You know how I run out of breath just climbing the one stairway in my house."

"But you always used to come before!"

"But that was before Amin died and the diabetes got me."

"But," said Umm Ali to me, "even when our friendship was blooming, it was usually Umm Magdi who came to visit *me*. Now she never comes, either because she's angry or because she has loads of problems in her family."

Then there was a more serious confrontation, which wove itself into Umm Ali's car nightmare. When Umm Ali organized a savings club to put money away for the car, Umm Magdi joined as one member. They agreed that she would withdraw her savings in the eighth month. But Umm Magdi came after the first month and asked to have her money in the third month. Umm Ali said it was impossible. Umm Magdi knew that she had promised that month to her brother-in-law, but Umm Magdi insisted, for she had suddenly got it into her head that her son should marry his fiancée immediately. Umm Ali pleaded with Umm Magdi to be patient; she knew full well her own desperate situation. But Umm Magdi would not budge. Either she would receive her bonus in the third month, or she wanted her installment back.

Umm Ali had to swallow her pride and go out and borrow money to pay Umm Magdi her fifteen pounds. "And even then Umm Magdi was angry. Though it was me who had *reason* to be angry! That time when Umm Magdi came crying to me because that woman had switched the order of payment in the savings club Umm Magdi had joined, I said to her right away, 'Don't cry, I'll help you. Look, I've got two golden brace-lets. . . .'"

And this was how the story of the golden bracelet came to light.

Umm Magdi, who was a pious woman, had long nurtured a dream to make a pilgrimage to Mecca. But she needed 100 pounds. So she joined a savings club, and simultaneously registered her name on a list of applicants to whom the government allotted turns. She was told that she could make the trip in eight months, and she agreed with the leader of the savings club that she would withdraw her money on the first day of the eighth month. September came with permission from the government, but no money. The woman had broken the agreement. Umm Magdi raised a big ruckus and finally got fifty-five pounds, but not more. That was when she came crying to Umm Ali and Umm Ali consoled her, "Don't cry, look here, I've got two golden bracelets. . . ." Umm Magdi refused to accept them both, but agreed to take one. So Umm Ali sold the bracelet for its weight in gold, sixteen and a half pounds. And Umm Magdi could—barely—travel to Mecca.

Umm Ali's heart must have been heavy when she took the momentous step of selling her bracelet. The bracelets were her insurance against crises and emergencies. She originally had four bracelets, but then Ali needed money for a fine, and she gave him one; and Amin needed clothes for school, and he got one. That left just two bracelets. Umm Ali treasured them. She never wore them but kept them hidden so none of the relatives would know about them. Not that she ever *wanted* to hide anything from them, she explained, but if any of her siblings knew about the bracelets, they would come running asking to have them as soon as they were in difficulties. It was therefore an unequivocal declaration of love Umm Ali gave Umm Magdi when she offered her the bracelets.

What the two friends could not envision was that the price of gold would shoot up rapidly soon afterward. Umm Magdi owed Umm Ali sixteen and a half pounds or a golden bracelet. The problem was that the two were no longer commensurate. Both friends agreed that it was the object rather than the money that should be replaced, and Umm Magdi chose to wait for the price of gold to decline. Instead it continued to rise. Finally, Umm Magdi gave Umm Ali twenty-five pounds and said that she would pay the rest so that Umm Ali could buy herself a bracelet as soon as she got hold of some more money. But when she *did*, she bought herself both a *butagaz* and cotton fillings instead of paying off her debt to Umm Ali.

In 1979, Umm Ali complained that a golden bracelet now cost fifty-five pounds, and that Umm Magdi *had* promised to pay her more as soon as she could afford to. A year later I think Umm Ali had given up all hope of ever getting more money. By then Umm Magdi had moved to a house by the Pyramids that she had built using her savings. Umm Magdi had managed to realize Umm Ali's lifelong dream of a house of her own at a cost far in excess of the price of a golden bracelet.

And here we are at the core of the problem, I think. The bracelet was the wedge that drove the two friends apart. This was something they simply could not handle. As the price of gold skyrocketed, Umm Magdi must have felt defensive and thought that when she had paid twenty-five pounds, she had more than cleared her debt. After all, *she* could not be blamed for the rising prices, she who had not even asked to have the bracelet, it was all Umm Ali's initiative. Umm Ali, on her part, probably felt a sting of conscience that she had accepted twenty-five pounds instead of just the sixteen and a half that she herself had given. She kept waiting for the price of gold to decline so she could buy herself a new bracelet and return the difference to Umm Magdi. The story of the bracelet must have become so painful for them both that it colored all their contacts, especially from September 1974 to April 1976 when Umm Ali was desperately in need of money due to the car affair. It is not unreasonable to think that Umm Magdi may have been looking for an excuse to break up. Was that perhaps why she went alone to buy the gas tank and the cotton filling? Or did she feel insulted when Umm Ali sent her daughters in her own place to visit Umm Magdi's son when he was sick—something she would never have done had the friendship been flourishing. But as a rationalization to break off the relationship, the incident came in handy. Umm Magdi would receive the community's support that she *had* reason to be offended.

Thus it happened that a precious friendship fell apart. As in a numerous other wrecked relations, the root cause was money—or its lack. Just how painful the break really was, is revealed by the following story:

One day in September 1979, Umm Ali asked Umm Fathi, a new neighbor who was fast becoming a new friend, to accompany her to the co-op to help her carry her groceries. There was quite a crowd waiting in front of the door at the store, and suddenly Umm Ali felt someone strike her back hard and scream, "Oh yeah, is the *sick* woman out and about! And you who couldn't walk a step!" It was Umm Magdi. With her hands on her hips and head tossed back she cornered Umm Ali, her face burning with disdain. Umm Ali almost fainted, so Umm Fathi had to support her. Umm Magdi continued her harangue, causing a great deal of commotion, while Umm Fathi supported Umm Ali so she would not collapse.

That was the last time Umm Ali ever saw Umm Magdi, "And even if she came here and tried to make amends, I would refuse, because there is no love left. The love is gone."

But the broken friendship still hurts today. Umm Ali still talks a lot about Umm Magdi and the bracelet. In the autumn of 1981, she sadly noted that the price of gold had broken every record. One gram now cost twelve pounds, compared with one pound and seventy piasters when she bought the bracelet. The bracelet weighed thirteen grams. She has not made the big calculation and figured out how much it would cost to replace the bracelet today. But I have. It would be one hundred sixty-six pounds and forty piasters—more than four times Mustafa's monthly wage with the government.

Some Who Were Not Mentioned

Ahmed and Amira, Farida and Umm Magdi—those are the four who figured most prominently in Umm Ali's life over the years 1969–82, next to her own husband and children. Until she died, in 1972, her sister Shaddya also had a special place in her heart, but she lived more than an hour away by (jammed) bus, so they did not see each other much, just once a month or so.

But Umm Ali's circle of acquaintances is large. It comprises many relatives, neighbors (though nowhere near all the people who live in the lane), and acquaintances' acquaintances, besides the children's friends and enemies. Many are those who, over the years, have been in and out of her house, many more in number than she has visited. Partly it is because she has been sick and somewhat immobile. But more important, she is known as someone who understands about life. When they have problems, many people seek her out for advice, whereas she relies more on her own judgment. In addition, she almost always has a savings club or two running.[1] The members bring their deposits to her and use the occasion to sit down and talk.

To say that Ahmed and Amira, Umm Magdi and Farida have been most important to her, means that Umm Ali talked about them the most, not that she saw them often. Amira, for instance, she used to see just a couple of times a year, yet she is intensely preoccupied with her. And years after her friendship with Umm Magdi broke up, Umm Ali continued to talk about her a lot. She seemed more important than any current friend.

But others have mattered too, first and foremost her father, the father's wife, her sister Feyza, and her sister Khadiga's children to whom Umm Ali was a foster parent after their mother died. But generally speaking, her relationship with her kin is a sad chapter—for Umm Ali as for so many others. The notion is widely shared that "relatives never love one another"—a stark exaggeration that is more revealing of the discrepancy between people's expectations and their experience than of the facts.

For the last fifteen years of his life, Umm Ali's father lived only ten minutes' walk away from her. She used to visit him once a month, whereas

---

1. This refers to the time before Umm Ali lost her sight.

A neighbor of Umm Ali's who is reputed to have ended her life the same way as Amin did, by setting fire to herself.

he never came to her house except to arbitrate in a marital conflict. Umm Ali could never forgive him for remarrying after her mother's death. She felt that at his age, he could have managed without sex, "for that was of course why he married her! His wife used to come to me and complain that he always wanted to sleep with her. But then I told her, 'And what d'you think, that he should *first* pay bride-price for you and *then* pay another to sleep with him? Do your duty!'"

Umm Ali blames her sisters Feyza and Farida for persuading their father to remarry. "They used to tell him, 'You're still young, you need a wife!' just because they didn't want him being a burden on *them. I* would have been happy to have him with me the rest of his life."

When her father was alive, Umm Ali's stepmother used to come and visit her about once every fortnight, "and then only for her self-interest:

to borrow money, or sell something, or to ask me to arbitrate a conflict." The relationship between the two improved considerably after her father's death. Umm Ali must admire her stepmother for the way she struggled to provide for her four children—Umm Ali's own sisters and brothers. And when one of the children died suddenly and inexplicably, Umm Ali grieved deeply with his mother. Now the two are friends, and Umm Ali often stresses how the stepmother loves her. She visits Umm Ali about once a week, as do only those who really love you. In conflicts (with Mustafa, Ahmed, and others), Umm Ali often uses her stepmother as mediator.

Umm Ali's relationship with her other relatives is poor. Her eldest sister, Feyza, lived only a ten minutes' walk away (until her death in 1990), yet I have never even seen her. Umm Ali never visited her, and Feyza came to her only very rarely "and then only to borrow money!" The relationship between the two suffered irreparably when Feyza's daughter broke an agreement to marry Ali. In addition, Umm Ali suspects Feyza of having stolen five pounds from Hoda once.

Among her other close relatives, her sister Khadiga's two children have been important to her, but in a sad way. Their mother died at the age of twenty after falling from the balcony while hanging out wash to dry. Umm Ali took care of the children and breast-fed the youngest. They have shown themselves most ungrateful. Sami, the boy, refuses to lend her money when she is in need, though he is a government employee. Samira, the girl, agreed to marry Ali, but then went ahead and became engaged to another! Since then, Umm Ali's family has not been on speaking terms with her.

In the alley where Umm Ali lives, there are eighteen houses and approximately 200 persons, all told. The lane is just about 125 meters long, and from her balcony she has a view of most of her neighbors. She is on greeting terms with perhaps thirty people, and on talking terms with perhaps ten.[2] The others do not concern her. Only in the event of a death does neighborliness become an obligation involving clear-cut duties, for example, everyone should sweep in front of their homes for three days in a row, and people should offer their condolences. But when Amin died, there were people in her own house—the landlord's family—who did not do so. People live in such cramped conditions and are so mercilessly exposed to one another that they try to keep their distance. So Umm Ali's world—like that of most other women—is surprisingly small. The view

2. When Mona married in 1982, Umm Ali invited just two of the neighbor families to the wedding.

from afar is that women in Cairo's back streets are intensely social and companionable. In fact, they know they must set their limits. As they say themselves, "Nothing but problems come from involving yourself with the people."

Twenty-eight

Houseguests Holding Their Ground

Her sister Farida is not the only one who has lodged with Umm Ali. There have been numerous others over the years. Umm Ali does not remember exactly how many there have been. But she remembers those who remained for long—with or without her blessing. Lodgers who have inspired the fondest memories include her brother Ahmed, her sister Shadyya, her father, Mustafa's old aunt, and several friends of hers who sought refuge with her until the husband, subdued, begged them to return. There have been dozens through the years; for a woman's home is always open to her friends, relatives, and daughters' friends. They can pound on the door and request shelter at any time of the day or night. Sleeping space is never a problem—unless it is someone you really do *not* want to house. I have counted up to nine persons in a (narrow) double bed. If necessary, someone sleeps on the bare floor with just a bundled *gallabiyya* under the head. But this is a solution everyone deplores in the winter when the cement floor is ice cold and damp.

The house is the woman's domain, and so *her* friends and acquaintances have easy access. The man has little to say in that respect. He can thunder his screams of protest, as Ahmed did. So long as his wife's concern for the guests does not lead her to neglect her husband, she has command of the house as she wishes.

"Free" may be an exaggeration, however. The duty of hospitality is so compelling that the hostess may, in fact, have little choice. Thus when Nefeesa, Ali's fiancée, let herself be persuaded by his sisters to stay the night (they were friends), Umm Ali and Mustafa were furious. To think what the people would say if they knew that an engaged couple slept in the same house! But they could not ask her to leave. The problem was only solved when the girl's mother came charging in herself to fetch her.

Men, on the other hand, cannot bring friends home with them to stay the night. Considerations of decency and modesty preclude such a move. It would be unheard of to let a man sleep in a room with females who were not related to him. And as cramped as quarters are, that would be hard to avoid. Therefore, if a man has quarreled with his wife and needs refuge, he must go to a female relative.

The man's close relatives, on the other hand, can come and go as they will—welcome or not. Blood ties entail, as we have seen, extensive moral and material obligations. Throughout her life, a woman has a right to be provided for by men, and when in need, she can call on a father, son, brother, father's brother, or more distant male relative. When women often choose nevertheless to appeal to a sister or friend, it is because the man is usually not master of his home—as we saw with Ahmed. And for his wife, it is naturally more satisfying to be generous by virtue of her good heart than by the force of her husband's kinship obligations.

Umm Ali has suffered the yoke of kinship several times. Among the houseguests she remembers without any joy are her sister Farida, Mustafa's foster sister Karima, and his sister Amina. Countless times I have heard her tell the story of how Amina came charging to them with her two teenage daughters after her son had sold the furniture and everything they owned to get money to spend on his upper-class friends. "He mixes with rich boys. It's terribly wrong, for then he will always feel inferior. Relations between people must be based on reciprocity: the poor with the poor, and the rich with the rich. Anything else just breeds discontent."

Umm Ali felt sympathy with Amina, but she had never been close to her. She says it was because Amina did not love her. But joint living for five months was bound to frazzle everyone's nerves. Now, Mustafa was not Amina's only hope of rescue; she had another close kinsman, a half brother, and with winter drawing close, Umm Ali hinted that she could move to him. He had plenty of room. And it was only when Amina made no sign to move, that she got Amin, then twelve, to tell her, "Dear auntie, when you and your daughters are here, I and my brothers and sisters must sleep on the floor. Soon winter is coming, and it will be icy cold. Please auntie, for my sake, be so kind and move." Amina stormed out the door with her daughters on her heels. A tiny bundle of clothes was all they had to take with them, their sole possessions.

That was the last time Umm Ali saw her sister-in-law before she died, six years later. When Amina came to see Mustafa, she used to go to his workshop.

Time is a marvelous healer, however. Umm Ali often expresses regret that the family has no relatives from Mustafa's side. When the husband of one of Amina's daughters turned up eight years later with greetings from the family abroad, he was showered with hospitality. Umm Ali slaughtered all her pigeons except a breeding pair, eight in all, and gave him the best the family could afford. At last, someone from Mustafa's family!

Among her truly bad memories of houseguests is this story.

One day in the spring of 1978 Mustafa came home with a boy Anwar's age, twelve years, and asked to have him stay with them. The boy was greatly to be pitied, Mustafa said, for he had neither mother nor father and had run away from his father's brother's wife who let him starve and stole his earnings. The boy had come to Mustafa's workshop, asking for work. Umm Ali was hesitant. She did not like the looks of the boy. And even if he was thin, he did not look like someone who had starved. But Mustafa begged for him, and so she gave in.

She cared well for the boy. He was given exactly the same food to eat as her own children. After a while, he asked Hoda to write a letter for him to his mother in Aswan. So he was not an orphan, after all! His mother sent a reply saying his brother was ill and his sister divorced—"Send money!" "As if *he* had anything to send!" Umm Ali quipped. "It was his mother who made him a thief!" When Mustafa asked the boy what his mother had written, he said, "Just 'How are you' and such things!" But they knew it was a lie, for one day when Umm Ali was washing his trousers, she found the letter in his pocket and read it.

The boy stayed with them for a few months and learned their habits. But he could not do anything wrong, for there was always someone at home during the day to keep a watchful eye out, and Umm Ali hardly ever slept at night. But then there was a night when she fell asleep nevertheless. Suddenly she was awakened by a slam. She thought it must be Afaf closing the door of the toilet, and went to look. The front door was wide open! She let out a scream, for she was sure she had closed the door after they all went to bed. "Ali!", she screamed, "go and see if the boy's still here!" He was gone.

"Ali, did you have any money in your pockets?"

"Yes, twelve pounds from the taxi fares!"

He checked his pockets; the money was gone. She ran to Mustafa and shook him awake. "You have brought us a thief!" They searched the flat. Anwar's only pair of pants was gone and his pajamas too (Umm Ali laments again and again the heartlessness of taking his only pair), though they were soaking wet; they had been hanging on the clothesline to dry. The radio was gone and a school bag. Mustafa and Ali charged off on the motorbike in search of the boy. They searched the whole neighborhood, in vain. Then they went to the main train station—and there, through a compartment window, they saw him. They stormed in, but he had seen them and thrown himself out of the window. They ran after him in a frantic search, but he had managed to disappear in the crowds. Somebody yelled that the boy had left a bag in the compartment; it was a new bag, not their own, but inside they found Anwar's pants with eight pounds in the pocket and his pajamas. The boy must have bought the bag with the four missing pounds. They took the things and went home, distraught. Ali cried that the taxi owner would think *he* was a thief when he did not show up the next day with the full twelve pounds the taximeter showed he had earned. His father tried to console him saying, "*Ma'lesh,* your mother will help you to borrow the four pounds!" Umm Ali exploded, "Don't fool yourself! *You* brought us the thief, now *you* go get the money!" But in the end she did help.

One day as Ali was driving the taxi, he suddenly caught sight of the boy. He jumped out of the car and caught him and brought him to his father's workshop. They beat him until blood flowed from his nose and mouth. "Just as he deserved," Umm Ali says. She was summoned and told Ali, "Bring him to the police!" But Mustafa pleaded for the boy, "Pity on him, he's just a child, it is his mother who's to blame for not raising him well!" Umm Ali protested that if they let the boy go, he might steal from others as he had from them. But Mustafa still pleaded. And the boy insisted that he had stolen *ghasb 'annu* [despite himself]. At last Ali was compelled to let him go, but not until he had given him another harsh beating.

A couple of weeks later Hoda came home with a girl. Umm Ali told the following story:

Hoda said she had met her at the bus stop and introduced her as "my friend." She said that the girl would spend the night with us, for she had run away from her husband who had beaten her, and had no place to go. I didn't like the looks of the girl. She was shabbily dressed and looked dishonest. Who could know if she was not a thief who might pick us clean while we slept. I felt convinced that this girl, trouble trailed in her wake. So I refused to let her stay. Hoda was furious. "But I can vouch for her. She's my friend!" she screamed. "How can you say that about someone you've just met in the street?" I queried. "I wouldn't mind if we knew her family; then I would have embraced her and asked her to remain with us for as long as she liked as one of our family. But a stranger from the street!" Hoda protested that she could not possibly ask the girl to leave now that she had brought her home. I suggested that she might say something like, "Mama has two (teenage) daughters who are still virgins, and our brother must sleep in the room with us to guard our honor. She won't let you sleep in the bed with us. Just think if you moved in your sleep so your bottom showed!" But Hoda was adamant and accused me of lack of compassion and of wanting to throw her friend into the street. I made ready to go to the doctor and warned her to get the girl out by the time I came home.

Instead I found the girl dressed in my daughters' clothes and sandals while they were washing her clothes! I almost went mad. I grabbed my clothes and stormed out without a word. Two boys who were visiting us and Hoda herself came running after me—I was walking in the street, crying. One of the boys offered to take the girl to his sister and let her sleep there, "for we want you to be with us, and not to make you unhappy." But I said I wouldn't risk his sister getting a thief into her house, and so I shook them off and ran to my father's wife. There Ali and Farida came a bit later. They tried to appeal to my love for them to entice me to come home. But father's wife bade them let me be. I said to them, "You don't love *me* in the least! You just want me for your sake!" Farida urged me to at least come home the next day. By then she would have taken the girl and placed her in service with some rich people. And it's true, she did. And the rich people agreed to hire the girl. So they asked to see her identity card.[1] But the girl didn't have any, she said her mother-in-law had torn it. Then the rich people got scared that perhaps she *was* a thief or prostitute or something, and so Farida had to take the girl with her again. When I came back from the doctor in the evening, there she was—dressed in my daughters' clothes and combing her hair, which was wet from being washed, with *their* comb. I was so distraught, I burst out crying. My nerves were gone. A friend of Ali's who was visiting us insisted on taking the girl to his sister for the night, and I agreed. But Hoda was furious. "My friend is staying with me, and if you ask her to leave, so will I!"

"So you think *you* will command over me?" I screamed.

"Exactly!"

"Then get out of here! I don't give a damn what happens to you!"

A relative of Mustafa's who had just come by took Hoda to task and lectured her that she mustn't ever imagine that one let girls here do as they pleased. A girl must obey and respect her mother. To which Hoda fumed,

"Respect! As if I were in one and all to dance to her tune! I'm free!"

I raged, "Free! I bore and raised you, and still *you* try to command

---

1. All Egyptians have an identity card which they should always carry with them.

over me! If you think that *you*'re the matron of this house, I shall enlighten you!" We almost came to blows, and the neighbors had to separate us.

So there you can see, no one here cares about me. A whole long life I have only lived for the children and their best interests. When I now understand that they, just like their father, only care for themselves, I will leave them to their own dogfight. For what have they given me in life? Disgust!

Part Eight

Young Today

Twenty-nine

On Freedom, Choice, and Love

Through all these years, Umm Ali used to say, "*ilhurriyya, hiyya kulli haga*" [freedom, that is everything]. It has been like a life motto to her, and she has imprinted it on her children. Even Nosa, four years old, could say, "Freedom is the most important thing in life."

In her strong stress on freedom, Umm Ali is atypical of her time and place. Most people accept as fact that some things are shame in themselves, regardless of time and place. Umm Ali, however, says, "Nothing is shame in itself. One must look to the situation."

Shame and freedom, in this perspective, are two sides of the same coin. For if people did not have to guard themselves perennially against how others might twist and turn their every action, everyone would have freedom.

Many would agree with Umm Ali in that. But they would bow to life's realities, rather than resist. She, on the other hand, has tried to bring up her children to depend on themselves rather than always watch what people might say. They should decide for themselves. "Freedom," she calls it. "Shamelessness," many of her neighbors would call it.

Umm Ali's strong emphasis on freedom reflects both her special character and her special background. She grew up in a home that was ruled with an iron hand. Her mother's will must always be. Umm Ali has had to pay a high price for that. Were it not for her mother's pressure, she would not have married Mustafa.

She did "choose" him herself, but she chose under pressure. The fifteen-year-old complaisant girl who had never learned to make an independent judgment was asked to choose a husband herself. She has told how she wanted to marry a suitor "as lovely as King Farouk," but her mother said no. Now, however, her mother said, "for my sake" and "for Abdou's sake." The fifteen-year-old little girl did not have much of a choice.

Umm Ali has sworn this will never happen to her children. They will choose a spouse for themselves. She would never exert the pressure on them that her mother did on her. It is a human right to be able to choose one's own spouse.

Through all the years I have known them, Umm Ali's older children have been about to get engaged. Hoda had her first suitor when she was only fourteen. Umm Ali tried to arrange an engagement for Ali when he was sixteen. Mona has had suitors since she was fifteen.

241

Hoda chides her mother for wanting her to accept the suitor who came when she was only fourteen. Umm Ali criticizes her sister Feyza for not talking sense into her daughter when she was fifteen and Ali asked for her hand. Later, she tells me, her sister regretted it and came to her and said, "Please, tell him to ask her again. You have it in your hand." But Umm Ali bluntly refused. Ali must choose for himself.

But when Ali chose for himself and chose Nefeesa, Umm Ali and Mustafa broke off relations with their son.

Freedom is fraught with problems. Children should have their freedom, but they should also show their parents proper respect. And respect means first and foremost obedience. The attitude is ingrained that the person who is older knows better and has a right to respect.

Umm Ali's freedom ideology has become a boomerang that rebounds on herself. She was never able to make the children understand that it was not literally meant, that it was "freedom with responsibility" she meant, and that such responsibility naturally means showing respect and concern for the parents.

But freedom is not all

"Love" is another ideal she cherishes. "Love must be there from the start. And it is not enough that one party loves. Both must do."

Her daughters are more pragmatic. Mona says, "Love is like an un-opened watermelon. You cannot know what it's like until you open it."

Hoda says, "It is better to marry someone who loves you, than someone you love. For he will make life good for you. And then you will come to love him."

In harmony with her understanding, Umm Ali has let her daughters bring male friends home with them. Numerous are the boys—potential suitors—I have seen sit at her place through the years and savor good food and good company. But much talk and little action ensued. In the end, she was so exasperated that she exclaimed, "The people must think we are running a night club!" [*kazino*] Mustafa was furious.

Umm Ali has tried to arrange matters so that her children would escape her own pitiful fate and rather get to know a potential spouse before committing themselves. This is rather unusual. That a couple meets in the girl's home after the engagement is common, but not before. Umm Ali's practice reflects her breadth of vision.

Unfortunately, the outcome was not what she had expected. At ages twenty-four and twenty-seven, respectively, her two older daughters were about to be branded old maids. She was convinced that it was because they had set their sights too high. But was it also because she placed them in a position of choice that they could not handle?

In 1975, when Hoda was twenty, her mother complained that she came home with four suitors running, declaring that she loved each in turn and wanted to marry him. In 1981 she complained that Hoda was haughty and would not hear of anyone bringing her a suitor. She insisted on finding him herself. "As if you can buy suitors prepackaged!" Umm Ali snorted. She assured Hoda that there were no strings attached. She could just let someone come and see her, and then find out for herself what his position [*markaz*] and family were; if she did not like him, she could just say no. She did not see Hoda's point that you don't choose a spouse on the basis of looks and external characteristics.

Two generations were pitted against each other. In Umm Ali's youth, marriage was arranged by marriage brokers bringing together a couple whom they thought would suit each other. To a large extent, this is the case even today. In such a situation, physical appearance and other visible characteristics like position, income, and family connections become important.

The new generation has been nurtured on TV and love films. Love is the mainstay of marriage these days. But what is love when a thirty-year-old—a very intelligent girl—could burst into tears because her brother had shooed away a soldier, a total stranger, who turned up on their doorstep asking to marry her? The soldier had followed her all the way from Midan Ittahrir, an hour's bus ride away. And so, as she said to me, "Can there be any doubt how much he loves me?"

Nowadays there are two ways to get engaged. The most common is the traditional way: older women bring together two young people in the expectation that they will learn to love each other; love will grow forth. The other is the modern way: the parties fall in love—perhaps by exchanging glances in the street or meeting at an acquaintance's. In the latter case, one tries to hide the fact from the father and act as if the suitor had come in the traditional way. Mother and daughter are accomplices in this, often helped by the mother's brother. Most mothers believe in love and wish their daughters a better future than they themselves had, at a time when it was not unusual for fathers to say, "*Mish huwa ragil? Mish kull irrigala wahid?*" [But is he not a man? Are not all men the same?]

It is questionable whether mothers can succeed in their aspirations on their daughters' behalf. Irrespective of whether you believe that love will grow forth or must be there from the start, there is a fertile ground for problems. Umm Ali's three oldest children have had ample experience with that, and they are in no way unique. Their experiences resemble those of most young people I know.

The problems are aggravated for the young today because the time between the engagement and the wedding has been drawn out. Ten to fifteen years ago it was common for there to be only one year between the agreement and the wedding. Today it may take more than five years.

A marriage arrangement comprises four stages. The first step is the *fatha,* so termed after the opening verse in the Quran. The parties enter into an agreement to get engaged in the presence of relatives while the opening verse in the Quran is being read. The second stage is the engagement, *shabka,* marked with a celebration and engagement gifts to the bride. Third is the *katb ikkitab,* the signing of the marital contract. The couple becomes legally husband and wife; divorce is now necessary to break the relation. Also this step is marked by a party and the giving of gifts to the bride. The fourth and final stage is the *duxla,* "entry," the wedding with sexual consummation. Only then can the couple live together as husband and wife.

Some of these stages can be combined, for instance stages 2 and 3 or 3 and 4. By making one celebration instead of two, one saves a great deal of money.

The most severe problem facing young couples about to marry today is housing. With a population increase from six to fourteen million over the past twenty-five years, there is a crisis in the housing market in Cairo. The young are affected, especially the poor. To rent a flat, even in the cheapest quarters, one must pay a down payment of two to three thousand pounds (key money [*xilawil*]) in 1995; this amounts to two to four times the annual wage of a new government employee with a college education. No wonder people struggle for years, and that every young man tries to get work in the Arab oil countries where one can earn ten to twenty times that amount in a year. But the competition is stiff, and many do not succeed. One young couple I know struggled for seven years before giving up. Then the bride's mother took pity on them and put one of her three rooms at their disposal. Eight people were squeezed into the remaining thirty square meters; another marriageable daughter faces poor prospects.

Seven years on the housing market would have broken most engagements. The people's talk would have flourished and bred endless problems; the two parties' families would have quarreled; rivals and their families would have had an easy way with their intrigues. The couple in question withstood it all because of an exceptional love for each other. I know of few marriageable girls or boys who have not had a past history of at least two or three (often more) broken "engagements," meaning they had read the *fatha* (the oath to marry). In part because of these developments, average marital age has risen sharply. In Umm Ali's youth, it was unusual for a first-time bride to be more than sixteen or seventeen years old, whereas today twenty-five years or more is quite common. Many girls do not wed till they are close to thirty—as did three of Umm Ali's daughters. The youngest, Nosa, signed the marital contract at only twenty, but it will take the couple years to assemble the furniture and equipment and pay the down payment on a flat. Already, two years have passed.

Division of labor between the parties provides that the man is responsible for paying the down payment on the flat, while the burden of furnishings is shared by him and the bride's family. Fifteen to twenty years back, most of the furniture would have been bought for the bride-price [*mahr*] which the bride's family added to. (The size of the *mahr* used to be 100–200 pounds.) Today the *mahr*—that venerable institution which has been an integral part of marriage all over the Middle East—is history; and the groom pays key money [*xilawil*] for the flat instead. As people say, "we don't have *mahr* anymore, it's old-fashioned; now groom and bride furnish together." [*yigahhzu sawa*]

The groom also pays for the engagement rings and jewelry, the bridal dress, and the expense of the engagement party and the wedding party.

In this situation, many young girls are looking for work. In the mid-seventies it had become quite acceptable or even a necessity for a girl to work. Both of Umm Ali's oldest daughters worked in a factory for years. But then ten to fifteen years ago, backlash set in, and since the mid-eighties the fundamentalist or Islamicist movement has called women back to the home and hearth. Their role has been redefined from one of equal opportunities to one of subservience and submission. And though the fundamentalists do not have much support among the lower class, their impact is nevertheless felt through the media and the mosque, urging the man to take control of the wife. The vision Umm Ali and others held of their daughters embarking on a new path—the path of freedom—is being undermined. As one mother said, watching her daughter be locked up for years to await her betrothed husband's return from the Gulf, "*I* used to be allowed to go everywhere!" Nor was the daughter allowed to use her college education.

The majority of young men probably never shared the visions that mothers like Umm Ali—and fathers like Mustafa—held for their daughters, that they would be free to work outside the home if they wanted. Values have a tendency to mellow with time, and fathers probably feel less threatened by their daughters becoming "modern" than would a prospective spouse. The stories in the following chapters show that the struggle to dominate the wife and keep her home is an old one. It predates the fundamentalist movement. The drama of male dominance reenacts itself in every generation, but in the wake of the housing crisis, it is becoming all the more tenacious. Women like Umm Ali and Amira could at least look back on a happy engagement time. But with the long period that now intervenes between engagement and wedding, and the pressures of acquiring flat and furnishings, many young couples are locked in battle from the start, battles that are often exacerbated by their families. The stories of Umm Ali's three older children are illuminating.

Thirty

Ali: Freedom at a High Price

Ali moves with a slow and ponderous gait and is taciturn and shy before people. His gaze is shifty, his skin so dark, he is labeled "black," not "brown," and his features negroid. Umm Ali takes pity on him. Not only is he physically like his father, but he has also suffered from his father's harsh treatment. From the time he was ten years old, Ali worked in his father's workshop and followed his example. Also, he was constantly told how stupid he was.[1] His father used to place unreasonable demands upon the boy about discipline

1. Ali kept wetting the bed until he was ten years old. Umm Ali has told a moving story of how he was cured: "Children who are light sleepers learn to be dry quickly, while the heavy sleepers take much longer. Ali had the most difficulties of all my children. I used to say to him that he *must* wake me up at night when he needed to pee. He would answer, "Yes, Mama!" and sleep right through. Sometimes his brothers and sisters would wake up (because he peed on them) and make fun of him. I didn't know what to do, neither scolding nor beating nor ridicule helped. I just had to hope that one day, God willing, he would manage. It was a washerwoman who put her foot down. I had such terrible backaches at the time, and she used to come once a week to do the laundry. One day she said that the bedding smelled so of urine, she couldn't stand washing it. Who did it? she wanted to know. Then she said that something *had* to be done. It was a great shame for a ten-year-old to wet his bed. So we went to the doctor, the three of us. The doctor took an enormous needle, as thick as my little finger, and jabbed it into Ali's back. He screamed in panic and squirmed madly. I was terrified that the needle might break inside him! By God, had I known that the doctor would do like that, I would never have gone! We were told to come back for two more shots. But I wouldn't, not even if Ali had continued to wet his bed. But he didn't, or at least not very much. The fright of the needle accomplished what years of scolding and beating had not."

and diligence long before children can master such claims. In addition, Ali lived for a long time in the shadow of his handsome and bright brother Amin, to whom his father used constantly to compare him. Therefore, Umm Ali says, Ali is unsure of himself. "You can see it yourself, he always goes and looks down into the ground, away from the people."

On the marriage market, Ali scored low. Three things weighed against him: his African looks, his lack of education (he did not finish primary school), and his lack of salaried employment. His kindness and consideration could not outweigh such faults.

In the fall of 1973, Ali got engaged to Nefeesa. They had been in love for four years. She is as dark as he and very thin—a deplorable quality in a female. But the worst thing about her, Umm Ali used to think (later she developed even more serious reservations), was her age: she was two years older than Ali. "That," Umm Ali said, "means that she understands things better than him and can bully him around." But because she wanted to give Ali his freedom, she let him choose for himself.

Twice before she had tried herself to find him a girl—in accordance with his own wishes, as she points out—and failed dismally. Both times it ended with bitter enmity in the family. The first concerned Samira, daughter of her sister Khadiga.

I asked the girl if she agreed to Ali, and she said yes. So I sent Ali a letter with the happy news, he was in the army. Soon after, the girl went to my brother and said she was going to marry another but had been shy to tell me. She is so haughty, that girl, she had to have a government employee [*muwazzaf*]. But Ali would have earned much more than a *muwazzaf;* taxi drivers earn very well. I told Ali the truth little by little.

Then there was Soad, the daughter of her sister, Feyza.

The girl said she agreed on the condition that she got two engagement bracelets worth fifty pounds. I said she *would* get, but not now, a ring was all we could afford at the moment with Ali in the army. But I promised her by my own eyes that I would make a savings club and give her the bracelets later. The girl refused. So I asked her mother and father to talk sense into her, but they refused, saying the girl must choose for herself. They made a great mistake. *They* are older so they should know better. Also, it was stupid of them, for it is better to marry a relative than a stranger. The girl claimed that her friends would laugh at her if she did not get the bracelets. But now, after *so* many broken engagements, both she and her mother regret the decision. They have asked me to ask Ali to ask for her again, saying, "You have it in your power!" But I won't. Ali must decide for himself.

As the relationship between her son and Nefeesa developed, Umm Ali finally broke with her principle of noninterference: she cut off relations with her son. But before it got to that, they had had many angry confrontations.

When Ali declared that he wanted to get engaged to Nefeesa, Umm Ali tried to talk him out of it. When that did not work, she had a serious talk with the two young people and urged them that as proof of their earnest intentions, they should sign the marital contract [*katb ikkitab*] at once, rather than just get engaged. Ali agreed, but Nefeesa refused. That confirmed Umm Ali's suspicion.

She doesn't want to be tied down, because she doesn't love Ali at all. She just wants to get engaged so she can demand things from him and say, "Give me panties, give me sweets!" and so forth, and then break the bond when she pleases. Really, she loves a man she was engaged to in Jordan (where she worked for a time). She's still wearing his ring on the same finger as she wears Ali's! Can you imagine, two engagement rings on one finger! I have asked her why she doesn't sell the ring from the first guy, but she says it's because she paid so much for it and would suffer a loss by selling. Was it *she* or he who paid? Have you ever heard of a girl paying for her own engagement ring!

Umm Ali says people laugh at Ali because his fiancée wears two rings.

And now Nefeesa wants to go to Jordan again—to work, she claims, in order to help Ali with the furnishings. But really, that's an excuse, it is to be reunited with her ex-fiancé. Would a girl who loved a boy ever leave him to go to Jordan! Now she is busy trying to fix herself a passport, signatures here and signatures there and bribes everywhere. *That's* why she will not sign the marriage contract! *Katb ikkitab* ties. After that, she will need her husband's permission to travel, and Ali would naturally refuse her. But now, when they're only engaged, she can just take off her ring and swoop! she is free. Meanwhile she has Ali squander his hard-earned money on her.

Umm Ali criticizes both the girl and her mother for their gluttony.

They're always asking Ali for money and gifts: "Give me, give me!" they say. Whenever he asks Nefeesa, "What would you like to eat?" she answers, "*Kofta* [meatballs] or fish!" Had she cared about his interests or her own future she would have been content with *ful* or *ta'miyya* [beans] or such. When they've been to the movies and are going home, she says, "Get me a taxi!" As if *she* were too high-bred to ride a bus!

Umm Ali contrasts Nefeesa's mother's attitude with her own attitude to Khalid, Hoda's ex-fiancé:

Whenever Khalid brought us fruits or sweets, I used to tell him, "Don't trouble yourself! We have plenty of food. Put the money in your future instead!" I loved him like my own son. I also told him to put the money into the *mahr* [bride-price]. That's what Nefeesa's mother also should have done. But do you know what she says? She says, "*We* don't want any *mahr,* we want to furnish together!" [*nigahhiz sawa*] Together! As if *they* had anything to furnish from! What does she think herself—an employee? "Furnishing together"—that means that Nefeesa's mother will *lend* Ali the money, but he has to pay her back! He owes *me* money and was a member of a savings club I run, but he left it so he could manage his commitments to Nefeesa's mother. One hundred pounds has he borrowed from her, including seventy pounds for engagement gifts! I said fifty would have been ample—the same as Mona got. But he said, "I don't give a damn about Mona!" Moreover, it is wrong of him to save with Nefeesa's mother. A boy should save with his own mother.

The story of the engagement gifts was a sore point with Umm Ali, for she was enraged at the way the thing had been handled.

One day Ali came here with Nefeesa and Nefeesa's mother and said they were going out to buy clothes for Nefeesa. Would I come along? I said there was no use in me coming along, since the girl must choose for herself. Also, I was ill. What liars they were! Do you think it was clothes they were buying? Not at all! It was the engagement jewelry! Nefeesa's mother had brought with her seventy pounds she had cashed in from a savings club. It was of course *her* idea, this thing about the jewelry, Ali doesn't have a penny to buy for. Now she has lured him into a situation where *he* is up to his neck in debt, and *she* has got her daughter engaged! For months, Ali won't have a penny to contribute to his own household!

They didn't *want me* coming along, that's why they lied to me and said they were going out to buy clothes. I have accused Nefeesa's mother to her face of not wanting to share joy with the groom's family. It's a shame, I said, to be so stingy one cannot even share joy with others. She defended herself saying they *had* asked me to come along, and besides, it wasn't planned, this thing about the jewelry. But why then did she bring seventy pounds along? I said she would see that I wouldn't come to the engagement party!

I didn't either. Nor did I invite anyone from our family. I said I was sick, and went over to Umm Magdi's because I was so depressed. At eleven at night, Ali came. He was furious and said they hadn't got engaged yet because they were waiting for me. I excused myself saying I had been to the doctor, and that I was ill. Ali insisted that I must come. I said that in that case I would have to stand in the street for I couldn't possibly climb the stairs to the fourth floor. Then Ali said that if I didn't come, he would do like his brother. This was exactly a year after Amin's death, and Umm Magdi urged me to go—otherwise, I might always fear that Ali might do like his brother.

I cried all the way to the engagement house, and cried as I entered the room. And everybody flocked around me and asked why I cried. I said I was sick. Then Ali put the bracelet and the ring on Nefeesa and they both kissed me. I sat stiff and numb. They tried to treat me, first with juice. I defended myself with my diabetes, saying I couldn't possibly take anything sweet. They fussed terribly, and in the end I got them to mix me a glass of almost only water and *a little* juice. But I drank only a sip and gave the glass to one of the children [Umm Ali smiles at the thought]. And I didn't even taste the food![2]

Mustafa, too, went to the party by force. From our family there was otherwise only my father's wife and my sister Farida.

They were so extravagant with the food and drinks in the party, used eight bottles of juice and four kilos of sugar, whereas we, in Mona's engagement, used only three kilos, and that was ample! And we had masses of guests, whereas they had almost none! And I got so angry with Ali because he took three bottles of juice which *I* had got as a present and squandered them in the party. It happened like this: They had used up all the juice, and then Nefeesa's mother said, "Ali, we need more!" Then Samiha [Umm Ali's half sister] told them that Adel [brother-in-law] had brought me three bottles as a gift but left them at their place because I was out. I didn't even know about it! And without even asking, Ali told Samiha, "Go and fetch them!" Nor did he pay for them!

Every day Ali gives Nefeesa thirty piaster and he often brings her mother gifts, whereas he never contributes a penny at home. He excuses himself saying Nefeesa's mother doesn't know how to make nutritious food—if he didn't buy them some, Nefeesa would subsist just on bread and rice. That's also why he often brings her here to eat with us. I have nothing against that. I'm happy for everyone who shares our food. But I'm angry because the girl lets herself be persuaded by Hoda and Mona to spend the night. Mustafa is furious and blames me. But what can I do? *Ask* the girl to leave? Yesterday, luckily, her mother came and fetched her.

---

2. To decline hospitality can be a victory, a way of demeaning the hostess. But it can also reflect mutual accommodation to chronic shortage and carry no such dire connotations. The most common reason given for not accepting hospitality is fear of reprisals: the hostess might go around and say how gluttonous the guest had been. But this does not apply at special occasions, like a wedding, only in ordinary life.

Day after day this fall, Umm Ali overflowed with regrets about the prodigal son.

The man should *share* his love between his mother and his fiancée. But Ali has only thought for Nefeesa. He buys her medicines on the minute, whereas mine must wait for days. It's a week now since I asked him to give me one and a half pounds for medicines for my diabetes. But he said he didn't have, though I know that he had just paid two pounds for medicines for Nefeesa. I accused him of not caring about *my* health, though I'm the one who cooks and washes and does everything for him. He squanders *all* he earns on this girl and her mother, with no sense of saving and planning. Had he only been like Amin! Amin used to save his money and buy himself nice clothes, and he always talked about how he would repay me manyfold when he grew up and [would] let me go on pilgrimage to Mecca. Ali should have done like Mona's fiancé. He didn't even buy her new clothes for the engagement but saved everything for the furnishings. After all, that's what counts, so the two can get married. But Ali lets Nefeesa and her mother twist him around their finger. Yesterday I asked him for money. "One of your sisters is shoeless," I said, "the other has no good dress—no wonder they don't get married!" He said he didn't have a penny. But I know that he gives Nefeesa money every day, for she herself has told Hoda. Then I told him I wanted back the five pounds he owed me for a year. "I don't *have* any money!" he said. I reminded him how I had had to *borrow* money at the time to help him. Now it's time he helps me. He always promptly repays Nefeesa's mother!

Suddenly one day, a fortnight after the engagement, the bird had flown; Nefeesa had gone to Jordan—behind Ali's back. Ali himself took it in stride. What choice did he have? Causing an uproar would brand him a cuckold forever. Better to cover up the flight and act as if she had gone with his consent. To his mother he said nothing. But she came to know the truth soon enough. And she was furious. Her son was a blatant fool, a laughingstock before the world. He must immediately break the engagement! Nefeesa's mother was equally furious. She came charging to Umm Ali and accused Ali of forcing her daughter to travel behind her own mother's back. For if Ali had not *refused* permission, Nefeesa would not have had to travel in secrecy!

With tears streaming down her face she wailed about how Nefeesa now would not even dare to send a letter home with her address for fear Ali would set the police on her. Even if her own mother should die, Nefeesa wouldn't know it!

Umm Ali curtly replied, "May God let your daughter return safe and sound!"

She urged her son not to pay a thing on his debt to Nefeesa's mother until he saw if the girl came back again.

She did at last—after many false starts. Then she married an Egyptian and divorced him after two months. She was pregnant, and a son was born. She was brought to her knees now, both materially and attractionwise. A divorced woman has little appeal save to a widower or divorcé; men marrying for the first time will want a virgin. To Nefeesa, Ali was again attractive, and she started strolling past his workshop. One day people came to Umm Ali with explosive news: her son had married Nefeesa! Umm Ali confronted Ali when he came home at night. But he swore that he and Nefeesa were just good friends. The rumors were all malignant, he said. But the next day, while Umm Ali was out, he took all his clothes and belongings and moved out. All that was left was the color TV he had brought from Libya, which was too heavy to carry.

Mustafa hit the ceiling. He wanted to go straight to the police station and accuse his son—of what, I don't know. Ali was old enough to choose a wife for himself; he did not need his parents' consent. Mustafa's threat was probably provoked by blind rage at the humiliation he had suffered. Umm Ali held him back. She was equally enraged, but her reaction was different. She said, "Ali is dead to me, dead like Amin."

She swore that she would not ever again set eyes on her son.

Ali suffered gravely from the breach, and tried hard to arrange a reconciliation. A couple of times a week he would visit his two sisters at the factory where they worked. He also asked them to come and see him on their days off, and to bring his little sister, Nosa, whom he missed. He sent his greetings and good wishes to his mother. On Mother's Day, he sent three pounds to her with a message to buy herself a pair of sandals, which he knew she sorely needed. He also told Mona to tell her that he wanted to come and see her on Mother's Day. Mona said it was best to wait since the mother was still so angry. On being told what Mona said, the mother snorted, "Still! I shall be angry for as long as I live!"

She refused to accept the money for the sandals. What made it impossible for her ever to forgive her son, she said, was that Ali had fooled her.

When he was working in Libya, he said on the tape he sent home— yes, he said it several times—that he wanted me to find him a bride. "Find someone *you* like, Mama!" I showed him girl after girl—lovely girls with good manners. To everyone he said no. I suspected then that he might have signed the contract with Nefeesa, but he denied it. He used to sleep in my house while he was fooling me!

If he had been married before, I would not have minded if he married Nefeesa. But to be young and budding and then to take a divorcée who

is even *older* than himself! It's a shame! There ought to be celebration and joy when a boy marries. But a wedding to a divorcée! Impossible!

In 1980, Ali tried again to find someone to mediate in this family drama.
His sisters tried, but in vain. His parents would have nothing to do with
their son.

But in the fall of 1981, he succeeded. His parents took him back in favor.
What perhaps did it was that Ali went down on his knees to the extent of
sending his father a message saying he wanted to start working for him again.
More humble a son could not be. The wages at the workshop were meager
compared with what he could earn as a taxi driver. But the parents were
unyielding regarding Ali's next wish: reconciliation with Nefeesa. It did not
help that their daughters assured them of how honorable and pious she now
had become. They did not want anything to do with her.

In the summer of 1982, Nefeesa managed a reconciliation. She showed
up, with gifts and embraces, at the hospital where Umm Ali had delivered
the stillborn. Umm Ali had no choice but to be reconciled. A few months
earlier Nefeesa had borne a child, Umm Ali's first grandchild. But Umm
Ali did not go and greet her.

Thirty-one

Hoda: "As If He Could Decide over Me"

Before she was sixteen, Hoda had already had four suitors. The first came
when she was only fourteen. Her mother advised her to accept him, for
he earned very well. But Hoda declined, feeling she was too young to get
engaged. Then there was Mahmoud, best friend of her brother Amin. But
him she only loved like a brother. Then there was a neighbor, but he was
black. And then there was Khalid.

Khalid was Hoda's first consuming love. He was tall and thin with a
pale face, green eyes and light brown hair—beautiful, by local standards.
First, he courted a friend of hers, but her family forbade the girl to see
him. After that he took up relations with Hoda. His former girlfriend tried
to commit suicide and was barely saved. Said Hoda, "Now her family
accuses me of being the cause of it, but by God, my conscience is clean.
I never so much as looked at Khalid before they had rejected him!"

Hoda and Khalid were together for two years. They saw each other almost daily, either at her home or at some friend's place. After five months, they read the *fatha.* Hoda says they loved each other deeply, but the relationship was not without problems, especially after the *fatha.* "Then he started to bully me, 'Don't use makeup! Don't cut your hair! Your dress is too short! Your trousers too tight! Your sleeves too short!' I was angry, of course. Who did he think himself that he could command over me! I said, 'I'm free!' " But Khalid was adamant and threatened to leave her, so she gave in.

Khalid also demanded that she quit her education. Hoda had just completed junior high school—with good marks—and was eager to continue. Khalid (who had only primary school) threatened her, "Then you'll be better than me, and then you'll despise me one day." He said there was no sense in her continuing, since she was to be a housewife, so education was a waste. Or if she insisted, she would have to find herself someone of her own level—a state employee!

They quarreled hotly over the issue, but in the end Hoda won. She managed to convince him that it would be in his own best interests that she continue so she could help earn money for the furnishings. After that Khalid even encouraged her to continue. When Umm Ali heard it, she said that Khalid himself ought to pay for Hoda's education since he was the one who was to benefit from it. Her own family had already paid masses in school expenses, and it would be even more now, for with the conflict, Hoda had lost a year of school. When she was to continue, she turned out to be five months too old for government school, and private school costs a fortune. But Khalid refused to pay.

Hoda later related,

For seven months we were happy together. Then something happened. Suddenly one day Khalid came and demanded that we should make the engagement party [*shabka*] at once. Baba said it was impossible, only seven months after Amin's death. [Tradition requires one to wait a year after a death in the family.] Khalid was annoyed, but he didn't say anything. But after this he became quarrelsome and short tempered. Then there was a day I was sick. Mama and Khalid took me to the doctor. The doctor said my nerves were worn, so I should stay home and rest for a few days. Khalid said he would come to see me the next morning. But he didn't come till two days later, and then only to speak with Mama in secrecy. He said he wanted fifty pounds which he had paid to a savings club she led, because a friend of his was traveling to Libya the next day, and Khalid wanted him to buy me the china. Mama said she didn't have fifty pounds; moreover, it was not Khalid's turn to cash in. But Khalid implored her, "By the name of the Prophet, Auntie, please be so kind and help me, borrow from anyone!" Mama protested and said there was really no hurry. Lots of people travel to Libya and other places. We could ask someone else to buy me the china, Umm Magdi's husband, for example. But Khalid said that no one else knew his taste, just this friend. Then Mama said that the friend could borrow the money from Umm Magdi's husband in Libya who earned well. But Khalid only laughed at that, saying his friend and Umm Magdi's husband were as far from each other as Cairo was from Libya. "Then let your friend travel to Umm Magdi's husband at my expense!" Mama said. But Khalid was adamant. In the end Mama promised to try, and Khalid left, gloomy.

The next day he came and got his fifty pounds. And then we didn't see him again for three days. He had promised to take me to the doctor again, but didn't show up. Then one day Afaf was fetching a tray from an acquaintance, Umm Fathi. She came back reporting that Khalid sat in her house. We asked her if she hadn't asked him, "Why aren't you coming?" Afaf said no.

That same evening two other acquaintances, neighbors of Umm Fathi, came visiting. They were members of a savings club Mama ran and told us that Umm Fathi had said that Mama had ruined the savings club since she let Khalid have his money before his turn. Mama chided them for thinking so poorly of her; the money to Khalid had nothing to do with the savings club, it was a loan from her to him. Then the women said, "Khalid is never going to marry Hoda, he sits in Umm Fathi's house every day and takes his pleasure from her! Her husband is old and ailing and doesn't care a thing as long as he gets his food and drink!"

We were enraged, of course! Umm Fathi used to come to us and say to me, "That Khalid is awful, *fellahin* [a country boy] and dark and skinny; you who are beautiful and educated can get someone much better than him. I'll find you someone!" Now we learned that she had gone to Khalid and said about me, "She's awful, that Hoda, flat-breasted and skinny and roaming with the boys. I'll find you someone much better than her!"

The next day we sent for grandfather's wife, uncle's wife [Amira], Amira's sisters, two cousins, and Umm Magdi so we could go together and quarrel with the rat. To Baba we told nothing. And just as we had heard, there was Khalid sitting in the house of Umm Fathi! We attacked her and abused her as she has never been abused—while Khalid sat without saying a word. Uncle's wife started hitting her too, and then Umm Fathi's son who had just been summoned, started beating me. We sent a message to Ali who came charging over on his motorbike with a friend. Ali wanted to beat up the boy who had hit me, but his friend threw himself between them and averted it.

In the evening, there was a knock on the door. Outside stood a policeman. He wanted Baba. Baba didn't understand a thing, and so Mama had to tell him all. Baba had to go to the police station, but first he sent Ali to a friend in the police with rank far above that of constable. At the station Umm Fathi, her husband, her son, and Khalid waited. They accused us of having provoked a big fight without reason. "Without reason!" Baba screamed. "That guy was to marry my daughter and left her without reason! What does he think we are—a toy in his hand?"

"I left her because there was no mutual understanding," Khalid said.

"And that you discover only after four years—after you've eaten and drunk in our house like a son!"

Then the police officer with high rank came, and everyone was surprised that Baba had such good connections. The officer said, "Go home, and I'll fix this for you!" Later he came and said that he would arrange so Baba and Ali could go somewhere and beat up the whole gang. Papa agreed, but Mama said no, "The Lord will take them to account."

The breakup was a heavy blow to Hoda. She grew even more skinny and depressed. Twice she tried to take her own life. If she had been boy-crazy and provocative in her clothing before, she became even more so now. Her obsessions in life seemed to be boys, clothes, and sleep. During the next three years, her mother complained that she brought home three suitors in turn, saying she loved each one and wanted to marry him. But each time she changed her mind before it came to the *fatha*. In the fall of 1975 she was seriously in love again. She confessed the following to me:

His name is Sami. She loves him and he loves her, but they cannot marry for five years because he has to complete his education first and then serve in the army. Nor can they get engaged, for rings cost at least ten pounds and the party at least five. She often meets him in secret places, and then he wants to kiss her and hold her hand, but she is afraid. He is annoyed because he loves her and she loves him, and there is trust between them. Now she is ruining the relationship by not giving him what he wants. She lies to her mother when she goes to meet him saying she is just seeing a friend. But she feels that it is her mother who forces her to lie by refusing to allow her to go out and to bring boys home.

She suspects her mother of wanting her to get married to any well-positioned man.

Like that officer who almost ruined Mona [see chap. 32]. We knew nothing about him, and Mama felt it was unnecessary to ask since he had such a good position. He on his part did as he should and asked about our family. Mama let herself be deceived by his good position. His true character he revealed in that story with Mona and also once when he came here accusing me of being the cause of Amin's death. He said Amin had killed himself from shame over my reputation!

Her mother said,

> Hoda is stupid and obstinate. She doesn't know her own good. She has become a replica of her father, just worse. Khalid left her because she didn't obey him. "Who does he think himself that *he* can decide over me!" she used to say. I encouraged Khalid to beat her. I said, "Hit her in the face, you have my permission!" But Khalid would not for then Hoda might hit back. I have told her that I hope she will marry someone who will teach her, and that I will *not* come to her rescue when she is unhappy and her husband perhaps even takes a second wife because she's so stubborn!

Umm Ali is sorry that Hoda passed up the chance to marry a boy in a neighboring house.

> He was pious and well-bred and intelligent. He didn't smoke, just prayed, and took his university exams. Hoda loved him, and I told her to tell him that she would be happy to marry him—she was fifteen years then. Hoda often went to visit him. Every time I asked her if she had told him. But she said no, she was shy. I said it was nothing to be shy about, how was the boy going to know it then. Once he invited her to the movies, and I encouraged her to go; it was a good opportunity to tell him. But Hoda never got up her courage. But when her friend Afaf fell in love with him, Hoda was quick to tell him. Now he and Afaf are married!
>
> Hoda is always doing like that, arranging dates for her friends. It was that which drove Khalid up the wall. Hoda used to go in and out of the homes of one boy after the other. It didn't help her that she said she did it on her friends' behalf. People must say she was cheap! She also used to bring boys home with her to meet her friends. Always there were new faces cropping up. I was so furious, I screamed, "And what do you think you are, a marriage-broker [*xutba*]?"
>
> "I only do good, Mama [*ba'mil tayyib, ya Mama*]," she said.
>
> "Not at all! You're reducing your home to a nightclub and driving your fiancé crazy and making the people talk and your father and brother mad! *You're* not responsible for getting your friends married—you who have not even got the sense to look out for yourself and do as your mother and your fiancé say!"

Hoda did not get engaged until she was nearly twenty-eight, and she married the man two years later. Her husband is kind and caring, but the marriage is fraught with problems. And no wonder. She is better educated than her husband, better employed, and older. Even a love marriage cannot stand up to such superiority on the wife's part.

Thirty-two

Mona: "Marriage Is Like an Unopened Watermelon"

In the summer of 1975 Mona got engaged to Foad. He is the brother of her uncle Adel who was married to her favorite aunt, Shaddya. Forty days after Shaddya died, Adel remarried. There is nothing wrong with that by Egyptian standards. Forty days is the traditional mourning period, and Adel needed someone to take care of his five children. Moreover, he is still young, and young men need a wife. But the children faced grim prospects. Nothing is worse, according to Egyptians, than to be saddled with a stepmother. Thus when Umm Ali first told me of the engagement between Mona and Foad, she said that Mona would marry him so she could be in a mother's place with the children. (Foad lived with his brother, so they would all be together.) But, Umm Ali said, she herself had *not* put any pressure on Mona and said, "For the children's sake" or "For my sake," as her own mother had done with her. Mona had been free to choose for herself. For love must be there before the marriage. And it is not enough that one person loves; both must.

Mona's story was rather different.

No, I don't love Foad, not yet. For I don't even know him. I've just been out with him twice, to a café, together with Hoda and Ali and some others. But he behaves well and is very caring and wants to give me everything I wish, so I believe love will grow forth. And I was so sick in my soul from men that I was happy to accept him. He's like a relative, not a stranger, it was Auntie Shaddya who brought him up [since he was six, when his mother died]. We know his family and know that we can trust him. That was the most important thing. All I wanted was a man there would be no problems with, someone I could trust—after all I have been through.

And she related,

Two years ago some acquaintances of Mama's came and said an officer of good family was looking for a bride. They wanted him to see Hoda and me. Mama agreed, and the officer came. He was tall and white and beautiful, with yellow hair and green eyes. He saw us both, and liked me. Mama asked whether I agreed, and I said, "Wait till we have seen what character [*axlaq*] he has."

Then he started to visit us. He behaved beautifully. He used to kiss Mama's hand and bring presents and he befriended Ali. But something troubled me. Always he was talking about how rich his family was, and how much he was going to inherit, and how one brother was an engineer, and another an inspector and so forth; and how he hoped that his father would die soon so he could come into his inheritance.

I was annoyed. I too could have bragged about how we were related to so and so, and how grand our family was, but what's the use?

True, the officer was polite and generous, but he had no personality [*shaxsiyya*].

When Ali asked her if she had made up her mind, Mona said yes, she would *not* marry the man. But the officer would not accept her refusal. He insisted on knowing *why* she would not marry him. And he continued to inundate her with tender and loving words. When this also proved useless, he said that they should part like brother and sister and asked her to go out with him just once. She refused, but the officer pleaded with Ali and Hoda to persuade her, and they kept saying, "Just go once, for our sake!" In the end, Mona gave in.

They met at seven in the evening at a café by the Nile. The officer treated her to cocoa, cakes filled with cream, and other goodies, and to a stream of tender words. The next thing she remembers she woke up in a flat. He must have put something in the cocoa!

"But where am I?" she screamed.

"In the flat where I was to have taken you as my bride!"

"You rascal! Have you no breeding?"

"Yes, I am a rascal, and I have no breeding, and when you don't want to marry me willingly, I shall force you! I'm going to take your honor tonight!"

She screamed in fright, "You thousand times son of a bitch! Have you no shame [*damm*]?"

"Yes, I have no shame!"

"And you who used to go in and out of our place and kiss Mama's hand, and befriend my brother, are you utterly lacking in respect [*ihtiram*]?"

"Yes, I have no respect! Do you see this knife? With it I'm going to tattoo my name on your bosom tonight. Or do you submit willingly?"

She screamed in terror.

"You can scream as much as you like—no one is going to hear you!"

The noise was deafening from the traffic below; it was already ten at night and winter when the people go to sleep early to escape the cold. She cried desperately. When the officer went to the toilet, she rushed to the door, but it was locked. He saw it and smiled mockingly, "The key is with me, and you won't have it till I have had my desire. Or do you want to be tattooed?"

She cried hysterically, and jabbed her arms wildly when he tried to touch her, but there were no objects she could use in self-defense; the flat was empty save for a sofa. She tried to appeal to his mercy.

"Don't you have any breeding [*zoq*]? Baba will be home by now, and he will be furious because I'm out!"

"I don't give a damn about your father!"

Suddenly there was a knock on the door. The officer pushed her into the next room, and opened it. It was his brother who lived on the floor below. She prayed, "Oh Lord, help me!" She tugged at the door gently. It was unlocked! She swallowed a scream of joy and tiptoed out and plunged down the stairs and ran like a madwoman till she was home. It was three o'clock in the morning. Hoda was up waiting for her and scolded her for being so late. But she collapsed in tears. Hoda tried to get her to tell what had happened. But she could not. She just cried until she fell asleep from exhaustion.

Mona told nothing about her trauma to her mother or elder brother. "For then there *must* have been a big fight. Ali would have had to defend the family's honor [*karamit ilusra*], and then the officer might have attacked him with a knife, which we could never risk after Amin's death. We ourselves would have had to quarrel with the women who had recommended him, and that would have caused a lot of trouble. But the officer's behavior was the utmost sin. He who enters a house as a guest is under a holy duty to respect the daughters."

Before this there was a painful story about Mahmoud, Amin's best friend. Mona related the following story:

He was in love with Hoda and wanted Amin to intercede for him. Amin said it was no use, Hoda loved Khalid. Mahmoud was very sad, but Mama said, "Don't be sorry. Instead of Hoda, take Mona, they are both like your sisters!" Mahmoud answered, "As you please, Auntie."

After this he always came to us. And little by little I came to love him. We used to sit together, and he spoke loving words to me. Sometimes I and Hoda went with Amin to visit Mahmoud's family. There we got to know a girl in the neighboring house. She was dark, and tall, and thin. Then she started to visit us. One day she said to Hoda that she and Mahmoud were in love and used to go out together. Hoda told it to me, and I was upset, naturally. The next time Mahmoud came, I was curt and abrasive. He wanted to know what was wrong. I said, "Nothing!" He insisted on knowing. "The last time I saw you we were happy together, and now your face is contorted. What's the matter?" I told him what the girl had said. Mahmoud said it was all lies. "She always comes to us and tries to make me fall in love with her. But I love you. *Bass*" [that's all].

Then Amin died. Every time Mona saw Mahmoud after that, she cried, and he cried. Then he stopped coming for a long time. She did not know why, but she was so depressed after Amin's death that she did not care to find out. Then Ali broke his leg and sent her to a friend of his to let him know. The friend lived near Mahmoud and so Mona thought she would go and ask his mother why Mahmoud did not come. His mother said it was because Mahmoud was so busy in school, but soon he would be coming again. Which he did; and he and Mona agreed to get engaged. Mahmoud talked with his parents and his father agreed, but his mother was angry because she wanted him to marry a relative. But after a while Mahmoud came and said that he had convinced his mother. They set a date for the engagement party, two months later.

Two days later the skinny girl, Mahmoud's neighbor, paid them a visit again. She said she and Mahmoud had now read the *fatha*. They asked her when. "Four days ago!"

When Mahmoud showed up, Mona didn't speak to him, but Hoda said, "Congratulations!"

"On what?"

"On the *fatha!*"

"Oh that, that's nothing. It was just something to stop the women's nagging. [His mother and the girl's mother were friends.] It's not for real."

But Mona had had enough. It didn't help that he said he would break the *fatha*. She was sick and tired of men. (Mahmoud later married this girl.)

Not long after, Mona met Magdi, the brother of Khalid, Hoda's fiancé.

He had just come to the city from the countryside and didn't know how to behave. For he was a *fellahin* [a peasant]. I went out twice with him to a *kazino,* once with Hoda and Khalid, and once with Ali and Nefeesa. But it was a flop; I sat and looked around at people like I always do when I am out, I enjoy watching the people. But Magdi was insulted and accused me of treating him like an animal since I let him sit and talk to himself. So we started quarreling, both times.

But Magdi remained in town and learned to behave like a city boy. Mona went out with him again, and fell in love with him. He was serious, and said he would come and ask for her hand as soon as he got a proper job.

Then everything was wrecked because of Hoda's misfortune! After what Khalid did to her, it would be impossible for Baba for accept his brother. Magdi was in despair. He sent a friend to implore me to marry him in secrecy. "*W'ana ragil?*" [And am I a man] I retorted. True, a man can marry without his parents' consent, but a girl? Never! Hoda said, "Take him! It is better to marry someone who loves you than someone you love for then he will kiss your feet and make life good for you, and then you'll grow to love him." But it was impossible—behind the family's back.

Then followed another unhappy love relationship.

He was a Jordanian, Hani was his name. Some acquaintances of Mama's brought him. He was handsome beyond words, white, with yellow hair and green eyes, and tall. He came and saw me and liked me. He behaved beautifully. For instance, he was always punctual so I could tell Mama precisely when I was going out and when I was coming home. And he was always bringing gifts: makeup, perfume, panties, or cakes for Mama. Mama said, "Don't bother yourself. Here's plenty of food." And she told me, "Tell him that Baba brings us everything we need." I told him and he was very happy. He said, "All others look only to the money, not to the man."

For five months they saw each other almost daily, and went out together once a week. Then they were both going to have their exams, he at the university, she at junior high school. He suggested that they should not meet during the next two months. "Otherwise, I'll think only of you and cannot concentrate on my studies." Mona agreed, but she missed him so much, she could not concentrate, and so she failed her exams. But before the two months were gone he came again, with a wig as a delayed birthday present for her. (Wigs were popular at the time, and very costly.) He looked completely changed, emaciated and worn. The reason came spilling out.

During the exams a fellow student had whispered to him, begging him for help. Hani had refused, barely audibly. But the inspector caught him "cheating." He was brought before an exam court, and sentenced to expulsion for three years. The only way to escape the sentence was to appeal to a higher court and bribe the judges. So he had written a letter to his father, a rich landowner, asking him for 700 pounds in bribes. Simultaneously he told his father about Mona, that he wanted to marry her and settle in Jordan. He got a furious reply. He would not get a penny in bribes and, moreover, he would be disowned if he didn't come home immediately and marry a cousin.

He did not have any choice. They cried in each others' arms before separating for good.

Before that again, two years before, there was another suitor, a neighbor who was a student. There were two of them, one white and one black. The white one and I used to greet each other from the balcony, and sometimes I made tea for him and brought him. In the end he took courage and proposed that we meet on the last evening before he was to move away, a Sunday evening at eight. Some days before I had to travel to my aunt in the country on an errand. I was supposed to be back on Sunday afternoon. But then the train was late, and I didn't come till Monday evening. By then he was gone. I cried when I came home, and never saw him again. *Hazzi wihhish. Mashuftish gher mashakil.* [My luck is bad. I haven't met anything but problems.] *That's why* she accepted Foad, Mona says.

He is calm and polite, we know his family, and know that we can trust him. His family doesn't have any objections, he has a good income, and is responsible and reliable. That there is still not love between us doesn't matter. For marriage is like an unopened watermelon. You cannot know what's inside before you open it. Many who love each other before the marriage curse each other afterward, and vice versa; there may be problems from his family or hers, or the people's talk may spoil everything; or the mother-in-law may be jealous; the fathers have quarreled, and so on. I was so sure that I was assured peace and happiness if only I took Foad. But three days after the engagement there arose problems worse than anything I had ever experienced at home because of a suitor.

We got engaged on a Thursday. On Saturday Foad came visiting, and Sunday too. Both times he found Hoda's tutor sitting on the bed [because of lack of space, beds are used for sitting] while I was sleeping beside. He got angry and said it was a shame that a man sat there while I was sleeping, even though I was covered with a blanket. On Monday he came again, and found both Hoda's tutor and the tutor's cousin! He was enraged and exclaimed, "What's this, always men sitting here! It's a disgrace, for you live in *hayy baladi,* [a native quarter] not *hayy afrangi.* [foreign quarter] I have traveled to other quarters in Cairo and seen such things, but here in a *baladi* quarter, it's a terrible shame!" He said we had to watch the people's talk, "For people here don't judge by what things are, only what they *appear to be!* [*ilmanzar*] They will say that men hang around at your place." He himself was not used to such things, he said, for Auntie Shaddya never let friends of her husband enter when he was out. She used to look from the window and tell the callers to wait at the café; that's how Foad was accustomed. And he implored me to talk to Mama so she could tell the men to stay away.

Mona could well understand Foad's concern. And she was happy that he was so protective. She talked to her mother who agreed with Foad, and her mother talked with Hoda's tutor who was also understanding. But Hoda hit the roof and complained to Ali who complained to their father who was furious. "What does he think himself, that he can command over us! As if there weren't men in this house before, and we can run our own affairs!" Mona and her mother protested that Foad did not command, just recommend. To no avail. The father scowled, "If he wants to keep you hidden from all men, then he'd better rent a room in a hotel and keep you locked up there!"

Mona was ordered to take off her engagement ring and bracelets immediately. Her mother protested that the engagement had only lasted three days,
and the people's talk would have a feast if it were broken. "We've already
too much of that, what with one suitor [Hoda's Khalid] having left us!"

But Ali went to Hoda's tutor and urged him to ignore Umm Ali's pleas.
And Hoda whined and fawned that she was sure to fail in her exams if she
did not take private lessons. Mona and Umm Ali chided her for caring only
about herself and ignoring her sister's interests. After all, it was only a matter
of fourteen days all concerned. Then Foad would return to work in Libya,
and the tutor and others could resume their visits. What's more, they said,
Foad was guarding Hoda's own interests—which *she* was incapable of. "You
know yourself how people here talk even when two who are *maktubin ki-
tabhum* [have signed the marital contract] go out together. Can't you imagine how they must talk now when they see men going in and out of here
nonstop!" And she should remember how jealous Khalid used to be. "And
that I'll tell you," Mona said, "he who is jealous about your daughter, you
should carry him on your head instead of dipping him in the mud, for he
shows how dear she is to him and that he will care about her."

But Hoda didn't give in. "Stubborn as a donkey, she continued to prattle
and whine and lay it on thick so as to incite Baba and Ali."

Mona was forbidden to see Foad. But she did not tell him. Instead, she
took her schoolbooks along when she went to meet him and lied at home
saying that she was going to a girlfriend to do homework. Foad wanted to
know why she was always bringing her schoolbooks. "Because people don't
know yet that we're engaged, and then it looks better like this," she said.

Mona's story continues.

Shortly after, Baba traveled to the countryside and was gone for a
week. When he came back he berated me because I was still wearing my
engagement ring and bracelets. Ali and Hoda joined in. Then there was
an evening when we were going to eat. I had no appetite at all. Baba and
Mama and Ali had already sat down at the *tabliyya* and Baba yelled at me,
"Aren't you going to eat?" I answered, "I'm coming at once!" Then I went
into the other room to wake up Hoda and as I came out a torrent of beatings hit me in the face. "I shall teach you for not answering when I ask!"
Baba yowled. He hit me with his fists so the blood streamed from my
mouth and my lips swelled horribly. It was the first time he had ever
beaten me since I was Anwar's age, and I cried for hours. It is a *shame* to
beat someone as tall as yourself! Mama consoled me and said, "It's my
fault," and so did Ali. Ali wanted to give me money to console me, but I
refused. Mama sat with me till three in the morning trying to calm me.
Then only did I sleep, completely exhausted.

The next day Foad came visiting. He was shocked to see my mouth, and wanted to know what had happened. I said I had been washing the floor and stood bent by the door when someone suddenly opened it and hit me in my face. "That's what I say," he admonished, "you're working so hard in the house you'll harm yourself."

Mona did not want Foad to know the real reason for her swollen mouth lest there be more hard feelings (*za'l*) between Foad on the one hand, and her father and brother, on the other. She observed, "There is enough *za'l* between people already." Mona thinks the real reason for her father's bad temper was that he never wanted her to marry Foad in the first place. Therefore he grasped the first and best excuse to try to get rid of him.

That time when Foad came together with his brother, Uncle Adel, to see me, Mama and Baba were not on speaking terms. The situation had lasted for three whole weeks. Foad was pleased with me. Myself, I didn't know why he came until after he was gone. Then Mama asked me what I thought of him, and if I agreed to marry him. She said Auntie Shaddya's children wanted me to, but that I must decide for myself. I said it was okay. I was so sick and tired of men, and so worn out by all the quarreling at home that I happily took anyone just to have peace.

It was a Monday they came. Uncle Adel asked Baba to give them an answer by Friday. Baba promised but didn't go. He did not agree, for Foad had put as a condition that I quit school, and Baba wanted me to complete my education. Foad doesn't have education, just three years of primary school, and he was afraid that I would be better than him. But Baba felt that with all we had spent on my education, it would be a shame for me to quit now with only two and a half more years to go [to complete senior high school].

When Baba didn't go with a reply, Adel called on Uncle Ahmed and asked him to go and talk to Baba. Uncle Ahmed asked Baba, "Now, what's your opinion?" Baba said he didn't agree. Uncle Ahmed got angry and said, "First you've driven your wife crazy, and now you want to undermine your daughter's interests! As the girl's mother's brother, I now take the matter into my own hands. But don't you come afterward and blame me for what I must do!"

Then Baba regretted himself. That night he said to Mama, "What do you think of Foad?"

"Which Foad?"

"Adel's brother."

"Oh him. What about him?"

"Do you agree to him?"

"Yes."

"So do I!"

Her father wanted a reconciliation with her mother, Mona thinks, for this time he was really afraid that she might make good on her threat of divorce.

Actually, he was far from agreed, and there were lots of quarrels between him and Mama about it afterward. Baba said I was to continue school *no matter what* Foad said. Mama asked [him] whether he had money to keep *me* in school when Hoda had just had to quit [and study privately] because he did *not* have. He said he had. Then Mama said that Foad wanted me to be a housewife, so education was a waste in any case. But Baba was adamant. In the end Mama said that it was no problem, I could continue school even if I got engaged, since Foad would be away in Libya and it would take years before we could marry. But Baba warned her not to talk nonsense. "You know full well that when a girl gets engaged, she loses all interest in school." And that's true. It's just like Baba said.[1]

Mona recalls,

I was so tired and my nerves so frazzled that tears kept pouring all the time—without reason; and I had to blow my nose constantly when I was out with Foad so he wouldn't notice. I don't know why I cry— tears just come pouring. Look at all the problems I have met in life, and I'm only eighteen years.

But more was to come. Two years later the engagement was broken. Only then did Mona confess to me that not even the engagement day had been a happy occasion. I think she could not bear to admit it to herself while she was still in love.

Already at the engagement party, there was more commotion and quarrels. The engagement day, you know, should be one of the happiest in a girl's life. But I was only distraught. Foad didn't buy me a new dress or new shoes. Instead he and his brother said to Mama, "Just dress her in anything!" I was upset and wept. But Mama said, "Don't be sad, he is just thinking about your best interests; he saves his money so you can buy yourselves good furniture and equipment." I borrowed a long white chiffon dress and white patent leather shoes from a friend. But the dress was too wide and the shoes too tight. I returned home from school on my engagement day tired and depressed. Foad ought to have been there waiting for me to take me to the beautician and bring me home in a taxi. In-

---

1. There is a law in Egypt forbidding girls who have signed the marriage contract to continue their schooling. The reason, people say, is that the girl would stir the envy of her classmates who would also then be thinking only of getting married.

stead Hoda and a friend and the friend's fiancé had to accompany me. I was so desperate. I had not eaten since breakfast, and I didn't came home from the beautician till eight at night. Foad and his brother consoled me saying, "Don't be sorry, we'll take you out to eat tonight."

There were lots of guests at the party. We had hired a belly dancer and three musicians to entertain, and especially one of Mama's friends brought lots of relatives to watch. We held the party inside,[2] and the guests filled both rooms, the men in one and the women in the other. Foad and I sat in the seats of honor in the room with the women. Suddenly, Foad's stepmother grabbed the ring and pushed it down my finger and rammed the bracelet up my arm, scoffing at Foad, "You're too clumsy to fix this!" I was upset. Then Foad and his brother said, "Come, we're going out to have your photo taken!"

I thought we were just going out to the main street, but they brought me by taxi all the way to the center of Cairo. There they had me photographed first, and then they took me to the theater! The theater! Can you imagine a girl who wants to go to the theater on her engage-ment? They play was not to start till half-past ten, and we passed the time sitting in a café. I ate cakes and drank cocoa, and afterward two glasses of beer, and then my head started spinning. Later both I and Mama said, "What a waste! He should have bought *shoes* for what the food and theater tickets cost, to make the bride happy. Imagine, an engagement without a happy bride—what a shame!" Mama hadn't even noticed that we left the house; she hadn't even seen me wear the engagement ring and the bracelets. She was in the kitchen preparing food for the guests, and when she came out, we were gone! And the guests were angry and made a big to-do and all left. They wouldn't even taste the food. "Whom do *you* think we came to sit together with?" they snorted. And they were right.

Foad had gotten Baba's permission to take me out, but neither Baba nor I could imagine that we would be leaving so soon or staying so late. They did not bring me home till four in the morning. Then I was dead tired and so distraught that I didn't feel that I had got engaged at all. And Baba scolded me. But by God, I was excused. . . .

Then Foad left for Libya, fourteen days later. He was gone for two years, and all this time he didn't send me a single gift, only letters; and

2. It is common to have the wedding or engagement party in the street, due to the cramped quarters. But educated people have started to regard such an arrangement as *baladi* [backward]. And Mona's fiancé had traveled and was acquainted with modern ways.

in one he said that we must come to the baker's one evening at eight for he wanted to talk with us on the phone. Then he told Mama—Baba refused to go—that they should take me out of school immediately, and spend the money on furnishings instead. He said he wouldn't let me work in any case so education was a waste. Later he sent a letter to Baba saying the same. Baba was furious, but Mama said it was best to give in, otherwise there would only be problems.

For two years I sat and waited. Then he came back. For a gift he only gave me five pounds which he slipped into my hand. And for the family, just two kilos of meat and rice and vegetables. I didn't get even a single piece of clothing, not even a panty or a pair of stockings. Then he said we must marry immediately, within a month, before he must go back to Libya. Mama said it was impossible. We would have to wait another year till Ali returned from Libya, for Baba couldn't possibly do everything [connected with the wedding], take me to the beautician, fetch the chairs, and so on. Besides, the furnishings weren't ready yet, just for one room. Foad said one room was enough. "And where will the guests sit?" scoffed Mama, "on the bridal bed?"

Foad said he couldn't possibly wait a year, and accused us of breaking an agreement to have the wedding that very month. We excused ourselves, saying we couldn't possibly imagine then that Ali would have deserted from the army and fled to Libya [which he had]. Foad must understand that I couldn't marry in my brother's absence. Foad replied that not only had we broken the agreement, but I had even gotten myself engaged to another while he was away. We were dumbfounded; and then the story came spilling out: his brother had written him saying we had sold the engagement gifts! He wanted to cause discord.

Foad blubbered out a litany of other lies, too, to throw mud on us. It was obvious that he wanted to break the engagement but put the blame on us so he could demand his engagement gifts back. For if *he* breaks the engagement, he forfeits the jewelry, if she breaks it, *she* loses the things. We on our part had lots of things we could have said against him, but we let it be to avoid trouble. For instance, we could have accused him of stealing half a suitcase full of clothes which Ali had asked him to bring for him from Libya. Foad stole half of all kinds of clothes: sweaters, trousers, bras, and all, claiming they had confiscated the things in customs. But it was a lie, for Ali had asked him to advance the customs fee for him. Ali had sent us a letter listing every item he sent, so we knew exactly what Foad had taken. Ali was so furious when he heard about it that he wanted to kill Foad. But Mama urged him to control himself since he is in Libya illegally. If the Libyans repatriated him, he would get *that* punishment for deserting from the army.

All this, and much more, we didn't mention. Foad and his brother, however, kept insisting that we must marry immediately. Then suddenly Foad got up and said to his brother, "Come on, let's go!" "But it's still early [*lissa badri*]!" Mama said. They just ignored her. Mama got angry with Baba, thinking he must have offended the guests while she was in the toilet for an instant. But Baba said, "In the name of the Prophet, I have shown them all respect!" And do you know what they did? They went straight to Grandfather's wife and lied to her that we had broken the engagement! Then they asked her to go to us and request a return of the engagement gifts plus twelve pounds which was all I had gotten as gifts these two years. Grandfather's wife believed them, of course, and did as requested; and she was shocked to discover the extent of their baseness when she learned the full truth from us. Still, she advised us to return the jewelry and the money, otherwise, she said, they would pester us forever. Foad's brother was a member of a savings club Mama led, and he had already cashed in his turn. If we didn't pay Foad the twelve pounds voluntarily, Grandfather's wife warned, they would take the money by force by refusing to pay the fee—which was true, of course. Then Baba said, "Here, take the jewelry, and here are four pounds. Tell them that's all I've got, but they'll get the rest as soon as I have my salary next month." Then he went into the kitchen and returned with the meat and the rice and vegetables wrapped in newspapers and said, "And here is the food!" Grandfather's wife protested, "But they didn't ask for the food!" Baba said, "And what do you think, that we'll wait till we have eaten the food, and they *then* come to claim it?"

As for the eight pounds, do you think they were content to wait less than a month? Never! Already the next week Adel deducted it from his savings club fee! And that though it wasn't even to him but to his *brother* we owed the money!

It was a terrible time afterward with lots of quarreling between Mama and Baba. Baba accused Mama of being to blame since she had accepted Foad from the start. Baba curses Foad for having destroyed my future by insisting that I quit school. Foad lies to people and says it's not true, he didn't insist. But I have the proof in his letters. I still keep his letters—here, in a shoe box. A friend of mine has advised me to tear them up, but I can't, not yet. They are all I have left from two years of life.

I think Foad still loves me; he has told it to Grandfather's wife. It was his brother and brother's wife who manipulated him to break the engagement. His brother did it because he loves me himself,[3] and his wife because she wanted Foad to marry her sister. In the end Foad did, and got his deserts. We have heard that her family are tireless in their claims, "give me, give me!"

Four years later, in the spring of 1981, Mona got engaged again, this time to a relative on her mother's side. In mid-August that same year Mona was married, at breakneck speed.

I was back on my yearly visit and was highly surprised to find that Mona's wedding was to be in only three weeks. Umm Ali insisted that I stay for the wedding, so I postponed my departure. She was exasperated and angry. It was crazy of the couple to rush the wedding like this. Three weeks before the wedding day they had assembled only a fraction of the furnishings. And who did they expect would come up with money for the rest? *She,* of course!

Mona was also hesitant. She, too, felt that they could have waited. The last two weeks before the wedding she lay sleepless night after night, worried that they would not get everything ready. And she sighed, "The wedding day is a day for the *groom* to be happy, not the bride."

She also said that she hoped that she wouldn't have to go through with intercourse the first night, "for I am so exhausted, and those things take nerves."

Not that she did not love her fiancé. He is kind and considerate, well educated, has a good job, and they know him well. Even her mother has only good things to say of him. "What I like about Hamdi is that he sees through his family, his mother and sisters. He knows what they are. . . . [here she listed their qualities] Therefore Mona has nothing to fear from them. Otherwise, I would never have let him have Mona."

Mona's predicament was that she would be living next door to her in-laws. Hamdi had managed to lay hold of the flat right across from theirs. Indeed, the flat was the reason why he insisted on rushing the wedding. By then he had already paid rent for it for a year while leaving it vacant (since an unmarried man does not live alone). Now he was tired of throwing money to the crows, he wanted real value for his expenditure.

To obtain a flat without paying a substantial advance is such a feat that it would have been foolish of Hamdi to forgo the chance when it came

---

3. Mona says he told her so during an incident when she slept in his home and he tried to seduce her. (Foad was in Libya.) It is not unlikely that he wanted to break the engagement for fear she might tell Foad.

up, even though he had just gotten engaged. His luck was the result of tragic events in his family, however.

One day the house where his family lived collapsed. One sister was killed in the fall from the fourth floor. The government had to provide the family with a new flat. This was located in a recently settled area, so remote from public transportation that it was regarded as highly unattractive. But the flat itself is of good quality. By chance, the flat across the hallway was empty. And by some stratagem, Hamdi managed to lay hands on it.

It did not mean he could marry. A wedding requires that the *furniture* be put in order. Traditionally, and even today, many families parade the bridal furnishings atop a lorry or cart to the accompaniment of drums, so people can see with their eagle eyes that everything is up to standard. Umm Ali was annoyed that Hoda and Mona refused to do it when they married. It was she who had pinched and scraped to get it all together; she would have liked to savor the acclaim for her achievements.

The furnishings were, I think, a main reason why Hamdi was bent on rushing the wedding. He put Umm Ali in a tight spot by fixing a date for the wedding and hiring a night club [*kazino*] for the occasion so the date could not be changed after the deposit was paid, thus presenting her with fait accompli. She had four weeks to get everything ready. He knows she is a master of the art of the impossible; he knew she would manage if given no other choice. Besides, he himself would help her. If, on the other hand, he yielded to her, and waited to fix a wedding date until the furnishings were ready, he would have to be patient for years.

Umm Ali succeeded by the skin of her teeth. I was with her daily during these weeks, and she was beside herself with despair at the foolishness of the couple. She worried day and night about managing *her* part, and she fumed that they expected her to do even more. They must have china, for example; and she felt that the cheapest kind would do. But they set their hearts on a costly set and left her no respite until she came up with the money for that. When she at last got her daughter married, she was up to her neck in debt. And she complains, "Lucky are those who have only sons. But I shall have to go through this three times more!"

When the wedding day dawned, her own and her daughters' dresses were still not ready from the seamstress. They had to *borrow* clothes to wear. And she herself did not even have a pair of shoes, only her raggedy sandals. "And it's a shame," Hoda said, "for at the wedding all the guests will be staring at the clothes of the bride's family. They will be talking and making fools of us." Umm Ali agreed, but said she couldn't care less.

As it was, nobody stared at Umm Ali's shoes; most of the guests hardly even saw her. She sank down in a straight-back chair in a jammed hall where chaos reigned and most of the guests were friends of the *groom*, and she did not know them. The bride's family was not even photographed on stage with the bridal couple, as custom requires. But when the photographer came, the *groom's* family and the *groom's* friends thronged forth and did not budge till the film was finished! Umm Ali's family was so furious at such lack of simple good manners that they did not even try to exert their own rights. Nor would they have managed to push their way through the crowd anyhow. The groom had invited far too many guests, because it gives prestige to have a big crowd.

This might sound like an overly grim picture of an event that surely had its bright side, too. To that the response would be that if there were a bright side, neither Umm Ali nor Mona saw it. The wedding party degenerated into a disaster. The bride's brothers and the groom's kin almost came to blows over the food. According to custom, the groom's family provides the food; they had made sandwiches with cheese and eggs and put them in prepacked boxes, two sandwiches in each. But they distributed the boxes to *their* guests only! When the bride's brother, Anwar, asked to have some for himself and his family's guests—many of them had come from afar and were starving—he was refused. So Umm Ali's guests marched out, insulted. The wedding party which began at ten and was to have lasted till around two, was over in just an hour.

Other sad things happened, too; the large candles which Umm Ali had bought for five pounds to decorate the entrance to the bride's home on the wedding night (according to custom) were stolen from Ali's car. And the bridal dress was torn when Mona, weeping, stumbled across the threshold of her new home. And it had been rented for forty pounds!

I accompanied Mona's parents and sisters the next morning when they went to bring her the wedding breakfast, bestow their good wishes, and "see" her honor—a bloodstained kerchief which testifies to the bride's virginity. Mustafa, poor man, shy as he is, refused to come up to the flat with us. And Umm Ali had to tell him, mildly but firmly, "What nonsense, is there a father who does not want to see his daughter's honor?"

The time was noon. The door of the flat was closed. The newlyweds were still asleep. Mona had been a nervous wreck the last few days. But across the hall, with the door wide ajar sat an expectant crowd of in-laws, eyes and ears alert, ready to burst in and grab the longed-for testimony to the bride's honor (there are two kerchiefs, one for the bride's family, and one for the groom's) and surely also ready to meddle in the smallest detail of Mona's and Hamdi's lives. He will have to be more than a man, Hamdi, to keep them at bay.

A quarrel blew up between Hamdi and his mother when she wanted to dance in the street with the blood-stained kerchief on her head. This is old tradition, but is obsolete according to modern young people. He managed, just barely, to stop her.

Mona has been blessed with a good husband—there is every sign of that. She sits in a beautifully furnished flat. But life is bound to be hard: she has to leave home at half-past five in the morning to get to work at seven. Not till five at night will she be home. Then all the housework awaits her. I have asked if she can't ask Hamdi to help her with that, since they are both working. No, she cannot *ask;* it is the woman's job. But she can hope that he will voluntarily help her when he sees how tired she is.

She would have preferred to stay at home. But it is impossible, with a rent of twenty-five pounds. With her salary, she can cover this and a bit more.

Hamdi suggested that she start taking the contraceptive pill even before the wedding, so they won't have a child at once. They need her income. Both she and her mother protested that it was impossible, like interfering in God's plan. Horror stories circulate about women who took the pill from the start and became barren.

Hamdi plans that when Mona has a child, she will place it with his mother so she can continue her job. The plan sounds unrealistic. It is extremely rare for a woman to be on good terms with her mother-in-law. Admittedly, Mona is an exceptionally gentle and accommodating person. Still, leaving her child with her mother-in-law would be asking for trouble.

Had Umm Ali lived close by, everything would have been different. But she is a two hours' journey away—outside rush hours.

Mona has had the dream of every young girl come true. She is married, well married. Thanks to the education which her parents struggled so hard to let her have, and which her ex-fiancé only partly managed to spoil, she also has a job. She works in a clothes factory. But double work in a city as jammed and hard to get around in as Cairo is back-breaking, not a means of self-realization, for a woman unless she lives close by her place of work. As Mona says, "I don't expect to be happy. Happiness, what is that? All life is problems. But Hamdi loves me, and he will try to be good to me."

Her mother would have added, "Yes, all life is problems. What counts, is how you tackle them. God helps her who helps herself."

As equipment for life, Mona has been blessed with a cheerful outlook and her mother's rich intellectual powers. She is an unusually wise, balanced, and sociable person. But what she makes of her life will depend to a large extent on what her husband proves himself to be. Will he stay loyal to her or seek support for himself from his family? Will he be economically responsible, or spend money on "being a man"? It is impossible to know. She has said it herself, "Marriage is like an unopened watermelon."

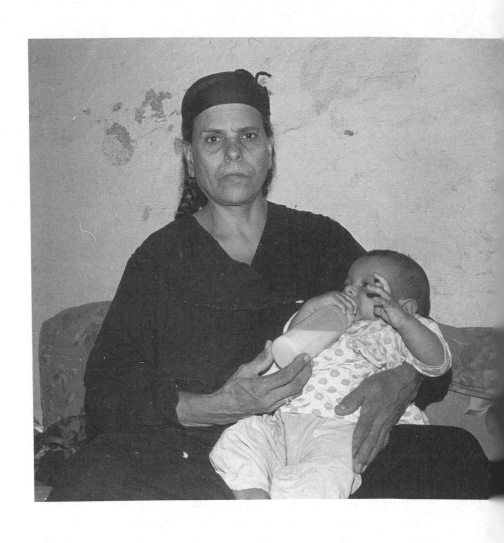

Part Nine

A Hope for the Future

Fulfillment

In February 1979 I visited Umm Ali for the eighth time. It was a year since I had last seen her. I knew exactly how our reunion would be—after eleven years, the pattern was clear. First she would embrace me and kiss me seven times on each cheek (the mark of our special relationship and my long absence; otherwise three kisses times two is the norm); next she would tell me how she had dreamed that very night that I would be coming; and then she would embark on a long journey back in time to bring me up to date on last year's events. It meant hour-long confessions about all that concerned her the most, including ever-new variations on the theme, Mustafa, manchild forlorn. Always new, elaborate stories about his carelessness, neglect, and deceit.

I was totally unprepared for what I was to find, a happy Umm Ali who praised Mustafa for how good he now had become. Gone was bitterness, gone condemnation. She gave Mustafa full recognition for his new and blessed ways. Every month he now gave his monthly salary into her hand. A fixed sum at a regular time. Her highest wish had been granted.

She knew full well, she said, what had spurred his change of heart. When she gave birth to the stillborn boy, her own life had been in danger. Mustafa had panicked that she was actually going to die. What would he have done? He is lost without her. Now that Hoda and Mona are working in the factory, there would have been no one at home to care for him. He would have had to remarry and face the problem of giving his children a stepmother and so forth. For the first time he realized his total dependency on her. "And now he has become so good! Before when I was sick and so tired that I couldn't get up in the mornings, he would kick me in the side and scream, 'Get up, you daughter of a slut!' But now he just says with a mild voice, 'Please, get up, just a little, it would be so good for you!'"

I was completely unprepared for Mustafa's change of heart, but more so for hers. I would have sworn that as bitter as she had been for twenty-five wearisome years, the bitterness must have struck roots in her heart. I was mistaken.

Many more years have passed. Mustafa continues to give his monthly wages into her hand. She continues to praise him for his good and responsible ways. She also makes it a point of telling *him* how she praises him before others. She wants him to be sure of that. The family as a whole

functions better. The atmosphere is calmer, conflicts fewer and more easily resolved. When Mustafa had a relapse last year and smoked hashish
again, it did not lead to angry confrontations. Umm Ali took him to task
and lectured him on the sinfulness of his behavior. Mustafa came to his
senses.

Umm Ali has always emphasized how her heart is white. Unlike most
people, she does not bear grudges. What she says is not quite true. Her
sisters Farida and Feyza she cannot forgive. But perhaps that is because
they have not reformed themselves. Mustafa, on the other hand, has given
her undeniable proof of his good intentions. Through all the years she
used to say to him, "It's not you I condemn, it's your behavior." Mustafa
doubted it, I doubted it. We thought that she also held things against *him*.
She has once more proved that she practices what she preaches. Her
speech and action are one.

People among the poor are convinced that money is the source of all
happiness. Umm Ali has had proof of that. With forty pounds in her hand
every month, she can face life with assurance.

Thirty-four

Talking Is Therapy

The question I ask myself is, How could Umm Ali manage—after years of
despair with Mustafa for ruining and wasting her life—to meet him half
way when at last he changed his course? Why was she not locked in
bitterness? Why did she not carry a grudge? She does not talk much any
more about how bad he was for so long but rather about how good he
now has become.

Is it because of the conviction that runs like a leitmotif through her
life that you can rid yourself of bad feeling by talking it out? She always
emphasizes how talking about one's despair is a means of getting it *out*
of the body; not completely, of course, but enough to preserve one's
health.

Through all these years she had a safety valve for her bitterness. It was
not left to settle like a stone in her heart.

In my country, Norway, we also believe that it is valuable to talk about
one's suffering. Yet we are careful not to do it. We dread saddling others
with our own problems and exposing ourselves. Therefore we rarely talk

intimately, and then only to very special friends from whom we extract a vow of confidence. Much—perhaps most—that truly matters to us we suffer silently in loneliness or in the desolation peculiar to twosomes. We hide behind a conviction that everyone has enough with her own [*enhver har nok med sitt*]. We who live in great affluence, are so poor in terms of time, trust, and companionship that everyone has enough with her own.

Not that we know what "her own" actually implies. The shield around privacy and the preoccupation with keeping one's façade make us effectively strangers to one another. We do not give each other the *opportunity* to be really concerned with one another.

For the people I know in Cairo, life implies suffering and problems to a degree we can hardly fathom. And yet *they* do not have enough with their own. With them, there are practically no limits to people's willingness and ability to engage with one another. Is it because they are mentally more resourceful than we are? have more time than we do? or more compassion for their fellow beings?

The answer lies elsewhere, I believe. What they do have that makes a real difference is a conviction, a tried and true belief, in the frailty and fallibility of human beings. Whereas in my society, we stick to the pretension that being perfect is possible—so we are reluctant to expose cracks in the nice façade—they take it as a matter of course that "all life is problems [*ilhayah kullaha mashakil*]." To strive and struggle and yet fall short, that is the human lot.

So they rush to their fellow beings and pour their hearts out whenever they are distressed, without fear of intruding on their time or tiring them with repetitions. Today it's me, tomorrow you. That a person talks about the same things over and over just shows you how important they are to her, and then it goes without saying that others must listen. I cannot count all the times I have heard Umm Ali tell the same stories in great detail to close and distant acquaintances alike. It is like a purging or cleansing each time. In the West, it is commonly believed that victims of trauma can experience a catharsis by telling their stories. For people like Umm Ali, however, life seems an endless trauma, and the way to endure it is to tell it again and again. Her close ones and I, we know these stories by heart. And yet we listen anew each time. It strikes me that if any of my friends at home carried on the way she does, I would be annoyed. As a Norwegian in Norway I meet people with expectations of self-discipline and moderation. Cairenes take a different view. For don't we all harp on the same strings when they represent what truly matters? And community and belonging, do they not stand for what actually lives on in our hearts?

The Egyptian acknowledgment of human frailty and weaknesses and of life's innate complexity relieves people of the pressure of playing up to each other's pretensions. Now it is, of course, quite feasible to know that everyone struggles, and yet to pretend that all is well. But that is not a course the people I know in Cairo have chosen. In their world, a façade of flawless success would be seen as hollow self-deception. Perfect marital harmony is inconceivable. Marriage is uniformly recognized as hard work, indeed, as a perpetual tug-of-war, and quiet spells are expectations at best. The hurt that all parties in a family may cause each other will become known to others, and they will feel free to respond. Neighbors intervene unasked (but not necessarily unwished for). Friends and relatives are mobilized. There is security in such facts. A person does not stand alone against a superior force; the other side cannot completely overwhelm her. Conflict can be contained within reasonable bounds in most cases. Hence while overt marital violence is common, *covert* violence—a main problem in my society—is practically unknown.

When people meet to resolve conflicts, everyone present will offer advice. All have their opinions, for they all have relevant experience—indeed, they all seem to have all manner of experience. Everyone has seen conflicts and been present during mediation from the time she was small; no one is ever shielded from disputes because "this is not suitable for children." So everyone has a broad range of knowledge about conflicts of all kinds. What they did not meet in their own home, they encountered in the lives of aunts, uncles, cousins, and others as they tagged along with their mother or father on missions as mediators and peacemakers. Over the years they have learned a variety of scenarios for conflict resolution. That does not mean that all conflicts can be, or are, settled, but at least they have been aired and the opposing views have been confronted.

In my society it is considered best always to manage by oneself, and somehow demeaning to ask the support of others. In Cairo, on the contrary, seeking the help of others is seen as the only natural and sensible course, for men as well as for women. Far from being regarded as a sign of weakness or a failure to cope, asking the advice and help of others shows your respect for them and your acceptance of their insight and wisdom.

In consequence, people become involved in each other's lives, for better or worse. Everyone knows a great deal about many others, and the information they have is personal and intimate. Never mind that much of it may be wrong; the point is that everyone *assumes* she knows a great deal, and involves herself and makes judgments accordingly. The fear of

A neighbor of Umm Ali's with her child.

interfering and meddling—so prevalent in my own society[1]—would simply not make sense to Egyptians. Indeed, it would be seen by them as indifference and a failure of compassion.

A sinister side effect of such an involment is, however, that gossip and "the people's talk" flourish. Lives become inextricably intertwined. These are costs the people deplore, and that they try hard to protect themselves against by a degree of concealment and distance. But the costs of isolation

1. Take the following as an example: a friend of mine appeared one day with a big blue and yellow bulge on her cheek. I knew her husband to be a reasonable person yet could not suppress my shock and asked her what had happened. She had had dental surgery. But, she told me, she had been like that for four days, and last night had participated in a discussion group on wife battering. Everywhere she went, people stared at her. But only one person before me had asked what was the matter!

would be even greater; it would exhaust one's psychic resources. So nearly everybody prefers the social course. And though they all complain about how others meddle in matters that are none of their business, they are spared the sense of meaninglessness that plagues many people in our part of the world. People in Cairo's back streets are not "alienated." They have roots in a social world, and a clear sense of belonging.

They are also remarkably strong psychologically, and that is especially true of mature women. Compared to Scandinavian women of the same age, Cairene women have smooth skin (and not only because they are fat), despite many deliveries, little physical activity, and unhealthy food. Their backs are straight, their faces clear. They rarely use pills for headaches or sedatives for sleep, and never alcohol or cigarettes. Without access to therapists and social workers, problems are tackled by people themselves helping each other by "talking together."

That everyone talks and consults so much does not mean, however, that they feel free to confide in anyone. The people I know in Cairo have their own conception of privacy and discretion, but it is so different from ours that it can be difficult to understand. Their concept of privacy does not embrace what we call the private sphere; women in Cairo's back streets will freely compromise their husbands and expose the problems of their marriage. *Such facts do not reflect unfavorably on them.* In this respect, they are indeed more independent than many married women in the West. Marriage in Egypt does not entail a merging of personhoods and does not set off social pressures toward social and spiritual unity. Women retain a sense of their own separate social identity which stands impervious to the failures and blemishes of their nearest and dearest; for they are not brought up on an ideology of happy families and shame on her who falls short in that respect. But they can be hurt, harshly and pitilessly, when the world sees signs of their *material* defeat. Shortages, rags, and unpaid rents, these are the dark secrets of their lives which it matters most to keep private.

In the West, it may be fashionable to wear dirty and torn jeans, as if one were indifferent to looks and standards. We have the wealth, so we can do that. The studied carelessness and denial of material things remains only a pretense, a shell that others see through. It does not compromise or tarnish one's person.

To this day I become annoyed whenever I see people playing such games. I think to myself that they do not know what they are doing, or they would be ashamed. For people who fight a daily battle against the blemish of poverty, material things (including a pretty and neat appearance) are of the essence. Nothing can expose a person as completely as appearing to be short of material essentials. Thus, to [...] pain that comes from a lack of money is their most p[...] pain—as we have seen time and again in Umm Ali's lif[...]

How could Umm Ali manage to meet Mustafa halfway [...] changed his course? I think several factors are relevant. [...] ortant, she had had a safety valve, an outlet, for feelings of sorrow and anger that might otherwise have overwhelmed her. By always talking about her desperation, she had not only been able to rid herself of some of her frustrations, but she had obtained support from her circle that reassured her that she was nonetheless a good and valued person. The talking sustained her sense of self-worth and self respect.

But there was another reason, I believe, and this has to do with what marriage is in this society and how spouses affect, and do not affect, each other's self and identity.

Mustafa had hurt Umm Ali terribly for twenty-five years and, as she says, laid all possibilities waste. But he had not hit her in her deepest soul or damaged her sense of self-respect. For marriage in this society was never conceived as the ideal unity and community of fate that middle-class Western culture constructs, in which two persons in their "twosomeness" [*tosombet*] are maximally vulnerable to *each other* and *each other's* judgments of self. In Egypt, as everywhere, spouses need each other to realize themselves as woman and man. But they do not need each other to think well of themselves. The confirmation of self and one's own value can—no, should—largely be had from persons other than one's spouse. Among my friends in Cairo, marriage is above all a relationship between two persons who enter into a partnership of work and other commitments, but who retain strong ties to several other persons. For the woman, her mother, siblings, and other close kin continue to be of prime importance throughout life, as will the children and the close friends she has. The wife never assumes her husband's name; she retains her father's name as "surname" through life, whereas she takes her given name from her firstborn child. She is dependent on her husband for her status and rank in society. But he will influence her personal sense of value and identity only to a limited degree. Far more important in this respect is her reputation in a circle of close friends and kin and especially in her children's eyes.

Therefore, Mustafa's contemptible behavior through the years reflected primarily on him, and not on his wife. She was far less prone to suffer feelings of inadequacy, guilt, and personal defeat than would a Western middle-class woman, at least in my society, Norway. It may be illuminating to pursue this contrast a bit further.

Among many westerners, particularly in the middle class, a woman will typically experience it as a personal failure if her husband fails, and her own sense of value is diminished.[2] This is intimately connected with the mutual vulnerability and defenselessness that is a part of the very structure of an urban, middle-class Western marriage—handicaps that Muslim women largely escape. Marriage among us is based on love and the ideology that love is all and conquers all. With this as their doctrine, young couples are launched into a reality that is both harsh and complex, where the conclusion is inescapable: if they fail, it is their love, that is, the core of themselves, that has failed. What a pitiful foundation on which to build a life and a partnership, say women in Cairo.

For them, marriage is hard work—too important to be determined by the fickle attractions of two immature persons. Even with the emphasis on love these days and on young people choosing their own spouses, a number of practical considerations enter and are made relevant to the decision process. The choice is rarely in the hands of the young people alone. Too much is at stake. Marriage is not a means to realize a great and preestablished love; rather it is a means to create love. The expectation is that love will grow forth provided both parties behave. Umm Ali answered her son, Ali, when he asked if she loved his father, "I neither love nor hate him. But it was *he* who did not let me [love him], the way he behaved." In other words, she had been prepared to; it was her duty as his wife. Who knows—perhaps Umm Ali will finally succeed in feeling such love, now that her husband has become so good.

Umm Ali has grown up in a society that we would call sexually segregated. There are strict limits on how, where, and when persons of the opposite sex can meet and interact. But such an organization of society may also offer certain advantages to women. Women in segregated societies have never seen themselves as second-rate specimens of *man*kind. They do not struggle to acquire a man's capacities and style so as to be able to compete with him in his world. Women and men are acknowledged to be different kinds of human beings with different strengths and weaknesses. And though sexual segregation regrettably has been used often enough to keep women in the domestic sphere—as Umm Ali's daughters came bitterly to experience when their fiancés demanded that they quit school—this is an arbitrary and unnecessary use of the system.

---

2. The most glaring evidence of this is seen when women in my country let themselves be battered for years without even telling their closest kin. Reportedly, they feel shame with themselves for bringing out such qualities in their partner.

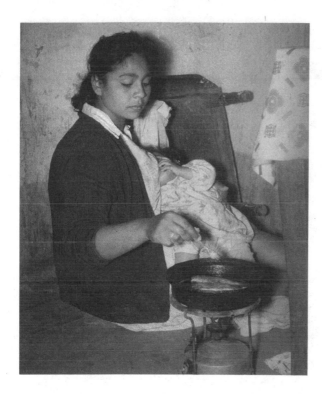

The development of the female role is from insecurity toward strength. A young woman in 1970. See the following page.

What is more fundamental is the emphasis on the distinctive character of womanhood, and thus the force of women's society.

Many western women who have spent much time in sexually segregated societies have been struck by the personal force and self-assurance women there often act out. Whereas in the West, adherents of feminism have had to fight a battle to get society to recognize the value of feminine qualities, in sex-segregated societies this seems never to have been an issue. Women know they have positive value by virtue of their female qualities, and that lends them an assurance and strength which, in my judgment, middle-class women in the West less often achieve. Umm Ali has that assurance and strength, as do many others I know.

There are many sides to women's liberation, some of them deeply cultural. My own society, Norway, is recognized (and rightly, I believe) as a model of a society promoting equality among the sexes. And yet I think that in some respects we socialize girls to seek a more dependent emotional relationship to men than does Egyptian lower-class culture. Girls among us are taught to stand on their own feet, but also to aim at a

The same woman in 1982.

marital relationship that merges the identities of husband and wife and creates social pressures toward unity, fusion, and family harmony. Umm Ali's daughters are brought up to think of themselves as separate persons with separate identities and qualities, distinct from those of their husbands. There is no doubt about their respective boundaries, no merging into "oneness." They are, and remain, "he" and "she," with, in large part, separate social circles; they do not become a "pair." An Iranian scholar has observed how in the West, people come in pairs, like shoes (Minai 1981). The sisterhood that Western women discovered through feminism in the late sixties and have since tried to solidify has been a basic institution among Egyptian women for centuries.

As the years have gone by, and I have seen women in Cairo grow old, I am struck by their vitality and strength. They have a phoenix-like capacity to rise from the ashes after every hardship and defeat in the many trials life sets them. Their resilience is truly impressive. During the course of her life, a woman tends to move from weakness toward strength. Marriage starts with hardships and problems; being mother to small children is exhausting. But seeing children through school is even harder, since they require more money then (for private tutoring) than at any other time—except for daughters, whose wedding expenses are simply overwhelming. But once the children move on—and some start working, others get married, and one is left with only a late and loved straggler or two—life starts improving. The marriage of a daughter quickly leads to the cherished status of grandmother. They have an experience and wisdom, these women, that is highly appreciated. And because they never saw themselves as attractive because of their sex appeal, the loss of youth is not a great loss to them. No one likes to grow old. But I am quite sure that these women dislike it less than most.

For some years I feared that Umm Ali would suddenly die before my next visit to Cairo. She was so shrunken and so miserable in those years after Amin's death and until her daughters started working and Mustafa changed his ways, that I feared she might simply succumb. But during the last few years, she has picked up remarkably. And she is not alone in this—many women of her generation seem to be doing the same.

Now that they are pushing fifty, their worst struggles are over. God willing, they can look forward to better times.

Part Ten

Epilogue

Thirty-five

What Happened Next?

The preceding text took us up to 1982, an arbitrary cutoff point, it seems, until we realize that there are no final endings. Life goes on, but the same stories repeat themselves on a human level. It is in this sense that the lives of Umm Ali and her circle illuminate a human plight that transcends the vicissitudes of history. Still you may want to know what has become of Umm Ali and the others over the years. I have been back yearly to see them, and briefly, this is what I can say:

Umm Ali is still living fairly well, but she has become almost blind. Her diabetes at last took its toll, and she panicked when she realized it was going to happen. The core of her despair, as I understood it, was not losing her sight as such, but the thought of the chaos that would invade her and make the whole family life into a mess when she was not there to *see* and keep an eye on everything. Her lifelong preoccupation with *nizam* [order, plan, system]—that key to happiness which she had craved and never achieved due to her husband's consistent failure to provide— now turned into almost an obsession. How would the daughters manage? She knew they would not. Who would cook, sweep, tidy, take charge? And how would she know who entered and left the flat? A lifetime's battle for *nizam*—which was mostly lost but which kept a few sweet and hard-earned victories—now threatened to do her in as the disasters that would descend on her paraded before her mind. Had she not courted calamities before when she was merely absent a few hours a day while holding the job? What now when she could never oversee anything but must rely on hearsay and fabrication? We all tried to console her that losing one's sight is not the worst thing in life, given that she was other- wise relatively healthy. But she would not be consoled.

She insisted on undergoing an eye operation which was outrageously expensive and gave her a minimal chance of saving fifty percent vision on one eye. I arranged for her to have it done gratis with an eminent eye specialist whom I contacted through friends. We went together to the hospital and got it all arranged. But I had to leave Egypt before the day of the operation. As it turned out, she did not show up. She later told me I must understand that nothing that is free is good, and that a doctor would never treat a person like her conscientiously unless he was well paid. When I protested how well we had been received when we had been at the hospital, she said of course; it would be different when she came alone. A lifetime's experience was distilled into one formula. There was nothing I could say to rebut her conviction, part and parcel of poor people's wisdom of life.

So she had her son Ali, her son-in-law Hamdi, and her brother Ahmed struggle to borrow a fortune so she could carry through with the operation at a private clinic. It was mostly in vain. For a while, she saw a bit better. But then she turned practically blind and has remained so. She can discern shimmers of light, but not faces or colors. And yet, says my son, after seeing her last year, she acts as if she saw everything! Nothing ever seems to elude her. Her gaze is focused, her remaining senses razor sharp. She continues to be in charge and compensates for what she cannot keep track of visually by a stream of shouted commands. But I sometimes think I am glad she cannot *see* the state of affairs. It would sadden her. Afaf and Nosa fight constantly over who is going to do what and when, and much is left undone.

When I last saw her, in January 1994, Umm Ali was "mute" and had not spoken for three months. She told me it was because she was driven nuts over the bickering of the girls. The state of muteness—rendered in Arabic simply *hiyya mish bititkallim* [she does not talk]—is not as literal as it sounds: the speechless one can whisper and by giving her your full attention, you can barely hear what she says. Umm Ali's power over her family was clearly enhanced by her muteness. If they had disregarded her before, her daughters now rushed to her the moment she beckoned. If before they had turned a deaf ear to her, they now had to bend close and listen attentively to her every word. Silence, in a world bursting with clamor, can be an ingenious weapon. Umm Ali came out of her muteness just before I left, to the immense relief of the family. Mustafa glowed as he gave me the news.

Mustafa has aged, naturally, but is otherwise his usual self. He is pensioned from his government job and spends more time at home, having left the workshop more or less in Ali's charge. But he is in good health and seems relatively content. The relationship between him and his wife is rather peaceful, all things considered. There is less to fight about—only three children at home—and the economy is less strained. He and Umm Ali stand together against the daughters' betrothed husbands, who bully the girls while failing to act up to a man's duty to exert himself tirelessly to assemble the furnishings so they can wed. Afaf has already had an apartment for more than a year without being able to move in. Mustafa roars at the attempts of his sons-in-law to reap the benefits of marriage without paying the costs, as when they demand total obedience and refuse to permit his daughters even to see their own sisters at will. He clearly resents the men's attempts to turn his bright and well-mannered daughters into docile instruments of *their* will, perhaps even more than their mother does.

For Mustafa, traditional as he is, is also broadminded. He has lived through the "days of the British" and is proud of that; he has seen changes come to Egypt that promised to make a new life for his daughters also; and he loves them dearly, there is no doubt about that. His lifelong experience and fatherly pride now put him at odds with his sons-in-law who seek a return to traditional ways when it comes to a woman's position. Umm Ali looks on with mixed approval but marked respect when he takes them to task. She and he seem to have become reconciled to each other, aware that they will soon be alone—with all the children out of the nest.

Looking back, I realize now how a running theme of Umm Ali's life over the past two decades has been getting the girls married. The boys presented little problem, they would take care of themselves since they earned their own money. But girls require endless thought and maddening expense. She has succeeded, almost. Two are married, whereas two are all but married, having signed the marital contract [*katb ikkitab*]. The furniture and equipment necessary for marriage in the full sense with sexual consummation and cohabitation virtually threaten to break the backs of many girls' parents. Only two more girls to go, and Umm Ali will have acquitted herself of her responsibility. But how she will manage, practically speaking, without a girl to help her now that she is blind, I cannot envision. Or will the youngest son, Anwar, move in with his wife? Her daughters are prevented from helping her out, since they live far away in Cairo; nor could they move in with her, for a son-in-law must be master of his own home whereas a son is obligated to his parents.

Ali, Umm Ali's eldest, is established in his mother-in-law's house, in a separate flat. His parents are reconciled with his wife, though both parties keep their distance. The marriage between him and Nefeesa is working out well. She has become very pious, whereas he works hard against heavy odds to provide for the family. They have two children together plus the boy she had from her previous marriage—a boy Ali treats like his own son.

Hoda has proved herself an impressive woman when it comes to managing husband and house. I admire her for her acumen, ingenuity, and sheer hard work. She carries a double load, working in the factory by day and at home morning and night. Her husband insisted that she quit her job and they fought hard over the issue, but she won. She now keeps her two children in a nursery by day, having their father bring and fetch them as his hours are more flexible than hers. She would have preferred to keep them at her mother's with her sisters looking after them, but it is impossible. She tried it with the first boy, but traveling the long way was so strenuous that she had to leave him there during the week, fetching him only for weekends. Also, her sisters neglected him, she says. (And he did look miserable.) Now with the day nursery, both children seem to be thriving.

Hoda is almost losing her mind from financial problems. In addition to the high cost of the nursery, she is still paying off debts on the furnishings assembled five years ago. She admits that she may have been too acquisitive then, but the time before marriage is the only time when one can afford to think of the house. After the children come, they take everything. Nor would it work to sell the things now, for they would fetch only a fraction of their value. Much as Hoda would have liked to stay home from work, she has no option. Her husband cannot get regular employment, so her work is the only security they have. (It offers both job security and welfare benefits.) The thought of the children keeps her going. She puts her faith in God and is pious in prayer.

Mona is lucky compared to Hoda in that her husband has security of employment and a well-paid job. Her prediction that he would strive to make life good for her has come true. Hamdi exerts himself tirelessly for his wife and children. Mona quit working in the factory after her second child was born. She tried going back for a while after maternity leave, but the strain was too much. She had to leave her children at her mother's during the week, fetching them home only on weekends. Now Hamdi works for two to make up for the loss.

With an exceptional husband and three fine children Mona might have reaped happiness from life were it not for her hard-pressed economic situation, which necessitates acrobatic skills to stay afloat and a clearly unenviable living situation: her mother-in-law lives across the hall, which is bound to beget trouble. When one is also far from public transport with three small children, it is really too much. Mona tries to take it in stride but suffers from mental stress. In her mother's day, a person in her circumstances could have opted out of the situation by moving to another place. But with the present housing crisis, that solution is out of the question. So she sticks it out, hoping that tomorrow, God willing, she will get a reprieve, meanwhile seeking solace in her children.

She wanted to have another child, but her husband categorically refuses. With the cost of educating children these days, having three is really more than enough.

Hoda and Mona live far apart, more than three hours' round trip on jammed buses, so they see each other rarely, only once every week or two at the parents' place, which is midway between them. With Ali working for their father, they see him, too, now and then, but his wife only on very special occasions.

Afaf has come of age, and has emerged a stout and assertive young woman. She has had many relapses of her mental illness, in the process trying out an arsenal of medication that doped and dazed her but otherwise did little good. There were antidepressants and stimulating drugs to take the edge off the antidepressants plus a host of others, but none of real help. For years she heard voices that tormented her with accusations that she was not a virgin, and she decided that she wanted to wed in the traditional [*baladi*] rather than the modern [*afrangi*] way to put a stop to these allegations. With the *baladi* way there will be women present to see that she is actually a virgin, whereas with the modern way, the groom can just produce fake blood as proof.

Afaf bears the imprint of the upbringing in her mother's house in her emphasis on freedom. I have heard her lecture her betrothed husband in public in ways that earned her my and her parents' respect, though Hoda was aghast. "You just want to keep me caged in as if I were a doll," she screamed, "but I'm a human being!" She promises to make a powerful housewife—to her betrothed husband's dismay.

Nosa—the "little one"—has just signed the marital contract. She seems to be in for an especially difficult start. When I asked her why she wanted to marry a man with whom she fought constantly even before the engagement, she simply said, "*Ilwahda mish bititgawwiz kulli yom*" [It is not every day a girl has a chance to marry].[1] Her remark testifies to the fundamentalist winds blowing over Egypt these days. At twenty, Nosa fears becoming an old maid. Boys nowadays want nothing of the perils their older peers suffered (cf. the ups and downs of Hoda's and Mona's engagements), but desire instead to speed up the marital process, carving out a domain where *they* can be in charge—long before they can bear the costs of marriage. And so they look for young brides with whom to contract a marriage, years before the wedding. Sexual relations will be prohibited till then, but obedience and respect are theirs to command.

Nosa's struggles with her betrothed husband center on precisely such issues as who is to be in control of what. She resents his dictating her dress and demeanor and refusing to let her take a job when she has spent a lifetime exerting herself in her studies. But a man has the legal right to refuse. For someone like Nosa who could say, since she was a toddler, "freedom is the most important thing in life," marriage, *anno* 1994, comes

---

1. There is an almost equivalent old Norwegian saying used well into this century, "Du aldri blive gift hvis det ej skjer idag."

with a cost. So far hers has been a tug of war. Her husband will have to desist and she to smooth out a few rough edges, but in time, they will probably find a modus vivendi. As people say, "Divorce is for the rich who can afford it."

Anwar has caused his parents least distress of the children so far. He continues cheerful, with intelligence and drive, and is also very good-looking. He too has married—but is not yet cohabiting with—a girl of only sixteen. They are looking for a flat in the vicinity of his work, which is hours away from Umm Ali. Fortunately, he is letting his wife continue her school. I would not be surprised if in due course he moves in with his parents, though Mustafa says, no way! He and Umm Ali will manage by themselves.

Ahmed and Amira continue to live in the neighboring lane. Umm Ali rarely sees them, and last time I saw her, she and Ahmed were not on speaking terms due to a quarrel between Ahmed and Ali. When I asked Ahmed why this had to destroy his relation with her, he simply shrugged and said she was the mother, enmity with one family member means enmity with them all.

Amira has managed exceedingly well by any standards. She has raised four children up to or through university, and the three others will probably do well in their time. She owns the house which she is working hard and systematically to have demolished by securing a permit of condemnation so she can build anew. She will then be able to make a small fortune in rent, as with the neighborhood's now central location (Cairo has expanded at the margins), flats here are very attractive. She has also bought the taxi Ahmed once craved, but now he heaps curses upon it. The deal is that he drives the car but the women, Amira and her sister, own it; he earns five pounds a night as a regular wage, whereas they take the rest and pay for all repairs. What Ahmed failed to realize in his eagerness for the car was that the women would be on his neck always, nagging him to drive. He does not have a moment's rest and looks haggard, to tell the truth. I do pity the man, much as I admire Amira. Her old mother lives on, in glowing health. She says she is seventy-six, but her alleged age has not changed for years.

As for the others who figure in this book, most of them have dropped out of Umm Ali's life because they moved or fell out with her or died. Her relationship to her father's wife, however, is good and constant. So is her friendship with Umm Fathi, the friend who replaced Umm Magdi twenty years ago. And her relations to neighbors have improved as the children grew up and stopped fighting. Her sister Farida, however, she hardly ever sees, nor her children or other nephews and nieces. At Nosa's marriage recently, the only relatives who turned up were distant kin of Mustafa's from a remote part of Cairo, none of hers.

Such, in a nutshell, were the destinies of Umm Ali and others after we left them in 1982, which is as far as the main story took us. But their lives continue unfolding, a neverending story that goes on and on, but with the same themes repeating themselves on a human level. This is not to deny that fateful events occur as disasters or blessings through time: Amin's death; Mustafa's change of heart granting Umm Ali her lifelong wish for money; her father's remarriage; the story of the car; these and other events dispel any illusion of an "ethnographic present"—a motionless time, not to speak of Umm Ali's *sukkar* [diabetes] and resulting blindness.

But such is the spirit of the human being that people manage to pick up the pieces and carry on somehow, largely because they have no other option, barring opting out completely—as Amin did—or turning mute as Umm Ali and other women do from time to time. As a result, their lives may read like an ethnographic present—a recursive story of unchanging fates and circumstance. But that is because of life's "urgency and necessity" (Bourdieu 1990)—the things that have to be done and the ways of doing them that lend regularity and continuity through time. In a life of poverty, basic concerns tend to be the same, day in and day out. *Money* takes on the force of a specter, relentlessly in pursuit, dominating one's consciousness. When things fall apart, the eternal need for money is always there to reimpose direction and motive to one's struggle.

When Ali and Ahmed now fall out, the particulars are new, a specific happening, but the basic story is the same: the grueling effect of want of money. When Amin took his life; when Umm Ali cannot treat her diabetes; when her treasured friendship with Umm Magdi went to pieces; or when Ahmed wears himself out shouldering his family's expenses—the reasons are always the same: lack and want of money. And you can't give up, give in. For there is no one else to help you. In that sense, and that sense alone, the tales of Umm Ali, Mustafa, Ahmed, Amira, and the others reflect an everlasting present. In every other sense, they have seen dramatic changes in their lives, many of which were connected to the political economy of the nation-state in which they live.

Thirty-six

Cairo—City Victorious?

Four political regimes
Umm Ali and Mustafa have lived through four political regimes: the British and King Farouk, President Nasser, President Sadat, and President Mu-

barak.[1] It is a common opinion among the people who recall the days of the British that their own lives fared better then. There was little *fawda* and *ihmal* [chaos and neglect], corruption was absent, order reigned. Now, this may be nostalgia for a past that seems everywhere to embody the good things in life. But it is a shared opinion among the people I know that their own governments have neglected them and selectively favored the rich.

Mustafa talks of how, in the days of the British, he felt treated like a man, whereas Egyptian bosses are vain and condescending. Be that as it may, the people were in for grave disappointments with the Nasser regime, and used to heap abuse on it and him. What promised to be a salvation from oppression and poverty turned instead into a pursuit of national vainglory that cost them many of their sons as *they* were the ones who had to man the army and fight his war with Israel.[2] Indeed, the war intensified their condemnation of the government. As one man said, "They were two million and we were thirty-four [million] plus the rest of the Arab world. And they won—because of the exploitation and lack of cooperation among us" (Wikan 1980, 161).

During my fieldwork in 1969, two years after the June war, I was astonished to hear people's praise of Christians [*Mesahiyyin*]—a label used to include Copts and Jews. One message people had extrapolated from the Israeli victory concerned the superior compassion and cooperation of Christians—a lesson in keeping with what they observe of their own Coptic neighbors: "Christians love each other," versus "Muslims eat each other like the fish do" is a common formulation of this contrast. The war served as a foil to highlight the insufferable faults of the government, and as an opportunity to express their own idea of what a good society is like.

The hysterical mourning when President Nasser died in 1972 must be read as love and admiration for a man of great charisma, not as support for his policies. He was seen as favoring his own companions, building a political regime based on fear, and letting a corrupt bureaucracy swell to the detriment of ordinary people who have neither the connections [*wasta*] nor the bribes [*rashwa*] to keep them afloat.

Education

What Nasser did do for the people that changed their lives for the better was to improve access to education. That the children of the families I

1. For source of this chapter title, see Abu-Lughod (1972).
2. The poor had to bear a disproportionate share of the burden of the war because there is an inverse relationship between level of education and length of military service.

know have an average of six years more education than their parents is thanks largely to the Nasser regime and its emphasis, in ideology and practice, on education—for *both* sexes. Particularly impressive is the rise in education for females: in the course of one generation it has more than tripled, from two and one-half to nine years, whereas for boys it has just doubled (Wikan 1995). Umm Ali's family is typical in this respect. Whereas she has only two years of school, her daughters have twelve, twelve, eight, and seven years, respectively. Primary education was instituted in Egypt in 1923, but it was not until after the revolution, in 1952, that it became generally available to the people. By the early seventies, most children of the people I know attended school, and by the mid-eighties everyone did.[3]

But education came at a great cost. With the population explosion and a strained economy, classes had many more pupils than a teacher could effectively teach, so private tutoring became the norm, imposing new and heavy expenses on the people. The cramped living quarters, which hardly afforded a child the space or peace to study, made remedial tutoring all the more necessary. Amira has gotten three of her children through university partly because of her ingenuity in arranging for their study. The home was filled with ear-splitting racket, so she simply moved out, renting another flat (equally cramped) to live in, leaving the first for the children's study. It cost her thirty pounds extra per month—a third of her husband's regular salary at the time—but it was worth it. The same option is closed to most others, however. With the housing crisis in Cairo it required the ingenuity of someone like Amira (and some luck) to find a way out.

Still the people's motivation for education continues unabated and many go to enormous lengths to secure their children this stepping-stone to middle-class life. But disillusion has set in. Whereas in the early seventies people used to say, "Egypt has become the country of testimonials," by now it is all too plain that education does not pay off in the sense of securing a high-salary job. Unskilled labor earns much more.

What education does provide is status and esteem plus—for high school graduates—a guarantee of employment, job security, and social security (in sickness, old age, and so on). The government has committed itself to hiring every graduate, though at present there is a waiting period

---

Since university and high school graduates have shorter terms of service (see chap. 7, n. 1 above), it is the sons of the poor who make up the rank and file of the army.

3. Primary education was extended from six to nine years in 1981, but it has recently been reduced to eight years by the elimination of sixth grade. For valuable insights on education, see El-Hamamsy 1970; Ikram 1980, 124–41; Howard-Merriam 1979, 256–70; Khattab and El-Daeiff 1984, 169–87; and Singerman 1995, 160–61.

A young man from a
very poor family who
made it through
engineering college and
is now in a prestigious
position in Kuwait.

of up to nine years, and the wages are ridiculously low. As a result everyone has two jobs. And so the circle is closed: teachers have to give private
lessons to survive, and pupils have to take private lessons to succeed.
What this means, in effect, is that Egypt has an informal education system
that underpins the formal system and prevents its total collapse (cf. Singerman, 1995; Wikan 1995). The system of tutoring, largely paid for by
the people, is the necessary complement to "compulsory free education."
It is a tribute to the people, parents and children alike, that they persist.

But does it pay? Is it worth it? Clearly not, if one considers the enormous sacrifices families make to get their children through school, sacrifices that entail deprivation in every aspect of life: fathers working themselves to despair to pay the cost of tuition or private school (which is
necessary if the children fail in public school); mothers scrambling to
save and borrow; children studying around the clock; and the whole family forgoing proper nutrition and other life necessities; and so on and so

forth. People bemoan all this, and yet they persist in their quest. As one mother said, education is the only thing that parents can pass on to their children which cannot be lost. It is an investment in the children's future which is bound to bear fruit. Many of the children I know no longer consider themselves "poor" [*faqir, fuqara*] because of the enhanced self-esteem they derive from having an education.

Standard of living

The reign of President Sadat was accompanied by changes that produced great improvements in living standards among the people I know, and he went down in history among them as the provider of some good things in life: a blooming economy, enhanced life chances, and improvements in the position of women. This is not to say that all praised him equally, or benefited equally, or even that they saw the president as a prime mover in it all. As regards the position of women, for instance, later developments revealed a severe reaction in some segments of the population against the expanded rights which he maneuvered to launch. But positioned by the twists of history between President Nasser bent on pan-Arab glory and President Mubarak fighting economic recession, President Sadat's reign is associated with a time of glory, if not on a national, then on a personal scale. People also welcomed his peace journey to Israel.

What was the secret of President Sadat's politics, as seen from down below? First and foremost was his open-door policy [*ilinfitah*], which flung wide Egypt's doors to foreign trade, capital, and tourism.[4] As a result, there was a boom in the building, transport, and service sectors of the economy with major job opportunities for people who subsist, even when they have regular salaried jobs, on what they can earn from subsidiary work as taxi drivers, painters, carpenters, and so on. Add to this the possibilities for labor migration to oil-rich Arab countries, and the picture of better times is even clearer.

Labor migration provided the chance to earn in a year ten to thirty times more than in Egypt. Consequently, many men, and especially the young, struggled hard for the opportunity to go. In many cases, it required bribes and connections to obtain the necessary work permits and papers,

---

4. The question of the impact of the open-door policy on the lives of the poor has been hotly debated. Some scholars contend that it aggravated their difficulties as the gap between the rich and poor increased. But in my opinion, there can be no doubt about its positive impact. My research shows significant improvements in employment opportunities and standard of living. That the rich grew richer is of much less importance to the people than that they themselves became better off.

but the effort was well worth the gain. Even one year's stay abroad could drastically improve one's status at home. Overall, about one-third of the families I know have had at least one member go abroad, as did Umm Ali's brother Ahmed, her son Ali, Mona's ex-fiancé Foad, and the husband of her former friend Umm Magdi. But labor migration served the population as well as it did because the men generally did not take their families abroad.[5] Thus the wage retained its very high value, and the family was also spared the cost of displacement, physically and mentally.

The details of what people were able to achieve during Sadat's reign have been set forth elsewhere (Wikan 1985). The change as registered from below was impressive and subjectively marked in people's vocal praise for their bettered lives. When this improvement did not find its way into international statistics on the standard of living, it was because of a failure to value what mattered to people themselves, and a failure to measure real income (ibid.). Most men, as we have seen, derive their main income from jobs in the informal economy that often do not enter macrostatistics.

When an enhanced standard of living also translated into improved quality of life, it was due not only to an ingrained conviction that money makes happiness but also for objective reasons. My most spectacular example is provided by a donkey-cart driver who ascended to a horse and cart, then a lorry, then a second lorry, and in the end a white Mercedes, as good as new. In the process, he also acquired two four-story houses. He had risen from the most destitute conditions, pitied even among the poor. But he had drive and ambition, and step by step built his entrepreneurial "empire." His children eat better, dress better, and have better health than many children whose parents were lucky compared to him in being favored with an education.

The irony of the open-door policy was that it came to the aid of primarily the poorest among the poor who were not committed to education (because of the cost of uniforms, shoes, pencils, and so on), and so were "free" to expend their resources elsewhere (meticulously saving a penny now and then through savings clubs). But even many of the educated gained, since most had a stake in a subsidiary manual job even when they held regular employment.

In Umm Ali's life, the enhanced standard of living—fruit of a boom in Mustafa's workshop—could be seen in such treasures as a fridge, a butane

5. Men did not bring their families in part because they were not allowed to, but also because of the harsh living conditions in Saudi Arabia and the Gulf. Bringing the family is done only by some white-collar workers from the middle class.

stove, a fan (to take the edge off the stifling summer heat), an iron, and in due course a washing machine and a color TV. When these things became obtainable at all, it was thanks to another effect of the open-door policy, the manufacture in Egypt of commodities that in Nasser's time were laden with import taxes, making them exclusively the possessions of the rich.

But if the years of Sadat (1970–81) were times of relative hope and optimism, why do such achievements not stand out more clearly in the stories we heard? Partly because of a rhetoric of complaint that foregrounds the ceaseless shortage of money. Joys and pleasures appear more obliquely as victories in the constant competition to shame others. More important, the objective circumstances did not change that much. The open-door policy did not remove poverty; it just made it more bearable and eased the sense of deprivation. The drastic *political* changes necessary to redistribute resources more equitably were not initiated by either Sadat or any other president—apart from Nasser's land reform, which did not help the urban poor.

Recession

With President Mubarak, recession has set in, linked with the larger world economy. For the lower class, the effect is experienced as diminished job opportunities, spiraling inflation (about 25 percent annually), rising cost of basic amenities, and escalating distress. The president is given the blame, not because he is expected to be a magician with the ability to change the world, but because people can see with their own eyes that recession hits unequally, and the rich appear to be spared. Their complaint is with the injustice and inequality of the system that has them pinching and scraping while others wallow in affluence. Why doesn't the president *do* anything? they ask. In other respects, he is seen as a decent man, but one lacking force and courage.

Mustafa has little work at the workshop now, which does not really matter to him as he is on pension and all his children will soon be out of the nest. But Ali is hard hit. Ahmed too complains gravely. He has to drive the cab for eight hours or so just to earn four or five pounds ($1.2–1.5), whereas he used to make three times as much in a night. Hoda's husband is out of work every so often due to the slowdown in building activity. So far no one I know is entirely unemployed, just underemployed. But even the Mercedes Benz owner is struggling and has had to sell one of his two lorries.

Given an official unemployment rate in Egypt of 14.6 percent, what is surprising is not that people are underemployed, but that most men I know manage to find work most of the time. The informal economy explains how. Because most jobs in the informal economy are in the service sector, the more people there are, the more jobs there can be, barring technological developments that substitute machines for men. But with recession, men have to spend more time searching for jobs and must work longer hours for lower wages. The search for work abroad, in Saudi Arabia and the Gulf, is intensified under these circumstances, and those who get a chance to go are considered very lucky.

The quest for education—though it does not promise a reasonable salary, and despite its high costs—is still pursued, understandably, in this climate of recession. What education offers that nothing else can give is employment in the formal sector and social welfare benefits—of inestimable value in a society without any general social welfare. And though a high school diploma is not a prerequisite for such employment, it certainly helps. The social security is the reason why Hoda hangs on to her job for dear life though at one point it meant she had to leave her two little ones, aged two and four, alone in the flat for four hours a day! The question is how long this can go on, the government's promise of salaried jobs to all high school graduates coupled with the swelling ranks of these graduates. Already a number of deplorable side effects are seen: a sprawling bureaucracy, diminishing salaries in real terms—perpetuating the quest for two jobs—and an expanding school population that has long since exceeded the carrying capacity of the system. With up to ninety pupils in a class, the system has virtually collapsed. The recent reduction of free compulsory education from nine to eight years is just one more evidence of this backlash.

The Contract with Egypt
The World Bank and the United States, which give Egypt $2.3 million in aid annually, have been urging Egypt for years to privatize public-sector companies that remain afloat only because they are receiving large government subsidies. But President Mubarak and his government are understandably reluctant for fear of its political consequences (Elon 1995). Privatization inevitably means widespread unemployment since the government guarantee of tenured employment to high school graduates would come to an end. This could prove disastrous for the regime since there is no government safety net of unemployment or other welfare benefits, save for a nominal 20 pound per month pension for the aged and for widows.

Privatization could undermine not just the political but the social structure. We have seen how people command an arsenal of skills, knowledge, and practices that enables them to cope and persevere in their life situations. It is useful to think of this body of knowledge and practices as "cultural competence" (Wikan 1995). But obviously, cultural competence

A government employee
at his second job—
making rosewater for
sale to local people.

requires a corresponding structure of opportunities to which it fits, or
adapts, the efforts of people. This structure has been provided in Egypt by
a succession of Arab socialist governments through their enduring Contract
with Egypt. This contract includes food subsidies, free educational and
health services, rent controls (see below), and employment guarantees
(with social security) contingent on an achieved level of education. It is
striking to note that several of these benefits have the characteristics of "bonuses": they require a degree of effort or expenditure from the recipient
and are not simple entitlements. Employment, job security, social security,
and home tenancy are within reach of those who labor hard. And because
the level of self-help required is attainable by almost all, people in general
devote their energies to laboring for such goals. The bonuses thereby match
and reinforce the set of cultural competences on which the buoyancy of
the lower class in Cairo depends, in contrast to the more inertia-producing
welfare efforts directed at the disadvantaged in western countries.

Egypt is a country of paradoxes. Stark social inequality, lack of real political participation by the poor, and lack of general social welfare, coexist with
a system of benefits and bonuses that is of crucial importance to the people;
vital food subsidies relieve them of hunger: poor people in Cairo are rela-

tively well nourished. There is free health care and education, and though the services can be quite inadequate, there is no denying their value. There is job security and social security for all public sector employees; and home tenancy is guaranteed to all who can rent a flat. What this means, in effect, is that the Contract with Egypt offers an enhancement of status for citizens who exert themselves in persistent efforts at self-help. And though the terms of the contract leave much to be desired for ordinary people, it channels their efforts in the constructive ways that are so characteristic of this population. Let us see how it is done in the field of housing.

Population explosion

From the point of view of the younger generation, the most pressing crisis facing the population concerns housing. With a population growth in Cairo of approximately eight million over the past twenty-five years (from about six million to about fourteen million people), it is exceedingly difficult to find housing—without which the young cannot marry.[6] But everyone feels the pinch as people become stuck in their dwelling, with no freedom to move away, whether to escape troublesome neighbors (as Umm Ali could in her time) or to be close to one's place of work or relatives. Nevertheless, most young couples do manage to find a home; they are not forced out on the pavement, and only rarely must they remain with parents in the old flat. The prevailing pattern in Cairo is one of *housing* in the real sense—with each family occupying a separate flat or room with a lock on the front door. We shall see how the Contract with Egypt plays a role in promoting this pattern. First, let us see where people settle.

Cairo's famed "City of the Dead"—a cemetery that has now been transformed into a real urban quarter with perhaps one million people—is one favored solution.[7] Another is provided by Cairo's "Second City"—the rooftop dwellings so common in lower-class quarters. A third option, and the one that young couples I know have chosen is a place in one of the

6. Egypt is making significant progress in stemming population growth. Over the period 1950–93, the total fertility rate for Egypt has declined from 6.6 to 3.9 children per woman (Cochrane and Massiah 1995, 8–9). The present growth rate of 2 percent per annum is one of the lowest in the Middle East, having fallen from 2.6 percent in 1980–85 (ibid., 1). But even with an expected further decline to 1 percent by 2025, the population of the country is expected to reach 87 million by that year, up from 54 million in 1992 (ibid.).

7. This cemetery now resembles a real town with houses, electricity, schools, and so on (Friedrich 1984, 22–23).

new settlements rising with lightning speed on the fringes west of the Nile on formerly agricultural land. The building boom since Sadat's time has created a tremendous areal expansion: Umm Ali's home is now quite central, whereas it used to be on the periphery. The city has mushroomed in all directions, covering good agricultural land and moving right up to the edge of the desert. When I now visit Gamila, I have the Pyramids in full view a stone's throw away, and it is all very picturesque. But she does not think of it as such. She would rather go back where she came from, an area once scorned even by her for its backwardness and squalor but now praised for its amenities and atmosphere. Indeed, a super high-rise building has just been erected in the main street abutting Umm Ali's lane, with all that implies of rising real estate value. Little by little, I am afraid, the whole area may be demolished as capitalists see their chance to buy up a plot with a derelict house and make a fortune by building a new house and renting it out. What the area has to commend it besides good transportation and markets and shops, are functioning sewage and water supply—most of the time. Such amenities are sorely lacking in the new settlements.

Such new flats will be effectively out of reach of the children of local residents. The only one I know who has managed to lay hold of one—not in the super high-rise, but in another new house, quite posh—is the daughter of the donkey-cart driver turned Mercedes boss. Thanks to her father's affluence and her own lovely looks and demeanor, she married an affluent man.

The caprices of Fortune are apparent in her case. She will live right next door to her mother's childhood home, in a prosperous position that none of her mother's neighbors from those days can hope to replicate for their children. Hoda and Mona—once triumphant because they were going to school and would be choosing their own husbands whereas Laila, the girl's mother, was kept at home and married off at an early age—have been pressed out to the margins of the city into the new settlements springing up to accommodate the surge of people. Nor can they have realistic hopes of landing *their* children in a much better position.

Even when old flats become vacant "back home," they are beyond the means of local people. The young are being banished from the areas where they grew up and where their parents continue to live. What we see is a steady stream, a one-way movement, of youngsters driven out. What accounts for this new demography that reveals the old quarters losing, little by little as they must, their previous composite character? And how are people able to find a place to stay at all in a city with eight million extra people to be accommodated since only 1969?

Building and renting out

The government did not do much to help. Most was left to private initative. Indeed, "the gap between the urgent needs of the urban lower classes and the state's ability to provide low-cost housing constitutes one of Egypt's major crises" (Khalifa and Moheiddin 1988, 251). Cairo, like many megacities in the developing world is being built primarily by the informal sector; roughly 84 percent of all housing units built from 1970 to 1981 were in this sector.[8] What is remarkable is that "Cairo's housing stock has expanded at a rate high enough to accommodate new household formation and in-migration" (Brennan 1993, 83).

Who were the builders and how did they build? Umm Ali's plot provides a clue. Many were ordinary people like her who had acquired a plot by buying in installments facilitated by savings clubs, or by the earnings of family members working abroad. Many moved out, as she said one could, to their plot even though the walls opened to the sky and there was neither water nor electricity. But by placing themselves in a forced savings situation where the hardships were maximal, improvements followed little by little until these places were transformed.

In this way many of Umm Ali's friends and acquaintances became house owners, her former best friend, Umm Magdi, for instance; or her present best friend, Umm Fathi. The Mercedes Benz owner also started out in this way and was doubly ingenious; he bought a plot in an area then considered *fellahin* [rural] where most urbanites, proud of their heritage, would not venture. Consequently, the price was low. In time, he bought a second plot. With the city's expansion, he is now well within the borders of Greater Cairo, and indeed closer to transportation and markets than many of those who bought an "urban" plot.[9] The real value of his property has skyrocketed.

The 1970s saw a boom in such building activity, consistent with the optimism and general plentitude of the Sadat years. It was the poorest who made best use of this option for they were the most desperate to escape paying rent; nor were their resources tied up in education. Were it not for Umm Ali's struggle to educate her children, she too could have built.

Savings clubs: A reprise

Here it is necessary to interject a further note on savings clubs, this impressive economic institution that provides the foundation for savings and

8. Compare, e.g., De Soto 1989 and Hardoy and Satterthwaite 1989.

9. "Greater Cairo" refers to an area comprising 29,000 square kilometers, perceived by the people as "Cairo," and encompassing Cairo city and Metropolitan Cairo. Greater Cairo incorporates such areas as Imbaba and Giza.

investments. As we have seen through Umm Ali's story, all members pay weekly, biweekly, or monthly contributions that are pooled, each member appropriating the whole amount by turns. By organizing such savings clubs (and thereby receiving the first pooled result), the more forceful and foresighted women are able to raise capital for down payments on lots. They also help others by organizing clubs on their behalf.

The pressures and stimuli mobilized are vital because of the necessity to enlist members. In need of money yourself, you start a club and have the right to draw the first installment, but you have to assemble a membership of others who are willing to pay their shares starting now but who do not draw their bonuses until later. Alternatively, you go to someone recognized for being good at running such clubs, asking her to start one on your behalf. So the organizers circulate, encouraging one to save for tuition here, shaming another into saving for a new bed there, creating the network of commitments and motivation to manage to set aside some trifling yet burdensome daily, weekly, or monthly sum for a set long-range purpose. Most members can only succeed in saving in their precarious situation because of these mutual commitments and pressures; and the house plots, school fees, key money for flats, and so forth could probably never have been paid without them.

This social organization for saving, and the interest-free character of loans, deposits, and installments, prove powerful tools even in the hands of the most economically marginal households. It constitutes a basis for people's remarkable ability to respond to opportunities.

Many of those who built did not, in the end, move themselves, though they had originally intended to. With time, it became increasingly apparent that the old run-down area where they lived still had its attractions and advantages; the new house became a place to lodge one's sons when they married, or so one hoped. As it turned out, Egyptian housing laws do not really permit such a strategy for the impoverished, so their houses were rented out. Beneficiaries were people like Hoda and Mona; the story of how such young couples find a home must now be told.

It is generally assumed that much of the financing for housing in Cairo comes from earnings of workers abroad, sales of inherited land or jewelry, and savings in informal credit associations (Brennan 1993, 90). My own research shows that this is only the obvious part of the story. An ingenious form of cooperation is at work between builders and tenants centered on the "key money" [*xilawil*] or advance [*muqaddam*]. It comes about in this way:

Picture a person having acquired a plot of land by paying in installments facilitated by savings clubs. She intended it for the children's future, to build on and move to in time. Perhaps she has moved. Or perhaps she realizes that she is too old; better build for the children—when she gets capital.

Picture then a couple wanting to get married and looking for a place to live. They hear of this woman with the essentials for a home, a plot, but no money to build. So the two team up. The couple offer capital in the form of a two- to three-year advance payment of the rent.[10] In return, they are promised the flat. Or the process can start the other way around, by the owner approaching the client.

In this way, houses get built and people obtain a home. Perhaps the most common procedure is for the owner to save or borrow capital from friends or kin to build one floor, then rent it out, and use the advance to repay the loan or to finance the building of the next floor. In this way, step by step, stories are added. I believe this is how Greater Cairo came to be, largely through the efforts of ordinary people who turned capitalist in a joint venture with tenants.

But by so doing, both parties are in fact contravening the law: only one year's advance on the rent is permitted. Still the practice can be seen as social cooperation, for if people were to keep to the law, Cairo might collapse under the weight of the housing crisis. Now, despite state neglect, the poor manage to find a home; and I have little evidence that tenants feel exploited.[11] True, the advance weighs heavily on them, but it does obtain them a home for life.

The rent freeze

A home for life? This is the paradox of rented housing in Cairo: that it *is* for life, or even the afterlife, in that one's sons can inherit the flat in turn, with no increase in rent. Umm Ali still pays what she has always paid, five pounds ($1.5) per month. Likewise, when Amira was able to rent a second flat, it was because the first flat costs her only three pounds a month. The

---

10. Standard practice is to reduce the rent by half until the advance is used up.

11. I know of only one case where the tenants filed a complaint in court against the landlady. They were very ingenious. First they asked for a receipt for what they had paid (normally receipts are not used), which the landlady, a naive and illiterate woman, gave them. Then they filed a complaint, also requesting a reduction of the rent. The landlady was sentenced to reduce the rent by 30 percent, and to receive no rent until the advance had been used up. She thinks that if she had not been clever enough to register the house in the name of her eldest son, an engineer, she would have been jailed. The tenants in this case were highly educated white-collar workers. Their act was widely condemned.

rent freeze (in force since 1948) ensures that the rent cannot be increased after the contract is signed, nor can the tenant be evicted save by gross breach of the contract. Even Mustafa's abuse of his rental contracts, at home and in the workshop, did not result in eviction. Egyptians are mercifully compassionate, and many go to great lengths to avoid evicting a tenant.

But these regulations and practices have repercussions in two ways. First, with these restrictions, owners are naturally reluctant to rent, preferring to keep the flat for their own children. Second, the rent freeze leads owners to demand the maximum rent from the start, since that is the only time they can set the price. As a result, tenants are squeezed to begin with, which hits the young especially hard, as they are the ones who enter into new contracts. Let us explore these complications.

When Amira, or the Mercedes owner, keep flats empty in their houses, they are in good company: an estimated one million flats are vacant in Cairo. The number is probably increasing. From 1969 to the early eighties, every flat in Umm Ali's neighborhood was occupied, and it would have been inconceivable to leave a flat empty. Today empty flats are common; in Umm Ali's house alone, there are four (out of eight). The owners I know all do this for the same reason: to make a future for the children. Different scenarios are possible, however.

Amira and her sisters were ingenious enough to buy a decrepit house in the area where they live rather than to opt for a vacant plot in a faraway spot. The drawback is that the house yields hardly any rent, for they got the tenants and the old contracts with the purchase. Their problem is to get the tenants out. One lady died, so her flat is left vacant (her children were settled elsewhere). The strategy now is to get a condemnation ruling which would leave the government with the task of lodging the houseless tenants.[12] It goes without saying that Amira is letting the house deteriorate. She has applied once already for the condemnation permit, without result. When last I saw her, she was appealing the decision in court. When she is finally successful, as I am sure she will be, she will truly make the children's future, giving her sons a good place to stay, and reaping considerable rents from the other flats.

The Mercedes owner's plan is different. His second house is brand new, and he is merely waiting for his sons to grow up and marry so they can

12. Government is obliged to provide housing for people whose homes collapse or are condemned, and it generally does. Some recipients take advantage of the situation by selling the new flat, generally provided in good buildings, for a good profit and renting a more moderately priced flat.

occupy the flats. Letting out meanwhile would be impossible. So he sits there in his fancy four-story building with his cars below, his family on the second floor, and two stories empty above. Even his wife's brother who is destitute cannot become his tenant in the interval, though it means that he cannot marry. (He is thirty-five years old and speaks of himself as pensioned.) But how could the owner be sure to get him out in time? Indeed, the law would side with the tenant.

Thus the macroresult of such micromovements is an artificial housing deficit in the city at large. The shortage drives up rents, high already because of the insidious effects of the rent freeze. Losers are young couples. The scramble for flats is without doubt the most pressing problem confronting them, and it is a testimony to their dignity and drive that they will not make do with anything less than a flat, a real place to live. But the cost to the people should not be minimized. They compensate with their vitality and resourcefulness for the failure of the government to help them out.

Project Home

The government does help in one important way, however. The fact that the law guarantees home tenancy for life to anyone who can pay the advance plus the subsequent rent has far-reaching implications. It creates the incentive people need to commit themselves to such projects. How well it works is best seen in the younger generation.

How do young men spend their youth? Not in leisurely pursuits or pranks but in hard work to acquire a flat so they can marry. One of my most astonishing discoveries through the years has been to see male children, spoiled and pampered by their mothers, turn into responsible, hard-working men. The drive to acquire a home is spurred by the wish to be independent and avoid the problem-ridden relationship between mother and daughter-in-law that makes living with the family a trial for the man as well. But because sizable capital is needed for the key money, young men are kept on a straight and narrow path, harnessing their energies to a constructive purpose. The housing crisis spurred this development. But the people's own priorities feed into it; were it not for a family orientation and notions of self-regard that make marriage the mark of the man, one might easily envision young men in Cairo being caught up in crime as are poor men in many other big cities. Now instead, their energies are channeled into a long-term undertaking, Project Home.

Life at the margins

The new settlements were built on agricultural or virgin land, with great speed and a consequent lack of infrastructure and basic amenities. From the outside, the houses look good, but in terms of building regulations they are substandard: the foundations are poor, lanes are exceedingly narrow in violation of the law, the sewage floods and blocks regularly, and the water supply is unreliable. Also, the areas suffer from want of such basics as street names which might help relatives locate a person. Most new settlements resemble a labyrinth, with one alley a replica of every other and no way to find one's way. The landmarks of the old central quarters are lacking, such as an open square here and there, or houses of different sizes and shapes, reflecting the area's natural development. In the new quarters, houses look more or less alike, having been built at top speed in the course of just a few years, with no breathing space to break the feeling of confinement. Umm Ali, with her vision intact, could not locate Mona's house by herself. And Mona tells of her own panic when she was new in her place and could not find her way home after she had been shopping! She walked crying up and down the lanes until she happened on her place.

If we compare siblings with each other, further problems spring to light. The rent freeze works to drive a physical wedge between them; with the city's rapid expansion, a relationship is set up between location and price that has a centripetal effect: a place barely within economic reach of a sibling marrying one year will be effectively out of reach for the one marrying the following year except if the two are already on clearly unequal footing, as are Hoda and Afaf. Afaf will live in the same lane as Hoda but in a much cheaper and more squalid flat. This is quite different from the situation obtaining in Umm Ali's time when siblings could all live close to each other in comparable flats, and it is presumably a new development in the history of Cairo. Its effects on coping and mental health are worrisome. Bereft of a supporting network, how will people manage?

The question may seem strange considering the troubled relations of many kin (cf. the complaint "relatives are never ever fond of each other"). But there is also abundant testimony to mutual compassion and care. Egyptians talk worse than they act: the rhetoric of complaint masks the reality of cooperation. Relatives do provide sources of help for each other in need. And sisters in particular support each other, however much their relations are ridden with conflict at times.

Hoda and Mona would dearly love to live close to each other, but there is no way. Even should Mona, who is the better located, want to sacrifice centrality for nearness to her sister, she would have to pay four times more in rent than she does now (due to the inflated new rental contracts) plus the substantial advance. As a result, people are frozen into their homes and kinship networks are fragmented.

It would not be so bad if people like Hoda or Mona had other sources of support close by: friends and acquaintances. With time, that may come. But at present, mutual suspicion and disinclination to form bonds is what I observe. As a signal of this, shutters are closed all day, even in winter, and families retreat to the innermost recesses of the flat, dark but for the neon tube. In the old quarters, much as people railed about each other, they used to sit in the rooms facing the lane, and they constantly "spilled over" as curiosity or passion got the better of them. In the new areas, much less goes on in the lanes as people keep more doggedly to themselves, and an atmosphere of estrangement prevails.

One effect of this pattern is seen in the paucity of savings clubs. Even with ten to fifteen years' residence, people in the new settlements continue to turn back "home" for such clubs. The networks and trust necessary for their operation have not evolved, and thus the scope for solving daily problems is reduced. What would Umm Ali have done without a rich supply of recruits for savings clubs? Hoda and Mona are much more constrained; with the distances in Cairo today, no one runs home for help. Nor is the mother mobile enough to go and check on her daughters. An exception is Amira's mother; the old matron drags herself out to the Pyramids, forever railing about her daughter's bad luck in being exiled to such a place (which in fact is quite posh).

The structure of new settlements thus reduces people's ability for self-help in a society where strong human supports are needed, given the lack of general social welfare. I regard the dispersal of kin networks as a distinctly counterproductive effect of the housing laws, which were actually intended to aid the people.

Safety and human supports

Yet with all its problems, Cairo emerges victorious in several respects; most remarkable are her people. Their resilience and good humor seem to enable them to keep going against all odds—though the Contract with Egypt improves the odds and creates a structure of opportunity of some value. Through their myriad small acts the people create a city that is a miracle in the sense of being spared some of the most harrowing problems that beset many big cities throughout the world: violent crime, homelessness, and street children. How are these feats achieved? Looking at Umm Ali's life offers a clue.

Think of the two youths picked up from the street, who were brought home, the first by Mustafa, the other by Hoda: the boy who had run away from his family, and the girl said to have quarreled with her mother-in-law. There have been several such "guests" through the years, both in Umm Ali's home and in the homes of others I know. In Egypt, caring does not stop with the family; and so, when a child has run away, her or his family can rest moderately assured that somewhere there will be someone who will take care of her or him—as did the Aswan boy who met Ali on the train when Ali had run away. The guest will be provided with shelter, food, and clothing—even a comb and toothbrush shared with others—as women know from personal experience. All of them have a history of seeking refuge with a relative or friend after a quarrel with the husband and receiving such compassionate care. They need not take to the street.

How basic is this notion that every human being needs a home is best seen from the case of the girl Hoda brought home. When Umm Ali refused to lodge her because her nerves were spent from her recent experience of being picked clean by the boy Mustafa brought, the reaction of friends and kin was not that the girl should be sent back where she came from, into the street. That was somehow ruled out. What they tried instead was to find her another home, as when one man offered to take her to his sister, another to place her as a servant with some rich people. But the simplest solution of all, telling her to go away, was inconceivable, given a culture where hospitality is a holy duty.

These reactions go a long way toward explaining the absence of homeless people. The aggregate effect is to set up a mutual "insurance system" that supplies some of the basic human supports. Did Umm Ali think of the Aswan boy who lodged Ali when she took an Aswan boy, much as she disliked his looks, into her home? Doing unto others as you would have others do unto you is indeed part of an Egyptian ethos, expressed in the values of compassion and generosity [*insaniyya wa karama*]. I find an explanation for the absence of street children in the efforts of so many individuals to live their lives with self-respect. Caring for others and sharing what little one has is part of such self-respect.

But the relative absence of homelessness depends on other features of the social system as well: Who in the United States are most likely to end up on the street? Unemployed young men on drugs and poor unwed mothers (Jencks 1994). In Egypt, as we have seen, real unemployment is not such a problem even if official unemployment is high; drugs are little used by the lower class; unwed mothers are exceedingly rare, and fathers in general embrace fatherhood.[13] For these and other reasons, homelessness and street children do not emerge as critical social problems in Egypt.

13. In the United States, by contrast, several observers note a "nationwide abandonment of paternity" (Freedman 1993, 135). Unwed mothers make up a very large percentage of the poor.

Cairo has been characterized as a city of villagelike settlements constituting an organic whole. Little by little, this character is changing as we get cities within the city displaying some of the ills of Western satellite settlements. A prototype for this contrast is provided by Umm Ali's and her married daughters' neighborhoods. But even in the daughters' neighborhoods, life is sufficiently transparent that a child who had run away would stand a good chance of being found.

News travels quickly in Egypt. A pervasive communication system is set up by the twin institutions of gossip and "the people's talk"—the latter a magnificent purveyor of information, albeit in twisted form. Genuine interest in the lives of others—an intensely social orientation—and an eloquence that turns every happening into a drama, a story, also work to spread information far and wide. Such processes in turn shape the face of the city.

One effect can be seen in the remarkable safety that obtains in the city. Reliable statistics on violence are not available, but as two observers note, "Cairo, despite all the minuses it gets when considering the specifications of a sound and comfortable urban life, enjoys a definite surplus when it comes to social conduct, security, and street safety" (Khalifa and Moheiddin 1988, 257–58). The people themselves refer to Cairo as "*balad amm w'amana*" [a country of safety and security]. They have a clear perception of what the basis for this is: it is in the strict social controls and in bystanders' propensity to always intervene in a fight. That they might not do so seems inconceivable to them.

Such violence as there is is mainly a private phenomenon; its arena is the home, its combatants family members or relatives. Sometimes neighbors fight in the streets. But this is usually kept in check by the people's intervention. The Egyptian propensity to meddle in each other's lives has the positive effect of making no home, no relationship inviolable. People are rarely allowed to suffer or fight in peace, and while domestic violence is frequent, hidden violence is rare.

The police also serve to curb violence, as in the fight following the betrayal by Hoda's fiancé when the women en masse cornered the seductress. But they will only interfere between strangers, not kin. Thus when Ahmed reported Ali to the police for cheating him of money, the police refused to take action, saying, "You are relatives, you have to sort this out for yourselves." Thus conflicts are handled without appeal to the courts—much too time-consuming and expensive a stratagem—and the people themselves also perform a policing function by their ever-present readiness to intervene.

With all their suffering and problems, people like Umm Ali are thus spared the agony of living in a city with violent crime. Their children will not be abducted. Their daughters will not be raped. Their sons will not be killed, nor will their men be mugged or murdered. One can walk about even at night in safety. The most one risks is having belongings stolen at home or on the bus, as when Umm Ali lost the wash from the clothesline, or when passengers on the bus have their watches stealthily removed.

How is this feat accomplished—a city of millions nearly free of violent crime? No one really knows. But I see its concomitants in numerous small acts at the personal level in the neighborhoods I frequent. Macropatterns are the aggregate of a multitude of individual decisions and acts. Looking at the lives of the people I know, the following factors seem relevant. They can be subsumed under "Project Children" and "Project Home."

In every society, as is well known, poor young males are most at risk for perpetrating criminal acts. Girls pose little threat. It is men—almost exclusively men—who are the perpetrators. In the United States, 94 percent of all prisoners are men. Statistics for other countries are probably similar. Thus it is worth asking, What opportunities and constraints apply to poor young males?

It is significant that in Cairo, children from the earliest age have instilled in them a home orientation that foregrounds loyalty to the family and a notion of mutual honor vis-à-vis the world. But it is an honor not grounded in an ethos of bravado and revenge, but rather on propriety and respectability for boys also. Keeping the children off the streets is part of this respectability ethos; and the mothers' success in doing so counters the formation of gangs that could easily have bred deviant behaviors. Second, youths are strictly supervised; they are not allowed to roam; persons of the opposite sex meet in the homes, and living at home until they wed, there are no "free agents." Third, alcohol and drugs are little used among males and never among females. Fourth, family relations are stable, divorce is almost nonexistent, and boys grow up with fathers or father figures who serve them as models of family-oriented, hard-working men. Fifth, the family is perceived as a haven of warmth and support despite the turmoil and conflicts. Recall Ali's despair when he was thrown out of the family, and his desperate efforts to get back in. Also, the woman's role has features that solidify the family and make it a building block within a moral society. Children can generally rest assured where the mother's loyalty lies and of their own value to her. She will not sacrifice their interests for another man or for passing sexual liaisons. If feelings of self-worth and belonging deter criminal acts, then the mother's role in the family structure of Cairo promotes law-abiding behavior. Sixth, and this is crucial, there are jobs in the informal or formal economy, enabling men to marry and provide for a family, if with great difficulty. "Project Home" harnesses their youthful energies to a long-term constructive purpose.

Finally, the "people's talk"—that devastating social institution—serves also the positive effect of enforcing conformity to norms. It is like a secret police, always on guard and assembling information at top speed; but unlike the secret police, *kalam innas* has no patience; it seeks instantly to inflict harm by carrying information out into the open, where it soon reaches the family of the perpetrator. As a result, everyone is impressed with their dependence on this grim reaper and the necessity to stay within strict norms of propriety. It does not mean that everyone complies equally. On balance, however, *kalam innas* serves to contain deviant behavior and to police the community.

But why do people choose to conform? In part from a realization that those who will not are reduced to zero—degraded in the eyes of the world. Without a reasonable reputation, it will be hard to realize cherished goals like marrying; and marriage is a fundamental goal in Islam. But basically, the Egyptians I know are a law-abiding people whose self-respect depends on their ability to lead respectable lives.

Changing times

Can Cairo continue victorious in this respect? Already, there are some disturbing signs to the contrary. Trade in hard drugs has arrived, and whereas the afflicted come mainly from the upper classes so far, drug addiction may spread downward and launch the whole complex of associated crime. So far, I have not heard parents express their fears of their own children falling prey to narcotics—it is just not part of their world so far. But in other respects, new fears are arising, centering on the safety of children and girls.

While Cairo is still objectively safe to walk about in day or night, perceptions of safety are changing. Stories have started circulating about the kidnapping of children and increased molestation of young girls. The stories signal "the new times" in which law and order are vanishing. The political economy is blamed: demoralization from unemployment, shattered hopes, and delayed marriage (due to the housing crisis) create burning frustrations that incite criminal acts.

It seems that fundamentalists have a role in spreading such stories to fill people with despair at the breakdown of society and the impotence of government. But the portent of the stories carries mainly into the new settlements so far, for they are more scarred by distrust. Quarters like Umm Ali's are still perceived to be safe. However, the difference should not be exaggerated; I believe violence and crime exist more at the perceptual than the actual level. Cairo remains, also in the new settlements, a remarkably safe place to live, a testimony to the stronghold of families, the efficacy of social control, and the general law-abiding orientation of Egyptians.

The fundamentalist upsurge

What people in new and old quarters share is a general concern about the position of women. Stories abound of the atrocities to which they are now subject due to the men's misdemeanors on buses and streets. Again, the political economy is blamed: with more men out of work, people say, many have nothing better to do than accost women. Consequently, young women had better not ride a bus by themselves; this is used to explain why most men will not let their wives work outside the home.

Nosa, for instance, is eager to take a job, but her betrothed husband forbids it. And the trend is widespread among the lower class. The law is behind the men. Only if a girl was working when the marriage was contracted can she demand to continue her job, but even this right is nominal. Most men will make it a condition for marriage that the girl be just a housewife.

"Backlash" is a fitting word to describe the changes I have observed in women's position over the past ten to fifteen years—changes that people like Umm Ali or Mustafa could scarcely have imagined. Women's increased participation in public life which Nasser's regime advocated, and the amendments to the personal status law which Sadat launched have both been revoked: the first in effect, the other by law. Both are associated with the fundamentalist upsurge in Egypt.

Take the Sadat law as an example. By maneuvering expertly, he managed to give women a vital right in 1975 of automatic divorce if the husband took a second wife. Four years later the law was revoked; and the wife now has to prove that the new marriage hurt her—in practice almost impossible. Umm Ali's sister Farida can consider herself lucky that her husband mistimed his second marriage. Had he waited a few more years, Farida might have been trapped.

Fundamentalists are conspicuous by their absence in quarters where I work. Here people have always had to think of their daily bread first, and they scorn the extreme and violent ways of fundamentalists who are mainly found among the intellectuals and the middle class.[14] Still, their

14. I personally know only two men who support the fundamentalist or Islamist movement. The histories of both are instructive. One was an exceptionally gifted child, the only boy I know from a poor family to make it through school and university without ever failing a single year. Normally children fail time and again and have to

impact is felt. The fundamentalist message carries through the media, the mosque, and by word of mouth, exhorting people to stick to the letter of the Quran and to express their piety by certain everyday acts. The male–female relationship is seen as a field especially pertinent for the demonstrations of such piety. And so we are back with Nosa's and Afaf's struggles with their betrothed husbands, and their parents' exasperation at the arbitrary dominance of the men.

After a lifetime of freedom of movement, Umm Ali's two youngest daughters now cannot go anywhere, cannot even set foot outside the house, without their betrothed husbands' explicit permission. They can-

---

repeat classes over and over. Thus this boy stood out from the beginning. He was also (I have known him since he was five) unusual in being unsociable and blunt, lacking the charm and good humor of most children. He did not have many friends. He chose to train as a teacher but cannot support himself and his wife on the regular wage. He refuses to do private tutoring, however, regarding it as a sin. To make a long story short, he went to work in Saudi Arabia without taking a leave of absence from his job in Egypt and was punished with demotion and lower wages when he came back. How he will now manage, I do not know. His family (parents and siblings) criticize his extreme ways, as when he refused to let himself and his bride be photographed at their wedding or to shake hands with a female guest. They regard him as a loser, unfit for life, which in a way he is. Now he tries to add to his income by selling *gallabiyyas*, but it is a losing battle.

The second man I know who supports the fundamentalists is the Mercedes Benz owner, also a highly unusual man. Having risen from the most destitute of conditions to affluence, he is a man who does not "belong"; his wealth places him far above the people in his neighborhood, whereas he lacks the marks of real status by being unedu-cated and *baladi* (in the derogatory sense of the term, backward). His wife, their children, and his in-laws—down-to-earth, good-humored people without any preten-sions—distance themselves from his ways, which only adds to his fervor. When last I saw his wife, she pointed to the walls in her living room and showed me that the photos of the children had been removed. What did she think of it? I asked. She laughed and said she was sorry but what could she do? The sheikh at the mosque had said that photos were a sin. But she said it in a way that made me think she was hopeful that the situation would pass. After all, she has lived to see enormous changes in Egypt in the course of her forty-year lifetime: whereas she and her mother have no education whatsoever, her youngest siblings have even completed high school; she grew up in a tiny room in a basement in a family of eight but now lives in affluence in her own house; she has only four children, thanks to family planning, whereas her mother bore eight; all her children are living, whereas women of her mother's generation usually lost several. She says *ilhamd lillah* [praise be to God] for it all; and she trusts in God that some day, some way, her husband will come to his senses. I am less hopeful, unless the economic conditions for ordinary people improve. It has seemed clear to me that her husband's case is one of defeated aspirations; he did not turn to the fundamentalists until recession set in.

not even visit their own sisters. When asked what is at stake for the men, the answer is couched in the language of love. The issue of power or dominance need not arise so long as the girl complies. But would anyone who had met Umm Ali or Amira or Umm Magdi or Farida believe that compliance comes easily to Egyptian women? Self-assertiveness runs in their blood. The stage is set for endless dramas and much maneuvering and resistance on women's part; while the men, trapped in a world that beats them down, may well be committed to win on the home arena.

The fundamentalist message exhorts the man. Even when he has no particular sympathy with the movement and feels he is acting entirely on his own, he cannot escape its impact. The message is in the air that to be a man, you must take charge of your home and wife. Women are blamed for the demoralization of society and admonished to stick to their natural roles as wives and mothers. The public world and the labor market should be left to the men who want neither competition nor temptation—thus both genders can best fulfill their roles. The vision of a moral society advocated by the fundamentalists leaves no room for women in public: they should be as invisible as possible, covering all save face, hands, and feet.

I am amazed now when I read my description of women's dress and demeanor from the sixties to the early eighties (chap. 3). It seems like an ultramodern world compared to today. To think that women wore short skirts or pants and bared their beautiful hair. To think that they moved in public with an air of self-assurance—as if the world belonged to them and they would be using their education. This has all passed. Back to the home is the rule of the day. Or as the wife of the Mercedes Benz owner said on marrying off her daughter at sixteen, "No use in going for [higher] education for girls these days. Men just want a housewife."

But for someone like Umm Ali or Amira, who scraped and pinched and drove themselves to despair to give freedom and equal opportunities to their daughters, backlash hits like a fist in the face. Was it all in vain? Opinions are divided. Some, like Umm Ali, comfort themselves that the daughter will have gained in knowledge that she can use to live better and to teach *her* children; there will be less need for paid tuition. Others, like Amira, urge their daughters to persist in their course and work—even if it diminishes their chances on the marriage market. One woman said that the daughter should work "so she will feel she is present [*tihiss inni hiyya muwgoda*]," though the daughter had lost one suitor after another because of her refusal to give up her job (she had a college education). Another mother, herself illiterate, scorned her daughter as stupid [*qabita*] for giving in to her husband and quitting her job after marriage.

There is nothing new in men wanting a housewife. Men have always been afraid that the wife would be "better than them." What is new these days is the insistence of *educated* men that the wife should not work. Before it was the *un*educated ones who did so, whereas educated men had a broader vision and were happy for the extra income. Also new is a trend to accelerate the marital process so one acquires the status of husband long before one can provide for a wife. In this double circumstance—laying claim to a wife before one comes of age and forbidding her to work—lies the man's hope of ascendancy. Nosa at twenty has to abide by her betrothed husband's every wish. He, by contrast, has acquired a field of authority and an enhanced sense of his own power. No wonder Mustafa rages. In his time, a man was a man by virtue of assuming the duties of marriage together with its rights. Now young men boss and bully their wives without any sense of duty. Egyptian law permits this strategy by separating the marriage contract from the actual wedding. But this had always been the case. It is only now that men bend the practice to suit themselves. Signing the marital contract binds the woman for life, whereas the man is free to divorce.

Fundamentalism and these new practices find especially little favor with parents between the ages of about forty and sixty; they have lived through a time when they took for granted certain freedoms and basic human rights, such as a woman's right to have a job, to dress freely if properly, and to have freedom of movement. Now their efforts to instill these values in their children have been subverted. Sighed one mother (a meek, uneducated woman) on watching her college-educated daughter be locked up for a whole year while her betrothed husband was abroad, "*I* used to be allowed to go everywhere!"

Making a future for the children

Despite the threat from fundamentalists, I am optimistic that the interests of the people will ultimately prevail. The fundamental attitude of Egyptians is to keep struggling, principally in order to make a future for the children, letting that be their supreme orientation to life. And so, whether the regime is Nasser's, Sadat's, or Mubarak's, or whether thwarted by fundamentalist movements, the struggle continues unabated, much as we have seen in Umm Ali's or Amira's lives.

It gives strength to have a first-priority agenda in life. The Egyptian "Project Children" differs from that of many parents around the world in that it is not just an intention or plan; it is a dogged dedication to a particular long-term project that is pursued with relentless zeal and devotion. When this deeply embraced ideal becomes truly efficacious, it is

Making a future for the children. A child in her new home, still with earth floor and no ceiling. In time, the rest will come. By moving into the unfinished home, the family puts itself in a forced savings situation.

because it subsumes a repertoire of practical strategies, of long-term motivations, of inducements to sacrifice until body and soul ache, for the distant, future goal. The phrase also evokes the social sanctions and shame of doing anything less than making a future for the children (Wikan 1995).

And that is the moral of this book. Like the phoenix rising from the ashes, I see people in Cairo's back streets struggle and fail, struggle and fail, but never give up. Therein lies the hope and triumph of this city: the people and the people alone are her most precious resource.

Fieldwork

When in 1969 I made my first fumbling entry into an area of Cairo inhabited by people who called themselves "we, the poor" [*ihna innas ilfuqara*], I could not envision how this was to change my life for good. Twenty-five years later I continue to go back—as I have every year but two—feeling that it is here I have my deepest, most lasting friendships. A journey that was to have been merely for the sake of collecting material for a thesis in anthropology, turned instead into a lifelong commitment to a people and a way of life that earned my deepest respect.

How did it all begin? By coincidence and the twists of Fate.

I was in Cairo having completed a year's study of Arabic and was ready to go home when I received a letter from my department suggesting I proceed with fieldwork. I was not actually qualified; I had planned to do one more year of study before venturing into the field—among the Bedouins of Arabia, as I had hoped. But I was penniless—living off loans from the government—and my department was concerned to save me time and money. So I ended up in what I then perceived to be the slums of Cairo (I would not now use such a word)—worlds away from my romantic Bedouins. Fortune could not have favored me more.

Why the back streets of Cairo? Because at the time, all areas beyond the boundaries of Cairo or Alexandria were off limits to foreigners. This was in 1969, two years after the June war with Israel, and strict precautions applied. I tried to be allowed to circumvent them so I could do a village study, and I had friends willing to vouch for me (I had already spent two years in Egypt, also a year in 1964–65). But it was in vain. A compromise was struck that allowed me to do a fringe settlement—Shubra ilKhema—inhabited by villagers recently settled in Cairo. But soon this, too, came to an end. The authorities claimed that the area was unsafe for me, as indeed it seemed, and after three weeks I was obliged to give up. What to do next? The authorities had no suggestion—indeed it seemed as if they would prefer *not* to know—so I was offered a small scholarship but no research permit. The deal was clear.[1] I would do what I had to do and make no nuisance of myself. I was on my own, but where to?

---

1. It went without saying that the only use I had for a scholarship was to help cover my expenses while I did *some* sort of study. The stipend was offered by the Ministry of Higher Education.

Umm Ali and anthropologist, circa 1975.

Through the friend of a friend I came into contact with Umm Ali. She was his aunt, and lived in a poor quarter of Cairo. A formidable woman of thirty-four and the mother of six, she reached out to me with such warmth and hospitality, I felt instantly accepted. She suggested that I move in with her family, and that we, to counter the people's talk, should say that I had come with greetings to the family from a relative abroad. Thus began a month of co-living that taxed my powers of endurance so much that in the end I had to move out. The most persistent problem was sleeping at night. I shared a narrow bed with Hoda and Mona, squeezed in their midst, and itching madly from the bedbugs while feeling suffocated from the crowding and the heat. We slept eight people in a tiny room with no ventilation. Taking notes was also difficult. There was no place to withdraw, and no place ever to sit in peace. (I never take notes while talking to people.) So after a month, I moved out to a flat which I had to find away from the neighborhood. Lodging close by was precluded by the perception that no decent unmarried girl lives alone. I made my way back and forth every day by public bus (an ordeal that almost did me in, given the state of public buses in Cairo), coming into the area around nine or ten in the morning, since life starts rather late, and getting out at about midnight or two in the morning. Occasionally I slept there, with either Umm Ali's or other families.

Fortunately, Cairo was—and still is—a safe place to be. I have not feared robbery or rape in this city either in 1969, when the population was about six million, or now when it stands at around fourteen million.

How did I explain my reason for wanting to be with the people? First, by my genuine interest in their lives, and my wish to understand and to document their hardships; second, by my need to write a thesis to make a living; and third, by my need to improve my Arabic. When Umm Ali suggested that we "forget" about the two first concerns and center on the third, it was because of the general suspicion of foreigners that prevailed in the country at the time. She was afraid of how my intentions might be misinterpreted and twisted, so for safety's sake, we should just stress my interest in Arabic.

I was relieved at her advice as I was soon made to feel the curse of postwar hostility. I have elsewhere described my trials as I made my way into the area from the bus each day (Wikan 1980). I had to pass through crowded market streets where I was an anomaly, a darned foreigner—or worse, an American, as many misthought—and I had to pay for it by being a target of rotten tomatoes and slush water from above. Kids also threw stones at me. It was unpleasant but not dangerous. In the end we made peace with each other from sheer familiarity.

Within Umm Ali's neighborhood, reactions were also mixed. Most people went out of their way to be invite me home, but some kept their distance. With time, my most pressing problem became keeping my own distance as people competed with each other to have me as their friend. I felt as if I was drowned in friendship and hospitality and had no control over my own life and movements. I was also exasperated when people pestered me, as some did, with complaints that I had visited others before coming to them or had even paid a call on their enemy. In time a modus vivendi was worked out. I insisted on my right to have my friends, even if they were enemies of some of my friends. And I insisted on my freedom to come and go without being stuck in a house a whole day simply because the hosts grabbed hold of me. They evolved a plausible explanation for my strange behavior: "You know, she's a Christian. Christians love the people."[2] By seizing on a standard for-

---

2. The Copts living among them are seen as more compassionate and caring than Muslims, and the standard word for "Copt" is simply "Christian" [*Mesihi* (*yya*)]. Macropolitics also underpinned people's conviction of the superior qualities of Christians. Israel had just won the war, and the fact that they were two million as against thirty-four million Arabs stood as proof of the superior human qualities of Jews. Both Jews and Copts are popularly referred to as Christians.

mula which they use to explain their own relations, they managed to make sense of my deviant pattern. In their own world it was unheard of to go in and out of houses the way I did. There, friendships are strictly limited to a few—two or three—close relations.

My predicament was that, had I followed their way with respect to friendships, I could not have done a proper study. A thesis based on two or three families? Umm Ali was the broad-minded one. Never jealous of my relations with others, as far as I could sense, she encouraged me and helped me in every way. With her as a starting point, I soon formed a network of relationships, following natural ties. Some were her friends or relations, others she did not even know. Thus I came to form a fortuitous sample of seventeen families, comprising a hundred people, who constituted the "object" of my study. My chief constraint was that they had to be dispersed in space so that I could visit some without being observed by all the others, as otherwise I would unleash a fury of complaints when I came to *them*. It was compassion and generosity—not ill will—that lay at the back of these reactions. People naturally wanted me to have the best—themselves—and not waste time on anything less.

In time, all the families were informed that I was writing a thesis in social science [*il 'ilm iligtima'i*]. Though they could not know what this really meant, they had some idea since Egyptian radio used to broadcast educational programs on social science and psychology that were popular among some of my families. What mattered to them was that they felt I took a genuine interest in their lives. Thus, when the secret police were observed checking on my movements, my friends were angry on my behalf. One man reported having told the police: "She's a friend, not a foreigner. Can't you see, she *cares* about us, which is more than the government ever does!" Soon the police disappeared.

The intricacies of how the set of seventeen families was formed, and how people were connected or not connected with each other, have been elaborated elsewhere (Wikan 1980). A detailed description of how the fieldwork unfolded is also given there. Here, suffice it to note that I worked by trial and error, having no model of how one conducts fieldwork in an urban setting, and feeling utterly lost much of the time. Urban anthropology was still in its infancy, and discussions of method were nearly nonexistent. My most pressing problem I conceived as that of locating a community, a "field" to study. There were no natural borderlines, no visible signposts to circumscribe a community. People participated in different worlds, so to speak, and had only partly overlapping or even no relations with each other. To top this absence of a natural field, most things went on indoors, behind locked doors, and I envied everyone who did a village study as I dragged myself up and down stairs, pounding on doors. Had I been a man, things would have been so different. I could have sat at the cafés, and participated in a public world.

When despair hit me, and I cursed my bad luck at being confined to an urban setting and my stupidity in choosing anthropology, Umm Ali and others saved me. She did it by endlessly lecturing me on the need for interpersonal understanding—within the family, beyond the family, indeed in all the world. Her life philosophy which she never tired of laying out to me was that human beings must share their experiences with each other so they will come better to understand each other. So she and I were "into" the same project. When my perseverance faltered, she was there to spur me on and impress upon me the sheer necessity of doing what I barely could. And she sustained me also by giving me the exhilarating feeling that I mattered to her. However much I was a failure by professional standards, I could at least do something there and then. And so I kept going.

Beyond the world of the poor, there was also a vital source of support. Though I practically never saw her anymore, Dr. Laila Shukry El-Hamamsy of the Social Research Center at the American University in Cairo prevailed as an abiding presence. But for her, I might also have given up. I remember one moment in particular when she saved me. I had appeared on her doorstep after a long absence, looking wretched. I felt an utter failure as an anthropologist *and* as a human being because I could not bear my physical and mental surroundings: the filth, the stench, the misery. And now my last vestige of hope, my willpower, was also failing me.

Laila lectured me on the senselessness of thinking I could do it! She chided my teachers for instilling in me such a vain hope. No foreigner could possibly cope, when not even an Egyptian could. Recently there had been a man—of lower middle class himself—who tried to live among the poor, and even he had to give up. So what did I think myself?

That did it. From then on I felt a sense of accomplishment rather than doom. And so I kept at it.

Many others also lent me courage and hope. By their infectious good humor and never-ceasing warmth and generosity, as well as by their sheer inability, it seemed, to hide their true feelings, friends in the back streets drew me into their lives and kept me there when I felt an urge to withdraw. And so we have become bound to each other. I feel a surge of happiness when I hear people say, as if to bear witness, "just ask Unni, we have been friends for twenty years!" In their world, as in mine, such long-lasting friendships are unusual. And I treasure this testimony that at least I have brought something in return for all they have given me.

I never paid for anything, not even my food. The hospitality of the people is such that it would have been an affront if I had offered to. What I did, on occasion, was to give children and adults clothes that I assembled from people in Cairo or Norway. But on the whole, I simply gave my friendship. Nor was I ever asked for money, not even a loan. With the hindsight of later fieldwork in other parts of the world, I find this simply remarkable. They knew I would have given had they asked, and on occasion I helped in minor ways, but the hospitality of Egyptians is such that it overrides everything. And so it was they who went out of their way to give to me, as when I would board the plane loaded with freshly baked *kofta* [meat balls] sent especially for my family, or *kahk* [cakes] if my stay had coincided with the Feast after Ramadan, and *ne'ne* [mint] dried especially for me since they knew I loved mint in my tea. Clearly, I have been a burden on their meager resources with my comings and goings through the years. And yet they always made me feel that I could not come often enough or stay long enough.

My bond with them is deep, so deep that on my return to Norway after my first fieldwork, I found that I could not carry on with my academic project. The transition from life in the poor quarter to the halls of academe where lifeless analyses of systems and structures seemed to carry the day, was more than I could cope with. I wrote my thesis—in spite of myself, *ghasb 'anni* as Egyptians would say—but then withdrew it. It meant I had no degree. But I had been true to my own self. The thesis was rewritten and published as a popular book (Wikan 1980); and its reception convinced me I had done the right thing. Then, as now, I believe that if anthropology is to help build a better world, we must work *in* that world by reaching out to a broad audience and address critical social issues. Today I am happy I joined the ranks of anthropology again. But I could do so only because of an expanded freedom for anthropologists to address compelling human concerns in a voice that highlights the lived experience of people so it resonates in our world.

References

Abu-Lughod, Janet. 1972. *Cairo—one thousand one years of the city victorious.* Princeton: Princeton University Press.

Abu-Lughod, Lila. 1992. Writing against culture. In *Recapturing anthropology: Working in the present,* edited by R. G. Fox. Santa Fe, NM: School of American Research Press.

Ainslie, George. 1982. A behavioral economic approach to the defense mechanisms: Freud's energy theory revisited. *Social Science Information* 21:735–70.

Atiya, Nayra. 1984. *Khul-Khaal: Five Egyptian women tell their stories.* Cairo: American University of Cairo Press.

Barth, Fredrik. 1966. *Models of social organization.* London: Royal Anthropological Institute Occasional Paper no. 23.

Belmonte, Thomas. 1979. *The broken fountain.* New York: Columbia University Press.

Bourdieu, Pierre. 1990. The scholastic point of view. *Cultural Anthropology* 5: 380–91.

Brennan, Ellen. 1993. Urban land and housing issues facing the third world. In *Third world cities: Problems, policies, and prospects,* edited by John D. Kasarda and Allan M. Parnell, 83–101. Newbury Park, CA: Sage.

Clifford, James. 1988. *The predicament of culture.* Cambridge: Harvard University Press.

Cochrane, Susan H., and Ernest E. Messiah. 1995. Egypt: Recent changes in population growth. Human Resources Development and Operation Policy Working Paper, no. 49.

Crapanzano, Vincent. 1988. On self-characterization. Working Papers and Proceedings of the Center for Psychosocial Studies. Chicago.

Dahl, Tove Stang. 1992. *Den muslimske familie: En analyse av kvinners rett i Islam.* Oslo: Scandinavian University Press.

Das, Veena. 1994. Moral orientations to suffering: Legitimation, power, and healing. In *Health and social change in international perspective,* edited by Lincoln C. Chen, Arthur Kleinman, and Norma C. Ware, 139–69. Cambridge: Harvard University Press.

De Soto, Hernando. 1989. *The other path: The invisible revolution in the third world.* New York: Harper & Row.

Early, Evelyn. 1993. *Baladi women of Cairo: Playing with an egg and a stone.* Boulder, CO: Rienner.

El-Hamamsy, Laila Shukry. 1970. The assertion of Egyptian identity in historical perspective. Paper presented to the Burg Wartenstein Symposium no. 51, 5–13 September.

El-Messiri, Sawsan. 1978. *Ibn el balad: A concept of Egyptian identity.* Leiden: Brill.

Elon, Amos. 1995. Crumbling Cairo. *New York Review of Books,* 6 April.

Freedman, Jonathan. 1993. *From cradle to grave: The human face of poverty in America.* New York: Atheneum.

331

Friedrich, Otto. 1984. And if Mexico City seems bad. . . . *Time*, 22–23 August.

Geertz, Clifford. 1973. Thick description: Toward an interpretive theory of culture. In *The interpretation of cultures*, 3–30. New York: Basic Books.

———. 1988. *Works and lives: The anthropologist as author*. Stanford, CA: Stanford University Press.

Hallowell, A. Irving. 1955. *Culture and experience*. Philadelphia: University of Pennsylvania Press.

Hardoy, Jorge E., and David Satterthwaite. 1989. *Squatter citizen: Life in the urban third world*. London: Earthscan Publications.

Hatem, Mervat. 1988. Egypt's middle class in crisis: The sexual division of labour. *Middle East Journal* 42(3): 407–22.

Hawkins, Darnell F. 1993. Inequality, culture, and interpersonal violence. *Health Affairs* (winter): 80–95.

Hoffman-Ladd, Valerie J. 1987. Polemics on the modesty and segregation of women in contemporary Egypt. *International Journal of Middle Eastern Studies* 19: 23–50.

Howard-Merriam, Kathleen. 1979. Women, education, and the professions in Egypt. *Comparative Education Review* 23:256–70.

Ikram, Khalid. 1980. *Egypt: Economic management in a period of transition*. Baltimore: Johns Hopkins University Press.

Jencks, Christopher. 1994. The Homeless. Cambridge: Harvard University Press.

Kasarda, John D., and Allan M. Parnell, eds. 1993. *Third world cities: Problems, policies, and prospects*. Newbury Park, CA: Sage.

Khalifa, Ahmed M., and Mohamed M. Moheiddin. 1988. Cairo. In *Mega-cities: The metropolis era*. Vol. 2, edited by Mattei Dogan and John D. Kasarda, 233–64. Newbury Park, CA: Sage.

Khattab, Hind A., and Syeda Greiss el-Daeiff. 1984. Female education in Egypt: Changing attitudes over a span of 100 years. In *Muslim women*, edited by Freda Hussain, 169–87. New York: St. Martin's Press.

Kleinman, Arthur. 1992. Pain and resistance: The delegitimization and relegitimization of local worlds. In *Pain as human experience: An anthropological perspective*, edited by Mary-Jo DelVecchio Good, Paul E. Brodwin, Byron F. Good, and Arthur Kleinman, 169–97. Berkeley and Los Angeles: University of California Press.

Lapierre, Dominique 1986. *The city of joy*. New York: Doubleday.

Lavelle, Robert, et al. 1995. America's new war on poverty. San Francisco: KQED Books.

LeVine, Robert, et al. 1994. *Child care and culture: Lessons from Africa*. Cambridge: Cambridge University Press.

Macleod, Arlene Elowe. 1991. *Accommodating protest*. New York: Columbia University Press.

Malinowski, Bronislaw. 1922. *Argonauts of the western Pacific*. New York: E. P. Dutton & Co.

Mernissi, Fatima. 1975. *Beyond the veil: Male-female dynamics in a modern Muslim society*. Cambridge: Shenkman.

Minai, Naila. 1981. *Women in Islam: Tradition and transition in the Middle East.* London: John Murray.

Rogde, Isak, trans. 1984. *Fargen bortenfor* (The color purple, by Alice Walker). Oslo: Gyldendal.

Rugh, Andrea. 1984. *Family in contemporary Egypt.* New York: Syracuse University Press.

Singerman, Diane. 1995. *Avenues of participation: Family, politics, and networks in urban quarters of Cairo.* Princeton: Princeton University Press.

Smock, Audrey Chapman, and Nadia Haggag Youssef. 1974. Egypt: From seclusion to limited participation. In *Women's roles and status in eight countries*, edited by Janet Zollinger Giela and Audrey Chapman Smock, 35–79. New York: Wiley & Sons.

Walter, E. V. 1966. Meanings of poverty in histories and cultures. Manuscript.

Wikan, Unni. 1980. *Life among the poor in Cairo.* London: Tavistock.

———. 1985. Living conditions among Cairo's poor—a view from below. *Middle East Journal* 39(1): 7–36.

———. 1988. Bereavement and loss in two Muslim communities: Egypt and Bali compared. *Social Science and Medicine* 27(5): 451–60.

———. 1990a. Housing strategies among the Cairo poor, 1950–1985. In *Housing Africa's urban poor*, edited by P. Amis and P. Lloyd. International Africa Institute Publications. Manchester: Manchester University Press.

———. 1990b. *Managing turbulent hearts: A Balinese formula for living.* Chicago: University of Chicago Press.

———. 1991a. *Behind the veil in Arabia: Women in Oman.* Chicago: University of Chicago Press.

———. 1991b. Toward an experience-near anthropology. *Cultural Anthropology* 6(3): 285–305.

———. 1992. Beyond the words: The power of resonance. *American Ethnologist* 19(3): 460–82.

———. 1994. Local communities, aid ideology, and the Bhutanese state. In *State and Locality*, edited by Mette Mast, Thomas Hylland Eriksen, and Jo Helle-Valle, 41–70. Oslo: Norwegian Association for Development Research.

———. 1995. Sustainable development in the mega-city: Can the concept be made applicable? *Current Anthropology.* (Aug-Sept).

Wilson, William J. 1987. *The truly disadvantaged: The inner city, the underclass, and public policy.* Chicago: University of Chicago Press.